Democratization by Institutions

In the two decades since the publication of Robert Putnam's landmark book *Making Democracy Work*, the argument that democracy requires high levels of social capital has held sway. In this pioneering study of democratization in Argentina, Leslie Anderson challenges Putnam's thesis. She demonstrates that formal institutions (e.g., the presidency, the legislature, the courts) can serve not only as operational parts within democracy but as the driving force toward democracy.

As Anderson astutely observes, the American founders, in their own efforts to create a democratic nation, debated the merits of the institutions they were creating. Examining how, and how well, Argentina's U.S.-style institutional structure functions, she considers the advantages and risks of the separation of powers, checks and balances, legislative policy making, and strong presidential power. During the democratic transition, the Argentinian state has used institutions to address immediate policy challenges in ways responsive to citizens, thereby providing a supportive environment in which social capital can develop.

By highlighting the role that institutions can play in leading a nation out of authoritarianism, even when social capital is low and civil society may oppose reform, Anderson begins a new conversation about the possibilities of democratization. This book has much to say not only to Latin Americanists and scholars of democratization but also to those interested in the U.S. constitutional structure and its application in other parts of the world.

Leslie E. Anderson is a University of Florida Research Foundation Professor of Political Science.

DEMOCRATIZATION BY INSTITUTIONS

*Argentina's Transition Years
in Comparative Perspective*

Leslie E. Anderson

University of Michigan Press
Ann Arbor

Published in the United States of America by the
University of Michigan Press
Manufactured in the United States of America
⊚ Printed on acid-free paper

2019   2018   2017   2016   4 3 2 1

A CIP catalog record for this book is available from the British Library.

Library of Congress Cataloging-in-Publication Data

Names: Anderson, Leslie (Leslie E.) author.
Title: Democratization by institutions : Argentina's transition years in comparative
   perspective / Leslie E. Anderson.
Description: Ann Arbor, Michigan : University of Michigan Press, 2016. | Includes
   bibliographical references and index.
Identifiers: LCCN 2016020360| ISBN 9780472073238 (hardback) | ISBN
   9780472053230 (paperback) | ISBN 9780472122325 (e-book)
Subjects: LCSH: Democratization—Argentina. | Argentina—Politics and government—
   1983–2002. | Argentina—Politics and government—2002– | Executive power—
   Argentina. | Institution building—Argentina. | Social capital (Sociology)—
   Argentina. | BISAC: POLITICAL SCIENCE / Government / Comparative.
Classification: LCC JL2081 .A54 2016 | DDC 320.982—dc23
LC record available at https://lccn.loc.gov/2016020360

For my maternal grandparents,
Philip Clive Potts, PhD, 1930,
and
Mary Crosson Potts,
in recognition of their dedication to education

Contents

Acknowledgments

I have many thanks to offer, for I received a great deal of help in the creation of this book. Most of the earliest interviews were with members of the Alfonsín administration and with Raúl Alfonsín himself. These were done during a 1997–98 fellowship funded by the Gardner Foundation of Brown University. I am grateful to Will Harrison, former Dean of the College of Liberal Arts and Sciences at the University of Florida, who stepped in allow me to accept the Brown University fellowship. Without that fellowship the crucial early steps in the research for this book would never have been taken. I am thankful to former Associate Dean Lou Gillette for his support in my application to Brown.

I also thank the Fulbright Commission for a fellowship in the North American spring of 2008 that allowed me to conduct many of the interviews of members of the Carlos Menem administration upon which this book is based. Guillermina Seri provided invaluable assistance in helping me establish the academic contacts in Argentina that made the Fulbright Fellowship possible. James McGuire also supported that Fulbright application in important ways. I am particularly thankful to Carmen Diana Deere, former Director of the Center for Latin American Studies at the University of Florida, for supporting my application for the 2008 Fulbright Fellowship.

Part of the funding for other, shorter visits to Argentina came from my University of Florida Research Foundation Professorship. I appreciate Carmen Diana Deere, former Director of the Center for Latin American Studies, for nominating me to compete for the Research Foundation Professorship. I also thank former Associate Deans Allan Burns and Lou

Gillette for encouraging me to apply for the Research Foundation Professorship. Finally, I want to acknowledge the support for my scholarship that I received from former Dean Paul D'Anieri and from then-Associate Dean of the Faculty Dave Richardson, both of the College of Liberal Arts, University of Florida. I also thank Professor Pradeep Kumar, Department of Physics, College of Liberal Arts, University of Florida, and former Associate Dean Milagros Peña. These four individuals have helped create the peace of mind that made it possible for me to complete this book.

This research required many hours of work in various libraries in the United States that boast strong collections of materials on Latin America. In particular, I relied upon libraries for complete collections of the Argentine newspapers *La Nación* and *La Prensa*, two of the largest, most visible, and most internationally known newspapers in Argentina. A full understanding of events in this book relied upon coverage from these two newspapers. Gaining a complete view of these events kept me in the library on nearly a daily basis for about two years. I am appreciative of Richard Phillips and Paul Losch of the Latin America Collection at the University of Florida for their willingness to call seventeen years of newspapers, on microfilm, from various libraries around the United States so that I could reach the understanding upon which this book relies.

The research also took me to several research libraries elsewhere in the United States. In the early phase of this work I spent considerable time at the Library of Congress, the only library in the States that has a complete collection of the now-extinct Argentine newspaper *La Opinion*, which was edited by Jacobo Timerman. I thank Frank Carol at the Library of Congress for facilitating my research there. César Rodriguez, Curator of the Latin America Collection at Yale University also played a key role, working with me during my repeated visits to New Haven while I pored over the congressional transcripts of the Argentine Congress. Rodriguez also worked with Richard Phillips to send many dozens of microfilm reels to me in Florida, on loan from Yale. Pamela Graham, Curator of the Latin American Collection at Columbia University, tracked down Menem's 1989 inaugural speech. It was essential to my understanding of his campaign and the promises he made to Argentina during that time. While on sabbatical in 2010–11 and during intensive summer writing periods, I lived in Boulder County, Colorado. During those periods I have relied on the Lafayette Public Library for extensive research support through their interlibrary loan program. I would like to acknowledge Patty Frobisher and Bernice Hicks from that library for their perpetual willingness to chase down books I have requested from other libraries. Credit is also due to the City Council of Lafayette for creating and funding a warm, welcoming, and serious working environment at the Lafayette Public Library throughout the course of this work. Without them this book would never have been finished.

I have received a great deal of support in Argentina. Within the scholarly world Andrés Fontana of the University of Belgrano, Aníbal Corrado of the University of La Matanza, Pablo Alabarceres of the University of Buenos Aires, and Ana Maria Mustapic of Di Tella University have each provided countless hours of support and facilitation. They have opened many doors to me, put me in touch with many invaluable contacts, looked over my research design, and prevented me from making errors. They have also read my work, listened to my arguments, and offered me opportunities to present my work to various audiences in Argentina. This book would be much more limited without their involvement. I also thank Nora Seilicovich for remaining outside the academic world and for distracting me, taking me to plays, movies, to the beach at Punta del Este, Uruguay, to watch and dance the tango, and to bicycle along the Constañera. Without someone to coax me away from my work while in Buenos Aires, I surely would have gotten less work done.

I would also like to thank my interviewees, whose names will come out in the text of the book. During the first phase of this research I concentrated upon the former members and ministers of the Radical administration; during the second phase of this research I worked primarily with former members and ministers of the Peronist administration. During all phases and all times I have worked closely with members and former members of Congress and with labor union leaders. These individuals were and are important, powerful, and influential people, and finding time for an academic interview was extremely difficult. They were always gracious, polite, and facilitative. Obviously, without them, this book could never have been completed.

I owe a debt of gratitude to students and scholars who have read all or part of this manuscript in its various stages: Stephen Boyle, Richard Conley, Aníbal Corrado, Rodolfo Diaz, Ana Margheritis, Andreina Nash, Leigh Payne, Vanessa Siddle-Walker, Wendy Slater, and Eric Yamamoto. I would like to thank Lyle and Teresa Sherfey, Tinker Harris, Helen Gould, Kate Jackson, Vickie Doler, and Anne Lane for keeping me riding (horses) and keeping me sane. Dan O'Neill provided books on institutional theory. Conor O'Dwyer and Bryon Moraski helped refer me to relevant literature on Eastern Europe. Aníbal Corrado helped me understand the power and limits of presidential decrees and guided me in sorting through the multiple kinds of decrees. As always, all errors are mine. Melody Herr skillfully guided this book through the review and board approval process. Thank you.

I thank my husband, Larry Dodd, who has supported my work on this book throughout these many years. Our ongoing dialogue about American politics and American political institutions has helped inform the research and writing throughout the project. I also appreciate Meredith and Cris Dodd for putting up with having yet another academic in the family. This book is dedicated to my maternal grandparents, Philip Clive Potts and Mary Crosson Potts. He wrote a dissertation on educational policy in Maryland in the colonial and postcolonial years and defended it at Johns Hopkins University in 1930. She taught in a one-room schoolhouse. Without them I would not be the person I am. Thank you for your love and support and for pushing me, always, toward education.

Boulder County, Colorado
June 2015

PART I

The Presidential System and Democratization

ONE

The Presidential System as a Resource for Democratization

Argentines are second to no other American [citizens] when it comes to the capacity to understand the institutional game.[1]
—Domingo Faustino Sarmiento, 1853, on writing Argentina's Constitution

The process by which authoritarian nations become democracies is the subject of extensive study in political science today. One prevalent line of argument links democratization to a strong role played by civil society. One version of this argument suggests that the people act through revolution to remove the ancien régime.[2] Another version argues that the people cooperate with each other socially, building trust that translates into

---

1. Domingo Faustino Sarmiento, "Comentarios de la Constitución de la Confederación Argentina" (Santiago, Chile, 1853), iv. For a sophisticated study of constitution writing and building, as well as the factors determining constitutional durability, see Zachary Elkins, Tom Ginsburg, and James Melton, *The Endurance of National Constitutions* (Cambridge: Cambridge University Press, 2009).

2. Leslie E. Anderson and Lawrence C. Dodd, *Learning Democracy: Citizen Engagement and Electoral Choice in Nicaragua, 1990–2001* (Chicago: University of Chicago Press, 2005); Gordon S. Wood, *The Creation of the American Republic, 1776–1787* (Chapel Hill: University of North Carolina Press, 1969); Gordon S. Wood, *The Radicalism of the American Revolution* (New York: Knopf, 1992); Isser Woloch, *The New Regime: Transformations of the French Civic Order 1789–1820* (New York: W. W. Norton, 1994); and David Garrioch, *The Making of Revolutionary Paris* (Berkeley: University of California Press, 2002).

political skills.[3] A third version suggests that the people use a gradually expanded franchise and popular protest to reform their polity incrementally toward greater inclusiveness and democracy.[4] These are some of the kinds of democratization processes we have witnessed when the people involve themselves actively and positively in politics.

But what of nations where civil society is not necessarily or not always a positive source of influence, or where people do not trust each other and cooperate or where there has been no revolution? Argentina has been found to be low in trust and social capital. Where civil society is uninvolved or negative or largely nonexistent, nations must turn to alternative resources in order to democratize themselves. In such contexts, preexisting formal democratic institutions of the state, the elected presidency, the legislature, and the courts, constitute a potential source of authority, ideas, and innovation through which a formerly authoritarian nation can gradually transform itself into a democracy. This book is a study of how that can happen.

In studies of the democratization of previously authoritarian nations, the institutional path toward democracy has been explored less often than the civil society path.[5] What institutional studies we have emphasize the statistical contours of cross-national analysis but shed no light on the political process inside and among institutions as authoritarianism changes to democracy.[6] In contrast with such overviews, the founders of the United States institutional system tried to think through the various dilemmas for democracy that might be posed by a contest over power inside one new

3. Robert O. Putnam, *Making Democracy Work: Civic Traditions in Modern Italy* (Princeton: Princeton University Press, 1993); Leslie E. Anderson, *Social Capital in Developing Democracies: Nicaragua and Argentina Compared* (New York: Cambridge University Press, 2010).

4. Charles Tilly, *Popular Contention in Great Britain, 1758–1834* (Cambridge: Harvard University Press, 1995).

5. I suggest in *Social Capital* (2010) that institutions can become Argentina's path toward democracy, a viable alternative in view of its low levels of social capital. Chapter 7 of *Social Capital* presents an early version of the argument developed in this book. For two reviews that grasp my argument in favor of institutional democratization in Argentina, see Kirk Bowman, "Book Review of Leslie E. Anderson, *Social Capital in Developing Democracies: Nicaragua and Argentina Compared*," *Latin American Politics and Society* 53, no. 3 (Fall 2011): 188–92, and Elizabeth J. Zechmeister, "Book Review of Leslie E. Anderson, *Social Capital in Developing Democracies: Nicaragua and Argentina Compared*," *Perspectives on Politics* 10, no. 2 (June 2012): 507–8.

6. As examples of such statistical studies, see Arend Lijphart, *Patterns of Democracy: Government Forms and Performance in Thirty-six Countries* (New Haven: Yale University Press, 1999), and Pippa Norris, *Driving Democracy: Do Power-Sharing Institutions Work?* (New York: Cambridge University Press, 2008). Zachary Elkins, Tom Ginsburg, and James Melton study the written text of national constitutions and develop statistical tests of constitutional longevity and democratic durability. See their book, *The Endurance of National Constitutions* (New York: Cambridge University Press, 2009).

nation. They hoped to create an institutional design that would address those dilemmas and allow democracy to grow on a new continent.

The institutional design created by the founders of the United States has not been examined as a resource for democratization after dictatorship, yet such a study is key to understanding democratization in a presidential system. The United States is the institutional model for Argentina and for most Latin American countries. Yet scholars have rarely analyzed closely situations in which the process of democratization depends upon institutional initiative and design while civil society is weak or plays a secondary role.[7] Political scientists have studied the role of formal institutions as reforming mechanisms within established democracies. Numerous studies have investigated executive power, legislatures, and the judiciary. But those studies do not examine the use of those same institutions to accomplish the initial reform required to move an entire nation from authoritarianism toward democracy. Moreover, established democracies usually already feature a robust civil society, providing a supportive foundation for institutional contributions; thus, we do not know how formal institutions would function in the face of civil society resistance. The empirical evidence in this book reveals how institutions can be a path toward democratization without strong civil society support or in the face of citizen resistance.

This effort to understand the role of institutions in leading democratization fits with the polity-oriented approach pioneered by Theda Skocpol. Skocpol argues that we must understand the overall function of the polity if we are to understand the development of policy. To understand "the patterns and transformations of social policy" we need to analyze politics as being jointly influenced by "historically changing governmental institutions, political parties, and social groups." She defines a polity-centered approach as one that "looks at state formation, political institutions and political processes all understood in non-economically deterministic ways."[8] A polity-centered approach differs from a state-centered approach because the former looks beyond the bureaucracy to consider the interrelationships between states, political parties, and social groups. The polity-

---

7. An important exception to this pattern is Robert Mickey, *Paths Out of Dixie: The Democratization of Authoritarian Enclaves in America's Deep South, 1944–1972* (Princeton: Princeton University Press, 2015). Mickey emphasizes the crucial role of the courts, particularly the federal court system and the Supreme Court in democratizing the South.

8. Theda Skocpol, "The Origins of Social Policy in the United States: A Polity-Centered Analysis," in *The Dynamics of American Politics: Approaches and Interpretations*, ed. Lawrence C. Dodd and Calvin Jillson (Boulder: Westview Press, 1994), 182–206, esp. 189, 191–92, and 206, and *Protecting Soldiers and Mothers: The Political Origins of Social Policy in the United States* (Cambridge: Belknap Press of Harvard University Press, 1992).

centered approach also contrasts with a concentration upon civil society not by disregarding civil society but by also turning attention to the role of institutions in the creation of policy outcomes. A polity-centered approach necessarily incorporates a significant role for history, with the recognition that institutions and policies reflect historical connections to developments in the past. Throughout this book I understand political development and social policy as deeply shaped by social history, including both the history and background of Argentina's parties and the configuration of the state. History explains why democracy developed as it did and why specific policies emerged. As we go through these chapters, watching the development of both democracy and policy, we will refer to Argentina's history to understand this progression.

The polity-centered approach draws attention to four processes considered in this book: (1) the establishment and transformation of state and party organizations; (2) the effects of political institutions and procedures on the identities, goals, and capacities of social groups involved in policy making; (3) the fit, or lack thereof, between the goals and the capacities of actors within the historically changing points of access allowed by the nation's political institutions; and (4) the ways in which previously established social policies affect subsequent politics.[9]

Skocpol uses the polity-centered approach to understand the development of social policy in the United States. This book uses the same approach to understand democratization, a policy writ large that is relevant for many societies today. In this book we study Argentina in contrast with the United States, focusing on democratization policy in Argentina. The book uses U.S. history, both that of state institutions and that of political parties, to understand how these affected the development of Argentina's current democracy in its first, formative years. We concentrate here on Argentina's democratic transition years—1983 to 1999—and specifically upon the first two civilian presidencies of Raúl Alfonsín and Carlos Menem. The book reaches across several subpolicies within Argentina's overall policy of democratization, including human rights, labor reform, social welfare, and education policy. The results show us both how and why Argentina's democracy developed and also point toward reasons behind the limits on Argentina's democracy today.

In a democratizing nation that has recently been authoritarian the polity includes many authoritarian actors. The polity-centered approach in the United States allows us to comprehend the full range of actors involved in

---

9. Skocpol, "Origins of Social Policy in the United States," 191.

making policy, including state institutions, parties, party leaders, and sectors of civil society. But such a powerful microscope has rarely been used to understand the process and policy of democratization itself. Using a polity-centered approach to study democratization allows us to see inside the polity in a detailed fashion. There we find democrats and authoritarians engaged in a perpetual struggle on a daily and weekly basis. This is the essence of democratization, a policy like any other that may or may not succeed.

In recent years, and long after the transition period studied here, democracy in Argentina has remained troubled. Unlike the transition years, the nation now has only one party able to win national power, although that party is severely divided into oppositional factions that tend to coalesce around (for or against) the president at election time and disappear subsequently. In 2015, President Christina Fernández de Kirchner's faction of Peronism was defeated in an event that *may* be a step toward greater democratization. However, the 2015 winners are a personalistic coalition of anti-Kirchner Peronists and Radicals coalesced around the leadership of Mauricio Macri. They have strong support from the Peronist labor unions. This is not a victory by a different party. Additionally, Kirchner's factional victory over Menem's faction in the 2000s, widely heralded at the time, did not free the nation from autocratic efforts by the new president. Each Peronist faction that achieves power soon becomes autocratic and increasingly unaccountable owing to the lack of competition from a strong non-Peronist party. Corruption charges have been leveled at several recent Peronist presidents from different factions, including Christina Fernández de Kirchner. A public prosecutor who was apparently preparing an arrest warrant for President Christina Kirchner was found shot in his home.[10] While contestation between candidates in the 2015 national election appeared genuine, they are primarily contenders from factions of Peronism. While these recent events are beyond the focus of this study, the book will show why none of these developments should come as a surprise. Our scrutiny of Argentina's polity allows us to see how Argentina achieved the level of democracy it did and also why that democracy still faces serious limits.

An Overview of the Democratic Reforms

Before scrutinizing the design of Argentina's presidential system, let us look briefly at the daunting but exciting task that system faced. The demo-

---

10. Simon Romero, "Draft of Arrest Request for Argentine President found at Dead Prosecutor's Home," *New York Times*, February 3, 2015.

cratic transition studied here was one of the most exciting moments in the history of Argentina. If the presidential system could oversee reforms of this magnitude successfully, that conclusion bodes well for other nations seeking to democratize in more fortuitous circumstances.

In December 1983, Argentina returned to a regular electoral calendar from the most brutal dictatorship the nation had ever known. To date, that calendar has been honored, with momentous economic, political, and social implications for the nation. Although the evolution of Argentina's democracy is still underway, the nation has moved from pronounced crisis to reduced crisis to periods of relative normalcy. In the period of time this book covers, from 1983 to 1999, across two presidencies and seventeen years Argentina gained civilian control over its armed forces and applied the rule of law to them.[11] This alone is a significant and unprecedented achievement and it was accomplished through the nation's institutions of state. Argentina then conducted criminal trials of many members of the military for violations of human rights. In their scale, timing, and domestic initiation, these trials proceeded in a manner unparalleled elsewhere in Latin America and, again, relied upon national institutions. Beyond civilian control of the military, between 1983 and 1999 Argentina underwent extensive political, economic, and social reform that modernized the economy and took initial steps toward a modest welfare state. Additionally, Argentina gradually achieved a degree of democratization in the internal operation of labor unions, the most authoritarian enclave of society beyond the military itself. Finally, Argentina made extensive changes to its educational system, including the primary and secondary schools as well as the universities.

Reforms of this magnitude managed through national institutions have rarely been undertaken, much less accomplished in so brief a time. The accomplishment is all the more impressive given the problematic role played by civil society during this period. We consider the role of civil society more closely below. The political, social, and economic reforms studied here were spearheaded by two presidents, Raúl Alfonsín of the Radical Party (1983–89) and Carlos Menem of the Peronist Party[12] (1989–99), and by their cabinets, working in conjunction with the Congress and

11. The period under study here begins with late 1983 and the first electoral campaign after the dictatorship of 1976–83. The study ends with the end of Menem's presidency in mid-1999. The period is slightly less than seventeen years.

12. The Peronist Party is also known as the Justicialist Party or the PJ. In the last twenty years the Peronist Party has become more factionalized than it was during the transition years studied here. In this book I use the term "Peronist Party" to include all the factions that consider Perón to have been their leader and model.

the judiciary. These seventeen years of democratic transition merit special attention for several additional reasons. First, they constituted a period of political and economic crisis during which the survival of democracy was unclear and the immediate threats to its well-being were numerous. Second, in response to the crisis, the pace of reforms was swift. After Menem left the presidency in 1999, Argentina continued to reform itself in more incremental ways and to manifest significant disagreement over the direction that reforms should take. But nothing post-1999 has achieved the breathtaking speed of reform that characterized the period from 1983 through 1999. Third, the political structure of the nation during the seventeen years covered in this study can roughly be characterized as a two-party system in which Argentina boasted two national parties that could win the presidency and govern. Following the crisis of the Fernando De la Rúa presidency in 2001 and his resignation, this two-party system no longer exists. Argentina has now entered a troubled era of factionalized one-party rule. The only competition for national power exists between factions of the Peronist Party, a circumstance against which V. O. Key himself warned.[13] The demise of competition between at least two well-established national parties has had profoundly negative implications for Argentina's democracy and is an unfortunate side effect of democratization by institutions.[14] But during the years under study in this book, that development still lay in the future.

Why Argentina?

The magnitude, speed, and scope of the reforms studied here draw our attention to the Argentine case and are, themselves, reasons for its study. But Argentina is of concern in the overall scholarly inquiry into democracy because it has not benefited from a strong civil society in the democratization process. Instead, a formal presidential system modeled upon the United States led the reforms needed for democratization. Argentina has a long history of democratic institutions that have existed at least in name since the mid-nineteenth century. Those institutions became a resource to build democracy. We have few studies of such a process, and Argentina during the 1983–99 period offers a perfect opportunity to scrutinize an institutional and polity-centered democratization process. Civil soci-

---

13. V. O. Key, *Southern Politics in State and Nation* (New York: Knopf, 1949).

14. Leslie E. Anderson, "The Problem of Single-Party Predominance in an Unconsolidated Democracy: The Case of Argentina," *Perspectives on Politics* 7, no. 4 (2009): 767–84.

ety contributed to ending dictatorship but subsequently played a mixed role. There was no revolution, as in France or Nicaragua, and no gradually expanding franchise, as in Britain.[15] There is weak social capital,[16] low trust,[17] and high social antagonism.[18] While my work and that of others exhibits dismay about Argentina's low social capital, Argentina also offers an opportunity. By studying it we gain greater scholarly understanding of alternative resources for democracy because the nation has moved toward democracy anyway. That formal state institutions might guide democratization is hopeful because other nations may be in the same predicament. Such nations need alternative resources upon which to build democracy. This book helps understand how nations low in social capital can build democracy by other means.

The book draws on extensive evidence of the negotiations inside the institutions of state over seventeen years to learn how that became possible.[19] My use of the term "institutions" includes the formal institutions of state within the presidential system. These institutions themselves then reflect the relations among the parties and between the parties and civil society. The book looks at how the presidential system democratized the state without strong civil society support. In the face of the reform efforts that accompanied democratization, civil society opposed reform, sometimes for reasonable and legitimate reasons. At other times sectors of civil society were intransigent, unrealistic, ideological, or myopic. Civil society opposition owed partially to the fact that the reforms of democratization brought social hardship. History explains how corporate and paternalistic benefits that had accompanied the country out of the Peronist past had also brought a state monopoly on services and the promise of state-provided universal employment. This formula was unsustainable, bankrupting the economy and threatening democracy. Economic chaos itself brought a

---

15. Michael Brock, *The Great Reform Act* (London: Hutchinson and Company, 1973); Richard W. Davis, *A Political History of the House of Lords, 1811–1846: From the Regency to Corn Law Repeal* (Stanford: Stanford University Press, 2008).

16. Anderson, *Social Capital*.

17. Matthew R. Cleary and Susan C. Stokes, *Democracy and the Culture of Skepticism: Political Trust in Argentina and Mexico* (New York: Russell Sage, 2006).

18. Gabriela Ippolito-O'Donnell, *The Right to the City: Popular Contention in Contemporary Buenos Aires* (Notre Dame, IN: University of Notre Dame Press, 2012).

19. My emphasis on formal institutions of state within the presidential system contrasts with other uses of the term "institutions." The word is also used to include the study of relations between civil society and parties and to understand "systems of rules." For this use of the term, see Steven Levitsky and María Victoria Murillo, "Introduction," in *Argentine Democracy: The Politics of Institutional Weakness*, ed. Steven Levitsky and María Victoria Murillo (University Park: Pennsylvania State University Press, 2005).

long series of strikes, which themselves endangered democracy further. Economic modernization, essential to stabilize the country politically, deprived many citizens of employment and social services. That process incurred severe social costs and incited further citizen resistance and anger. But leaders inside the institutions of state pushed the reforms forward anyway because they could see the bigger picture and understood that these reforms were the most effective path toward a sustainable and functional democracy.

Again, the polity-centered approach allows us to understand Argentina's political circumstances. While this approach does not concentrate all attention on civil society, it allows us to look at the role of civil society while also considering the role played by political institutions and procedures, including the fact that these change. Given the role of civil society in Argentina's democratization, a polity-centered approach is more useful than an approach that concentrates only or even primarily upon civil society. The book then uses the polity-centered approach to study democratization at two different levels. First, throughout these chapters we will study the process of democratization itself, including the use of a presidential system of elected leaders to achieve an outcome of respect for human and civil rights, civilian control over the military, and the rule of law. At a second level, we will also use the polity-centered approach to study the unfolding and accomplishment of specific social policies that were essential to democratization.

The institutional path toward democracy has several distinguishing features. First, it is a top-down process of reform that introduces opportunities for power abuse, particularly in a presidential system where the executive has an independent electoral mandate. Second, just as civil society does not always constitute a democratic influence,[20] so institutions contain within them nondemocratic influences. The institutions of a democratic state are meant to be open and inclusive, so they ideally contain voices from all social sectors. In a former dictatorship they will inevitably include some nondemocratic voices. These voices can become a drawback to a democratization process driven by institutions. Third, institutions

---

20. Harry Eckstein, *Regarding Politics: Essays on Political Theory, Stability, and Change* (Berkeley: University of California Press, 1992); Sheri Berman, "Civil Society and the Collapse of the Weimar Republic," *World Politics* 49, no. 3 (1997): 401–29; Morris P. Fiorina, "Extreme Voices: A Dark Side of Civic Engagement," in *Civic Engagement in American Democracy*, ed. Theda Skocpol and Morris P. Fiorina (Washington, DC: Brookings Institution Press, 1999); Ariel C. Armony, *The Dubious Link: Civic Engagement and Democratization* (Stanford: Stanford University Press, 2004); Amaney Jamal, *Barriers to Democracy: The Other Side of Social Capital in Palestine and the Arab World* (Princeton: Princeton University Press, 2007).

reflect national history. The new democracy struggles forward weighed down by tendencies and patterns from the past. Any attempt to understand democratization must account for these historical patterns. These usually include institutional vestiges of authoritarianism manifested in the design of the institutions themselves and in the behavior of many actors who are involved in the democratization process.[21]

This book combines the study of the presidential system itself with an examination of the process of democratization through the use of the institutions of state. It explores how Argentina's institutions have been the source of innovative ideas about how democratization should proceed. It illustrates how leaders used institutions to push forward startling and much-needed reforms without which democracy would have died soon after its return. And it shows how institutions were used to restrain authoritarianism and rectify backwardness when no other authority existed to maintain the movement toward democracy. The book examines the inner workings of formal democratic institutions to determine how they had the strength and legitimacy to drive forward the democratization project. We investigate how they were able to accomplish such a task (a) while these institutions were still in their formative stages and weighed down by historical legacies and (b) while civil society initially resisted change and then reluctantly followed their lead. The scrutiny of this case has broader implications for the study of other democratizing nations that also seek to use state institutions to democratize.

The United States Comparison

Although the process of democratization by institutions has been understudied in new democracies today, the role institutions can play in developing and preserving democracy was the subject of thoughtful consideration and extensive debate when the United States was a developing democracy. The framers of the U.S. Constitution gave considerable attention to creating an institutional arrangement that would allow effective government and protect the new democracy from power abuses. For this reason, reference to the United States model is essential for this study. Like many Latin American nations but unlike Europe, Argentina's

---

21. Frances Hagopian has suggested that Brazil's contemporary democratic regime, which also came about through evolution rather than revolution, manifests many qualities of continuity with the previous regime, which was a military dictatorship. See Frances Hagopian, *Traditional Politics and Regime Change in Brazil* (New York: Cambridge University Press, 1996).

model of national government builds upon the U.S. example. The close scrutiny of interaction among the institutions of state conducted here is informed by extensive research on the United States. The book makes frequent comparisons between institutional interactions in Argentina and those in the United States.

However, because the United States emerged out of a revolutionary tradition that rejected centralized power, in the early founding period political leaders concentrated more on checks, balances, and representation than upon the specifics of presidential power. A revolutionary culture in the United States then produced a series of early presidents who were not power mongers and some of whom were even weak. But subsequent presidents were more willing to use presidential power; and later literature on American politics has developed a keener understanding of executive power, both its assets and limits. Real concerns about an imperial presidency emerged in the United States after World War II. That literature is useful for understanding the Argentine case and Latin American democracy more generally.[22]

In recent decades a burgeoning literature on the United States presidency has interrogated the question of constraints on the executive. Latin America is a region with a tradition of centralized power, and that was true long before the coming of democracy. As Latin American nations convert to democracy, they have typically chosen presidential democracy, following the example of the United States. Presidentialism poses a danger in a region of historically centralized power.[23] More so than parliamentary democracy, presidentialism concentrates power in one person. A president's separate electoral mandate increases his or her authority and visibility. That mandate becomes one of the tools that a presidential system uses to accomplish reform. That power is both an asset and a liability. The presidency can act swiftly, more so than any other institution of the democratic state, and a

---

22. James MacGregor Burns, *The Deadlock of Democracy: Four-Party Politics in America* (Englewood Cliffs, NJ: Prentice Hall, 1963).

23. Juan Linz argues that Latin American nations should be parliamentary rather than presidential democracies. See Juan J. Linz, "Presidential or Parliamentary Democracy: Does It Make a Difference?," in *The Failure of Presidential Democracy*, ed. Juan J. Linz and Arturo Valenzuela (Baltimore: Johns Hopkins University Press, 1994). This idea has generated an interesting debate. For example, contrary arguments were developed by Matthew Soberg Shugart and Scott Mainwaring, "Presidentialism and Democracy in Latin America: Rethinking the Terms of the Debate," in *Presidentialism and Democracy in Latin America*, ed. Scott Mainwaring and Matthew Soberg Shugart (Cambridge: Cambridge University Press, 1997). The debate over presidentialism or parliamentarism for Latin America was also considered earlier in Dieter Nohlen and Mario Fernandez, eds., *Presidencialism versus Parliamentarismo, América Latina* (Caracas, Venezuela: Nueva Sociedad, 1991).

self-confident, popular president can rally the nation and set it upon a path toward reform and recovery. Such power is convenient in times of crisis but can also be misused. This danger is greater in Latin America because of its tradition of centralized authority and greater still in Argentina, which has a harsh authoritarian past.[24]

Presidentialism in the United States has produced strong presidents, some of whom have stepped outside the bounds of their authority, particularly in times of crisis. Congressional behavior in the United States has also brought reasons for independent presidential action. This study uses a comparison with several strong U.S. presidents, ranging from Abraham Lincoln to Franklin Roosevelt and John F. Kennedy, to help frame our understanding of Argentina's two transition presidents, Raúl Alfonsín and Carlos Menem. We will scrutinize the use of executive power in Argentina during crisis against the backdrop of U.S presidential behavior.

Throughout much of the comparison here the United States looks like a good model of a well-functioning democracy. As an older democracy, it has wrestled with issues of power balance over more decades than has Argentina. But the United States is not without problems of its own, including the institutional relationship between the executive and Congress today. In recent years U.S. politics have faced many challenges similar to those found in Latin America. United States electoral politics have become increasingly polarized, and never was that polarization more evident than in the 2012 presidential election. That polarization now pervades congressional politics, inhibiting the nation's ability to govern itself. Today, more than ever, the United States is like many Latin American nations in that it faces a finite economic pie in a manner that has not been true for many decades. While the U.S. economy may be slowly recovering from recession, it is not expanding fast enough to accommodate the needs and demands of all economic sectors. This description fits Latin America and constrains political possibilities there just as it does in the United States. And finally, like Latin America, the United States today faces a growing gap between rich and poor, a circumstance that contributes to polarization and limits the number of potential solutions to problems. For all of these reasons a comparison between the United States and Argentina is instructive. While Argentina

---

24. Arend Lijphart argues that both presidential and parliamentary democracies are basically majoritarian and, by definition, are harsher and more exclusionary than consensual democracies. He favors "consensual democracy," predominantly found in small nations. This book will demonstrate that Argentina, and Latin America more generally, has done well even to achieve any sort of democracy at all. The goal of consensual democracy may be one for the next century, if at all, but nevertheless holds out an ideal goal. See Lijphart, *Patterns of Democracy*.

can learn from the example of the United States, there is also much we can learn about U.S. politics by studying Argentina.

Argentina's transition presidents used their power to respond to crises. However, they used power differently, a fact that has often led to negative assessments of Menem and more positive evaluations of Alfonsín. Differences certainly exist between these two leaders, but they are similar in ways that have gone mostly unrecognized. Menem's use of power was entirely appropriate at some times; at other times, democracy might have benefited had Alfonsín been more willing to use his power. To help clarify these distinctions we will scrutinize their leadership styles by comparing them to strong U.S. presidents who likewise acted to resolve severe crises. These comparisons help evaluate the utility of a presidential system for democratization.

This book concentrates on Argentina's democratic transition years of 1983–99. However, Argentina's democracy still struggles forward today, beset by continuing problems. The democratization process itself, conducted through institutions, has contributed to those problems. Institutional democratization imposes continuities from the past. In Argentina continuity has meant that the parties themselves are weighed down by their past. Party continuities have produced a single-party state dominated by Peronism, beginning after the transition period studied here. Free to maneuver without competition, many Peronist leaders now act in an authoritarian fashion. Peronism is also central because of its historic relation to social benefits, a subject we explore in chapter 6. Given that Argentina's institutions are still the nation's primary democratic resource and that they reflect authoritarian habits, we are left with the question of whether those institutions can continue to drive forward the democratic project in more normal times. On the other hand, civil society was less strident and more constructive by the late 1990s, the end of the transition period studied here, than it was in 1983. The changing nature of civil society then opens the possibility that civil society may play a larger and more positive role in the future than it did in the past.[25]

The Plan of the Book

Chapter 2 examines the design of Argentina's presidential system, assessing how it emulates and differs from the U.S. model. That chapter scrutinizes

---

25. Leslie E. Anderson, "Democratization and Oppositional Consciousness in Argentina," *Polity* 46, no. 2 (April 2014): 164–81.

several elements of the polity, including the presidency, the legislature, the judiciary, and the political parties. We see how the American design of these institutions brought both advantages and liabilities to Argentina's democratization process. The chapter etches clearly for us the elements of the polity that play the central role in democratization.

Parts II and III consider the use of the presidential institutions to enact democratic reforms. Part II assesses the Alfonsín years and the early establishment of the rule of law. Alfonsín's accomplishments encompass the early effort to gain civilian control over the military and address human rights, democratize the unions and privatize nonfunctional utility services and state industries. Chapter 3 addresses civilian control of the military and human rights policy, and chapter 4 addresses labor reform and privatization. Alfonsín was skilled at building a broad coalition of support for his policies across Congress and some sectors of society. That skill is essential in a presidential system where the branches of the state have enough independent power to check each other's actions. In Alfonsín's early years, the presidential institutions worked well together, producing sufficient institutional power to face down the military. Chapter 4 addresses Alfonsín's less successful efforts to gain legislative support for labor reform and privatization. An initial defeat on labor reform led him to regroup his efforts and claim a later success, still working with Congress. On privatization, Congress blocked his reform efforts entirely. These institutional successes and struggles took place largely without extensive civil society support for democratization, after the initial contribution of the human rights groups to ending the dictatorship.

Part III focuses on the Menem years and the specific policies that allowed democratization to continue. It examines how the institutions of state were used to accomplish policy reform. Chapter 5 finds Menem using his extensive powers, delegated to him by Congress, to conduct quick economic reform in the face of crisis. Congress began by accepting his actions and later challenged him more and more. Chapter 6 covers Menem's resort to the corporatist power relations left him by Perón to accomplish labor reform. That tactic mostly bypassed Congress and left a reform that was moderately successful but could have done much more. Chapter 7 covers Menem's efforts to reform the educational system. He was required to work with Congress more fully because educational reform lacked the crisis mode of privatizations and labor reform. Menem proved much less able to accomplish successful reform when doing so required working with Congress and building a coalition in support of his agenda.

Part IV presents an overview of power in Argentina's democratization process and conclusions about the study as a whole. Chapter 8 presents an empirical analysis of executive power and provides insight into the nature of executive leadership in the democratic transition, including the interaction between the executive and the legislature. The conclusion reexamines Argentina's institutional path toward democracy, considering both its achievements and its liabilities. It looks at similar institutional processes in other Latin American nations and shows that Argentina's lessons are also relevant for the United States itself. The book concludes that civil society dynamics in support of democratization are not the only possible resource for democracy; democratization can more forward without strong civil society support. Moreover, when the electorate elects a person who abuses or exceeds democratic authority, then the capacity of institutions to keep presidential democracy in place is an essential contribution. Yet institutional democratization would be even better if civil society played a supportive role. Where the democratization process benefits both from functioning democratic institutions and a participatory, constructive population, then the process has the best chance of success. The lessons found here offer guidance for other nations that might also use their institutions to democratize.

TWO

The Presidential System in a New Democracy

Argentina and the United States Model

[B]ut an enlightened statesman may not always be available. Therefore it is the fact of representative government itself, the institution
itself which is the key protection . . . and not the individual within
the institution.

—James Madison[1]

This chapter visits the institutional design Argentina had at its disposal for
the transition process that began in December 1983. That design models
itself upon the United States. For that reason, we will consider the details of
the American institutional model. Yet Argentina, a Latin American nation
with a long history of dictatorship, came to that institutional arrangement
out of a tradition of strong centralized, hierarchical power. A democratic
institutional model and an authoritarian history clash in Argentina in a
manner that was not resolved during these transition years and remains
unresolved today. These two powerful forces define the picture we study
here. On the one hand, the institutional plan is intended to constrain and
diffuse power across the three branches of the state, throughout the electorate itself, and among the geographical territories of the nation. That proto-
type also aims to be inclusive and deliberative. On the other hand, powerful

---

1. Federalist #10, 19.

traditions in Argentina and Latin America more generally encourage leaders to solve problems through the use of concentrated, centralized power, represented by the executive. Throughout the transition years, these two powerful forces battled each other, with the institutional design seeking to disperse and constrain power while history, tradition, habit, and willfulness tempted leaders, particularly in times of crisis, to concentrate power in the executive and use it to dominate every other institution.

The democratization process itself necessarily incorporated authoritarian players from Argentina's past. Democratization, both the process (elected power, deliberation) and the democratic institutions, allow openings for authoritarian voices to enter the democratic game. Authoritarian forces from the past contended for a say in the new democracy. Some of these forces, such as the military, could more legitimately be excluded or at least limited in their influence over the democratic institutions of state. Others, such as a president or political party with authoritarian tendencies, could not legitimately be excluded from governance. Instead, they must be both included and constrained, an effort that requires a delicate balancing act between the power of the institutional design, on the one hand, and the power of history and tradition, on the other hand. The tension between the democratic goals intended by the nation's institutional model and the authoritarian players within those institutions who want disproportionate power or who try to subvert or misuse those institutions underscores the complexity of democratization by institutions.

Juan Linz has suggested that a parliamentary democracy would be better for Latin America than presidential democracy.[2] But Latin American nations have preferred the U.S. model, in part because it does allow a nation to have one leader, an institutional outcome that fits with the tradition of centralized power. Whether or not presidentialism is optimal for Latin America, democratization by institutions in Argentina or elsewhere usually means working with the institutions largely as they stand, either on paper or from a previous democratic era. Few nations have the luxury that the United States had in which founders can ponder and deliberate over the best institutional design. Most Latin American nations already have a constitutional design from a previous era that has gone unused for decades. It is more likely that the crisis which accompanies the transition itself per-

---

2. Linz, "Presidential or Parliamentary Democracy." Also see the discussion of this argument and responses to it in note 23 of chapter 1. Part of Linz's argument is that presidential democracy is more likely to break down. The reader will remember, however, that the breakdown of parliamentary democracy in Germany resulted in the Nazi regime which started the Second World War.

mits neither space nor time to construct or reconstruct the nation's institutional framework. Nations and leaders go with what they have and make the best of it.

No institutional design functions perfectly, even when it results from the thoughtful, deliberative process that characterized the U.S. founding. Every institutional arrangement has weaknesses and can also be undermined by authoritarians who do not wish to follow the intent of the design. Therefore, the process of using institutions to democratize is a flawed and imperfect process that entails stumbling forward a few steps, making multiple mistakes, or encountering nondemocratic constraints along the way. The task of using institutions to democratize a nation requires extracting what is constructive and democratic from the institutional design while restraining the authoritarian tendencies introduced into those institutions by parties and players from the past. This difficult task requires democratizing the institutions themselves while also using them to democratize the country.

The extent to which the democratic design of the institutions predominates over the authoritarian behavior of some players is partly a function of the original institutional design and partly the result of the personalities inside the institutions. Any set of institutions can be used for authoritarian purpose by power holders and elected officials who subvert or bypass the checking mechanisms and by other power holders who allow them to do so. Likewise, personalities committed to democratic governance can make a poor institutional design function in a more democratic way. Whether democratization can be accomplished through the formal institutions of state depends upon who prevails: the democratic forces within the institutions or the nondemocratic ones. Watching this process unfold in Argentina shows that the nature of the president and the tendencies of the two major parties were key factors in whether institutions functioned democratically or pursued nondemocratic purposes.

The Separation of Powers

In proposing the institutional design of the United States, what would later be called "The Virginia Plan," James Madison wrote, "The accumulation of all powers legislative, executive, and judiciary in the same hands, whether of one, a few or many, and whether hereditary, self-appointed or elective may justly be pronounced the very definition of tyranny."[3] Therefore, in designing his Plan, Madison sought to avoid the accumulation of all power in one branch. He constructed a three-branch institutional arrangement where each branch would have a degree of independence while also having a margin of overlap in their powers. Independence would allow the system as a whole to balance authoritarian impulses that might emerge from any single branch while the margin of overlap would allow the branches to check each other.

But even though he wanted to avoid the concentration of power in one branch, some analysts think that it was Alexander Hamilton and not Madison who was more thoughtful about the design of the executive branch. While Madison was thoughtful about the composition of the legislature, Hamilton believed in the constructive power of the president and paid particular attention to the design of the executive office. "Energy in the executive," he wrote, "is a leading character in the definition of good government." Thus, Hamilton provides an initial blueprint for the style of democratization that we see in Argentina, and in Latin America more generally, one that grants a central role to the presidency.

Yet even in his enthusiasm for an energetic executive, Hamilton was fully aware of the potential dangers of that office and of the need to provide institutional mechanisms for checking and restraining the presidency. In his writings he considered several formats for the executive and rejected all but the solo executive because he thought the latter would be the most easily restrained.[4] Ultimately, however, the United States as a developing democracy did not have to contend with a powerful presidency. The United States emerged out of a revolutionary tradition that exhibited great caution about central power and began, instead, by locating primary power in the states. It would not be until more than one hundred years later that the United States began to confront both the potential and the dangers of a powerful, energetic executive. For that reason we need to scrutinize carefully the institutional arrangement of Argentina's executive to learn both how it is similar to the U.S. example and how it differs.

---

3. Madison, Federalist #47. On the overall discussion of the design of the Virginia Plan, see Federalist #10 and #47.

4. Federalist #70, Alexander Hamilton, "The President," in *The Federalist Papers*, by John Jay, Alexander Hamilton, and James Madison (New York: Washington Square Press, 1972), 133. In this paper Hamilton considers and rejects a dual executive, such as what France currently has, and an executive council.

The Presidency: The Dilemmas of Power

Most Latin American democracies come out of a long tradition of centralized dictatorship and Argentina is no exception in this regard. That historical background has meant that these new democracies are generally tempted to start with strong presidencies and then learn along the way how to use and control those executives. This challenge is the reverse of the decentralized starting point of the new United States. In fact, many Latin American "presidents" have not even been elected, and it is the actual *election* of a president that often marks the formal beginning of democracy. Democratization by institutions in a presidential system, then, makes the presidency a central focus. This institution has the greatest potential for strong democratic leadership but also poses the greatest threat of authoritarian power. Indeed, the two qualities are intricately linked. The president must have a forceful personality to resist the influence of outgoing authoritarians. He or she must envision a way through the crisis. A strong president can rally the nation behind a reformist agenda. But the president also controls the greatest number of political resources and can turn them in a nondemocratic direction. Additionally, the presidency is the place where the nation's tradition of strong, centralized control is most likely to emerge. In Argentina, the tensions between the positive and negative potential of the president are heightened by an institutional design that makes the presidency even more powerful than it is in other presidential systems.

The potential democratic contribution of the presidency and its tendency toward authoritarianism are greatest in moments of crisis, including democratic transition moments. The years studied here represent Argentina's transition moment. In times of crisis, a nation needs bold, forceful, self-confident leadership. But this type of leadership is also the most prone to overstep the bounds of democratic authority, push the edge of institutional constraints, and become autocratic.

This dilemma between the need for and the dangers of a strong president confronted the United States after its founding. Abraham Lincoln articulated the dilemma well. On November 10, 1864, upon the occasion of his second electoral victory, he said, "It has long been a grave question whether any government, not too strong for the liberties of its people, can be strong enough to maintain its own existence in great emergencies."[5] Lincoln faced the breakdown of the very nation he had been elected to lead.

---

5. Phillip Shaw Paludan, *The Presidency of Abraham Lincoln* (Lawrence: University Press of Kansas, 1994), 291.

When the South seceded, he saw the potential demise of the nation itself and he was determined to prevent it. In his response to Southern secession, Lincoln provided an agenda—keep the nation united at all costs—around which the remainder of the country (the North and the West) could rally and a self-confident determination that his view on matters was correct. He succeeded in imposing his view, indeed had been reelected for it, and his perspective on the situation was widely embraced. He played the role of a strong leader with an unflinching agenda and a self-confident assurance. He fulfilled the role we expect of the presidency, particularly in a time of crisis, and without it the nation would not have survived.

But along the way, Lincoln pushed the edge of his authority. He declared war and mustered troops single-handedly. He chose a commanding officer and began to collect resources for war. He took many of these initial steps toward military conflict while Congress was not even in session, so he passed none of them through the legislature. Faced with resistance to his agenda in the North he suspended the writ of habeas corpus, one of his most controversial decisions. But he was determined that the postal service and other forms of normal communication would not be used in the North to help the South or to undermine the military effort against the Southern states. He did not doubt the correctness of his purpose. He would save the union, and the means he found to do so were acceptable to him if they supported that goal.

Other U.S. examples also help us understand the dilemma of the presidency. Franklin Roosevelt confronted crisis, first economic collapse and then world war, and used the power of the presidency to face those catastrophes. Upon assuming office he drove through Congress a massive legislative agenda, transforming economic relations in the United States. When the Supreme Court ruled his reforms unconstitutional, he attempted to increase the number of justices on the high court and to name the new members. This last move was considered unconstitutional and was disallowed but Roosevelt had tried it anyway because he thought the Court decisions were wrong and bad for the country. His self-confidence was the kind often found in strong leaders facing crisis.

Both Lincoln and Roosevelt pushed the edge of the law or stepped beyond it, depending on one's perspective, when facing emergency or war. But other United States presidents who did not face war or economic depression have also used power in ways that courted unconstitutionality or pushed the very edge of presidential authority. John Kennedy used presidential discretionary power and funds to establish the Peace Corps, a single-handed reform of international relations in the face of an obstructionist Congress. Similarly, when a southern-dominated Congress resisted, Johnson leaned hard on legislators to pass the Civil Rights Act. Upon assuming the presidency after Kennedy's assassination, Johnson was told *not* to take on any effort to get the Civil Rights Act passed because doing so would alienate southern legislators who dominated Congress. Civil rights was a lost cause. Johnson famously responded, "Well what the hell's the presidency for?" and he then brooked no compromise in pursuing the passage of the Act. He walked the halls of Congress pressuring legislators individually in ways that even his former allies found to be overbearing and he kept lists of names of those who supported the Act and those who would not.[6]

These examples draw attention to one of the core dilemmas of the presidency as an institution and help us place the Argentine process in comparative perspective. Power is supposed to rest with the people, but democracies also need a leader who will make final decisions on momentous questions. That leader needs—and will use—power and discretion, sometimes to a considerable degree. The dilemma lies in the balance between government by the people and the need for humane, decisive, visionary leadership. This dilemma becomes particularly pronounced in times of crisis. At such moments the needs of the people might well be greater or more urgent than at other times. Yet the need for strong leadership that grasps the larger picture and enjoys discretion is likewise more pronounced. Thus, the strains and contradictions between democratic rule and the need for strong leadership become etched more clearly during a crisis. The tension between the need for strong power and the need to constrain power is particularly pronounced when popular sectors resist reform and cannot see the need for it. Such resistance is likely when the crisis is clear but reform requires painful sacrifices. Leadership needs to be determined and powerful, but not to the point of becoming authoritarian.

The tension between the need for strong power and the desire to constrain it is more pronounced in new democracies where the institutional setting is still untested and fragile.[7] The stakes are higher in newer democr-

6. See Robert A. Caro, *The Years of Lyndon Johnson: The Passage of Power*, especially the Introduction, page xv, and chapter 18. Also see Rowland Evans and Robert Novak, *Lyndon Johnson: The Exercise of Power*, especially chapter 17, "Taming the Congress."

7. Guillermo O'Donnell specifically addresses the problem of constraints on power in developing democracies by advocating institutional checks, which he calls "horizontal accountability." Melo et al. (2009) dismiss horizontal accountability in favor of the pressure and checking mechanism represented by elections, what O'Donnell would call "vertical accountability." Appearing to come down on the side of elections rather than institutional checks, Ian Shapiro calls for "competition" as the best method for constraining power within

racies because democratic habits are newer, institutional constraints are less practiced, and the crisis could well be greater. As we study Argentina's democratization process as led by its institutions of state, the presidency will be the center of our attention. It played the most central role over these seventeen years of transition. Certainly, the power of the presidency was misused at some points in the transition process, but, as the comparison with several U.S. presidents shows, strong power is not always authoritarian, and presidential discretion is not necessarily an enemy of democracy. On the contrary, power and discretion can provide the leverage that democracies most need to survive. Part of our task in this book is to understand the nature of presidential power as exercised in Argentina by Alfonsín and Menem. We will untangle the points where presidential power was misused, overused, and even authoritarian. But we will also scrutinize situations where strong presidential power was quite appropriate and consider instances where the power exercised by the president could and perhaps should have been even greater.

The Legislature: The Dilemmas of Power Constraint

Like the executive, Argentina's legislature is modeled upon the United States. Madison had reasons for wanting a separate, representative legislature. He and other founders had great confidence in the role of a legislature in maintaining democracy. One reason why they placed so much emphasis on the role of the legislature is that the transformation of the legislature into a democratic institution basically began "in colonial America in the seventeenth and eighteenth centuries." As such, legislatures "proved to be ideal instruments for contesting British authority."[8] For this reason, Madison wanted a legislature to play a central role in American government.

Additionally, Madison wanted a bicameral legislature that was supposed to fulfill several roles. It was intended to restrain the presidency, but the

---

democracy. See Guillermo O'Donnell, "Horizontal Accountability in New Democracies," in *The Self-Restraining State: Power and Accountability in New Democracies*, ed. Andreas Schedler, Larry Diamond, and Marc F. Plattner (Boulder: Lynne Rienner, 1999), and "Why the Rule of Law Matters," *Journal of Democracy* 15, no. 4 (October 2004): 32–46. For an alternative position, see Marcus André Melo, Carlos Pereira, and Carlos Mauricio Figueiredo, "Political and Institutional Checks on Corruption: Explaining the Performance of Brazilian Audit Institutions," *Comparative Political Studies* 42, no. 9 (September 2009): 1217–44; and Ian Shapiro, *The State of Democratic Theory* (Princeton: Princeton University Press, 2003).

8. Gerhard Loewenberg, *On Legislatures: The Puzzle of Representation* (Boulder: Paradigm Publishers, 2011), 9.

two chambers were also supposed to restrain each other. Madison argued for two chambers because he thought that each would make a different but essential democratic contribution. The lower chamber would most closely represent the people and, as such, would be more passionate and more subject to concerns of the moment. The Senate, by contrast, would represent territorial interests and be more removed from the passions of the moment. A different electoral calendar for each chamber would ensure that any single concern of the moment could not predominate in the election of all representatives. By requiring the agreement of both chambers for legislation to become law, the Congress would check the presidency and also restrain itself. Madison argued that the overall structure of the institutions would disallow any imbalance in any particular direction and would protect against any single branch becoming too powerful.

James MacGregor Burns has suggested that, in his concern to restrain power, Madison overdid it in designing the U.S. model. He created a scheme so complicated and mutually restraining that it became "a harmonious system of mutual frustration."[9] We need to remember this complexity as we examine the Argentine process of democratization because, to a considerable extent, Argentina's Congress did exactly what Burns says a Congress will do: it created frustration. But frustration was already in excess in a nation in crisis and only encouraged the executive to act alone, presenting the nation with the very danger Madison sought to avoid. Thus the institutional design imported from the United States brought both positive and negative attributes to the development of democracy.

Modeling itself on the U.S. presidential system, Argentina has a bicameral legislature, with a lower chamber, the House of Deputies, and a Senate. Deputies represent population districts while the Senate is a reflection of the federal system and represents the subnational units known as provinces. Deputies are elected for three-year terms while senators are elected for nine.[10] Half of the lower chamber is up for election each legislative electoral term while one-third of senators are subject to replacement each legislative electoral cycle. At the point of Argentina's return to democracy,

---

9. Burns, *Deadlock of Democracy*. In this quote Burns is quoting Richard Hofstadter (source not given).

10. In the 1853 Constitution, deputies were elected for six-year terms while senators were elected for nine. One-third of the lower chamber was subject to election every two years; one-third of senators were subject to being replaced every three years. This was the electoral calendar that prevailed for the first eleven years of the democratic transition studied here.

After the 1994 constitutional reform, deputies were elected every four years and senators every six. One-half of deputies are now elected every two years and one-third of senators are elected every two years. Reelection is allowed in both chambers.

the president was elected for a six-year term that fit with the three-year cycle defining the legislature. That would change in 1994 when Menem asked for and received a constitutional change allowing him to run for a second term. Beginning in 1995 the presidency followed a four-year cycle while both chambers now follow a two-year cycle.

At the time of the democratic transition studied here senators were not directly elected, as, indeed, they were not in the original U.S. plan. As in the early years of the United States, Argentine senators were indirectly elected by the provincial legislatures, the design that Madison thought would best represent territorial interests. When the United States moved toward direct election of senators in the early twentieth century, Argentina stayed with the original model. It was not until 1998, at the end of the transition years under consideration here, that Argentina turned to the direct election of senators.[11] During most of the transition years Argentine senators were not directly responsible to the electorate but were beholden to the legislatures and governors inside their provinces of origin.

This design contributed greatly to the frustration that accompanied any effort to conduct reform during the transition years and also introduced a powerful source of authoritarianism into Argentina's democratization process. Edward L. Gibson has shown that many of Argentina's provinces were and are authoritarian enclaves where democratic contestation for power is limited or absent. Moreover, writes Gibson, Argentina's Senate is malapportioned and overrepresents the rural provinces that have scarce population levels. These rural provinces are also the ones more subject to subnational authoritarians.[12] These influences introduced into Argentina's democratization process a Senate that reflected authoritarian interests but that, according to Madison's intention, had the power to restrain both executive and congressional efforts toward democratic reform.

Madison sought a legislature because he thought that it would provide a forum for dialogue over policy at the national level. Dialogue, then, would allow the representatives to see reason and choose the best course of action. This function of a representative chamber is essential to democracy. Using such a chamber early in the democratic transition process is

---

11. Additionally, at this time a third senator from each province joined the Senate, representing the first minority party winner from each province.

12. Gibson, *Boundary Control: Subnational Authoritarianism in Federal Democracies* (New York: Cambridge University Press, 2012). The U.S. Senate is also malapportioned, giving disproportionate power to the less populous states. See Frances E. Lee and Bruce I. Oppenheimer, *Sizing Up the Senate: The Unequal Consequences of Equal Representation* (Chicago: University of Chicago Press, 1999). The malapportionment in Argentina's Senate is even more extreme than that in the U.S. Senate.

central to democratizing the nation through its formal institutions. Argentina's legislature represented constituents and provided a check upon the executive during the transition years. Sometimes it played a positive and even heroic role, particularly in the early years, directly after the departure of the military. But legislatures function imperfectly, and the design of Argentina's Congress also introduced authoritarian interests, which could not legitimately be excluded. Therefore Congress also had periods when its behavior was problematic, imperfect, and counterproductive. It caused at least as many problems as it solved and then struggled valiantly to solve the very problems it had created. Later, it caused problems and did not resolve them at all. Several of its characteristics were particularly relevant to the transition process.

First, over its entire history, the Argentine legislature has functioned during very limited periods of time. Although it was established by the 1853 Constitution, it existed in name only and not as an elected, representative body for the remainder of the nineteenth century. It began to serve as a forum for dialogue during the brief democratic period of 1916–30, but at that time it was dominated by the Conservative Party and the president's new, reformist Radical Party held very few seats in Congress. The Congress was again officially a deliberative body during Perón's first two presidencies, from 1946–55, although deliberation then was restricted by oppression. Peronist deputies harassed and heckled opposition legislators and often refused to allow them to present their arguments in chambers. Because of these patterns inside the legislature, both of these periods saw serious problems with the representative and democratic nature of the Congress. Congress again functioned briefly in the 1950s and 1960s during the short presidencies of Arturo Frondizi (1958–62) and Arturo Ilia (1963–66), but at that time the proscription of the nation's largest political movement, Peronism, made democracy and therefore the legislature quite imperfect. We see, then, that the legislature had been unrepresentative and noninclusive in the 1920s, uncivil and hostile toward debate in the 1940s and the early 1950s and again unrepresentative in the late 1950s and the 1960s. The Congress was then closed entirely for the period of the military dictatorship immediately preceding the transition years studied here. For a legislative body that has officially existed for over 160 years, the Argentine Congress has actually only a few decades of real experience with debate, deliberation, policy-making, and governing. Most of those years followed the return to democracy in 1983. During the years of democratic transition, the legislature was a very inexperienced deliberative body. Representatives were eager to play a role in the transition, but they were often clumsy in their efforts to do so.

Second, the legislature necessarily reflected the parties themselves, including their nondemocratic elements, and it was never feasible to include the one while excluding the other. Our polity-centered approach requires that we incorporate an understanding of party history. In Argentina that is often a nondemocratic history. Democratic institutions are tools for democracy, but they can also be held hostage by the nondemocratic players within them. In the chapters that follow we will see how the legislature reflected both its democratic purpose and was sometimes crippled or misused by representatives who reflected nondemocratic interests.

Executive and Legislative Tension: The Ongoing Struggle

In the democratization process studied here, these two institutions—the presidency and the legislature—play the most consistent leadership roles. They reflected both the personality and the agenda of the players working inside them as well as the influences of their original design. One way in which Argentina's executive and legislative institutions are distinct is that they give the president more power than in most bicameral presidential systems and more power than the U.S. system gives to the president.

Scholars of the American presidency suggest that the U.S. president has three kinds of powers: (a) constitutional powers specifically given in the text of the constitution, (b) delegative powers transferred by Congress for a specific time or purpose, and (c) inherent powers, which are unwritten but essential to the office, to be used at the discretion of the president.[13] The executive and legislative branches in the United States disagree about how far the president's power actually extends and where the power of the Congress begins. The last of the three powers is the location of much of this disagreement. Some legal scholars have argued that this third category does not even exist and is, in fact, antithetical to the separation of powers upon which the United States government is founded. Their position, however, has not prevailed.[14] Over time, U.S. presidents have insisted

---

13. Kenneth Mayer, *With the Stroke of a Pen: Executive Orders and Presidential Power* (Princeton: Princeton University Press, 2001), 36 and chap. 2.

14. Some scholars who take this position say that inherent powers are incompatible with the notion of limited government in the Constitution. For an argument against prerogative powers, see Bruce Ledewitz, "The Uncertain Power of the President to Execute the Laws,"

that the office does have inherent powers that can be used to make law in special circumstances, such as instances when Congress is obstructing progress.[15] U.S. presidents have been more likely to make this argument in times of crisis.

Awareness of this disagreement between the legislature and executives in the United States is useful, especially considering that it is a much older and more experienced democracy than Argentina. The Argentine presidency is officially granted more power in all three categories than is its U.S. counterpart. Any consideration of the use of power by Menem or Alfonsín during these transition years must bear this difference in mind. With respect to the first kind of power, the Argentine Constitution grants more power to the president by allowing him or her to "regulate" a bill so that it becomes enforceable law. Beyond simply needing a presidential signature, as in the United States, a bill cannot become law in Argentina without presidential "regulation." In regulating a bill the president puts in place the bureaucratic mechanisms needed to implement the law. Without that step the bill has no effect. The involvement of the Argentine president in law implementation is therefore essential.[16]

This higher level of presidential power is a legacy of the centralized,

---

Tennessee Law Review 46, no. 4 (Summer 1979): 770. Also see Donald L. Robinson, "Presidential Prerogative and the Spirit of American Constitutionalism," in *The Constitution and the Conduct of American Foreign Policy*, ed. David Gray Adler and Larry N. George (Lawrence: University Press of Kansas, 1996), 114.

15. One such special circumstance was civil rights. As mentioned in the previous section, Johnson, as president, would eventually overcome senatorial opposition to civil rights legislation. However, before Johnson's determination to brook no compromise, the U.S. Senate had obstructed the passage of any civil rights legislation for eighty years. In 1957, when the Senate finally passed the first civil rights law, they "gutted" it into virtual worthlessness. The Senate managed this resistance as a result of being dominated by a minority of southern Senators led by Richard Russell (D-Ga), with a central role played by Lyndon Johnson. As Johnson saw his potential to be president fade due to his antagonism to civil rights, he reversed his position and began to maneuver inside the chamber for the passage of a civil rights bill. Then, as president, Johnson forced through the Civil Rights Act of 1964.

Prior to Johnson's presidency U.S. presidents Truman and Kennedy had responded to Congressional obstructionism on civil rights by passing civil rights legislation through executive order. On the use of executive orders for this purpose, see Mayer, *With the Stroke of a Pen*, chap. 6. On Senate obstruction of civil rights and the role of Russell and Johnson, see Robert Caro, *The Years of Lyndon Johnson: Master of the Senate* (New York: Alfred A. Knopf, 2002), 33–41, and chap. 7.

16. Other scholars of Latin American legislatures likewise note that Latin American presidents have more power than their U.S. counterparts. However, the fragmentation of many Latin American party systems can make it more difficult to work with the legislature than it is in the United States, where only two major parties exist. See Brian F. Crisp and Felipe Botero, "Multicountry Studies of Latin American Legislatures: A Review Article," *Legislative Studies Quarterly* 29 (2004): 329–56, at 348.

hierarchical Spanish colonial tradition inherited by most Latin American countries.[17] Whereas democratization in the United States began with a revolution that rejected centralized monarchical power, most Latin American countries have been less inclined to view centralized power with the suspicion that characterized the founders of the United States. The revolutionary origin of the United States resulted in widely dispersed power residing in the states and a central government that was originally quite weak.[18] The process of democratic development in the United States has been a negotiated movement from decentralized power resting with the states to the more centralized power of the federal government.[19]

The development of democracy in Argentina has consisted of movement in precisely the opposite direction, from highly centralized, sometimes authoritarian, power toward dispersed power. We will see that process in the democratic transition period studied here. We will also learn that Argentina is still in the very early stages of that process. In fact, power is still quite concentrated in Argentina's executive, having increased during the Menem administration. Some observers believe that power has become even more concentrated since the transition period studied here. Argentina's power dispersion away from the executive may never reach the level found in the United States.

The second kind of presidential power, delegated powers, played a key role in the transition process. The crisis period studied in this book caused the Argentine Congress to make a deliberate decision to delegate enormous

---

17. On the early Spanish colonial conquest of Argentina, see Chris Moss, *Patagonia: A Cultural History* (Oxford: Signal Books, 2008).

18. The states were so cautious about executive power that they even placed strong constraints on governors. Philip J. Cooper, *By Order of the President: The Use and Abuse of Executive Direct Action* (Lawrence: University Press of Kansas, 2002), 5–6. Argentine governors face no such constraints and have been quite expansive and even authoritarian in their use of power, including in naming senators.

19. On the negotiation of this process, see Thornton H. Anderson, *Creating the Constitution* (University Park: Pennsylvania State University Press, 1993). Relatedly, Paludan argues that the Civil War and the Lincoln presidency marked one moment when national power increased greatly and state power decreased. After the Civil War, and for the remainder of the nineteenth century, American presidential power did not again reach the level found under Lincoln; at the same time, presidential power never again declined to the level it had been before Lincoln. Paludan, *Presidency*, 316–17. After the Civil War and in the early twentieth century, the southern states became one of the strongest voices for state power. They held out for more power residing with the separate states, the so-called states rights position, while the North held out for greater federal powers. The state's rights position of the South was also a disguise for segregation and the denial of both human rights and civil rights to black citizens. Caro, *Years of Lyndon Johnson*; Mickey, *Paths Out of Dixie*. More recently the position has been used by Arizona to increase restrictions on immigrants. Arizona's position was struck down by the Supreme Court in 2012.

powers to the president in the Menem years. This response to crisis was not unprecedented in a presidential democracy. In the United States, Congress delegated special powers to Roosevelt in 1933, when he took office in the wake of economic collapse. Congress again delegated special powers to Roosevelt with the coming of war.[20] Part III of this book will show that Menem, like FDR, thought he faced an unusual crisis and asked Congress for special delegative powers, which it granted. However, requesting these powers is quite different from seizing them illegally, something Menem did not do.

With respect to the third kind of presidential power, inherent powers, Argentine presidents are clearly in agreement with their U.S. counterparts. They tend to believe they have a high level of inherent powers and act accordingly. The transition years studied here will illustrate that point, particularly with Menem. However, the debate about whether one or both of these two Argentine presidents used power inappropriately is best understood comparatively and institutionally. These power issues are not confined to Argentina, to Latin America, or to new democracies. They are contested issues in every democratic system. Nevertheless, factors specific to Argentina often determined and usually increased the extent of presidential power.

Crises usually result in greater concentrations of presidential power.[21] In the United States, crises have increased central power in a highly decentralized context and have often contributed to nation building. Because the Argentine political system was already highly centralized and nation building, including democratization, consisted of decreasing central power, the advent of crisis has had precisely the opposite effect: it contributed to greater power concentration in a nation that needs such concentration to

20. The U.S. Congress likewise permitted a wide latitude of power to President Lincoln in the face of war. Lincoln's case was different, however, because he was president at a time when the office was much weaker than it was in the twentieth century. As a result, Lincoln made a series of decisions in the early months of the war that were outside of his official authority. He did so partly because Congress was on a three-month break and partly because they served his purposes. When Congress reconvened, they ratified most of the measures that Lincoln had already taken. Paludan, *Presidency*, esp. chap. 4.

21. A notable exception is Russia where the crisis created by the dissolution of the Soviet Union brought about the construction of a dual executive based on the French model, including both a president and a prime minister (the latter was aligned with the Soviet/Russian legislature, the Duma). As it turns out, the new Russian presidency, held by Mikhail Gorbachev, was not strong enough to oversee the reforms necessary to keep the country unified and bring about major economic reform. As a result, the Duma and the prime minister turned against the president and ousted Gorbachev. See Eugene Huskey, *Presidential Power in Russia* (Armonk, NY: M. E. Sharpe, 1999), 7.

decrease. This irony is all the more poignant given that new democracies pass through crises more frequently than older democracies.

The Peculiarities of Argentina's Presidential System

In addition to having a higher level of involvement than the U.S. presidency in law implementation, Argentina's presidency has other peculiarities as well. Argentina's government is a presidential system with significant parliamentary attributes that further increase presidential power. While Linz and others have preferred a parliamentary system for Latin America because it disallows a separate electoral mandate for the executive, parliamentarism increases the power of the executive in a different way: it ties the executive and legislative branches together under the control of the same party. In that way the Westminster model gives legislative powers to the prime minister that the U.S. president does not enjoy.

Notably, the Westminster model leaves the executive driving the legislative agenda, whereas in the United States it is Congress that drives the legislative and policy-making agenda. That basic fact is one of the reasons why the U.S. Congress is considered one of the most powerful legislatures in the world. Moreover, the responsibility of creating policy has caused the U.S. Congress to build an extensive committee system through which expertise becomes available for making good policy. Argentina's presidential system gives the executive both the enhanced powers of the separate electoral mandate, derived from a presidential system, and the enhanced powers of driving the legislative agenda, derived from the parliamentary system. Despite existing in a presidential system, the Argentine Congress has very little space for fielding a legislative agenda of its own and is not expected to do so. Instead, the legislative agenda of the administration is expected to originate with the executive. Among legislators and presidential advisers, the Congress is often referred to in the vernacular as "el parlamento," Spanish for "the parliament."[22] This formally incorrect reference to the legislature tells us a great deal about the de facto powers of the insti-

---

22. For example, legislators use the term "el parlamento" to refer to the Congress, a term that is incorrect with respect to the institutional configuration of Argentina's legislature. Yet the use of that term betrays the extent to which legislators themselves expected the Congress to follow the executive's lead in presenting a legislative agenda. For an example of this term in academic parlance, see William C. Smith, "State, Market and Neoliberalism in Post-transition Argentina: The Menem Experiment," *Journal of Interamerican Studies and World Affairs* 33, no. 4 (Winter 1991): 1–17, at 5.

tution.[23] The expectation that the president will drive the legislative agenda gives Congress little institutional space for restraining the executive and more closely resembles a parliamentary system than a presidential one.[24] However, the Congress is not quite as weak as a parliament either because there are moments when the Congress seizes the initiative and runs with it in a manner quite unforeseen by the president. We will see moments like this during Argentina's transition years. When that happens the president needs to know how to work with Congress by building a congressional coalition. It is not a skill that Argentina's presidents have had much chance to develop.

Within the wide latitude that the president enjoys, the Argentine president is expected to appoint the cabinet. The president names the ministers but also the second and third person in command under each ministry. These are the subminister and the second subminister, respectively. The president often names these secondary level ministers in consultation with his or her chosen ministers but does not consult the Congress about these selections. In this way, all aspects of administration within the executive branch, including all of its ministries, fall under executive prerogative and outside the purview of Congress.

However, unlike a parliamentary system, the Argentine legislature does not have the authority to call for a vote of no confidence or to express its disapproval of the president in an electoral manner. Likewise, it does not normally have the authority to call a national election that would allow the electorate to remove both the executive and the party in power.[25] Instead, as in a presidential system, the Argentine president holds a set administrative term that can be foreshortened only by himself. Alfonsín chose to resign

---

23. The relative weakness of the Argentine Congress and its subservience to the president contrasts with the power of the U.S. Congress, which, as Michael Horowitz writes, "can do in the presidency. [U.S.] Presidents often have to accommodate Congress because Congressional power is real and it shoots real bullets." See Michael J. Horowitz, "Commentary and Exchanges on Politics and Public Debate," in *The Fettered Presidency: Legal Constraints on the Executive Branch*, ed. L. Gordon Crovitz and Jeremy A. Rabkin (Washington, DC: American Enterprise Institute for Public Policy Research, 1989), 318.

24. In the United States the power of Congress is such that neither the executive nor the legislature can accomplish policy goals without the cooperation of the other. In comparison with the Argentine system, the U.S. president is weaker, and the legislative balance of power is more even. Richard E. Neustadt, *Presidential Power: The Politics of Leadership* (New York: John Wiley and Sons, 1960), 37.

25. An exception to this general rule came in the early 2000s when Radical president Fernando De la Rúa resigned. Congress accepted the president's resignation and called for a new election to replace him. Unlike in a parliamentary system, the congressional vote was not a vote of no confidence toward De la Rúa, nor did it call for an election in order to remove the president.

six months early after a new president had been elected. Additionally, in the years under consideration here, the term for an Argentine president was longer than the term for a U.S. president; it more closely resembled the French presidential term, which was once seven years and is now five. In 1983, Argentina's presidential term was six years, without the possibility of reelection. It was shortened in the mid-1990s to a four-year renewable term as a result of changes that allowed Menem to be elected for a second term. In this way the Argentine presidency enjoys the strengths of both a presidential and a parliamentary system without the constraints of either.

This overview demonstrates that the Argentine presidency is an extremely powerful office within the national government.[26] Whether it should be that powerful could and perhaps should be an issue of concern for Argentines. But within the institutional configuration described here, many of the powers exercised by Argentina's presidents fall within the law. Citizens dissatisfied with this reality, including Argentine journalists, take issue with the system itself as much as with individual presidents.

One way to look at institutional relations between the executive and the Congress during the two presidencies under consideration is to place them in a 2 x 2 comparative matrix. Table 2.1 considers the relative weight of executive and legislative initiative across the policy areas examined in this study. These are privatization, labor policy, social policy, civilian control of the military, and human rights policy. The table summarizes executive/

---

26. Carlos Nino argues that Juan Batista Alberdi, who originally drafted the Argentine constitution, actually wanted the nation to have an elected king, a government that would have been democratic in its origins but not in its practice. See his *Radical Evil on Trial* (New Haven: Yale University Press, 1996), 49. Other observers have credited the idea of an elected king to Simon Bolívar who was influential in Latin America more generally but not a writer of Argentina's constitution. In the end, Argentina did not settle for an elected king. Instead, the constitutions already in existence in several Argentine provinces served as models for the 1853 constitution, along with extensive references to the United States Constitution, as well. Other constitutional models that influenced the Argentine 1853 Constitution were the 1812 Constitution of Cadiz, Spain, the 1832 Swiss Constitution, the 1826 and 1833 Chilean constitutions and the French constitution of 1783. From among the provincial constitutions that were influential, the 1826 Rivadavia Constitution was the most influential of all. The political leaders who most influenced the 1853 Argentina constitution later became known as "the Generation 80," referring to 1880. They included many provincial governors and several leaders who would become presidents of Argentina in the subsequent decades.

The tendency to embrace and encourage a strong executive contrasts with political thinking in the drafting of the United States Constitution where centralized power was suspect. Luis Roniger and Mario Sznajder observe that the executive has traditionally been predominant in Southern Cone nations more generally, a trend that fits with the regional subculture of hierarchy and centralized power. See Luis Roniger and Mario Sznajder, *The Legacy of Human Rights Violations in the Southern Cone: Argentina, Chile and Uruguay* (Oxford: Oxford University Press, 1999), 8, 10.

legislative relations with respect to the policies that comprised the transition process. It shows that the policies were not always characterized by independent executive initiative and a subservient Congress. Instead, policy sometimes reflected joint executive-legislative action within the design of the institutions themselves, as described above.

As the following chapters will demonstrate, many policies appear in the top left quadrant, indicating both congressional and executive attention to the issue. Sometimes that attention revealed different agendas, as with labor policy. Yet both branches wanted influence. The dialogue between the executive and the legislature over labor policy, for instance, consisted of a struggle between agendas. The top right quadrant represents a more modest executive involvement, at times because the executive wanted to hide behind the Congress (e.g., ending the draft). The bottom left quadrant holds the early years of privatization, periods where congressional initiative was low. During Alfonsín's term, Congress was primarily obstructionist. In Menem's early years, Congress was caught by surprise. The bottom right quadrant indicates policies that held the attention of neither branch, such as the social cost of many of Menem's privatization policies or reparations and social healing as part of human rights policy. On the first of these, the executive branch showed only limited initiative in addressing poverty, although it took some measures. Congress showed low initiative on poverty. As a result its policies were ultimately inadequate. On

TABLE 2.1. Overview of Presidential/Congressional Initiative by Policy Area, 1983–1999

Congressional Initiative	Executive Initiative	
	high	**low**
high	1. privatization in late Menem years (1997–99) 2. social policy, including education 3. civilian control of military/human rights policy under Alfonsín 4. labor policy (exec. agenda = control; leg. agenda = protection)	1. eliminating the draft 2. K-12 education reform
low	1. privatization under Alfonsín 2. early privatization under Menem (1989–90) 3. civilian control of military under Menem	1. social costs of reform, poverty alleviation 2. human rights policy: restorative justice, reparations, social healing

human rights policy, neither institution displayed interest in reparations or symbolic moves that would facilitate social healing.[27]

The Judiciary: The Dilemmas of Nonelected Status

Ian Shapiro says that the judiciary is unlike the other two branches.[28] On the one hand it is the only branch entitled to interpret the law. Where the law is respected, this special position places the judiciary above the other two branches of the state and able to constrain them both. Additionally, its nonelected status allows it to claim an independence and dispassion that the other two branches cannot assert. The judiciary can use this claim to bolster its authority over the other two branches. In this sense the judiciary is more powerful than either the executive or the legislature. On the other hand, in a new democracy the question of whether or not the law is respected is precisely the issue over which a struggle occurs. Patterns and habits come forward from the authoritarian past while contemporary actors are accustomed to operating where the rule of law does not prevail. Lawlessness matters for the judiciary because it is not elected, and for that reason has no separate, immediate electoral source of legitimacy all its own. It also has no independent powers of enforcement and depends upon the executive to enforce its decisions. Its disconnection from the electorate and its reliance solely upon the rule of law for its power makes it susceptible to making mistakes that reflect its secluded status. It is also vulnerable to the powers that the other branches have over it, such as nomination or changes in the law. In this sense the judiciary is weaker than the other two branches. Its vulnerability is etched most clearly while democratization is in process.

The dilemmas of the judicial position became evident during the transition years because respect for the rule of law varied over time. During

---

27. In discussing executive-legislative relations during the Menem years, Ana Maria Mustapic writes that party discipline or the willingness of legislators to conform to the president's agenda could not be assumed or taken for granted but had to be produced by deliberate action. The presidential system provides space within which legislators can defy or challenge the president's leadership. However, the political party's ability to distribute selective incentives and the bipartisan system that existed during the Menem period worked to encourage legislators to cooperate with the president. Mustapic writes that executive-legislative relations oscillate between these two different logics, one a logic of presidentialism and the other a logic of parliamentarism. See "Oficialistas y diputados: las relaciones ejecutivo-legislativo en la Argentina," *Desarollo Económico* 39, no. 156 (Jan.–Mar. 2000): 571–95.

28. Ian Shapiro, *Democratic Justice* (New Haven: Yale University Press, 1999); R. Shep Melnick, "The Courts, Jurisprudence and the Executive Branch," in *The Executive Branch*, ed. Joel D. Aberback and Mark A. Peterson (Oxford: Oxford University Press, 2005), 452–85.

the Alfonsín presidency the rule of law was respected. As a result the judiciary held a powerful position and its role during that period illustrates the judiciary's potential contribution to democratization. The judiciary pushed forward the democratization process in a daring manner that was unparalleled in any other Latin American democracy. Yet that boldness itself eventually became problematic; as problems arose, the vulnerability and dependency of the judiciary became clear. Judicial boldness caused problems for democracy itself. As an unelected institution whose members are not worried about reelection, the judiciary pushed forward with its agenda despite the emerging problems. Congress then responded in a manner reflective of its own elected status, limiting the role of the judiciary with new laws.

The early democratic Congress that limited the judicial role did not intend to relegate the judiciary to the sidelines for the remainder of the transition. But this was precisely the outcome because Menem came next and had a very different attitude toward the judiciary. Under Menem respect for the rule of law was not guaranteed, a posture that exposed the judiciary's dependency upon the executive. Menem resented and resisted the judiciary's capacity to halt his more authoritarian tendencies. His resistance found support in rules that allow the executive to name and remove justices. Faced with their newly rediscovered vulnerability,[29] many judges and magistrates did not push back against Menem but accepted or even embraced the subordination he imposed upon them. In the Menem years the judiciary played very little role in democratization.

The long-term results of executive power over the judiciary haunt Argentina's democracy today. Judicial subordination to the executive is a central problem, underscored by the death and possible murder of a public prosecutor who was investigating Peronist president Christina Kirchner. The loss of the two-party system has further debilitated the judiciary at the national level, although party competition inside some provinces has permitted the judiciary to remain strong there.[30] After the close of the transition years studied here, a new Peronist president, Nestor Kirchner, reopened the question of human rights trials. That policy could change the role of the judiciary in the future. Perhaps the judiciary has yet to write its own story beyond the years studied here. In other nations with extensive human rights violations the judiciary has sometimes taken several decades

---

29. During the dictatorship, Argentina's judiciary was not known for resistance to tyranny. Judges and magistrates felt threatened by the military, just as the rest of society did, and they responded in a self-protective manner.

30. Rebecca Bill Chavez, *The Rule of Law in Nascent Democracies: Judicial Politics in Argentina* (Stanford: Stanford University Press, 2004).

before attending to the questions of retroactive justice, reparations, and social healing. That was true in Spain where, thirty years after the return to democracy, the judiciary is now trying to play a role in democratization.[31] Its influence has been felt far beyond the borders of Spain.[32]

But that question lies beyond the study at hand. In the next part we see that Argentina's judiciary played a more central role in the immediate post-dictatorship years than the same institution has done in other new democracies following gross human rights violations.[33] In the transition period as a whole, the judiciary began by playing a key role in democratization and was then reduced to a much smaller role. That outcome is owing to the institutional design itself and to the historical patterns of the Peronist Party embodied in the behavior of President Menem.

The Main Parties inside the Institutions

We move now from a consideration of the state's formal institutions to an overview of the two main national parties that used those institutions. Whereas the United States did not have a developed party system of two nationally competitive parties at the time of its founding, Argentina came to the democratization process having two large national parties that had existed during the nation's authoritarian years. Their history of survival in authoritarian periods shaped their behavior now, during democratization.

The presence of two parties capable of winning national office separates the transition from the contemporary period because today Argentina's two-party system has been replaced by a single-party, factionalized system. While the struggles of a one-party state lie beyond the study at hand, the seeds of the single-party system were planted during the stresses

31. Omar Encarnación, *Democracy without Justice in Spain: The Politics of Forgetting* (University Park: Pennsylvania State University Press, 2014).

32. Cath Collins, *Post-transitional Justice: Human Rights in Chile and El Salvador* (University Park: Pennsylvania State University Press, 2010). Tom Ginsburg finds that, in Asian cases, the judiciary indeed serves as a protector of democracy. See *Judicial Review in New Democracies: Constitutional Courts in Asian Cases* (New York: Cambridge University Press, 2003). Ginsburg looks closely at the cases of Taiwan, Korea, and Mongolia.

33. Argentina's decision to put military officers on trial placed the judiciary in a more central role than would have been the case had the country chosen to confine itself to a truth and reconciliation commission, as was the case in South Africa. There, trials of human rights perpetrators were mostly avoided by the amnesty granted to those who confessed their crimes before the TRC. For an extensive discussion of the various roles played by a truth and reconciliation commission as opposed to judicial trials, see Robert I. Rotberg and Dennis Thompson, eds., *Truth v. Justice: The Morality of Truth Commissions* (Princeton: Princeton University Press, 2000).

of the transition itself. For the seventeen years considered here, the nation still enjoyed two-party competition from the Radicals and the Peronists.[34] Our comprehension of democratization necessitates understanding these two parties and knowing what assets and liabilities they brought from their own past.

Radicalism

The Radical Civic Union traces its history to the late nineteenth century. It was born as a popular social movement to expand suffrage rights to include all males and to make elections competitive. Prior to the arrival of the Radical Party, democracy had existed only on paper: parties were unrepresentative and most people were not allowed to vote. The Radicals wanted to gain universal male suffrage, make the president an elected official, and bring management of some of the nation's natural resources under the control of the government.

The Radicals called for elections over many years before they finally achieved universal male suffrage in a presidential election in 1916.[35] Their candidate, Hipólito Yrigoyen, won the presidency. The Radicals won the office two more times before they were removed, and a military coup ended democracy in 1930. That coup indicated that the contest over whether or not Argentina would be a democracy was not over. The Radicals, therefore, maintained their voice for democracy, and stood against tyranny for most of the rest of the twentieth century. In the process of taking that position for so long, they became a party that stood for ethics, clean government, and heroism. They stood for democracy but were less capable of formulating the specifics of policy to be used by a democratic government. They also became idealistic, rigid, somewhat detached from reality, and limited in their ability to launch a governing program. After their initial social agitation in the late nineteenth and early twentieth centuries, they also became a party with a very limited and declining grassroots base. They proved unwilling to do the hard work necessary to build and retain a relationship with average citizens, and they appeared elitist. These basic quali-

---

34. There are also small provincial parties present in both chambers as well as members of the Unión del Centro Democrático (Union of the Democratic Center), a small national party that represents the far right. To date, none of these has won national power. At the beginning of the 1990s UCEDE was replaced by MODIN, a nationalist party lead by Aldo Rico who had led an attempted coup against Alfonsín in 1987. Then, in the mid-1990s, a third party, FREPASO emerged. It joined with the Radical Party in 1999 to create the Alliance Party that won and produced the De la Rúa presidency.

35. Universal suffrage became law in 1912, four years before the next presidential election.

ties continued to characterize the party during the democratic transition.

The continuities that Radicalism brought to the democratization process consisted of a set of priorities and a style that rapidly became outdated as the nation modernized itself. They remained an elitist party, held closed primaries, and failed to expand their electoral base. They campaigned on normative issues and lacked pragmatic specifics about how policies would be implemented.[36] Their problems were then greatly compounded by the fact that they faced a nondemocratic adversary in the form of Peronism, which, if prepared to play by democratic rules in elections, still used the institutions of state as an opportunity for nondemocratic behavior. The Radicals were unequal to the task of besting nondemocratic opponents using democratic means. They were a party that prioritized ethics and normative vision, taking the moral high ground while neglecting the pragmatic necessities of party survival. Their strengths and limitations have had a long-term impact on Argentina's democracy.[37]

Peronism

Peronism is not as old as Radicalism but nevertheless enjoys a long history. Its history is tied to the influence of one man, Juan Perón, who was a military officer. Perón began his rise to national visibility by being part of a military junta during World War II. As minister of labor, Perón oversaw many reforms for the benefit of labor and developed a large following as a result. Calculating that he could win an election on the basis of that following, he then challenged his military superiors and became an unexpected voice for elections. He won his first election as president in 1946 and a subsequent electoral victory in 1952.

However, Perón was not a democrat. The advent of elections brought many other democratic processes that he was much less willing to embrace. He resisted forming his movement into a political party because he understood that doing so would open the door to competition against his own control. Peronism eventually became a party anyway, but Perón always dominated both the social movement and the party in a hierarchical, caudillista fashion, eliminating opposition voices and demanding absolute loyalty from both followers and secondary leaders. During his nine years in power, Perón engaged in considerable abuse of power and misuse of the

---

36. Peronism also holds closed primaries but has taken great care to build a popular electoral base with labor. On the obsolete nature of many Radical Party tactics, see Anderson, "Problem of Single-Party Predominance" (2009).

37. Anderson, "Problem of Single-Party Predominance."

democratic institutions of state. He arrested and jailed opposition leaders from the Radical Party and eliminated Socialist Party leaders within the labor movement.

He also undermined the democratic function of Congress. He encouraged Peronist representatives in Congress to denigrate opposition voices inside the institution, undermining the institution's capacity to serve as a forum for dialogue. As a party, Peronism disallowed opposition input into any aspect of policy while Perón was in power. The domineering posture of Peronism within Congress caused the decline of the institution itself during Perón's presidency. It began as a vibrant forum for debate and dialogue but debate was soon stifled by Peronist bullying, disrespect, and discourtesy toward opposition legislators. By the end of Perón's first nine years in power, Congress had become nothing but a rubber stamp for Perón's policies. Energetic opposition legislators had retired and meaningful debate had died. In the months before Perón's ouster, Peronist legislators themselves tried belatedly to undo many of the destructive laws they had driven through Congress in Perón's early years, but it was too late. Eager to demonstrate subservience to Perón, Congress had deprived itself of the opportunity for debate and of the self-corrective mechanisms debate allows. A military coup removing Perón then deprived the nation itself of any chance to return opposition legislators to Congress and revitalize debate there.

Perón also tolerated no opposition from labor. As part of his effort to control labor, he instituted a system of corporate welfare benefits distributed through the unions he organized and controlled. This arrangement not only provided benefits to workers beyond what many other countries had at the time but also gave the president extreme powers over the working class. Control was also exercised by union bosses who held the purse strings of the benefits and could use them to pressure workers into following their orders. Vertical dominance, intolerance, limited democratic loyalties, and corporate welfare came with Peronism into the democratization process of 1983–99. They were visible in the behavior of President Carlos Menem; his brother, Eduardo Menem, who became Senate Majority Leader; and the Peronist legislators in both chambers of Congress.

In contrast to the Radicals, the Peronists have always been willing to do the hard work entailed in building a grassroots base. But these grassroots ties are clientelistic rather than democratic. At all levels of the party, ties have been vertical, hierarchical, and unfree. A grassroots base has allowed Peronism to remain in contact with average citizens but has undermined the capacity of those citizens to participate in politics in the independent fashion necessary for democracy. These characteristics of continuity then came forward into the process of democratic transition. Indeed, the historical baggage of each party would allow it to contribute to the democratization process in some ways but detract from it in others. This contradictory role would be even more pronounced for Peronism, the party with the largest influence coming out of the transition years. The contradictory influence of Peronism was most visible with respect to the incorporation of social services into the democratization process.

The continuities of Peronism consisted of a set of inconsistent and contradictory behaviors: grassroots contacts combined with vertical control and antidemocratic behaviors. These behaviors dated back to the party's past and to Perón himself, but they caused Peronism to be a contradictory and inconsistent influence upon the democratization process. Some reforms that Peronism oversaw were profoundly democratic and could have important long-term implications for democracy's continued survival. Other behaviors were deeply nondemocratic, and they have left the nation struggling with a contradictory set of influences at it moves into the twenty-first century. As a contradictory, untrustworthy party, Peronism has prioritized power over every other concern and has shown no discomfort in reversing itself repeatedly. It has played by democratic rules when those rules increase Peronist power, and broken democratic rules when those rules jeopardize that power. These contradictions mean that the party and its leaders lack moral authority or vision and are often distrusted. They have prioritized pragmatics and power over all other considerations, and their priority scheme has had profound implications for Argentina's democracy today.

Conclusion

This chapter has considered the polity and institutional design derived from the United States as potential resources for democracy. It is an appropriate comparison because issues of power and power constraint that were central in Argentina's democratic transition were also prevalent during the U.S. founding. These concerns are reflected in the institutional design. The two nations begin at dissimilar points because the United States began with a decentralized political system undergirded by a suspicion of centralized power while Argentina has always relied upon strong, centralized power for crisis resolution. Yet over its history the United States has looked to the presidency for crisis resolution, and the presidency has delivered on its promise, as Hamilton knew it would. The strong presidency in Argentina helped democracy begin as it helped American democracy survive. We begin with the first years after dictatorship to learn how the president, working with Congress and the judiciary, used the institutions to wrench Argentina away from authoritarianism and start it on a path toward democratization.

PART II

The Alfonsín Years

THREE

When All Three
Branches Cooperate

Human Rights Policy and Civilian Control of the Military

Alfonsín obtained the rule of constitutional law; Menem obtained
the subordination of the military to that law.

—Horacio Jaunarena, former minister of defense under Alfonsín[1]

When we focus upon the checking mechanisms of Madison's system we
neglect something equally important about his arrangement: the extent
to which good government can emerge when all three branches work in
tandem. This chapter illustrates how policy can result from cooperation
across all three branches of state. In the history of the United States, one
such cooperative moment was World War II, specifically the immediate
aftermath of Pearl Harbor. Argentina's emergence into a postdictator-
ship world was a similar moment because the nation faced an enormous
challenge from a nondemocratic adversary: the military. The early years
of Alfonsín's presidency witnessed cooperation and mutual reinforcement
across the branches of state in the effort to contain the military and confront the issue of human rights violations. The result was a government
more capable than it would have been had one branch worked alone. Even
so, the new democratic government needed all the institutional resources
it could muster to make democracy prevail.

---

1. Interviews, Buenos Aires, October 1, 1997, and October 28, 1997. I am indebted to Raúl
Alfonsín for helping to arrange the first of these interviews.

One of democracy's greatest challenges is the effort to discipline, overcome, or halt the behavior of a nondemocratic adversary. In advanced democracies this challenge has rarely presented itself short of war. Lincoln contended that he faced a nondemocratic adversary in the treasonous Confederate states who had assaulted the nation's democratic system by their secession. That assessment led him to suspend the writ of habeas corpus and supervise the mails so that disloyal individuals in the Northern states could not sabotage the war effort there. Contending against nondemocratic enemies causes even democracies and democratic leaders to push at the edges of the law or to suspend it entirely.

But except in the institution of slavery itself, even Lincoln did not face violence against civilians without a declaration of war. Situations where democracies confront terrorism are closer to that scenario, and democratic leaders have suspended the rule of law in such circumstances.[2] That contrast makes Argentina's democratization all the more remarkable because the nation faced the challenge of disciplining the military by using institutions within the rule of law. "Energy in the executive," wrote Hamilton, "is the essence of good government."[3] Alfonsín began his presidency exemplifying that energy. Precisely because of the danger democracy faced, Argentina needed strong, brave, determined leadership. This chapter demonstrates the progress Argentina made by drawing upon strong presidential leadership. Yet Alfonsín exercised that leadership within the confines of the nation's democratic institutions and drawing perpetually upon the support and additional leadership of the other institutions. Using law to fight lawlessness was part of Alfonsín's agenda for restoring democracy. The president determined that the crimes of the military would not be set aside as they had been by earlier civilian regimes. Although the president, his cabinet, Congress, and the judiciary were forced to create law along the way, Alfonsín's effort was successful. Congress created law to enable investigation of human rights violations and possible punishment of the military.[4] The process of creating law, of implementing military

2. In the trying circumstances of 1978, during the desperate search for Italian prime minister Aldo Moro, who had been kidnapped by a terrorist group, the Red Brigades, some observers thought to use torture to extract information from Red Brigades' prisoners. In a famous response the Italian chief of police is said to have rejected that suggestion because it would only serve to make the police as bad as the kidnappers themselves. On the Moro murder, see Richard Drake, *The Aldo Moro Murder Case* (Cambridge: Harvard University Press, 1995).

3. Alexander Hamilton, Federalist #10.

4. I see the involvement of Congress and the judiciary as positive indications of institutional inclusion in the efforts to gain control of the military. However, David Pion-Berlin suggests that Alfonsín's lack of total executive authority actually meant that Alfonsín lost control of his own human rights policy and was himself moved forward at critical points either by the

and human rights policy, remained within democratic bounds and was the essence of democracy.

Reestablishing Democracy by Institutional Means

Between 1976 and 1983 Argentina suffered the most brutal military dictatorship in its history of repeated military dictatorships.[5] The military took power in 1976 by ousting Isabel Perón, who had been the vice president for her husband Juan Perón and had become president upon his death. After overthrowing Isabel, the military ended elections and outlawed political parties. They named their government the Process of National Reorganization (Proceso de Reorganización Nacional) and called the government "the Proceso" for short. The Argentine people called it the "Dirty War."[6]

A famous Roman dictum reads "inter arma silent leges"—"in time of war the laws are silent."[7] This dangerous spirit helps explain the attitude of the military during the dictatorship. Upon assuming power in 1976, Argentina's military maintained that the nation was at war against leftist subversives.[8] They said this because terrorists had targeted the military and

---

Congress or by the judiciary. Both of these institutions acted in ways that caused problems for the administration and threats to the new democracy. See *Through Corridors of Power: Institutional and Civil Military Relations in Argentina* (University Park: Pennsylvania State University Press, 1997), chap. 4.

5. Carlos Nino argues that Argentina's cultural configuration of power concentration, ideological dualism, corporatism, and anomie actually set the stage for the massive human rights violations that came with the Dirty War. See *Radical Evil*, 49.

6. On the military in Argentina, see John Samuel Fitch, *The Armed Forces and Democracy in Latin America* (Baltimore: Johns Hopkins University Press, 1998); David Pion-Berlin, "Between Confrontation and Accommodation: Military and Government Policy in Latin America," *Journal of Latin American Studies* 23, no. 3 (October 1991): 543–71; David Pion-Berlin, "The Limits to Military Power: Institutions and Defense Budgeting in Democratic Argentina," *Studies in Comparative International Development* 33, no. 1 (Spring 1998): 94–115; and Pion-Berlin, *Through Corridors*. On Alfonsín's human rights policy, see Alison Brysk, *The Politics of Human Rights in Argentina: Protest, Change and Democratization* (Stanford: Stanford University Press, 1994).

7. Cited in Scott C. James, "The Evolution of the Presidency: Between the Promise and the Fear," in *The Executive Branch*, ed. Joel D. Aberbach and Mark A. Peterson (Oxford: Oxford University Press, 2005), 16.

8. The military subscribed to a set of beliefs known as the "National Security Doctrine." By these beliefs, the military saw themselves and all of society as threatened by leftist insurrection. They were convinced that they themselves would be the first victims of leftists who were about to take national power. See Fitch, *Armed Forces*, esp. chap. 4. Videla, head of the first ruling junta, described subversion as not only guns and bombs but also the spread of ideas contrary to Western and Christian civilization. Included in the group of subversives were the Mothers of the Plaza de Mayo. See Michelle Bonner, *Sustaining Human Rights: Women and*

police during Isabel's presidency. During the seven dictatorship years the Argentine military murdered people.[9] Figures for the number of missing Argentine citizens vary between 10,000 and 30,000. Because no records were kept, we will never know the precise number of citizens who died. The pattern the military used was to single out individuals they claimed were "subversives" and to kidnap them, either at night, in their homes, while they slept, or when they were alone in a relatively isolated place during the day. "Arrested" citizens were taken to clandestine military prisons. The military and the police subsequently denied any knowledge of these arrests, and most victims were never seen again. The military, police, and judicial establishment never conducted any civil or criminal trials of those who had been arrested. Instead, those detained were tortured in an effort to extract information from them. Sometimes, prisoners died under torture. After torture, many dead prisoners were dumped into mass graves in isolated areas of Argentina. In other cases bodies, and sometimes prisoners who were still alive, were flown out over the South Atlantic and dumped into the sea. A very few prisoners escaped or were released. What we know about the clandestine prisons draws on information from those who survived. At the time, those arrested became known as "the disappeared" because there was no information about their fate and the authorities (both the police and the military government) denied any knowledge of them.

Part of the task during the early Alfonsín years explored here was to reconstruct the events that had occurred between 1976 and 1983. That reconstruction discovered that, apart from murder and torture, in the pattern described above, the military had also kidnapped children from their victims and had sold them or given them away to military families and

---

Argentine Human Rights Organizations (University Park: Pennsylvania State University Press, 2007), 65, 68.

Pion-Berlin writes, as well, that the military saw themselves as privileged members of society and the military itself as a privileged corporation. By contrast, the Radical government rejected the military's special view of themselves. The Radicals saw military men as citizens first and soldiers second. See "Between Confrontation and Accommodation," esp. 552.

Roniger and Sznajder suggest that the political discourse of the Proceso years was about a version of collective well-being, an international struggle against a common enemy that justified the infringement of collective rights. This immediate discourse fit well with a subculture of hierarchy, corporatism, and barbarism. See Roniger and Sznajder, *Legacy of Human Rights Violations*, 7–8.

9. After the downfall of the military regime, many military men insisted that they were and had been heroes in a war. By their actions, they had saved the nation. On the other hand, some members of the armed forces never supported the human rights violations that predominated in the Dirty War. Some officers opposed the Dirty War even at the time. Fitch, *Armed Forces*, 138–39, 141.

friends.[10] The effort to reconstruct the campaign of disappearances concluded that the military had captured and killed most of the leftist terrorists within the first few months of the dictatorship.[11] Yet the repression continued.[12] Although the military labeled all of its victims "subversives," most had had nothing to do with terrorism.[13]

In the face of dictatorship there was no civilian uprising. The contribution of civil society was to elect Alfonsín. Argentina had suffered military

---

10. A fictionalized account of the fate of such babies was poignantly portrayed to international acclaim in the Argentine movie *La Historia Oficial*, or *The Official Story*. The English translation loses the double meaning of the Spanish title, which also captures the fact that the main character is a high school history teacher. The movie won the Academy Award and brought international attention to the crimes of the military. For a dramatic fictionalized account of the human aftermath of the repression in Chile, see Ariel Dorfman, *Death and the Maiden* (New York: Penguin Books, 1991), and the review of Dorfman's work by Sophia A. McClennan, "Beyond *Death and the Maiden*: Ariel Dorfman's Media Criticism and Journalism," *Latin American Research Review* 45, no. 1 (January 2010): 173–88.

11. National Commission on Disappeared Persons (CONADEP), *Nunca Mas: A Report by Argentina's National Commission on Disappeared People* (London: Faber and Faber, 1986); Alison Brysk, *The Politics of Human Rights: Protest, Change, and Democratization* (Stanford: Stanford University Press, 1994).

12. Iain Guest argues that international pressure from the United Nations and the United States might have brought down the military regime by 1979 and that pressure from those quarters had already saved a number of lives by that point. However, the international dynamic changed with the arrival of the Reagan administration. Through Jeanne Kirkpatrick, Reagan put pressure on the UN to stop its human rights policies and eventually caused the removal of Theo van Boven, the Dutchman who had been a key player in the UN human rights policy. Argentina's representative to the UN, Gabriel Martinez, steadfastly defended the junta for seven years and attacked Van Boven even though Martinez certainly knew about the killings happening in Argentina. Subsequent investigation revealed that Martinez dutifully forwarded to the junta in Buenos Aires all of the UN questions and inquiries about the disappearances. As a result of the pressure from Reagan, Kirkpatrick, and Martinez, the Argentine junta was given a reprieve, allowing it to remain in power for another four years. Guest concludes that the UN betrayed the human rights movement in Argentina by yielding to U.S. pressure. See Iain Guest, *Behind the Disappearances: Argentina's Dirty War Against Human Rights and the United Nations* (Philadelphia: University of Pennsylvania Press, 1990).

Robert H. Holden has argued that "public violence," particularly by the military against civilians, was even more extreme in Central America than anywhere else in the continent, although the same argument about a war against leftism was also used there. See *Armies without Nations: Public Violence and State Formation in Central America, 1821–1960* (Oxford: Oxford University Press, 2004).

13. In the first two years of the military dictatorship, international pressure against the regime was so strong that Argentine diplomats abroad began to be affected by it. Some of them even pressured the military government to step down. This situation changed with the arrival of President Reagan who announced that he admired the junta for their security policies. He was later embarrassed by junta General Roberto Viola who, upon a visit to Washington, suggested that there would never be any investigation of military crimes because one does not investigate a victorious army. Viola also remarked for the press that had the Nazis won the Second World War, there would have been no Nuremburg Trials or the Nuremburg Trials would have been held in Virginia! See Guest, *Behind the Disappearances*, 237, 278.

dictatorships in the past, and each time the civilian government gave the outgoing military regime impunity.[14] Alfonsín's election was a choice *not* to repeat this pattern.[15] As the Radical Party candidate, Alfonsín had promised that this time it would be different. "We cannot act," said Alfonsín, "as if nothing has happened." In his campaign he said that there would be no impunity for the military. His promise was courageous, unprecedented, and problematic. Even practiced and well-oiled democratic institutions move slowly and encourage disagreement. Whether unpracticed institutions could accomplish the complex task of uncovering the truth was much more uncertain. But the electorate had chosen Alfonsín because of his promise to address the past.

The electorate rejected the other candidate, Peronist Italo Luder, who preferred to forget the past. The Peronists anticipated that investigation

---

14. Pion-Berlin writes that in the fifty-three years between 1930, when the military ousted President Yrigoyen, and 1983, when the military allowed democracy to return, Argentina experienced a period characterized either by direct military rule or by military tutelage. During that time, the military had cut short every democratically elected government that had ever taken office. Yet Argentina's militarism originated in society itself, including rural landowners who began by holding power through fraudulent elections. *Through Corridors*, 46–47.

On the long-standing militarism of Argentine society, see Alain Rouquie, *Pouvoir militaire: Societe politique Republique Argentine* (Paris: Presses de la fondation nationale des sciences politiques, 1978). Rouquie argues that the military has historically been central in Argentine political life and that the centrality of the military is the fruit of a long, slow germination of cultural patterns (62). In particular, the army was central to the idea of state formation, and army generals were chosen by civilian authorities rather than by procedures internal to the military itself (63, 67). This process created close ties between the military and civilian leaders and led to the military assuming that it had and should take political responsibility for the nation. The culture of Argentina's army is strongly influenced by admiration for the German military, with some superficial imitation of French military uniforms (76, 81). The autonomy of Argentina's military gave it the chance to become an enormous bureaucratic force in its own right, enjoying considerable freedom to maneuver outside of civilian constraints (89). The army's centrality had become pronounced by 1930, when Argentina made its first steps toward democracy and when the first elected president, Hipólito Yrigoyen, was ousted by a military coup (103).

Nino writes that the human rights trials caused the military to change their attitude and to stop assuming that they had a right to oversee the function of society and government in Argentina. This effect was quite apart from the actual outcome of individual trials. See the conclusion in Nino, *Radical Evil on Trial*, esp. 166.

15. One difference lay in the fact that military coups between 1930 and 1976 had always had support among at least some segment of Argentine society, and the 1976 coup did as well. By 1983, however, military behavior had moved outside the bounds of what Argentines considered acceptable. The Proceso forced citizens to rethink whether the military was really a solution to their problems. See Pion-Berlin, *Through Corridors*, 50–51, 53, 57.

This same question was also in the background of early electoral politics and the democratic transition in Chile and Uruguay, whose first elections in the current electoral calendar came after 1983. For a comparison of how these three nations handled the question of investigation versus forgetting, see Roninger and Sznajder, *Legacy of Human-Rights Violations*.

of the past would produce confrontation with the military, decreasing the chances that an election would be held or its outcome honored. Calculating that a policy of forgiving and forgetting was the path most likely to produce an enduring civilian regime, Luder promised no investigation of the military. Peronism has often seen the military as a partner, so that position fit with Peronism's historical military ties. The close relationship between Peronism and the military dates back to Juan Perón's early years in the 1940s and resulted from his own background as a military man.[16]

In the face of Peronism's mild attitude toward the outgoing military regime, the Peronist Party and its labor union supporters were suspected of pacting with the military: if Peronism won, labor would support the new government and hold no strikes against it while the military would face no criminal investigation.[17] David Pion-Berlin writes that General Leopoldo

---

16. Fitch, *Armed Forces*, 91. Several examples of military accommodation toward union leaders emerged in my interviews with union leaders themselves. For example, Oscar Lescano, head of the Light and Power union (the famous Luz y Fuerza union), offered himself for arrest in exchange for the freedom of forty-three members of the union, which itself had 70,000 members. The chief of the Buenos Aires police, Suarez Mason, refused Lescano's offer and thereby saved Lescano's life. We do not know what happened to the forty union members that Suarez Mason refused to release, nor do we know the fate of most of those disappeared during the Dirty War. Most prisoners died; however, at least one survived (name unknown) because that individual was able to testify subsequently that he had seen Oscar Smith, former head of the Light and Power Union, in a clandestine prison. Through this testimony, we learned that Smith had, indeed, been kidnapped and murdered by the military.

José Pedraza, leader of the powerful railroad workers union (Union Ferroviario), had a similar story. (Since my interview with him, Pedraza has been tried and found guilty of murdering a young leftist union activist and is currently serving a jail sentence. See http://www.wsws.org/en/articles/2011/02/arge-f25.html, accessed 2/29/16.) Oraldo Britos reported that military men told him to remain in Buenos Aires and not return to his home province where, as a labor leader, he would have been disappeared. Instead, the military told him to find a low-level job in Buenos Aires and keep his head down. That way he would survive. Britos took this advice and it saved his life. In order to make his uninvolvement in "subversive activity" visible, he walked five kilometers each way to work and back, five days a week, to keep himself obvious in an innocuous fashion. Interview with former deputy Oraldo Britos, Buenos Aires, October 11, 1997.

Alison Brysk argues that, when faced with a potential military coup, the unions joined with the human rights organizations and with many other sectors of society in supporting a generalized social atmosphere that protected human rights and demanded respect for them from the military. While Brysk's argument does not itself refute the possibility that some unions would have supported a generalized amnesty for the military, it certainly raises questions about any assumption of absolute loyalty or collusion between the military and the unions. On Brysk's argument, see *Politics of Human Rights in Argentina*. This union behavior is in keeping with my position that sectors of Argentina's civil society did come together to stand for and protect human rights but did not go beyond that to exhibit strong mobilized action in support of other reforms that accompanied and were necessary for democracy.

17. According to Pion-Berlin, the meetings that produced these agreements were made between labor and some members of the military but were "unbeknownst to the rest of the

Galtieri, the head of the third military junta in power during the Proceso government, met secretly with key Peronist labor leaders while the military was still in power. These meetings were held "in an effort to strike a deal" that would guarantee labor complicity in a military amnesty. But no written pact between the Peronist Party and the military has ever been unearthed.

Nevertheless, there was enough suspicion that the electorate rejected Peronism's offer and preferred Alfonsín's promise to investigate the past. As we look back now on the seventeen years under study in this book and as we consider the 5–6 years that lay before Argentina in 1983, we will see that there were high costs as well as deep satisfactions to the approach that Alfonsín advocated and the citizens chose. To opt for the investigation of the military human rights violations was, in many ways, the harder choice. It was a courageous and admirable choice that has made Argentina an example of retroactive justice after the return to democracy elsewhere in the world.[18] It was also a choice that would make democracy more precarious. The choice Argentina made might well have been the one that would lead toward greater inner peace for some individuals.[19] But it was a voluntary choice by this nation to prioritize investigation of the military

---

military." The meetings sought to relax military restrictions on union activity in exchange for labor support for a military amnesty. The idea was that the military would hold on to power indefinitely, supported by Peronist labor, by inviting into the military government some members of the Peronist labor unions. Pion-Berlin does not say exactly what was meant by "union support" for the military. But clearly there were secret negotiations, although their outcome was never made clear. These negotiations are the basis for suspicions both about the Peronist presidential candidate and about a pact between labor and the military. See Pion-Berlin, "The Fall of Military Rule in Argentina, 1976–1983," *Journal of Interamerican Studies and World Affairs* 27, no. 3 (Summer 1985): 55–76, esp. 68.

Argentine labor has a long history of association with the military in an antidemocratic manner, including an association that has helped end elected governments. For example, strikes of nearly four million workers against the Radical government in 1966 helped bring on the military coup that year. While the workers were not openly advocating a military coup against Illia, the chaos they created through strikes was used by the military as an excuse for armed intervention and Illia's ouster. See Santiago Senen Gonzalez and Yanina Welp, "Illia y la Toma de Fabricas," *Todo es Historia*, no. 383 (June 1999): 8–23, esp. 9. At the same time, Illia had won election under a context in which Peronism was proscribed, which gave workers limited loyalty to the democratic regime.

18. Cynthia J. Arnson, ed., *Comparative Peace Processes in Latin America* (Washington, DC: Woodrow Wilson Center; Stanford: Stanford University Press, 1999); Amal Jamany, *Barriers to Democracy: The Other Side of Social Capital in Palestine* (Princeton: Princeton University Press, 2007).

19. This option was not chosen by the electorate in Uruguay and was disallowed by the military in Chile. In the Southern Cone, Argentina stood alone in choosing this option. Roninger and Sznajder, *Legacy*. On Chile and Uruguay, see Alexandra Barahona de Brito, *Human Rights and Democratization in Latin America: Uruguay and Chile* (Oxford: Oxford University Press, 1997).

first above other problems (of which there were many), and to choose the leader and the party best suited to deliver that policy.[20]

Alfonsín's First Agenda: Congress and the Military Trials

Elected on a platform of ethics and honesty, Alfonsín assumed office with a high level of moral authority.[21] He moved swiftly to keep his campaign promises. When trials by the military of their own high-ranking officers found everyone innocent, Alfonsín appointed a commission to investigate the disappearances. Some still believed that the disappeared were alive. The commission was led by Argentina's renowned author Ernesto Sábato. As a result of its investigation the commission wrote the famous book *Nunca Más*, which established that the disappeared had been murdered as part of a systematic policy of the military regime. The report shocked Argentina and the world, illustrating that the disappearances had been no accident and had been deliberate and more widespread than previously imagined. The report also shattered any hopes that the disappeared would be found alive.

---

20. For a theoretical discussion of the legal basis for a policy of retroactive justice and for discussions of similar policies elsewhere in the world, see Nino, *Radical Evil*, chaps. 1, 3, 5. Nino asks whether the laws of the authoritarian regime itself should be honored and, if not, whether a democracy can go back and make a crime out of an act that was not a crime when it was committed (150, 160–61). Nino concludes that if democracy is based on self-interest alone, there are few grounds for retroactive justice. But if democracy also entails value judgments and the establishment of norms and morals is essential to democratic development, then the theoretical argument for retroactive justice rests there (134). Notably, Brazil has recently made advances in this regard. President Dilma Rousseff promoted a law, sanctioned in 2011, to investigate human rights crimes during the dictatorship of 1964–1985. The results of this investigation were published in December 2014. See Organization of American States, http://www.oas.org/en/iachr/media_center/PReleases/2014/151.asp; and Comissão Nacional da Verdade, 2014, http://www.cnv.gov.br/index.php/outros-destaques/576-verdade-e-reconciliacao-dentro-e-fora.

21. Relatedly, he staffed his cabinet with highly skilled individuals whose professional and academic accomplishments placed them at the top of their fields. His ministers were academics, scholars, and authors as well as internationally visible lawyers. It was an impressive group.

There is a parallel in U. S. history. John Kennedy assumed office in 1960, taking a position of moral authority in contrast with the outgoing Republican presidential regime and its close association with McCarthyism. Kennedy claimed that the United States had become a country without purpose or ideals, self-satisfied, materialistic, and ignoble. The parallels to Argentina are clear. Like Alfonsín, Kennedy increased the professional image and moral authority of his staff in part by turning to the academic world to help fill his cabinet. This group was prepared "to roll up their sleeves and make America over." Of the Kennedy cabinet, 18 percent came from the academic world while only 6 percent were business leaders. In contrast, the outgoing Eisenhower administration had been 42 percent from the business community and only 6 percent from the academic world. See Arthur M. Schlesinger Jr., *A Thousand Days: John F. Kennedy in the White House* (Boston: Houghton Mifflin, 2002), 210–12, 698, 726.

Now that the administration knew the truth, the next question was what to do with these revelations. In response to the truth commission report, Alfonsín supported a policy of trying the top generals in all three branches of the military.[22] He outlined three categories of guilty parties: (a) those who had planned the repression and given the general orders, (b) those who had acted beyond their orders, and (c) those who had complied with the orders.[23] Alfonsín had created these categories before the investigations of the past began. Now investigations of the disappearances revealed that the military could not be neatly divided into these categories and that human rights violations were both more complex and more widespread than Alfonsín had imagined. This complexity meant that the decision about who to place on trial was complicated. Alfonsín also had an agenda beyond trials. He specified backward- and forward-looking measures that he planned to take in favor of retroactive justice. As an example of the former, he planned to allow victims sentenced by the military to have their cases reviewed by civilian courts. This portion of the policy imagined that victims were still alive to challenge their sentences, and it assumed, as well, that there had been trials of the disappeared. In fact, there was neither. As an example of forward-looking policy, Alfonsín planned to make specific changes to the military code to weaken their ability to have legal authority over civil society.[24]

In these early weeks we see Alfonsín present a policy agenda as the Constitution says the president will do. His approach brought many other actors into participation and permitted many decisions that he would not have preferred. Had he retained tight control of policy, fewer actors would have influenced the policy. But Alfonsín wanted an institutional approach that would follow the rule of law. For example, he wanted to begin with a legalistic approach whereby the military would try themselves inside military courts according to the military code.[25] He anticipated that these trials would concern only the top commanders and would end quickly. He initially used a judicial approach that would have minimized the role of Congress because he thought that extended, public human rights trials

---

22. In the language of the human rights literature, this was a decision for "retributive justice" or punishment. Elizabeth Kiss, "Moral Ambition within and beyond Political Constraints," in *Truth v. Justice: The Morality of Truth Commissions*, ed. Robert I. Rotberg and Dennis Thompson (Princeton: Princeton University Press, 2000), 68–98, esp. 74–75.

23. Fitch, *Armed Forces*, 166–67; Nino, *Radical Evil*, 63.

24. Nino, *Radical Evil*, 69.

25. Roninger and Sznajder, *Legacy*, 59. Roninger and Sznajder argue that the military found, after the coming of democracy, that they were just one more political actor and could not get everything they wanted, as they had in the past (60–61).

would become an opportunity for legislators and the public to lambaste the military.[26] None of these early expectations worked out. Military tribunals refused to find anyone guilty. Alfonsín had given the military an opportunity to contain policy at a minimal level, but the military courts ignored the opportunity. By refusing to act, the military opened the door to far more extensive investigations than Alfonsín had envisioned.

The failure of the military to act made it harder for Alfonsín to contain his human rights policy on a small scale. A blanket finding of "not guilty" was not acceptable to the Argentine public. Too many people had suffered and died, and there was too much domestic and international attention on the issue. Having failed to contain human rights policy at a minimal level involving only judicial measures, Alfonsín decided to bring Congress into the process of policy creation. He asked Congress to write law to allow the civil courts to try the military.[27] That decision opened policy creation to the legislature.

Chapter 2 showed that Argentina's president is quite powerful even within the expectations of a presidential system. Part of that power lies in the president's prerogative to present a legislative agenda. Alfonsín led with a human rights agenda. But when his small-scale effort failed, he stepped back from the forefront of that policy and allowed Congress to assume some initiative. His retreat toward the background turned out to be a wise political move that made him less of an individual lightning rod for military resentment and probably decreased the chances of an immediate coup in 1984. Any effort by civilian authorities to punish the military had more legitimacy coming from Congress and enjoying support in both chambers. Yet the decision to have Congress write law was to have destabilizing repercussions for the new democracy.

Bringing the Congress to center stage was a slow and risky path forward. The details of how the policy unfolded illustrate the advantages and drawbacks of democratization by institutions. Democracy is always slow, and legislatures are a key part of that slowness. Deliberation over any law takes time. In fact, the U.S. framers of the presidential system intended Congress to be slow. They did not want rash decisions. Yet the solution that emerged from Congress was more than Alfonsín had anticipated or even wanted. Unpredictable outcomes are typical of legislation in any democracy, but the outcome represented a broader consensus than the more limited policy spearheaded by the executive would have achieved.

Turning the decision over to Congress brought a much wider group

26. Nino, *Radical Evil*, 71–73.
27. Nino, *Radical Evil*.

into the decision-making process. In particular, it brought the Peronist Party into the process in a manner that would not have developed had the decision been made in any other way.[28] It gave the opposition party a vested interest in the new policy. Since the Radical Party had won the presidency and the public had embraced their agenda of investigation into the past, these initial weeks of the new democracy appeared to unfold with the Peronist Party relegated to the margins of progress and not centrally involved in the agenda at hand. However, over the weeks of debate, as individual legislators in both chambers contributed to the decision process and the creation of new law, many Peronist legislators came to embrace the agenda of placing the military on trial for murder. The reader will recall Madison's argument that deliberation inside the legislature will bring forward reason and with it the best policy. Here we see that process at work. Peronist Party legislators from across the nation became willing to accept this agenda and support this law. Their support was a crucial part of the creation of law because it reflected broad agreement about what was to happen with respect to the military. No longer did this agenda belong to the Radical Party or its president alone. By bringing the Congress fully into the decision process Alfonsín was able to spread responsibility and support for the military trials across the leadership of the entire government and across both the executive and legislative branches.[29] The unity in action across executive and legislature, Peronists and Radicals created a coalition that stood together against military objections.

28. In public, the Peronist Party argued loudly for a policy of retroactive justice, but in private the party pressed for accommodation with the military. Meanwhile, the rightist Union of the Democratic Center, a small national party, initially supported ending the self-amnesty law but then reversed itself and started justifying the Dirty War. See Nino, *Radical Evil*, 111. Roninger and Sznajder, *Legacy* (57) write that military amnesty would have required the support of a substantial sector of civilian society but was mostly unavailable except in Uruguay, where citizens voted not to investigate military human rights crimes. However, Barahona de Britos, *Human Rights*, is careful to point out that the Uruguayan vote was the result of conservative rural voters who predominated over urban voters. Within Montevideo itself, the electorate voted to overturn the self-imposed military amnesty.

29. In the movement by Peronist legislators toward embracing retroactive justice, we see the results and benefits of deliberation. Students of Congress, which is itself a deliberative body, are quick to point out that the deliberative characteristic of legislative debate is one of the great strengths of legislatures: Lawrence C. Dodd, *Thinking about Congress: Essays on Congressional Change* (New York: Routledge, 2011). Advocates of deliberation suggest that through the process of dialogue parties move closer to each other, discover their true opinions, and arrive at better and more widely acceptable decisions. See Jürgen Habermas, *Communication and the Evolution of Society*, translated by Thomas McCarthy (Boston: Beacon Press, 1979), and Simone Chambers, *Reasonable Democracy* (Ithaca: Cornell University Press, 1996). Other scholars are less convinced of the advantages of deliberation. As an example of this position, see Shapiro, *State of Democratic Theory*, esp. chap. 2.

The lower chamber of Congress, which held a UCR majority, and the Senate, holding a Peronist majority, began by nullifying the self-amnesty laws the military had put in place before leaving power. Next they passed into law Alfonsín's forward-looking and backward-looking policy packages. The House also followed Alfonsín's policy lead and tried to restrict the trials to the top generals alone.[30] A bill restricting the trials originated in the Chamber of Deputies (House) and passed by overwhelming majority. Next the bill went to the Senate. However, a last-minute friendly amendment proposed by Peronist Elias Sapag changed the wording of the bill to include in the trials any officer who had engaged in "atrocious or abhorrent behavior."[31] Those words described a broad swath of the military, since inside the clandestine prisons the military had followed a de facto policy of requiring nearly every officer to involve himself in torture or some other aspect of repression. Therefore, Congress had now created a situation in which trials could take many years.[32] With the intervention of Congress and particularly of the Senate, a policy that could have been a short series of closed military trials of the top brass now became a policy giving the civilian courts authority to try all members of the military down the chain of command. This was democratization through the use of institutions, but it was certainly yielding surprising results.

Alfonsín had originally proposed using military tribunals as the first line of investigation. Congress accepted this first line of action. Under the

---

30. Nino, *Radical Evil*, 74–75.

31. Sapag was a representative of a provincial party, the Popular Neuqueñian Movement (Movimiento Popular Nequeño). He had, himself, lost two children in the Dirty War. His friendly amendment from the floor of the Senate inserted language into Article 514 of the Military Code to say that trials could also extend to any junior officers who had committed "atrocious or aberrant acts." That language allowed the law to include nearly all officers no matter how junior they were. Pion-Berlin, *Through Corridors*, 79.

Andrés D'Alessio, president of the Court of Appeals, downplayed the importance of the Sapag amendment. He suggested that the courts themselves would have gone deeper into the ranks of the military and into military responsibility even without that last-minute friendly amendment. D'Alessio's position was that the application of law was the purview of the courts alone and that no other branch of government had any authority to decide who was guilty or to limit the number of individuals to whom the law could be applied. Instead, argued D'Alessio, only the legal process of investigation and the collection of evidence could determine who was guilty, and the process of the application of justice needed to move forward of its own volition. Interview, Buenos Aires, July 23, 1993; I am indebted to Andrés Fontana for helping to arrange this interview.

32. Pion-Berlin does not see Congress as having been constructive in this role. He argues that, in fact, Congress became part of the problem. The law that emerged from Congress prolonged the trials beyond anything Alfonsín had intended. In the lower chamber, the new version of the bill that had come from the Senate was supported by thirty Radical deputies and all of the Renovationist wing of the Peronist Party. See Pion Berlin, *Through Corridors*, 564–65.

new law the military would again have an opportunity to try themselves. But there was a difference from the first time around. Congress stipulated that if the trials were not proceeding fast enough, the federal courts would have the authority to intervene and remove specific cases from the military tribunals and place them in the civilian courts. This language brought the judiciary into the democratization process and gave courts and federal judges considerable latitude since they would be the ones who would define "too slowly." The law removed control from the military and even limited congressional control over events. The institutional path had proved to be not only more inclusive but more expansive than any other approach.[33]

Considering what we now know about the extreme nature of the human rights violations during the Dirty War, it is easy to conclude that Argentina made the right choice. But much of this truth was still undiscovered when these early laws were passed. The level of human rights violations was found to have been beyond what many Argentine leaders had anticipated, so the extension of the trials had a greater impact than was known at the time the law passed.[34] The choice to expand the trials greatly increased military resistance to the policy; even as citizens and elites from both parties began to unite around that agenda, the military viewed the situation differently. Most members of the armed services did not believe they had done anything wrong. An institutional path had produced both a more expansive policy and more military opposition to that policy, both results emerging from the institutional dialogue.

Since Congress had empowered the civilian courts, the judiciary now exercised their own authority, expanding the scope of the trials still further. The Federal Court of Appeals pronounced that lower echelon officers had held complete discretionary power over the fate of captives, including decision-making authority over whether to kill them or set them free. Now

---

33. Nino argues that the policy choice of the Alfonsín administration was for "some measure" of retroactive justice, or justice surrounding past crimes. Any policy could be criticized for being inadequate in the face of the magnitude of the crimes committed. Yet any action could also be condemned for being legally problematic. The term "some measure" allows Nino to argue that the administration had attempted to address the crimes of the military, a position that he suggests is supportive of democracy. He explores the various arguments for or against retroactive justice from a legal and theoretical perspective but concludes from a policy perspective that the policy, however imperfect, was a good one. Nino, *Radical Evil*, vii–x and chap. 2.

34. On human rights violations and responses to them, see National Commission on Disappeared Persons (CONADEP), *Nunca Mas: A Report by Argentina's National Commission on Disappeared People* (London: Faber and Faber, 1986), and Leslie E. Anderson, "Of Wild and Cultivated Politics: Conflict and Democracy in Argentina," *International Journal of Politics, Culture and Society* 16, no. 1 (Fall 2002): 99–132.

under way was an institutional solution in which no single individual any longer controlled either the course of action or its outcome. Argentine society underwent an intense period of euphoria, fear, and frantic work overload.[35] The human rights groups approved. The new law empowered them to take the actions they had deemed appropriate all along. Working overtime, they and the families of the disappeared built cases against individual officers and soldiers.[36] Over several months, much new evidence emerged. This systematic investigation into the facts is what the military had wanted to avoid and what Peronist candidate Luder felt was dangerous and risky.

The enormity of the crimes was beyond anything anyone had guessed when the investigations began. Military complicity in torture and murder was widespread and inclusive.[37] As the trials got under way and the evidence was presented in support of individual cases, it became apparent that the law passed by Congress was so broad and military complicity so extensive that the courts could try nearly every member of the armed forces. The potential task was gigantic. The years it would require appeared to stretch endlessly into the future. Human rights trials of thousands of individuals on a case-by-case basis could tie up Argentina's legal system into the next century. Was this bottleneck really what society wanted? Was this long-term commitment what Congress had intended? Perhaps, but perhaps not. After all, when Congress passed its new law the magnitude of the task was not fully known. Now that more information had become available, proponents realized that Congress, and particularly Senator Sapag, had allowed this task to become potentially much larger than anyone had guessed.

The legal process itself also lengthened the implementation of the policy. The trials became serious legal mechanisms within which attorneys

---

35. An additional procedure further expanded the potential scope of the trials. Victims were permitted to file claims against specific officers directly with the court system, and those claims were then placed on the court dockets for trials. This procedure differs from the court system in the United States where the police and the district attorney undertake to investigate a claim that is only considered "alleged" when it comes directly from citizens. The police and DA, not citizens themselves, then decide which cases should be investigated and whether to prosecute. This procedure was put in place in Argentina because judicial authorities were aware that Argentine citizens did not want to approach the police and request investigations of crimes. The police were considered complicit with the military, and individual police officers had engaged in human rights violations. Allowing civilians to file charges directly greatly enhanced the ability of victims to place their cases under judicial authority. Pion-Berlin, *Through Corridors*, 89–90.

36. On the frenzied effort to file cases with judicial authorities before the deadlines imposed by the Final Point Law, see Chavez, *Rule of Law in Nascent Democracies*.

37. For an excellent overview of military human rights violations and policy, particularly as viewed from abroad, see Guest, *Behind the Disappearances*.

for the defense offered legal arguments. Attorneys representing military defendants made five specific defenses. Each was countered in court and ultimately rejected by civilian judges. Table 3.1 below presents the defenses offered and the reasons for rejecting them.

Once an institutional approach had expanded the number of actors, the press and public became involved. Mark Peterson has written that some issues are or become so salient that they elicit a "full court press."[38] The human rights investigations and trials had become precisely such an issue, appearing on television and in the newspapers and consuming national attention. Such intense focus upon one issue brings advantages and disadvantages. In Argentina it allowed the democratic government to press forward more thoroughly and successfully than would otherwise have been possible. On the other hand, it also caused the Alfonsín administration to neglect other important concerns.

As a realization of the time commitment gradually dawned, responses were varied. Among many of the human rights groups and the families of the disappeared, the size of the task was unimportant. These groups prioritized the discovery of the truth and the full punishment of those responsible. That the judicial process could take decades, would cost mil-

TABLE 3.1. Reasons for Defense of Military Defendants and Grounds for Rejection

Plea Offered	Grounds for Rejection
1. lawful self-defense	lack of proportionality (self-defense must remain on a par with the original threat made while military violence far exceeded the original threat)
2. necessity (to preserve the survival of the military)	unnecessary (the harm caused was greater than the harm avoided)
3. compliance with orders	No law authorizes torture and murder
4. state of war	Double rejection: (a) No war existed, and (b) had war existed, the military should have applied rules that apply to prisoners of war. Military failed to apply these rules.
5. accelerated end of terror	Yes, the repression did end the terror, but the means did not justify the ends—the military had used excessive force.

38. See Mark A. Peterson, *Legislating Together: The White House and Capitol Hill from Eisenhower to Reagan* (Cambridge: Harvard University Press, 1990), 167. Peterson's words here are only a manner of expressing that there is extensive public attention to the issue. He is not referring to judicial involvement in an issue. In the United States, an example of an issue that reached such a salient level was civil rights. Martin Luther King and his social movement, combined with violent southern opposition, together made civil rights a salient national concern. Johnson then knew how to capitalize on the atmosphere of the times to press forward with extensive civil rights legislation (175).

lions of dollars, would tie up the court system, and would occupy the primary attention and energy of the new government was secondary. This was one perspective.[39] From the perspective of the administration, on the other hand, it became increasingly evident that other problems needed attention and that the government could not afford to concentrate all its energy on the human rights trials. The nation had a future as well as a past. Provision for that future was urgently needed. In particular, just as they had violated the nation's human rights, the military had likewise violated every rule of sound economic management. The new democratic government needed to attend to the foreign debt, a rising number of strikes from the labor unions, inflation, and dysfunctional public services and industries.

From the perspective of the military, the magnitude and sweeping breadth of the human rights trials swiftly became intolerable. The military had greatly underestimated the nature of institutionalized democratic problem-solving. They had not guessed that their refusal to act would open the door to involvement by so many others. Having given up control of the agenda, the military now searched for ways to regain the upper hand. Early in the new government, and with Congress, the executive, the judiciary, and the voters united against them, the military had submitted to their fate. But as the trials stretched on and numerous other problems undermined support for the new government, the military calculated when they might stop the trials and regain leverage over the civilian government.

The Final Point Law and the Law of Due Obedience[40]

Analysts of national processes for confronting gross human rights violations have concluded that such processes are almost always "mired in the muck of compromise."[41] Argentina was no exception. In December 1986, Congress passed the Final Point Law, naming a date beyond which paperwork could not be processed to begin new trials of new defendants.[42] Sub-

---

39. Levinson argues that victims need social recognition as well as some effort toward justice. They and their families need to know that society acknowledges what happened to them. From this perspective the human rights trials served a social purpose as long as they continued. Sanford Levinson, "Trials, Commissions, and Investigating Committees," in *Truth v. Justice: The Morality of Truth Commissions*, ed. Robert I. Rotberg and Dennis Thompson (Princeton: Princeton University Press, 2000), 211–34, esp. 247.

40. In Spanish these laws were La Ley de Punto Final and La Ley de Obediencia Debida.

41. Kiss, "Moral Ambition," 70.

42. On the details of the development of this policy from someone intricately involved in it, see Nino, *Radical Evil*. Fitch argues that the Final Point Law may actually have increased the number of human rights trials because, in response to the deadline it imposed, federal

sequently Congress passed the Law of Due Obedience, which stipulated that officers or private soldiers who had been ordered to torture prisoners or otherwise engage in human rights violations would not be tried or punished for following orders.[43] Minister of Defense Horacio Jaunarena proposed and Congress passed the Full Stop or Final Point Law. Jaunarena argued that "democracy does not rest upon vengeance and persecution."[44] These laws placed an end point upon the human rights trials process when it had otherwise appeared that it might stretch into the next century.[45] They represented an imperfect solution to an enormous problem. Whether it was satisfactory or fair, the Final Point Law should have relieved military fears and allowed democracy to move forward.[46]

The new laws also created problems: they left some perpetrators at large and they failed to finish the human rights policy. Alfredo Astiz, who had been involved in the murder of several Mothers of the Plaza de Mayo and in the death of a Swedish teenager, Dagmar Hagelin, was acquitted under the new Law of Due Obedience.[47] Other perpetrators also escaped consequences. Additionally, the new laws ended human rights policy for

---

courts in many provinces worked through the traditional January holiday period in an effort to book as many cases as possible within the sixty-day deadline given in the law. See Fitch, *Armed Forces*, 161. Chavez also argues that provincial judicial structures responded by working overtime to apply human rights laws. See *Rule of Law in Nascent Democracies*.

43. Congress passed the Final Point law in December 1986 and Alfonsín promulgated the law on December 24, 1986. The Law of Due Obedience was passed and promulgated in June 1987. Many observers believe that the Law of Due Obedience resulted from the attempted coup of Easter, 1987. Observers suspected that the Law of Due Obedience resulted from military pressure upon Alfonsín, who preferred to have this law rather than have an armed conflict between parts of the military who supported the democratic government and parts of the military who defended the Dirty War. Peronist senator Vicente Saadi of Catamarca opposed the Due Obedience Law, arguing that the government should not give in to military pressure. Nino, *Radical Evil*, 74–75.

44. Cited in Pion-Berlin, *Through Corridors*, 92–93.

45. Nino argues that the Final Point Law only accelerated the number of cases filed in the provinces, where previously there had been only slow movement forward. Nino, *Radical Evil*, 92, 94, 100.

46. I am indebted to Jacobo Timerman, former editor of the now-defunct newspaper, *La Opinion*, and to Andrew Graham Yooll, former editor of the newspaper, the *Buenos Aires Herald*, for the perspective of the human rights community on these laws and the struggle for justice after the return to democracy. Both of these courageous men spoke out against the dictatorship in the early years of The Dirty War and both paid an enormous personal price for their courage. Both men were forced to flee Argentina: Timerman went to Israel while Graham Yooll fled to Britain. *La Opinion* was destroyed by the dictatorship; the *Buenos Aires Herald* survives. Interviews with Jacobo Timerman, Buenos Aires, July 23, 1993, and with Andrew Graham Yooll, Buenos Aires, November 10, 1997. On Timerman, see also Jacobo Timerman, *Prisoner without a Name; Cell without a Number*.

47. On Astiz's acquittal, see Pion-Berlin, *Through Corridors*, 95; Nino, *Radical Evil*, 93. For a fascinating eyewitness account of the shooting of Hagelin by Astiz on a downtown street in Buenos Aires, see Guest, *Behind the Disappearances*, 46–48.

the period of Alfonsín's presidency. The trials had gone a considerable distance toward uncovering the truth about what had happened during the military dictatorship. While some observers maintained that they had not gone far enough, much truth had come to light. But the overall policy did not include any systematic effort to provide reparations or begin reconciliation. These further policies, essential in other nations, had never been the intent of Argentine policy. The inattention to reparations and reconciliation was probably necessary given the climate of the times. Argentina certainly did not have the financial means for economic reparations, but it also may not have had the emotional resources to face nonmonetary steps toward reconciliation. For the transition period, Argentina had done what it could do. Any further effort at grief recovery, social healing, reconciliation, or reparations would have to wait for the solutions to the other crises the nation faced, if it ever came at all.

In the 2000s and beyond the transition studied in this book, some aspects of this unfinished business would be addressed during a period of greater political and economic normalcy. A new Peronist president, Nestor Kirchner, would reopen the human rights issue and encourage the courts to pursue new investigations.[48] Kirchner also declared a day of national mourning, a day off work to remember the start of the military dictatorship in March 1976 so that the Dirty War is not forgotten. Official actions such as a national day of remembrance avoid the financial cost of reparations but nonetheless recognize grief and ask the nation to stop and remember. They are considered important nonmonetary steps toward healing. But for the crucial years of democratic transition and consolidation explored here, the laws of Due Obedience and the Final Point, as well as the military unrest to which they responded, marked an end to pursuit of the first item on Alfonsín's campaign agenda. Supporters of the government inside the executive and legislative branches felt that enough time and energy had been spent on retroactive justice. The nation needed to turn to other matters. The military felt that even the limited degree of punishment meted out had gone too far and should be rescinded. They pressed for pardons and amnesty, as they had done all along. The various positions in this debate were irreconcilable.

Civilian Management of Military Affairs and Conscription

The laws allowing and then limiting investigation of the military for human rights abuses had been unprecedented actions by a civilian regime in the

---

48. Bonner, *Sustaining Human Rights.*

aftermath of human rights violations. They were a first step toward civilian control of the military. Yet if civilians were fully to control the armed forces in Argentina, they also needed to make many other decisions about support for and entry into the military. These decisions fell under different branches of the democratic government. Many were within the purview of the executive branch, particularly the Ministry of Defense, while others, such as those requiring or amending a law, included Congress. These decisions were less visible than the trials but equally important because they decreased military autonomy and power. Pion-Berlin argues that unity and single-mindedness within the Argentine government enabled Alfonsín to impose and enforce policies unpopular with the military.

Between 1983 and 1986 defense expenditures were cut by 40 percent.[49] These cuts kept military salaries low, reflecting both the economic crisis and deep civilian distaste for the military.[50] The government retired officers who had been highly visible in the human rights violations while younger officers more inclined to respect civilian decisions were promoted.[51] The Ministry of Defense eliminated the cavalry and improved military training.[52] The military had also built for itself a huge industrial complex where they produced arms for profit. They owned other industries as well.

---

49. Pion-Berlin, "Between Confrontation and Accommodation," 553. Also see his "The Limits to Military Power." Other studies have shown that efforts to cut military budgets throughout Latin America have been associated with attempted coups against civilian governments. Likewise, military demands for higher budgets that have not been met with a favorable civilian response have elicited coup attempts by the military. See Barry Ames, *Political Survival: Politicians and Public Policy in Latin America* (Berkeley: University of California Press, 1987), and Eric Nordlinger, *Soldiers in Politics: Military Coups and Government* (Englewood Cliffs, NJ: Prentice Hall, 1977).

An interesting parallel exists in the Kennedy administration in the United States. In 1960, James McNamara took the position of Secretary of Defense under John Kennedy at a time when McNamara thought that military spending and autonomy had run wild and needed to be brought under control. "This place is a jungle, a jungle," he said, describing the Department of Defense when he entered it. He demanded much greater oversight and accountability with respect to military spending as well as constraints upon the budget. See Schlesinger, *Thousand Days*, 315–18.

In his comparative study of military spending and democracy in Costa Rica and Honduras, Bowman finds that military spending has had a direct negative effect on the development of democracy. See Kirk S. Bowman, *Militarization, Democracy and Development: The Perils of Praetorianism in Latin America* (University Park: Pennsylvania State University Press, 2002).

50. Pion-Berlin writes that Argentina was unusual in the low level of esteem in which the armed forces were held by civilian society. In particular, Argentina's upper classes had little respect for the military. See Pion-Berlin, "Between Confrontation and Accommodation," 546.

51. Pion-Berlin writes that approximately fifty generals closely associated with the dictatorship were expelled from their military posts but that, primarily, this expulsion affected the upper ranks of command. See "Between Confrontation and Accommodation," 553.

52. The inability of subunits to work together in combat contributed to Argentina's rapid defeat in the Malvinas conflict. Argentina's military was good at killing civilians but not so good in war. Pion-Berlin, "Between Confrontation and Accommodation," 555.

The military even had private resort complexes. They had become an elite social sector with access to property, luxury, and resorts beyond anything available to much of the rest of society. All of this property now passed to the state under Ministry of Defense control. Many of these properties were sold, and the private military resorts and country clubs were slowly eliminated. The privileges and special lifestyle the military had created for itself came to an end.

These steps challenged both the foundation of military power and their special social status. They coincided with the trials and were bold decisions by a fledgling democratic government. Yet initially the military found themselves unable to resist these new policies.[53] As long as the government stood united across parties and across institutional branches, as they had done on human rights policy, then the military was less likely to oppose the decisions or the process. Two years into the Alfonsín presidency, he still enjoyed broad popular support for these policies. In the 1985 midterm election, the first after Alfonsín's election, the Radical Party won 43 percent of the lower chamber to Peronism's 34 percent. Radicalism also won twenty of twenty-four electoral districts nationwide.[54] But many members of the military, particularly older men and high-ranking officers, disagreed with these decisions.[55] The military stood watchful and ready, prepared to strike if the government showed any signs of weakening or if civil society showed declining support for the government.

The institutional arrangement played a role here. As long as the institutions worked in tandem, they produced strong government and high legitimacy. Unity protected the new democracy from military resistance. But the presidential system is also one of checks and balances. As the different state institutions began to disagree on policy, the military used these divisions to press its demands, playing one part of the government off against another. The very arrangement designed to limit power also limits democratic power and opens access points for nondemocratic actors.[56] The dissatisfied military sectors found openings in the last two

---

53. See Pion-Berlin, "The Limits to Military Power." Pion-Berlin further argues that one of Alfonsín's most important mistakes was his failure to give the military an alternative task. See Pion-Berlin, "Between Confrontation and Accommodation," 556–57.

54. Pion-Berlin, "Between Confrontation and Accommodation," 560.

55. Pion-Berlin argues that some of the policies Alfonsín's administration followed were unwise and unnecessary, provoking nonessential opposition from the military. For example, the Ministry of Defense excluded the military from having a representative among those advising the president on defense issues. He argues, as well, that Alfonsín did not try to cultivate military respect but simply tried to enforce obedience. See Pion Berlin, "Between Confrontation and Accommodation," 567, 570.

56. In addition, a leftist guerrilla attack on a military barracks, La Tablada, in January 1989 weakened the cause of the human rights trials. See Nino, *Radical Evil*, 102–3.

years of Alfonsín's presidency. Sectors of the military who rejected civilian control attempted three coups against the state. One was small and limited, but the others were more threatening. In one coup attempt, several officers tried to take control of the small domestic airport, Jorge Newberry, located near downtown Buenos Aires. Other coup attempts were larger, included more officers and soldiers, and sought to control a major military complex. In April 1987, over Easter week, the military attempted their first major coup, led by Colonel Aldo Rico, against the Alfonsín government. Many members of the army were ambivalent about the Easter coup attempt. But if they did not join it, they also would not suppress it. Instead, they surrounded the Campo de Mayo military base where Rico had taken power forcibly but refused to fire on him or on his rebel troops.[57] These underlying views only encouraged armed defiance of the democratic government.[58] A third attempt against Alfonsín came in December 1988. This third coup attempt was led by Colonel Mohammed Ali Seineldín, commanding the Albatross Special Unit. Following Seineldín's orders, the Special Unit took control of the Villa Martelli military barracks.

This military pressure placed the democratic government in a nearly impossible position. If the government yielded to military pressure they would forfeit part of their own governing agenda and betray some portion of their campaign promises to the voters. But if they made no concessions at all, they ran the risk that military defiance would grow, move beyond one airport or complex, and take control of the offices of government. Defiance could also spread to a larger portion of the armed forces.

Alfonsín's government sought a balance between military demands and democracy. Newspaper coverage of these events reveals an atmosphere of desperation, fear, and uncertainty that prevailed in Argentina while an attempted coup was under way and while the civilian government tried to save democracy. At one point, while Alfonsín engaged in negotiations with rebel military officers, under his instructions his minister of defense, Horacio Jaunarena, flew to Mexico City to try to obtain the support of the Mexicans for the democratic regime. One has to wonder why Alfonsín appealed to the Mexicans. Mexico in the 1980s was not a democracy, and the support of authoritarian Mexico was of limited value.[59] But the flight to

---

57. Pion-Berlin, *Through Corridors*, 71.

58. Pion-Berlin, *Through Corridors*; John S. Fitch and Andrés Fontana, "Military Policy and Democratic Consolidation in Latin America," working paper (Buenos Aires: CEDES, 1990).

59. On authoritarianism in Mexico, see Susan Eckstein, *The Poverty of Revolution: The State and the Urban Poor in Mexico* (Princeton: Princeton University Press, 1977); Jonathan Fox,

Mexico drew international and domestic press attention to the attempted coups. Argentina's democratic leaders knew that Latin America and the world would not condone another military coup in Argentina. The Mexicans were willing to offer symbolic support for democracy (abroad), which was better than nothing.

In this power struggle between the armed forces and the democratic institutions of state, the limits to democratic power are also visible in the government's decision not to end conscription. The government had already reduced the number of conscripts per year by 15 percent. This decrease, combined with a decline in volunteers and applicants to military schools, produced an even greater overall drop in the number of soldiers.[60] The Senate Committee on Defense, led by the Radicals, next considered eliminating the draft entirely. The bill never emerged from committee. The Radicals themselves were divided over the policy,[61] but the anticipated military reaction proved decisive. One Radical senator, Ricardo Lafferriere, summed up his party's position: "We thought that if we did away with the draft they [the military] might well do away with us. So we decided to let it go." The comment starkly portrays the limits of institutional power and the governing party's full awareness of those limits.[62] Congress was watching the military closely and calculating which policies could be pushed forward and which ones could not. The very system that introduced limits upon power, kept power too weak to push military reforms further.

While policy and power struggles were primarily institutional, civil society also played a role. Some sectors of society attacked the government relentlessly over its decision to end the trials. In the face of military aggression and a weakening democratic administration, some human rights groups pushed steadily for more trials and punishment. Some activists became as critical of Alfonsín as they had been of the military govern-

"The Difficult Transition from Clientelism to Citizenship: Lessons from Mexico," *World Politics* 46, no 2 (January 1994), 151–84; Jonathan Fox, *Accountability Politics: Power and Voice in Rural Mexico* (Oxford: Oxford University Press, 2008); Beatrice Magaloni, *Voting for Autocracy: Hegemonic Party Survival and Its Demise in Mexico* (New York: Cambridge University Press, 2006).

60. Pion-Berlin, "Between Confrontation and Accommodation," 558–59.

61. Interviews with Antonio Berhongaray, La Pampa, May 19, 2008; Victor Martinez, Cordoba, March 10, 2008; and Ricardo Lafferriere, Buenos Aires, October 6, 1997, November 17, 1997, March 3, 2009, and March 23, 2009. Berhongaray was chair of the Senate Committee on Defense.

62. Interviews with former deputy Ricardo Lafferriere, Buenos Aires, October 6, 1997, November 17, 1997, and March 3, 2008. Former deputy Lafferriere was continuously helpful to me in understanding the balance of power during the Alfonsín years and also facilitated several other interviews. I am indebted to Andrés Fontana for helping to arrange my first interview with Lafferriere.

ment itself.[63] Iain Guest argues that the Mothers of the Plaza de Mayo, led by Hebe de Bonafini, became strident and undiplomatic, seeking vengeance rather than resolution.[64] These pressures from civil society helped weaken democracy and encouraged the military to attempt a coup. On the other hand, once a coup was under way, civilian leaders of varying political colors united against the military. Both Saúl Ubaldini of the Peronist General Confederation of Labor (CGT) and Alvaro Alsogaray of the Unión del Centro Democrático (Union of the Democratic Center, or UCD), a small, far-right party, spoke out against the 1987 coup attempt.[65] While Alfonsín negotiated, thousands of civilians gathered in the Plaza de Mayo in silent vigil for the democratic government.

A polity-centered approach frames Argentina's struggle to democratize itself and tame its military. This chapter has traced the establishment of a democratic, presidential government and watched that government transform itself. It went from being an inexperienced new regime not even fully aware of the problems it faced to becoming a practiced, pragmatic, policy-making force able to yield on policy particulars to nondemocratic adversaries if necessary while keeping the main democratic project on track. Part of that transformation took place inside Congress where both parties moved from idealism and intransigence toward policy-making competence. In that move they remained united on the broad democratic agenda but increasingly opposed to each other on some of the particulars of policy. The years of success in controlling the military allowed the government to survive subsequent attempts to bring it down. Over Alfonsín's administration we also saw changes in the fit between the goals of different actors and the access they had to the institutions of government. Early in Alfonsín's presidency the human rights groups had more access to the government and more influence over policy than they had late in that same administration. The position of the military was the reverse. Each struggled through-

---

63. Here I draw upon interviews with several of the leaders of the Mothers of the Plaza de Mayo: Estela Carlotto, Buenos Aires, May 9, 1992; Hebe de Bonafina, Buenos Aires, May 17, 1993.

64. Guest, *Behind the Disappearances*, 403, 407. Guest suggests that the Mothers are still revered outside of Argentina but that domestically they have lost a great deal of public respect, particularly the portion of the groups associated with Hebe Bonafini. Other scholars are more sympathetic toward the Mothers' perspective. See, for example, Roniger and Sznajder, *Legacy*. A more recent study of scandal and corruption finds that some newspaper coverage claims that Bonafini and other members of the Mothers have been involved in corruption scandals. See Nuno Coimbra Mesquita and Aníbal Corrado, "Corrupción, sistemas mediáticos y gobiernos: Contextos de acusación y respuestas del poder public en Argentina y Brasil," *Politai: Revista de Ciencia Politica* 6, no. 11(2015): 89–110, esp. 105.

65. Pion-Berlin, *Through Corridors*, 72–73.

out the Alfonsín years to press forward their own agenda; they were more or less successful, depending upon their own changing position of power. Failure to end the draft defined the limit of the power of the democratic institutions at that time.

An Empirical Analysis of Presidential Power

We turn now to an initial empirical evaluation of presidential power during Alfonsín's presidency. If the state's institutions and particularly the presidency were the main arena for democratic struggle, we can follow the example of students of the American presidency who have studied executive orders to scrutinize presidential power. In Argentina the counterpart to an executive order is the decree. Table 3.2 enumerates the decrees issued by Alfonsín for democratic purpose. Here we look at how Alfonsín used presidential decrees to enhance both presidential power and democracy itself. We saw in the struggle against attempted coups that Alfonsín used symbolism to draw attention to and support for his government and the illegal military challenges it faced. We begin our analysis by studying symbolic decrees. Throughout his presidency he used symbolism to attract domestic and international attention to the democratic nature of his government. He used presidential decrees as part of this image.

TABLE 3.2. Presidential Decrees Issued by Alfonsín for
Democratic Purpose

Year Issued	Number of Decrees Issued	Percentage of Decrees Issued
1983	1	2.2
1984	11	23.9
1985	13	28.3
1986	6	13.0
1987	4	8.7
1988	6	13.0
1989 (Jan.–June only)	5	10.9
Total	46	100

For example, on December 13, 1983, three days after his inauguration, Alfonsín issued Decree #158, mandating the initiation of legal accusations against and trials of members of the first three military juntas, a total of nine men. Those tried and sentenced to life in prison in response to this decree included Jorge Videla, Emílio Massera, Roberto Viola, Armando Lambruschini, Raúl Agosti, Rubén Graffigna, Leopoldo Galtieri, Jorge

Anaya, and Basilio Dozo.[66] Between December 1983 and July 1989, Alfonsín issued 46 presidential decrees (5.6% of the overall total) deliberately aimed at fortifying Argentina's democracy and enhancing the nation's democratic image.[67] The subject matter of these decrees exemplifies the use of decrees to enhance and protect the democracy and legitimize the democratic institutions. These laws demonstrated Argentina's commitment to democratic norms and actions and its willingness to enact laws to establish democracy. Some of these decrees made important changes to existing laws while others had value primarily as symbolic statements. Such decrees demonstrated to the world and the voters that the government was committed to democracy. The international attention generated by the decrees might also have helped discourage the military from coup attempts early in Alfonsín's presidency.[68] Alfonsín was particularly inclined to issue these decrees early in his presidency (see table 3.2). Just over half of these symbolic decrees came in 1984 and 1985, his first two full years in office. As his presidency aged and his popular following weakened, Alfonsín issued fewer decrees of democratic importance.

Let us consider the content of some of these decrees more closely. On January 6, 1984, less than one month into his term, Alfonsín issued Decrees 125/84 and 126/84. The first placed the ships of the Navy under executive control while the second did the same with all air transport. While the constitution states that the armed forces stand under civilian control, these two decrees expanded and specified the extent of civilian control by detailing that the Ministry of Defense (part of the executive branch) also controlled the properties and services performed by the armed forces. These domains had previously been controlled by the armed forces, specifically by the Navy and Air Force, respectively. As president of the country and commander in chief of the armed forces, Alfonsín now assumed control over properties and services as well. These two decrees accompanied Law 23.023, passed by both chambers of Congress on December 8, 1983. Law 23.023 charged the executive with transferring these properties and ser-

---

66. All nine were later pardoned by President Carlos Menem. See chap. 5 for Menem's military policy in greater detail.

67. International image matters for all nations, even for the most powerful. Yamamoto, Kim, and Holden write that the United States has lost international moral authority because of its recalcitrance in embracing international calls for reparations for slavery and for its use of torture and its refusal to sign international agreements on human rights violations. This refusal to join the world community on these issues has caused disdain toward the United States and an "intensifying disbelief in America's actual commitment to genuine democracy." See Yamamoto, Kim, and Holden, "American Reparations Theory," 69–74.

68. Brysk, *Politics*; Margaret Keck and Kathryn Sikkink, *Activists beyond Borders: Advocacy Networks in International Politics* (Ithaca: Cornell University Press, 1998).

vices to executive control. In this sense, Alfonsín was acting in close coordination with and at the behest of the Congress. These two decrees had an obvious democratic effect, but they had a powerful symbolic value as well. They were part of the initial steps whereby civilians assumed control of Argentina's government.

On February 22, 1984, Alfonsín likewise issued Decree 648/84, which ended the executive power—which had been taken by the military—to expel people from the country for political reasons. While decree 648/84 made reference to Law 21.259, put in place by the military, no counterpart congressional law was passed in 1984 in conjunction with Alfonsín's decree ending the executive's power to drive people into exile. Again, the power of this decree was substantive as well as symbolic, having both a real effect upon the development of democracy and a powerful symbolic effect on ending repression. Yet from the books alone, the decree looks as if Alfonsín was acting alone, and, in some narrow and literal sense, he was. At another level, however, he was acting with the full support of the Congress and of civil society itself.

On August 2, 1985, Alfonsín issued Decree 1430/84, which authorized the police to carry out any penal sentences against members of the police that were handed down by the military tribunals authorized by Congress to try human rights violators.[69] No companion law was passed or had been passed in conjunction with Decree 1430/85. Similarly, Decree 675/86, issued by Alfonsín on May 6, 1986, authorized the purchase of equipment for the customs and migration authorities to speed and facilitate the repatriation of Argentine citizens returning home after exile. No companion law was passed. Decree 531/87, issued by Alfonsín on April 3, 1987, said that members of the military or security forces, or police officers and prison guards awaiting trial for human rights violations and not actively in flight or in rebellion would be allowed to retain 100 percent of their personal effects and possessions up until such time as the tribunals had reached a decision about the individual on trial. This decree accompanied Law 23.492 of December 23, 1986, the Full Stop Law.

This empirical overview of presidential power expands our understanding of institutional democratization by allowing us to scrutinize the

---

69. We know in retrospect that the military tribunals authorized to carry out these trials failed to issue penal sentences to anyone. In fact, these tribunals concluded that no laws had been broken. For that reason, the trials were moved from military to civilian courts. But in these early days, the civilian government had hopes that the military would take juridical responsibility for trials of its own members, and this decree facilitated the military's capacity to do so. On the evolution of this policy and on the removal of the trials from military to civilian courts, see Nino, *Radical Evil*.

decree, one of the most potent kinds of presidential power. What we find is a generally democratic use of this power. In contrast to the notion that all presidential decrees exemplify unchecked and even authoritarian presidential power, here we see decrees used for democratic purposes. Just as Lincoln used the powers of the presidency to preserve the union, Alfonsín used presidential power to enhance democracy and distance the nation from its repressive past. The decrees referenced here had value primarily as symbols of Argentina's growing or continuing democratic image and its effort to become a member of the international community of civilized nations. They were not acts of authoritarianism or of unchecked presidential power; they used the single-handed power of the presidency to support democracy. As the new democratic government aged, and particularly as the nation moved beyond the human rights trials and the early sensational struggle that surrounded those trials, new problems elbowed their way onto center stage. Alfonsín's ability and latitude to issue decrees of substantial and symbolic democratic importance was reduced. Yet, as we see from table 3.1, throughout his presidency he continued to issue decrees that had democratic impact, even in the final, embattled years of his presidency. In this analysis, decrees were a friend to democracy rather than a threat to it. They were often necessary bureaucratic steps toward putting democracy in place.

Conclusion

As in any new democracy emerging from military dictatorship, Argentina's early transition years pitted unarmed, elected civilian leaders against the armed power of the military. Moving that struggle inside the institutions of the state fortified democracy and gave it the strength to overcome military resistance and address human rights. Democratization by institutions brought with it the force of law and the rule of law. These were essential in distancing the new government from the lawlessness of the past.

In this struggle, the power and authority of the president were central. But the support, cooperation, and involvement of the other institutions of state protected the president from the fate of Salvador Allende. Raúl Alfonsín was able to unite a broad coalition of forces that included powerful support from both parties in Congress as well as the judiciary. This support allowed many of his policies to become reality. An institutional configuration that concentrated power in the presidency permitted him to initiate the legislative agenda, an essential beginning. But he did not use that power to reach toward nondemocratic ends or to bypass democratic process. Despite the need to act swiftly and definitively, Alfonsín worked with Congress while Congress itself involved the judiciary.

As the American designers of the presidential system had hoped, the combined institutions served the nation well. The institutions reached an unusual level of accomplishment in addressing the crimes of the past. No other nation faced with this record of human rights violations has generated from within itself the impetus to address such crimes to the extent that Argentina did under Alfonsín's guidance in the immediate aftermath of dictatorship. While Argentina's effort was incomplete with respect to reparations at the time of this study, the thoroughness with which the nation addressed retroactive justice without the support or pressure of international actors is unusual. It stands as one of Argentina's finest achievements and is a powerful recommendation for the force of institutions in democratization.

Argentina's Congress played a key role in human rights policy. It seized the initiative and provided a forum for deliberation, as a representative assembly should do. It hammered out a policy that addressed the nation's needs and placed the next policy steps with the judiciary. When its initial policy became problematic, it accepted responsibility and rewrote policy into something more workable in the moment. Moreover, it did all of this while also being a relatively new and inexperienced legislature that had been recently reconstituted after years of closure and oppression.

Nelson Polsby has proposed placing legislatures along a continuum from those that are arenas of deliberation at the low end of the continuum all the way up to legislatures that are "actively transformative of governmental decisions" at the high end.[70] The Argentine example challenges Polsby's continuum and illustrates why we need to study developing democracies in order to understand better the institutions of our own democracy. In human rights policy it was the deliberation itself, including the last minute Sapag amendment in the Senate, that caused the Argentine legislature to become "actively transformative of governmental decisions." Thus Argentina's Congress was not only deliberative or transformative. It was both, and it was transformative precisely because it was deliberative.

Many other Latin American nations lacking this combination of institutional power, including an active legislature at the moment of transition, have been less successful in early democratic efforts to address human rights crimes. In a referendum, the citizens of Uruguay voted not to pursue

---

70. Nelson W. Polsby, "Legislatures," in *Handbook of Political Science*, vol. 5, ed. F. I. Greenstein and N. W. Polsby (Reading, MA: Addison-Wesley, 1975), 277–78.

human rights investigations at all. The Central American nations have done the same, but without a popular vote. Chile did nothing to punish the military until it had experienced prodding from international actors and had fortified its domestic institutions. Mexico and Brazil have done very little to investigate human rights abuses. Argentina's example remains unusual, owing in large part to its early combination of institutional strength behind a visionary leader.[71] There was still more to do with respect to reparations and memorials. But, as with military reform, Argentina had gone as far as it could go with human rights policy at the time. Other matters demanded attention.

While the institutions of state primarily supported democracy in these early years, civil society behaved in contradictory ways. The human rights groups were key in ending the dictatorship. Their grassroots mobilized action had helped create opposition to the dictatorship and continued to be influential throughout Alfonsín's presidency. They demanded trials of the military and opposed limits on retroactive justice. Their contribution was positive at first and exemplified grassroots support for democratic reform. Several massive spontaneous demonstrations also supported the Alfonsín government by standing silently before the President's House during the attempted coups. These demonstrations were crucial in sustaining the democratic government against military takeover.[72] But as the administration aged the human rights groups became a part of the problem, creating chaos that endangered the new democracy. Steeped in grief, families of victims could not see the bigger picture or the broader solution that Alfonsín and congressional leaders perceived. The early popular coalition that had supported Alfonsín at the time of his election disintegrated in the face

71. Observers writing about the final months of the Alfonsín presidency have noted that many Latin American democratic regimes did not fully gain control over their military forces, a key problem in these early democracies. Fitch and Fontana make this argument, suggesting that clarification was needed with regard to the military mission. See "Military Policy."

72. The Argentine military has a long history of coups against Radical governments that dates back to the 1930s. On the other hand, military aggression in the 1960s was facilitated by factionalism within the Radical Party wherein some factions had a mixed and unreliable commitment to democracy and elections. In part, Radicalism's ambivalence toward elections was related to the hostility of some sectors of the party toward Peronism. See Cesar Tcach, "Radicalismo y Fuerzas Armadas (1962–1963): Observaciónes desde Cordoba," *Desarollo Economico* 40, no. 157 (April–June 2000): 73–95. When Radicalism itself produced a president, Arturo Frondizi, who sought accommodation with Peronism, the more anti-Peronist factions within Radicalism moved against Frondizi. See Alain Rouquie, "Le Mouvement Frondizi et le Radicalisme argentin" (Paris: Fondation Nationale des Sciences Politiques, Centre d'etude des Relations Internationales, 1967); Celia Szusterman, *Frondizi and the Politics of Developmentalism in Argentina, 1955–62* (Pittsburgh: University of Pittsburgh Press, 1993); and Pedro Sanchez, *La Presidencia de Illia* (Buenos Aires: Centro Editor de America Latina, 1983).

of the incomplete task regarding human rights. That disintegration left the institutions of state pressing forward with the task of democratization while civil society either protested the priorities of that process or watched from the sidelines.

Beyond human rights and civilian control of the military, Alfonsín had two agenda items that have received less attention. One he brought with him when he took office: a promise to democratize the labor unions. The other he realized was essential as he watched the economy deteriorate: the need to privatize crucial industries and services. These goals also made key contributions to democratization. Both policies needed congressional support, just as the civilian control and human rights policies had done. The next chapter scrutinizes these policies.

FOUR

Presidential Innovation and Congressional Constraint

Labor Reform and Early Privatization Efforts

Ultimately we thought we were smarter than we actually were. It is very difficult for a person who comes from a nation that has had two hundred years of democracy even to understand what we were up against in the early 1980s. We came out of a history of coups and interruptions of democratic politics dating back to 1930. We had no experience with democracy or with democratic negotiation. We had no background with democratic politics or administration. Of course, we were going to make mistakes.

—Juan Manuel Casela, former Minister of Labor under Alfonsín[1]

Alfonsín's democratizing agenda reached beyond human rights policy and civilian control of the military to address union democratization and privatization. We look at those policies in this chapter. The process of democratization extends beyond holding elections and gaining civilian control of the military. It also tackles authoritarian enclaves in society wherever they exist.[2] One of Argentina's most undemocratic sectors, apart from the mili-

---

1. Interview, Buenos Aires, November 16, 1997. I am indebted to Horacio Jaunarena for helping to arrange this interview.

2. Manuel Antonio Garretón coined this phrase in his description of Chile after its return to a restricted democracy in the aftermath of the Pinochet dictatorship. He argued that the continued existence of authoritarian enclaves or nondemocratic spaces within Chilean society meant that the nation had not fully democratized. See *Incomplete Democracy: Political Democratization in Chile and Latin America* (Chapel Hill: University of North Carolina Press,

tary itself, was the labor unions, particularly their hierarchical leadership. The relationship between the union leaders and the military dictatorship was ambivalent. Some union leaders had been targets of military repression but others had received favors or protection from the military during the Dirty War. It is not known whether the unions had actually pacted with the dictators for military amnesty. But the unions were a deeply non-democratic sector of civil society, powerful national organizations that had internal authoritarian practices and enormous power over the economy. They were on Alfonsín's list for reform. He saw control of the military as half of a double-pronged strategy for democratizing Argentina. The other half entailed changes in the system of leadership inside the unions to make them transparent and accountable to members.[3]

In the later years of his presidency, Alfonsín initiated the first steps of a privatization policy, but this had not been part of his campaign. It emerged in response to the growing economic crisis inherited from military mismanagement. Privatization was a more difficult task for Alfonsín because it lacked the noble purpose of human rights, civilian control of the military, or union democratization. In fact, for many observers the moral high ground lay in opposing rather than supporting privatization because of the hardship privatization would impose upon the poor. Economic reform and privatization lay entirely outside the Radical pattern of taking positions based upon principles; it was a pragmatic task.

Alfonsín's strength and leadership would prove to be much more limited here, and the capacity of the nation's institutions to democratize was weaker, owing to characteristics inherent to the democratic institutions themselves, including representation as well as checks and balances. The representative institutions of the democratic state incorporated nondemocratic players who resisted democratic reform. The legislative initiative again came from the president, but here Congress was less supportive or opposed, reflecting different interests. Alfonsín's power was adequate to begin these next tasks but not to complete them. This chapter uncovers some of the limits of democratization by institutions.[4]

2003). For the use of this term to understand authoritarianism and democratization inside the United States, see Mickey, *Paths Out of Dixie*, 2015.

3. David Pion-Berlin has argued that the military and labor represented the two greatest threats to democracy early in the Alfonsín presidency. Both, argues Pion-Berlin, required an autocratic executive that was the only kind of authority capable of restraining those twin threats. We will see in this chapter that, unlike the military, labor was indeed successful in using the Congress against the executive and in containing democratizing reforms. See Pion-Berlin, "Limits to Military Power," 94–115, esp. 108.

4. Harry Eckstein argues that Weimar Germany, democratic at the level of the state itself,

Historic Leadership Patterns inside the Labor Unions

Most of the unions had been established by and for Perón while he was minister of labor during the military dictatorship of 1930–46 and after 1946, when he was elected president. He had established his political power on the basis of labor support and had organized labor into gigantic unions, one for each major economic sector. Each was vertically organized under one leader, and a single leader of the General Confederation of Labor (CGT) was the top man representing all labor unions. This structure allowed Perón to control labor. He could gather about twenty labor leaders, one from each sector, in one room and issue orders or command obedience. Perón cemented this vertical structure in place by allowing the labor unions to provide benefits.[5] By funneling pensions, health care, and unemployment compensation through the unions, Perón made workers dependent upon the unions even after union leadership ceased to represent their interests. This system allowed cooperation between labor and the government[6] but it was also a method of corporate control modeled on Benito Mussolini's fascist state. Once this structure was in place, vertical control extended from the state downward into all unions while representation of worker interests assumed a secondary position. Perón's system also allowed the national government, rather than the workers themselves, to select a single union that would be permitted to negotiate for a sector. Unions were tied into the state rather than the working class. In the decades after Perón's ouster in 1955, this structure survived.[7]

nonetheless contained numerous enclaves of authoritarianism within its subgroups and social organizations, including families, schools, and companies. He writes, "Insolence, gruffness, pettiness, arbitrariness and even violence were so widespread that one could certainly not consider them mere deviations from normal patterns" (198). German society was "shot through with large and petty tyrants in every other segment of life [apart from the state itself]" (198). Germany was a country of "paramilitary organizations, trade union militants [and] beer hall conspirators" (198–200). For this reason, there was incongruence between the authority patterns of society itself and those of the state. This incongruence made democracy vulnerable and ultimately contributed to democracy's downfall. See Eckstein, *Regarding Politics*. Democracy and elections at the national level do not immediately democratize all of society in all its different subsections. The democratization effort goes on, including in established democracies.

5. Similarly, in 1883, Chancellor Otto von Bismarck established an early form of national health care in order to fend off more radical measures and to retain corporatist control. See Alter, *Defining Moment*, 309.

6. The period following World War II in Latin America witnessed a generalized expectation that the state should play an expanded role in national life. This expectation could be found in Chile as well as in Argentina. Ricardo Ffrench, *Economic Reforms in Chile: From Dictatorship to Democracy* (Ann Arbor: University of Michigan Press, 2002), 2.

7. Subsequent to Perón's presidency, his verticalist system of control through one union per sector became law under the presidency of Arturo Frondizi (Law 14.250).

While labor unions officially conducted elections for their leadership, in reality workers were denied choice through intimidation, the absence of a secret ballot, and the lack of an alternative. Leaders of different unions worked together to keep each other in power. Members of other unions were allowed to vote for the incumbent in each union, a practice known as "cross-over voting." Union leaders denied this practice and concealed it carefully.[8] But the outcome of these various machinations was always the same: decade after decade, the same individuals remained in the top positions of power inside the labor unions, particularly in the larger unions such as Light and Power (Luz y Fuerza), the Railroad Workers (Unión Ferroviaria), and the Metalworkers Union (Unión Obrera Metalúrgica). This system excluded non-Peronist leaders, particularly the socialists who had sought to organize Argentina's working class long before Perón. The exclusion of the socialists dated back to Perón, who had arrested, jailed, and tortured socialists, even if they had supported his rise to power.[9] His antip-

---

8. The leadership of Argentina's labor unions vigorously resisted this reform. They used every excuse imaginable to disqualify their own unions from coming under the reach of reform. One such ploy was to claim that only unions having a national presence should be forced to submit themselves to internal democratic elections because only those unions had a large pool of potential candidates. When the reform took place this kind of exception exempted many unions from having to submit to democratic elections for leadership. Those unions that could not find such an excuse were required to hold internal elections. Because of the large number of exempt unions, the democratization of the labor unions was only partial and incomplete. Even today, Peronists and labor union leaders who are part of the old power structure will deny that crossover voting occurred. But for the Ministry of Labor during the Alfonsín years, extensive crossover voting was a basic fact of life with which the government had to contend.

When external democratizers change the rules of the game by passing new laws or applying old laws in new, more democratic ways, nondemocratic forces inside authoritarian enclaves will predictably respond by trying to find or create loopholes to get around the new law. In Argentina this is what we were seeing inside the labor unions. In the United States, in 1944 the Supreme Court struck down the whites-only electoral primary that had been used since the 1870s to exclude blacks from electoral participation in the South. Like the Argentine labor unions, Southern states responded by looking for other ways to exclude blacks from voting in primaries. In different places of the South, whites used the poll tax, educational requirements, constitutional interpretation requirements, intimidation, and violence to prevent blacks from voting in primaries. See Mickey, *Paths Out of Dixie*, 2015, especially chapter 4.

9. Perón had arrested labor leaders of socialist sympathies, Luis Gay and Cipriano Reyes, and had consistently undermined and ultimately destroyed the political career of Juan Atilio Bramuglia, a Peronist labor leader of more consistently leftist political leaning. Bramuglia had sought to take Peronism toward electoral democracy. See Raanan Rein, *In the Shadow of Peron: Juan Atilio Bramuglia and the Second Line of Argentina's Populist Movement*, translated by Martha Grenzeback (Stanford: Stanford University Press, 2008), originally published as *Juan Atilio Bramuglia: Bajo la sombra del líder: La segunda linea de liderazgo peronista* (Buenos Aires: Ediciones Lumiere, 2006).

athy to socialist leaders came from their independent ideological position, which caused them to be more influenced by ideas than by strict loyalty to him. Perón refused to recognize any labor union represented by a socialist leader. He saw socialists as alternative leaders with ideas that challenged his personalist dominance, and he would not tolerate any challenge to his leadership. Although socialists had continued to try to influence the course of events inside some of the labor unions, they had had little success.[10]

This system of control was a key factor in the functioning of the Peronist Party itself. It allowed the party not only to depend upon but also to direct and control worker support. As long as the party controlled top labor leaders, it could use them to control the workers, calling strikes against a Radical government and preventing strikes against Peronist governments. This system was also capable of honoring a pact with the military to guarantee no labor strikes if the government gave amnesty to the military. This was one reason why Alfonsín saw civilian control of the military and democratization of the labor unions as two parts of the overall project of democratizing the nation.

Democratizing the Labor Unions[11]

Alfonsín began by choosing Antonio Mucci as minister of labor. Mucci was a worker, a strong unionist (a member of the graphics union), and a socialist. The choice of Mucci as labor minister was ideologically consistent with the social-democratic position of the Radical Party, but in a world where Peronism controlled the working class, Mucci was considered an outsider.[12]

Early in the Alfonsín presidency, Mucci sent Congress a labor reform bill that became known as the Mucci bill.[13] A detailed consideration of the fate of this bill tells us about the limits of democratization by institutions. It also uncovers the basic characteristics of the nation's two principal parties and

---

10. Anderson, *Social Capital in Developing Democracies*.

11. This perspective on the labor reforms of the Alfonsín years, both the reforms that failed and the reforms that succeeded, has been informed by numerous interviews across many years with political leaders, union leaders, members of the cabinet, and legislators. However, the most useful and influential interviews, and those I have relied upon to the greatest extent, were interviews with the following individuals: Jorge Triaca, Juan Manuel Casela, Rodolfo Diaz, Enrique Rodriguez, Oraldo Britos, Oscar Lescano, Jose Pedrazo, Antonio Venegas, and Antonio Caló.

12. Peronism has historically been characterized by bonding social capital, making members of the party/social movement hostile toward and suspicious of others, "outsiders" and non-Peronists. See Anderson, *Social Capital*.

13. La Ley Mucci, also Law 23.071/84.

allows us to see how history shaped the democratization process. As with human rights policy, the Alfonsín administration had an agenda with respect to union democratization, but it was not one Alfonsín was prepared to dictate into law by decree. Instead, Mucci presented his bill to Congress for consideration, debate, and passage, as indicated by the presidential system.

The bill was a major reform. It mandated transparent elections inside the unions, including the proposal of alternative candidates, the notion of one person/one vote, and an end to cross-over voting.[14] Mucci's bill also proposed proportional representation inside the unions so that leadership would include minority voices, like the socialists. A third key point to Mucci's bill concerned benefits. He and Alfonsín knew that control of social services inside each union was a significant part of the power of each union leader. Workers who voted against incumbent Peronist leaders could be denied health coverage, accident insurance, or a pension out of a general pension fund they had themselves paid into. The bill would move the provision of social services from the unions to the state. This was one of the most democratic measures in the bill. If it passed, rank and file members would be free to vote their own conscience. In the immediate term, through proportional representation, and over the long term, by granting political freedom to workers, the bill would democratize the unions. Mucci's coupling of democratic reform with transferring benefit provision to the state demonstrated the interconnected nature of democratization and welfare reform. In the Mucci bill Argentina would take its first steps toward broad inclusion of workers in state services. The bill would have undermined the foundations of Peronist control over workers and moved Argentina a first step toward a contributory social service state.

The Defeat of the Mucci Bill

The bill passed the lower chamber easily and went to the Peronist-controlled Senate.[15] The upper chamber was much less democratic, rep-

---

14. Peter Ranis writes that the authoritarian leadership structure of the CGT had been protected behind its ability to drive a hard bargain. Workers accepted authoritarian leadership inside their unions because of the extraordinary wages and benefits that leadership was able to command. See *Class, Democracy, and Labor in Contemporary Argentina* (New Brunswick, NJ: Transaction Press, 1995), 57.

15. Alfonsín thought he had a slender majority in the upper chamber, but he was sufficiently nervous that he chose not to attend the funeral of Yuri Andropov in the Soviet Union. Instead, he sent Vice President Victor Martinez, who chose to take with him one Peronist senator and one Peronist vote: Oraldo Britos, a strong union supporter. This information comes from an extended interview, over lunch, with former vice-president Victor Martinez, Cordoba, March 10, 2008.

resenting voices and historical patterns of authoritarianism. There were three reasons for potential problems in the Senate. First, the bill asked Peronists to vote against their own interests by ending a corporate control system that was responsible for putting many of them in power.[16] For that reason, many Peronist senators had little interest in the proposed labor reforms. Second, like the U.S. Senate, the Argentine Senate represents the subnational units in a federal territory: the provinces. Also like the US Senate before the seventeenth amendment, the Argentine Senate was not directly elected at the time of this debate. Instead, senators were elected by the provincial legislatures and had made little effort to win popular support or to be accountable to an electorate. Third, as Gibson has shown, Argentina's provinces can be bastions of authoritarianism so that indirect election opened the door to crony-ism and nepotism.[17] Peronist governors often prevailed upon state legislatures to elect to the Senate the governor's brother (or wife, or son, or cousin).[18] We see, therefore, how the demo-

16. It is unlikely that a legislative chamber will vote against its own interests, but there have been moments when that happens, because failing to do so would bring even worse consequences. One historic example is the 1832 vote in the House of Lords to expand the British franchise. A more recent example and one from the United States is the 2008 decision by House Republicans to support the bailout of the banks, a position that was against the interests of the party's historical constituency. On expanding the British franchise, see Brock, *Great Reform Act*, and Davis, *Political History of the House of Lords*.

Prospect theory helps to anticipate these types of votes. In prospect theory, legislators vote in ways that anticipate impending (economic or political) disaster and seek to avoid it. Prospect theory is a major field of study in psychology, economic and political decision making, and legislative studies. See, for example, D. Kahneman and A. Tversky, "Prospect Theory: An Analysis of Decision under Risk," *Econometrica* 47 (1979): 263–91; Jack S. Levy, "An Introduction to Prospect Theory," *Political Psychology* 13 (1992): 171–86; and Kurt Weyland, "Risk Taking in Latin American Economic Restructuring: Lessons from Prospect Theory," *International Studies Quarterly* 40 (1996): 185–208. Weyland's article is about Latin American presidents who chose to make difficult neoliberal reforms, not about resistance to those reforms by Peronists inside Argentina's Congress, but his analysis is relevant to the mind-set Peronists would have had when faced with Alfonsín's proposals.

17. Edward Gibson, *Boundary Control* (New York: Cambridge University Press, 2012).

18. Dating back to the 1940s, most provinces were dominated by Peronism, and the legislatures were dominated by the Peronist governor. Indirect election of the Senate has been a nondemocratic historical holdover from the past in the United States as well, one that was finally eliminated with the Seventeenth Amendment. Likewise, Argentina's Senate eventually moved toward direct election in the 1990s but that change came after the vote discussed here. On the problems of Argentina's Senate, see Mariana Llanos and Francisco Sánchez, "Council of Elders? The Senate and Its Members in the Southern Cone," *Latin American Research Review* 41, no. 1 (2006): 133–52; and Mark Jones, *Electoral Laws and the Survival of Presidential Democracies* (Notre Dame, IN: University of Notre Dame Press, 1995). On the history of the U.S. Senate, including the early years of indirect election of the chamber, see Lee and Oppenheimer, *Sizing Up the Senate*.

cratic institutions of state can include powerful nondemocratic voices. Passage of the bill in the Senate would be much more difficult and would depend upon a coalition of votes, including the support of several Peronist senators from small provincial parties. The struggle became a moment of truth for Argentina's new democracy. It was the first point at which the democratic forces of the new government stood head to head against the nondemocratic forces of Peronism, testing the relative strength of each.

Peronist legislators had other reasons for opposing the bill. They opposed bringing proportional representation to union leadership, saying that unions had to be able to act swiftly in moments of conflict. Proportional representation would force leaders to debate over actions, which would take time, weaken unions, and render workers more vulnerable. The debate also resurrected old hostilities between Radicals and Peronists. Some Peronist senators simply thought that Alfonsín was trying to destroy Peronism. Others suspected that the bill was a payback scheme against union leaders suspected of pacting with the military prior to the 1983 election.

The Senate defeated Mucci's bill by one vote. Unexpectedly, at the last moment Senator Elías Sapag of Neuquén Province voted against the bill and took with him the other Neuquén senator, Jorge Solana. Alfonsín had expected both to support the bill, two votes that would have made it law. The reader will remember that Sapag had been the senator whose last-minute amendment of the law on trials of the military allowed investigations to proceed beyond the top commanders. Now he moved again at the last minute, single-handedly shaping the legislative outcome.[19]

The conflict over the bill underscores distrust among political leaders and parties in the early months of the new democracy.[20] Both parties sus-

---

19. This paragraph draws upon several lengthy interviews with Jorge Solana, former Senator from Neuquén province. Unfortunately, former Senator Elías Sapag had died by the time I did the research for this book, but Solana had worked closely with Sapag for many years and understood Sapag's political perspective well. I drew upon Solana's interviews for understanding the role played by these two senators in the defeat of the Mucci bill. Solana was never convinced that there had ever been any pact between the military and Peronism. Interviews with Jorge Solana, Neuquén, April 1, 2008. I flew to Neuquén for the first interview but conducted three subsequent telephone interviews with Solana on April 12, 2008, May 2, 2008, and May 8, 2008.

20. Trust has historically been low in Argentina. Recent studies have found that the same is true today. On distrust among Argentines early in the nation's history, see Nicolas Shumway, *The Invention of Argentina* (Berkeley: University of California Press, 1991). On distrust today, see Cleary and Stokes, *Democracy and the Culture of Skepticism*. Cleary and Stokes find that distrust is higher in regions where Peronism is predominant. Similarly, my work shows that social capital and cooperation are low in Argentina generally and low among Peronists in particular. See Anderson, *Social Capital*

pected each other of the worst possible motives. An atmosphere of mutual hostility, recrimination, and suspicion characterized relationships between the two major parties as the nation moved out of authoritarianism. Authoritarianism is more than a political system; it is a culture of hostility, suspicion, and noncooperation, and it had predominated in Argentina and in party relations long before the Alfonsín years.[21] Distrust makes it difficult for a legislature to find reason and reach compromise. This atmosphere of suspicion and mutual recrimination would gradually yield to one of greater cooperation and mutual respect as democracy aged and the two main parties worked together to accomplish political and economic reforms. But as the nation took its first steps away from authoritarianism, distrust and suspicion prevailed, with negative ramifications for democratic and economic reform. The defeat of the bill underscores the limits of democratization by institutions.

The Aftermath of the Mucci Defeat

The failure of the Mucci bill was seen as a defeat for Alfonsín's government, but subsequent events have altered that view. The defeat was a reversal for the Radical government, but all democratic governments suffer reversals. The essence of democratic government lies in the give-and-take approach to policy development, and the defeat of the bill represented only one more step in the long-term development of labor policy. It also underscored more clearly which kinds of reforms would be possible. The defeat of Mucci's bill caused Argentine politics to recongeal along party lines, with Peronism closely allied with labor and the Radical Party pushing for democratization. These respective positions are historically typical of the two parties, and their divergence over the law represented a step toward more robust party differences than had been present when both parties united against the military.[22]

But the vote also had larger and contradictory implications for democ-

---

21. On Argentina's authoritarian culture of intolerance toward others, see Shumway, *Invention*, and Anderson, "Of Wild and Cultivated Politics," 99–132. In the years immediately before and after the end of the dictatorship, Edgardo Catterberg was able to measure these authoritarian characteristics through the use of public opinion polls that showed that Argentines were extremely intolerant toward those holding different opinions. Subsequent polling has shown that Argentine citizens have gradually become more tolerant as democracy has aged. On Catterberg's work, see his *Argentina Confronts Politics: Political Culture and Public Opinion in the Argentine Transition to Democracy* (Boulder: Lynn Rienner, 1991).

22. On the historical positions of both parties, see Anderson, "Single-Party Predominance."

racy. On the one hand, it had become an issue over which the two parties could take opposing positions, a step toward political normalization. Democracies are more healthy when at least two parties exist and are able to take opposing positions on key issues.[23] On the other hand, nondemocratic forces had prevailed. Acting in part on the basis of factors that predominate in any democratic legislature—the need to respond to constituents—Peronist legislators had voted to retain the heart of the vertical control system upon which they and their party depended. Democratization of labor might have been more possible had Alfonsín imposed the Mucci bill by presidential decree. But he was unwilling to use a decree to impose democratic reform.

Instead, he and his Cabinet began anew. That the law had been so narrowly defeated meant that there was strong sentiment in the Congress in favor of reforming the internal governance structure of the labor unions. Some Peronist legislators supported union transparency. Alfonsín decided to scale back his aspirations but not to relinquish altogether the agenda of union democratization. He replaced Mucci with a minister who had a better image among Peronists. Juan Manuel Casela, whose words open this chapter, was a Radical with strong working-class ties to labor who had the respect of many Peronist legislators and labor leaders. Casela shared Alfonsín's opinion that democratization of the labor unions was necessary. He also had a high level of personal knowledge of the inside functioning of many labor unions, knowledge that allowed him to know about specific cases of cross-over voting from one union to another. Yet Casela was a supporter of the unions, and they perceived him that way. His position was that labor unions were an essential prop for any society because they are the first defense of the working class against large companies and powerful economic interests.

Casela actually supported workers more than did the Peronist union bosses. He wanted the unions to represent the workers instead of being control mechanisms for Peronism. Casela told the unions to distance themselves from any political party and to work with either party if doing so served their interests.[24] He told them that the Peronist Party only used the labor unions to achieve and maintain political power. He said that, once the Peronists were back in office, the party would be more

---

23. Anthony Downs, *An Economic Theory of Democracy* (New York: Harper, 1957); Michael Holt, *The Political Crisis of the 1850s* (New York: W. W. Norton, 1978); Anderson, "Single-Party Predominance."

24. On the need for unions and parties to distance themselves from each other in the Italian case, particularly in times of austerity, see Miriam Golden, *Labor Divided: Austerity and Working Class Politics in Contemporary Italy* (Ithaca: Cornell University Press, 1988).

concerned with power than with defending labor interests. Casela said that the Peronist labor bosses never fully understood this argument and never took his advice, but they might have remembered it once Menem took office.

The battle over the Mucci bill had created great tension between the government and the unions. Alfonsín presented Casela with three specific tasks: a law of labor reform, a respectable international image of Argentina at the upcoming International Conference of Labor in Switzerland in June 1984, and reestablishment of positive relations with the unions. Casela approached these tasks with a combination of hard-nosed pragmatism and fundamental support for labor interests. He understood that the law governing the Peronist unions gave considerable power to the national government. The state could choose among labor unions, thus determining which unions and which labor leaders would be allowed to represent a specific industry. Casela preferred to talk with the unions and to include them in the negotiations over creating a new labor law. But in his conversations with them, he reminded union leaders that the government had this power and could use it. Faced with a union that absolutely refused to support any type of reform, the state could choose another, more agreeable union and make it the official representative of that industry. Casela preferred to avoid such measures, but he was speaking a language the union leaders could understand: the language of centralized, vertical control with power concentrated in the hands of the state. Perón had set up this system to control the labor unions, and his intentions had not been democratic.[25] But now, in the hands of a democratic state, that same power could be used to democratize the labor unions.[26]

Casela also used Peron's style of dialogue with union leaders. Mucci had gone directly to Congress with his bill, operating as if he lived in a fully

---

25. During World War II and while he was still minister of labor, Perón sent one of his assistants, José Figuerola, to Italy to study Mussolini's system for organizing labor unions. Seeking to follow Mussolini's example, Perón wanted to establish a corporatist state that he called "social cooperation." It was to include a system of vertical labor control. See Rein, *In the Shadow*, 55–57. Paul Buchanan argues that a legacy of corporatist control over labor, such as the Peronist system described here, actually made market-oriented reforms more likely to succeed because the state could use preexisting control mechanisms to punish dissident unions. This situation is precisely the one I am describing for Argentina and is another ironic legacy of Peronism's authoritarian past. On this pattern in Chile and Uruguay, see Paul G. Buchanan, "Preauthoritarian Institutions and Postauthoritarian Outcomes: Labor Politics in Chile and Uruguay," *Latin American Politics and Society* 50, no. 1 (Spring 2008): 59–89.

26. Franklin Roosevelt likewise dealt with unionized labor, but he made no effort to limit representation to only one union per industry. He lacked Perón's desire for control over labor. See Burns, *Roosevelt: Lion and the Fox*, 218.

democratic country where the institutions of state could make law. But the world of Argentine labor was not fully democratic. Casela used corporate means to achieve a democratic end. He went directly to the labor bosses and gained their consent first. From there congressional support would come more easily.

Working with the labor bosses, Casela wrote a new bill that eliminated cross-over voting and assured competition between at least two lists of candidates. It opened the door for Socialist Party leaders to compete in internal elections. But the corporate method also placed limits on what the government could achieve. The labor bosses were unwilling to accept proportional representation, and the unions retained control of benefits, retaining economic power over workers. The new bill was much less than Alfonsín had hoped for but more than the labor bosses wanted. Casela had promised Alfonsín that he would serve as Labor Minister for only six months, just long enough to write the new bill. His successor, Hugo Barrionuevo, would now be responsible for shepherding the new bill through Congress.

Reform is often slow, especially when conducted by legislative means. Even using the corporate method of bringing labor leaders on board, it took four years and most of the remainder of the Alfonsín presidency before the new reform bill became law. But Peronist opposition to the new bill was now reduced, partly because of its reduced goals and partly because the union leaders had themselves been involved in writing the reform. On March 24, 1988, the new bill, known as the Union Law, passed Congress. Its official name was the Law of Union Associations.[27] The date was symbolic because twelve years earlier, in March, the military had overthrown the elected Peronist government and instituted the Proceso dictatorship.

The text of the Union Law reads like a law to protect the labor unions. It reflects labor's deeply-engrained, self-protective tendencies. Between Perón's ouster in 1955 and his return to politics—with military acquiescence—in the early 1970s, the Peronist Party was proscribed from participation in elections. As a result, labor now felt very self-protective. It preserved the integrity of the unions, protecting them from intervention by the state. But it also required them to have regular elections among real alternatives in which voters were limited to members of that specific union. These two provisions alone represented movement toward democratization. The Union Law retained single-man control over the decision to

---

27. For an example of the understated nature of press coverage of this extremely important step toward democracy, see the newspaper report of the law's passage in *La Nación*, March 24, 1988, 1. The full text of the law is presented on pages 12–13 of that issue.

strike and union control over social benefits. Workers who refused to strike upon command could still be deprived of their benefits. A key problem with removing benefits from the control of union bosses was that, given the economic crisis, Alfonsín's government could not offer any alternative source of social support.

Democracy Comes Quietly

In the aftermath of the union reform law, union elections have become more democratic. They are now subject to oversight by the Ministry of Labor. There are more elections than there have been in the past, and more levels of union leaders are elected. The stipulations for calling rank and file assemblies have been loosened, and there is more representation in the lists of minority groups such as the socialists.[28] Yet by the time this bill passed Congress, economic and military crises had swamped the nation. In the months surrounding the passage of the Union Law, inflation was above 12 percent per month, the teachers were carrying out a nationwide strike, and one of the worst murderers from the dictatorship, the chief of police for Buenos Aires, Suarez Mason, had just been extradited from the United States with the full cooperation of a San Francisco judge and the U.S. State Department.[29] The passage of the Union Law was barely noticed. Four months later, in July 1988, when the law went into effect, preparations for the next presidential election were under way and newspaper coverage focused on the fight for leadership inside the Peronist Party. Also attracting press and public attention was the opening of the trial of General Galtieri, the last of the three army generals who had headed up the three juntas forming the dictatorship. This highly visible trial had legal and symbolic importance.

On July 27, 1988, inside many labor unions, workers listed on their union's beneficiary list, as required by law, quietly voted for the leadership of their unions.[30] Those who were watching closely recognized the importance of this event. Some unions, such as the powerful Unión Obrero

28. Ranis, *Class, Democracy*, 60–62. Ranis also writes that some unions had contested internal elections even before the Union Law. Among these unions were ENTEL, the state-owned telephone company, and CTERA (Central de Trabajadores de la Educación de la República Argentina), the nationwide teachers union. We look more closely at CTERA in chapter 7. See Ranis, *Class, Democracy*, 83 and 86.

29. For coverage of these multiple events and crises, see *La Nación*, January–March 1988.

30. For quiet and understated coverage of this monumental event, see *La Nación*, July 26, 1988, 1 and 7.

Metalúrgica (UOM, the Metalworkers Union), had found a loophole in the new law and managed to avoid elections entirely.[31] But the pressure was on. The press covered elections inside the more open unions and focused a spotlight on those that were still avoiding elections.[32] Inside the unions that were voting, the competition was between two tendencies within Peronism itself: the orthodox line and the renovationist line. These two opposing tendencies also appeared in the Peronist Party itself as the nation looked toward the next election.

Carlos Menem represented the orthodox line, while his opponent, Antonio Cafiero, who lost the internal party elections, was a renovationist. The orthodox line was considered the more advantageous position, both because they were the incumbents in most unions and because Menem had won the internal elections inside the party. Inside the unions the orthodox line included the old strongman bosses, some of whom were the same caudillos who had been in control for decades. Their challengers, the renovationist Peronists, supported greater transparency and account-ability. Newspaper coverage of some of the union elections pointed out that the orthodox line candidates were resorting to intimidation of the vot-ers and to financial threats against opponents. They also noted that there was strong opposition to the orthodox line in key labor neighborhoods of Buenos Aires, such as La Matanza, Quilmes, Constitution, and Avellaneda, as well as in key cities outside Buenos Aires, such as Rosario, La Plata, Mendoza, and Cordoba.

The failure of the Mucci bill and the limits of the Union Law under-scored, including for the Peronists themselves, what work still needed to be done to democratize the labor unions and limit the power of labor bosses. Quietly, imperfectly, and hardly even attracting public notice, democracy had begun to enter the labor unions. It was no small accomplishment. It came in the face of extreme labor militancy.

---

31. The UOM is one of the most hierarchical of all of the major labor unions. The suc-cess of the UOM bosses in creating a loophole that exempted the UOM from application of the law violated the spirit of the law and represents the extent to which it was a partial and imperfect victory for democracy.

32. On the use of repeated elections to present choice and the opportunity for democra-tization, see Anderson and Dodd, *Learning Democracy*; Leslie E. Anderson and Lawrence C. Dodd, "Nicaragua: Progress amid Regress?" *Journal of Democracy* 20, no. 3 (July 2009): 153–67; and Leslie E. Anderson, "Poverty and Political Empowerment: Local Citizen Political Participation as a Path toward Social Justice in Nicaragua," *Public Policy Forum* 6, no. 4 (2010): 1–19. Also see Carrie Manning, *The Making of Democrats: Elections and Party Development in Post-War Bosnia, El Salvador and Mozambique* (New York: Palgrave Macmillan, 2008), and Guillermo O'Donnell and Philippe Schmitter, *Transitions from Authoritarian Rule: Tentative Conclusions about Uncertain Democracies* (Baltimore: Johns Hopkins University Press, 1986).

Labor Strikes Out

If reform of the labor unions underscored the problematic and limited nature of democratization by institutions, the behavior of labor throughout Alfonsín's presidency demonstrated both why reform was essential and how undemocratic some sectors of civil society could be. In the face of a government seeking to make the unions more responsive to their members, and in an economic crisis, labor conducted between thirteen and sixteen major strikes that crippled the economy and weakened democracy.[33] International labor statistics that separate sectors of the economy place that number much higher. Subdividing strikes by sector also shows which sectors were the most militant. Table 4.1 lists by sector the strikes that

TABLE 4.1. Labor Strikes by Sector, Second Half of the Alfonsín Administration, 1987–1989

Sector	1987	1988	1989
Agriculture, hunting, forestry, fishing	9	12	0
Mining, quarrying	8	10	1
Manufacturing	175	93	42
Electricity, gas, water	35	15	1
Construction	32	20	2
Wholesale, retail trade and restaurants, hotels	10	7	3
Transport, storage, communication	114	85	50
Financing, insurance, real estate, business Services	29	30	3
Community, social and personal services	224	191	91
Total	636	463	193

Source: Data from International Labour Organization, Laborsta Internet: http://laborsta.ilo.org/STP/guest

---

33. After the fact, observers disagreed slightly on these figures, depending upon whether they were more or less sympathetic to CGT leader Saúl Ubaldini and the workers. Differences also emerged surrounding whether some of the work stoppages that Ubaldini organized actually counted as strikes. By the time of this research in the 2000s, loyal Peronists had incentive to underestimate the number of strikes that Ubaldini organized while those less sympathetic to Peronism remembered 15–16 strikes. Ubaldini himself was dead and while he was alive he might have underestimated the number of strikes he launched in any event. Some observers thought that he came to regret his actions against the new democratic leader and repented of the fact that he became remembered as "the man who made so many strikes against Alfonsín." Even if we accept the lower estimate, thirteen strikes amounts to more than two strikes per year during the five and a half years of the Alfonsín administration. Many observers saw this high number as aggression by the working class against the newly democratic government.

In 2014 the Railroad Workers Union again conducted disruptive strikes in protest over the arrest of their top two leaders, Jose Pedraza and Juan Carlos Fernández, on charges of murder. Pedraza was later convicted. These actions then and now exemplify the nondemocratic nature of the labor unions. See http://www.buenosairesherald.com/article/59781/arrested-railway-union-leader-pedraza-asks-to-be-released (accessed February 29, 2016).

occurred during the second half of the Alfonsín administration.[34] In the past, this kind of chaos had given the military a pretext to intervene and remove civilian governments; as we saw in the previous chapter, an angry military was only waiting for its chance to move again.

Responsibility for labor's militancy lay with the head of the General Confederation of Labor, Saúl Ubaldini. The CGT was the peak organization for all labor unions. The hierarchical formation of labor allowed Ubaldini to call strikes whether or not union members agreed. One individual's ability to close down the economy was what the Radicals had sought to curtail with the Mucci bill. The fact that the bill had failed early in Alfonsín's presidency gave Ubaldini the duration of Alfonsín's administration to use his power. He focused on worker interests at the expense of the larger picture, including consumer interests and democratic survival. Our effort to understand Argentina's overall policy of democratization requires that we look closely at the personality of powerful authoritarians inside the polity. We look here at Ubaldini because his behavior and personality exemplify vestiges of authoritarianism with which the new democracy now had to contend. Ubaldini's position as head of the CGT had been an accident. Control over the CGT had fallen to him not because he was a good leader but because he was expendable. Normally the CGT head comes from one of the major unions. But as the 1976–83 dictatorship had teetered on the verge of collapse and labor leaders sought a representative during transition, they hesitated to choose one from one of the major unions. They feared that the tables might suddenly turn and the dictatorship would remain in power, giving the death squads one last chance for political murders. The CGT leader could be a target and possibly the first victim of any renewed repression.[35] The CGT wanted a labor leader who

---

34. Strikes also soared in number after the return to democracy in Chile, where workers engaged in 949 strikes in the first eighteen months of the new democracy. See Buchanan, "Preauthoritarian Institutions and Post-Authoritarian Outcomes."

35. In fact, a CGT labor leader and member of the powerful, important labor union, Luz y Fuerza (Light and Power), Oscar Smith, had already been disappeared, tortured, and murdered by this same military dictatorship. Smith had disappeared early in the years of the dictatorship, but the military and the police denied any involvement with or knowledge about his disappearance. In fact, the military were so fearful about the power of the Luz y Fuerza union that they created an elaborate charade designed to pretend that Smith was still alive. The military detained Oscar Lescano, second in command inside Luz y Fuerza, and held him at a police station on a temporary basis. They then brought forward so-called witnesses who assured Lescano that Smith was alive and well but being kept in custody. Lescano was convinced by this charade and by these witnesses and was hopeful enough about the return of Smith that he did not organize the light and power workers into a major national strike. In reality, Smith had been dead for several days before the police temporarily detained Lescano, but he would not learn this fact until more than a year later. At that point, calling a national

could speak for them but who was not so central to the labor movement that it would be left decapitated if that leader disappeared. They hoped to find someone so unimportant that the dictatorship would ignore him. They chose Ubaldini.[36]

Ubaldini came from the beer-producing industry. He lacked any broad following but was a fierce public speaker. He could appear before the press as a fearless fighter for labor rights. He stood before the cameras with tears running down his face. He gesticulated, shouted, and roared. He was uncompromising, dedicated, and steadfast. He was also myopic, short-sighted, and foolish. As the first euphoria of Alfonsín's victory faded and the new government began running the country, Ubaldini had only one goal: to defend the interests of the workers. He was never interested in the possibility that chaos might end democracy. He did not worry that a return to dictatorship might worsen rather than improve the position of the working class.[37] He never betrayed any respect for Alfonsín's accomplishments. He never cared about the human rights trials or the difficult choices the new government had to make. For him, the world revolved around the working class.[38]

---

strike around a man who had gone missing more than a year previously was too difficult. However, this horrifying story was widely known within the working class and particularly within the Luz y Fuerza union. Quite understandably, Lescano was not eager to become CGT president while the military was still in power, and no member of the working class was willing to risk the loss of so prestigious and beloved a leader as Lescano.

36. During the military dictatorship, the relationship between labor and the military varied. The leaders of some unions were arrested or killed while others were left alone. One group of unions known as "the 25" was associated with the CGT and was more confrontational toward the military; the unions associated with the National Commission of Labor (CNT) were more moderate. The CNT was associated with Jorge Triaca, who would later be chosen by Menem as minister of labor. Ubaldini's subgroup had positive relations with the Church and the military. Peter Ranis even found in the early 1990s that 43 percent of workers interviewed spoke positively about the Dirty War years while some said that the repression was acceptable but had been handled badly. Ranis also found that blue-collar workers were more positive about the military regime while white-collar workers were more negative. See *Class, Democracy*, 137–38.

37. While Ubaldini's behavior was extreme, labor in Latin America has often demonstrated antidemocratic behavior. A study of labor across Latin America finds that workers are not necessarily supporters of democracy. Instead, they have often organized against democracy and helped contribute to democratic breakdown. Moreover, labor interests are not necessarily best satisfied by democratic regimes. See Steven Levitsky and Scott Mainwaring, "Organized Labor and Democracy in Latin America," *Comparative Politics* 39, no. 1 (October 2006): 21–42.

38. My perspective on Saúl Ubaldini is informed by multiple interviews with labor leaders and members of the Ministry of Labor who knew Ubaldini. Unfortunately Ubaldini, a chain smoker, had died by the time that I was doing the research for this book. In particular I draw upon interviews with former deputy Oraldo Britos, Buenos Aires, October 11, 1997; with former Minister of Labor under Alfonsín, Juan Manuel Casela, Buenos Aires, November 16, 1997; and former Minister of Labor under Menem, Enrique Rodríguez, May 14, 2008,

The strikes he called involved many thousands of workers across all sectors of the economy and drew in hundreds of different unions and union subsections.[39] They closed down transportation systems and deprived the nation of telephone, rail, and subway service.[40] They ended electricity supplies and other utility and energy sources. They made commuting to work or school, shopping for groceries, and caring for the young, old, and sick virtually impossible. They exemplified the power of the working class, and they illustrated why reform was essential. They contributed to the destruction of the Alfonsín government.[41] Ubaldini's concern was the legitimate issues of inflation, loss of buying power, and the decline in the economic position of the workers as a result of hyperinflation. He was combative and single-minded.

Labor militancy against any non-Peronist government is a historic tradition in Argentina, particularly among Peronist workers. As shown in table 4.1, the categories having the largest number of militant Peronist unions—manufacturing and transport—demonstrated the largest number of strikes during the last three years of Alfonsín's presidency. A significant number of strikes also occurred among state employees providing social services. Ubaldini's strikes were useful for Peronism while it was out of power in the 1980s. The chaos they created soon diminished public sup-

---

and May 25, 2008. Of these three, Britos was the most sympathetic to Ubaldini and said that Ubaldini ultimately regretted deeply the number of strikes he had called against Alfonsín and the level of chaos he had caused in those years. The other two interviewees were much less certain that Ubaldini regretted his behavior at all.

In most Latin American countries and, indeed, in most places where labor is unionized, a majority of workers must support striking before a strike can be called. In contrast, because of the vertical nature of Argentina's labor organization, labor leaders did not have to solicit the support of most workers before calling a strike. Instead, the decision to strike could be made at the highest level of union organization, with much less regard for the opinion of the workers themselves. This hierarchical organization greatly increased the individual power of Ubaldini, who had a myopic view of labor's needs. On labor law and strike requirements throughout Latin America, see Mark Anner, "Meeting the Challenges of Industrial Restructuring: Labor Reform and Enforcement in Latin America," *Latin American Politics and Society* 50, no. 2 (Summer 2008): 33–65.

39. Argentine labor was relatively quiet in the first months after the dictatorship but became more and more combative over the course of the Alfonsín administration.

40. FDR likewise faced obstruction by labor at crucial moments in the war effort. As the administration prepared for national defense in late 1941, the railroad unions announced a walkout of 350,000 workers while in the shipyards welders, craftsmen, and other vital workers were locked in prolonged labor disputes. In response, Congress passed antistrike legislation that set strict guidelines for unions and strikes. See D. B. Hardeman and Donald C. Bacon, *Rayburn: A Biography* (Austin: Texas Monthly Press, 1987), 271–72.

41. The pattern of labor mobilization against a democratic government has been visible throughout Latin America in recent decades and is not confined to Argentina. Levitsky and Mainwaring, "Organized Labor and Democracy in Latin America."

port for the administration, increasing the chances of a Peronist victory in the next election.[42] The irony of Ubaldini's behavior was that it underscored, even for the Peronists, the need for labor reform. By the end of four years of labor strikes fomented primarily by one man, even Peronist legislators inside Congress could see how problematic the labor hierarchy had become. By the late 1980s even Peronism was tired of the disproportionate power that labor held in Argentine society. Peronism moved to decrease that power by supporting passage of the Union Law and later, with Menem, by removing Ubaldini altogether. By overusing his power and endangering democracy, Ubaldini helped reduce labor power in the years to come.

But Ubaldini was not only a Peronist electoral tool and a vestige of dictatorship politics. He was a reflection of the disastrous state of the economy. Economic reform was desperately needed, and Alfonsín would focus upon the economy only late in his presidency. Yet if his successes were incremental and limited with respect to the democratization of labor, they were even more so on the economy. Throughout his presidency, the economic crisis worsened. By 1988, the newspapers reported inflation rates of 9 percent, 12 percent, or even 17 percent in one month.[43] This increase in the cost of living had a devastating effect on the working class. Anyone depending on a regular wage found that it covered fewer expenses each month. Inflation exacerbated union militancy. Strikes then meant that travel, transport, and education were impossible and that utilities were unavailable while workers were out. Such perpetual interruptions increased the sense of crisis and weakened public support for the government. In many instances, the government responded to labor strikes by increasing wages, but as soon as wages rose, prices rose again.

Apart from the unions and national debt, Alfonsín had inherited another problem from previous governments: the central role of the state in the economy, particularly with respect to crucial industries and services. Power, electricity, gas, the oil industry, railroad transport, bus and subway travel, telephone services, radio and television, and the mail all had been nationalized, most during Perón's first nine years in power. The railroad

---

42. We saw something similar happening in Washington, DC, in 2013 and early 2014: Republicans hostile to the Obama administration closed down the government, creating chaos and sequestering much-needed funds while those finances were needed to start up the nation's new health care program, the Affordable Care Act. As a result, citizens decreased their support for the administration and Obama's popularity ratings fell.

43. *La Nación* and *La Prensa* for 1988 and 1989.

had been nationalized during the first Radical administration of President Yrigoyen. Many of these services are publicly owned and function efficiently in France, but in Argentina nationalization meant a lack of competition or accountability to the public. Over time, these services had deteriorated, and now many were nonfunctional. The telephone service was poor, and the number of lines inadequate for the usage load. Where a line existed, companies hired secretaries who dialed phone numbers up to fifty times before the call went through. Railroad transport was so slow that rail line usage was impractical. The mail service was unreliable and subject to theft.[44] Across most dimensions of basic services, the Argentine economy did not function; dysfunction was then compounded by spiraling inflation.

Employment policies dating back to Perón were bankrupting the state. Under Perón the nation had sought to provide universal employment. He had built this expectation with paternalistic policies, depleting the economy even during his own regime.[45] The state kept thousands of workers on the payrolls, further increasing the national deficit. Many of the industries and companies delivering poor services were also the ones whose workers were on strike. Yet a sense of entitlement was not the only problem. Inflation was high. Wages were fixed and could only be raised through union action while prices flew upward. Ubaldini blamed Alfonsín and ordered strikes to redress labor's economic woes.

Toward Privatization

The nation clearly needed economic reform.[46] Some thought that privatization of service companies would release the state from providing production and services and allow dozens of companies to upgrade. The state also needed emancipation from the expectation of universal employment. But these reforms would bring a high social cost, and the government had

---

44. Those that could remember the 1980s, prior to the privatizations, estimated that if one called the state telephone company and requested the installation of a new telephone line one would wait ten years before the company did the installation. Others estimated that a railroad trip from Buenos Aires to Tucumán took over twenty-four hours. The same trip by automobile was much quicker.

45. For an example of a mentality that the state should provide employment, see Martin Retamozo, "Los Piqueteros: Trabajo, Subjetividad y Acción Colectiva en el Movimiento de Desocupados en Argentina," *América Latina Hoy* 42 (2006): 109–28.

46. René Cortázar, Alejandro Foxley, and Victor E. Tokman, *Llegados del Monitarismo: Argentina y Chile* (Buenos Aires: Ediciones Solon, 1984), 9–13.

already spent considerable energy on the human rights trials and labor reform. Whether the administration still had the political clout to lead another major reform was uncertain. Additionally, the Radicals had not come to power with an economic policy in hand. Historically, the Radical Party has been weak in formulating policy. The Radicals are better at carrying the banner for democracy and ethics. Taking the moral high ground had allowed them to defeat the Peronists and confront the military, deal with human rights and democratize labor. But they were less prepared to reform and stabilize the economy. Privatization became a possibility only as the need for it emerged. The military had left the nation deeply in debt.[47] International lending agencies tried to lighten Argentina's debt burden, but the situation was so extreme that debt payments continued to be a debilitating drain on the economy throughout Alfonsín's presidency. Industrial inefficiency and labor strikes only made these matters worse.

As with the trials of the military and labor reform, Alfonsín approached the task of privatization using institutional means. He sought to include Congress rather than make policy by decree. But as we have seen with the military and labor reforms, legislating is a slow process, and the economic emergency required immediate action. Moreover, Congress housed nondemocratic as well as democratic actors. Economic reform was Alfonsín's least successful policy, largely owing to the institutional method he used. The development and fate of his economic policy offers an ideal place to scrutinize the role of the polity in a policy of democratization. In this scrutiny we see the presidential system used to prevent much-needed reform policy.

Toward the end of Alfonsín's presidency an opportunity for privatization presented itself. Scandinavian Airlines System (or SAS), the Scandinavian airline company, offered to buy Argentine Airlines (Aerolineas Argentinas) and merge it with their own services. A limited number of other possibilities for partial privatization also emerged at this time. Alfonsín received offers from foreign companies to buy shares in the Argentine oil company, Yacimientos Petrolíferos Fiscales (YPF), and in ENTel (Empresa Nacional de Telecomunicaciones), the state-owned telephone company. These offers seemed like golden opportunities to release the state from some of its financial burdens, pump foreign capital into inefficient industries, and improve services. Additionally, privatizing these industries would have permitted the companies to rid themselves of excess labor and make the companies productive.

But privatization was not guaranteed to improve efficiency and would

---

47. The military government had chosen José Alfredo Martinez de Hoz as minister of the economy with the approval of the International Monetary Fund. See Nino, *Radical Evil*, 54.

certainly exact a social cost.[48] Some legislators were committed to universal employment and extensive protection for domestic industry, regardless of the economic cost.[49] Others rejected any foreign interest in state industries. These expectations fit closely with a left-of-center international rhetoric that prevailed in Latin America during the Alfonsín presidency, and his party shared these beliefs when they entered office. Yet in the face of the growing economic disaster, the party and its president began to reconsider their position. If owning its own industries and employing all its own citizens was still ideologically preferable, it might not be economically possible. When Alfonsín saw an opportunity to sell a portion of the ownership of three national industries he began to talk about the need to make industry more efficient and the national economy more competitive internationally. The level of privatization Alfonsín proposed was limited. For example, in the contract between SAS and Aerolíneas Argentinas, SAS would own 40 percent of Aerolíneas. Alfonsín still believed that Argentina should own its own industries. He hoped that the national industries could become efficient and functional through partial privatization alone.

The Peronist Response to Privatization

Despite the economic inefficiency of state industries and the limited nature of Alfonsín's privatization policy, the program met with hostility from the Peronist Party. Even before the SAS contract had been sent to Congress, the Peronist Party announced their opposition. Predictably, Alfonsín's privatization policy met with immediate hostility from labor. Labor understood that economic efficiency would also mean the loss of jobs; workers perceived their interests to be with employment more than with democracy or an efficient economy. That privatization would be extremely difficult became clear early in the effort, and the difficulty of the task would be matched only by its urgency.

48. Chile followed this same privatization policy during the years of the Pinochet dictatorship. Political economists observing the Chilean case have argued that privatization did not necessarily improve productivity or efficiency, and, in any event, it came at the cost of a decline in living standards for the low-income sectors of society. In Argentina, greater productivity and efficiency were achieved with privatization, but the costs to low-income sectors of society were still there. On Chile, see Ffrench, *Economic Reforms in Chile*. On Argentina, see Rodolfo Diaz, *Prosperidad o Ilusion? Las reformas de los 90 en Argentina* (Buenos Aires: Editorial Abaco de Rodolfo Desalma, 2002).

49. Chile also followed a policy of state protection of domestic industry. Combined with excessive bureaucratic obstacles, this policy produced inefficient industries there as well. Ffrench, *Economic Reforms*, 27.

As Alfonsín's government began to clarify a position on privatization in its final year, the Radical Party made economic arguments in favor of the policy. Alfonsín spoke publicly about national bankruptcy. He suggested that the state could not provide universal employment. He linked hyperinflation to the state economy inherited from Perón. As Alfonsín and the Radicals began to crystallize their position in favor of privatization, Peronism stayed with Perón's original position: the state should provide all services and universal employment.

This section of this chapter and the next chapter use content analysis of the Senate speeches of Senate Majority Leader Eduardo Menem on privatization to understand the Peronist position and their role in privatization. Eduardo became the spokesperson for his party in its effort to block Radical privatization policy. This analysis reveals both the Peronist position on privatization and Peronist behavior inside a legislature. The scrutiny also helps understand the nature of Peronism as a party. I suggested in chapter 1 that Peronism includes some nondemocratic actors and a periodic disdain for democracy itself. Here we see the results of Peronism in action. In early 1988, while Alfonsín was still president, Eduardo Menem was already emerging as a power inside Congress. His dominance was linked to his brother's political climb toward the presidency. Carlos Menem would become the next president. But the growing power of these two brothers and the emergence of Eduardo Menem as a spokesperson for Peronism inside the legislature were evident before Carlos's election. In early 1988, the Peronist Party in the Senate was considering Eduardo Menem as one of three senators who could become the Peronist leader in the upper chamber. Then, in preparation for the electoral campaign, the Peronist Party held internal elections to determine who would become the party's presidential candidate. Carlos Menem won the internal elections and then the presidency in the national elections of March 1989; Eduardo became Senate Majority Leader.

The four speeches analyzed here and in the next chapter occurred over a period of fourteen months. Between April and September 1988, Eduardo Menem gave three speeches opposing privatization and offering fundamental challenges to the entire course of action that Alfonsín proposed with respect to the privatization of Aerolíneas, YPF, ENTel, and the arms factories. In this chapter we consider these three. In the next chapter we will analyze Eduardo's fourth speech, of July 1989, in favor of privatization.[50]

---

50. The full text of these speeches is in the congressional transcripts, Congreso de la Nación, Argentina, Cámara de Senadores, 1983–99, *Diario de Sesiones*. The text of Eduardo Menem's speeches is republished in his book, *Nueve años en el Senado de la Nación (1983–1992)*

Speech #1: Against Privatization of
Aerolíneas and ENTel, April 27–28, 1988

This was the single most important speech by a Peronist leader against privatization. Eduardo made this speech against Alfonsín's proposed sale of 40 percent of Aerolineas to SAS and against the partial sale of ENTel to Telefónica España, a Spanish telephone company. It emphasizes the sale of Aerolíneas, mentioning the sale of the telephone company only in passing. Eduardo gave this speech on the Senate floor in response to a letter of intent sent by Alfonsín to Congress. In his letter Alfonsín indicated that he intended to sell minority shares of these two companies to the foreign companies indicated. Alfonsín also sent one of his cabinet ministers to the Senate with the letter in order to discuss its contents, answer questions, and dispel confusion.

Eduardo's criticism of Alfonsín's plan was procedural and substantive. He suggested that the airline and telephone companies were of supreme national interest and that Aerolineas, in particular, was a lifeline connecting the country to the world and linking the provinces to the capital. Despite the importance of these companies, the executive apparently intended to act without involving the "people's representatives." Privatization, especially the sale of such a huge portion of the shares of these companies (40%), without involving Congress violated the principle of publicity with respect to governmental actions and might well be illegal. Having a minister from the executive branch present in the Congress to talk informally about the proposed sale violated parliamentary procedure. He accused the administration of acting in secrecy and asked whether this policy involved the sale of an airline or was, in fact, a move that would occur in a spy movie.

Eduardo criticized Alfonsín's inadequate attentiveness to the full play of market forces. He criticized the administration for moving forward on privatization without open bidding on the price of shares among competing companies. He suggested that, had there been a process of open bidding, there might well have been a superior offer to buy Aerolíneas shares. He also suggested that Alfonsín's reasons for selling to SAS were not clear.

(Buenos Aires: printed by author, 1992). The speech against the privatization of Aerolíneas and ENTel is found on pp. 396–414. The speech against the privatization of YPF is found on pp. 407–14. The speech against the privatization of various armaments factories is found on pp. 415–24. The speech in favor of privatization is found on pp. 424–59. I am appreciative of former Senator and Senate Majority Leader Eduardo Menem for helping me to understand these speeches. Here and elsewhere in this book Eduardo Menem was repeatedly helpful in facilitating my understanding of Senate power during these transition years. Interview with Eduardo Menem, Buenos Aires, May 6, 2008.

Eduardo characterized the sale of 40 percent of these two companies as a "process of denationalization," making the failure to invite open bidding even more problematic. Having made an argument against Alfonsín for not bringing full market mechanisms to bear, in the form of open bidding on the sale of shares, Eduardo then criticized the proposed operation of the airlines for placing too much emphasis upon market mechanisms. He said that once shares in Aerolíneas were owned by SAS, profit and the market would then determine decisions about air travel. He argued that SAS might not see value in servicing some remote provinces and that some would be cut off from the rest of the nation. He wondered why no effort had been made to look for purchasers among national companies. He asked, why look for buyers among people "from the other end of the earth?"[51]

Eduardo played to patriotism, emphasizing the sale of Aerolíneas because it was an important symbol. He took offense that SAS had sent a delegation to inspect the operation of Aerolíneas, and asked whether Aerolíneas had likewise been allowed to inspect the operations of SAS. He said that the Scandinavian airline company was not doing Argentina any favors with this purchase, and he implied in the speech that Argentina did not need SAS. Eduardo claimed that the proposed sale to SAS was a concession to imperialism. He argued that while normally one does not speak of Scandinavian imperialism, he wondered what, if any, precautions had been taken to make certain that SAS was free of British influence.[52] Eduardo culminated his nationalistic objections by claiming that the issue was one of national sovereignty. He questioned whether there was a market price for sovereignty, claiming that sovereignty should not be sold or endangered. Menem argued that, while 60 percent of the shares in Aerolíneas would still remain under Argentine ownership, the legal basis for some decisions required holding 70 percent of shares. Therefore, this proposed sale amounted to a forfeiture of decision-making power as well as the transfer of ownership of national property.

Eduardo Menem went on to challenge the idea of privatization itself, arguing that the inefficiency of state industries might come from poor administration rather than from public ownership. Might the functioning of these companies be improved by changing their administration? In this query, he issued another criticism of Alfonsín's administration because it was currently overseeing the state companies. He ended his speech by

---

51. Given what we know now about the provinces as enclaves of Peronist authoritarianism, Eduardo's sense of urgency in keeping the provinces linked to the capital takes on a different meaning. See Gibson, *Boundary Control*.

52. The British were considered enemies at the time because they had recently defeated the military government's attempt to take the Malvinas/Falkland Islands.

warning the administration not to take action that the next administration would have to annul on the basis of illegality. The implication was that the next administration would certainly be Peronist and that the position of the Peronist Party on this matter would be quite different from Alfonsín's. He asked Alfonsín not to place the nation in a situation where it would have to embark upon legal trials "that would cause great damage to the State, of which those responsible will be those who are now taking this grave responsibility to sell part of the national patrimony without observing the most elementary norms of political prudence and, even more seriously, the laws." He finished by saying that he had not made the speech for political reasons or to undermine the Radical administration, for the depreciation of the government had already gone so far that it could not get any worse. "We [the Peronists]," he claimed, "are simply seriously concerned about the destiny of the country." Table 4.2 summarizes Eduardo Menem's arguments against the privatization of Aerolíneas and Entel.

TABLE 4.2. Content Analysis of Eduardo Menem's Speech against the Privatization of Aerolíneas and ENTel, April 27–28, 1988, Senate Chamber

KEY ARGUMENT: *Privatization amounts to selling the nation's heritage to foreign interests. Anyone who supports privatization is a sellout to imperialism.*

Objection Raised	Number of Mentions
Procedural concerns about ignoring Congress	8
Nationalistic/patriotic/anti-imperialist	16
Legal concerns	3
Arguments against market mechanisms	2
Arguments for greater market mechanisms	4
Alleged secrecy/lack of information	1
Generalized criticism of Alfonsín administration	0
Criticisms of Alfonsín's economic policy	0
Total number of different concerns raised	6
Total number of objections made, including repetitions	42

Speech #2: Against Privatization of YPF (National Petroleum Company), May 11, 1988

Eduardo's second speech against privatization during the Alfonsín administration was also delivered on the Senate floor in the final months of the Radical presidency. Under the constitution, Congress has the prerogative to call members of the cabinet to a session of one of the chambers of Congress.[53] This speech was given on an occasion when the Senate had called

---

53. This congressional prerogative is similar to the Question and Answer period found in the British Parliament with the important difference that in the British system the prime

Alfonsín's minister of defense, Horacio Jaunarena. In this instance, the administration was considering selling shares in YPF to Shell, a U.S. oil company based in Houston, under an arrangement known as the "Houston Plan." Jaunarena was called to answer questions about the plan. In the speech Eduardo suggested that it had been difficult to arrange a time for the minister of defense to come to the Senate, and he expressed anger over the difficulty the Senate had confronted in finding a time to bring Jaunarena to the Senate.

This speech was as much a generalized attack on the Alfonsín administration as it was a criticism of one specific privatization effort. Eduardo began by criticizing multiple aspects of national petroleum policy under the Alfonsín administration. He claimed that the administration's petroleum policy was erratic and that the nation was now into its third or fourth petroleum policy.

As with the proposed privatization of Aerolíneas and ENTel, Eduardo complained that the administration was bypassing Congress. Having a minister present to inform Congress about what was happening was not sufficient. In particular he said that the administration had not even had a minister present to inform Congress about the Houston Plan. Instead, Congress had learned about the intended plan through the newspapers and had now called Jaunarena in through its formal interpellation powers. He again questioned the policy of privatization itself, pointing out that privatization of the petroleum industry might increase rather than decrease costs, and he asked for details about crude oil prices and production levels.

As in his speech against the privatization of Aerolíneas and ENTel, Eduardo objected to the sale of shares of YPF on nationalistic grounds. He claimed that a U.S. company knew more about the proposed Houston Plan than Congress did. Eduardo claimed that Congress would have given the minister support if he had asked for it. This claim seems particularly disingenuous considering the reaction recorded above to the visit from a cabinet minister to inform the Congress about the privatization of Aerolíneas and ENTel. Eduardo maintained that the proposed plan was economically unsustainable because, after selling the oil company, YPF would be paying more per barrel of oil than what it actually cost Shell to produce a barrel. Eduardo did not produce any tables or offer any statistics in support of this accusation.

---

minister himself is called upon to answer questions and challenges from the floor of the legislature. This power of "interpellation," as it is called in Spanish, is also found in other Latin American legislatures and can be used as an important restraint upon the power of the executive. Leslie E. Anderson, "The Authoritarian Executive: Horizontal and Vertical Accountability in Nicaragua," *Latin American Politics and Society* 48, no. 2 (2006): 141–69.

Although Peronism clearly opposed this sale, the May 11, 1988, speech was somewhat less hostile, accusatory, and inflammatory than his speech thirteen days earlier regarding Aerolíneas and ENTel. This second speech even contains a suggestion of greater openness to the possible benefits of privatizing YPF and the opportunities for increased production that might emerge from a deal with foreign companies. Eduardo's complaints focused repeatedly on the procedure used—the alleged effort to bypass Congress—and less on privatization itself. He also appeared to be beginning Peronism's electoral campaign by launching numerous criticisms of Alfonsín's administration more generally.

The criticisms made of Alfonsín's proposed privatization of YPF were more specific and are concentrated in a few categories, whereas in the speech thirteen days earlier Eduardo had ranged across seven different types of accusations in his objections to privatization. Here he concentrated primarily upon procedure and upon criticisms of Alfonsín's administration while also maintaining his earlier accusations of secrecy against Alfonsín's government and his nationalistic position that privatization was not patriotic.

TABLE 4.3. Content Analysis of Eduardo Menem's Speech against Privatization of YPF (National Petroleum Company), May 11, 1988, Senate Chamber

KEY ARGUMENT: *Alfonsín's administration was bypassing Congress and was inept both generally and with respect to economic policy.*

Objection Raised	Number of Mentions
Procedural concerns about ignoring Congress	10
Nationalistic/patriotic/anti-imperialist	2
Legal concerns	0
Arguments against market mechanisms	0
Arguments for greater market mechanisms	0
Alleged secrecy/lack of information	2
Generalized criticism of Alfonsín administration	3
Criticism of Alfonsín's economic policy	6
Total number of different concerns raised	5
Total number of objections made, including repetitions	23

Speech #3: Against Privatization and Sale of Arms Production Factories, September 8, 1988

Eduardo Menem's last antiprivatization speech came on the occasion of a proposed sale of several arms-production factories owned during the military dictatorship by the military itself. At one time, the military had made

money using these factories to produce arms for foreign countries, bypassing the civilian government, when one existed. These factories had a controversial history, and removing them from military control represented
a departure from a time when the military operated as a separate entity
above the law.[54] As part of the movement toward civilian control of the
military, these factories were no longer owned by the armed forces and had
passed to the Ministry of Defense. They were officially owned by the state.
Outdated and lacking improved production capacities, they were no longer
profitable and represented one more fiscal drain on the treasury. Alfonsín
proposed to sell them to private companies. Once again the Senate exercised its powers of interpellation and called Minister of Defense Jaunarena
to the chamber to answer questions about the proposed sales.

Eduardo said that there appeared to be a wave of privatizations of arms
production factories and his party was concerned about the implications of
such sales for national defense. He claimed now, in September 1988, that
the Peronist Party was not opposed to privatization per se, seeing it as a
means to an end. Instead, Peronism's real apprehension concerned where
decision-making power would lie in areas fundamental to the progress and
development of the nation. One such area was national defense. He argued
that this worry had defined his argument five months earlier on the privatization of Aerolíneas and ENTel.

He questioned the administration's decision to begin by selling the
most profitable companies first, and he wondered where the nation would
get the money to improve the enterprises that were functioning more
poorly. He suggested now that the state should sell off some companies
but that it should sell first the ones that were losing money. Having made
this point, he reiterated his party's concerns about selling national property, especially without open bidding. Some companies that were offering
an important public service ought not to be sold at all. With respect to
the military factories, Menem pointed out that they were already largely
in private hands and that only 30 percent of shares were owned by the
state. Therefore, the sale of state shares meant that these factories would
rest entirely in private hands.

Eduardo objected to Alfonsín's apparent willingness to privatize these
factories by decree and in a secret manner, which the administration
claimed was necessary for national defense. He noted that the Peronist
Party had asked for a copy of the sales agreement, and the administration
had refused to provide one. He acknowledged the need for secrecy, but

54. Fitch, *Armed Forces and Democracy in Latin America*, and Pion-Berlin, *Through Corridors of Power*.

argued that some information should be provided when national defense was at stake because of the need for transparency.

In the first speech analyzed above Eduardo made many objections to the policy of privatization and he repeated those multiple times. However, of all those objections, two stand out as being the most persuasive: the nationalist objections and the procedural objections. With respect to the first, and most emphatically in the first of these three speeches, Eduardo tied Peronism's objections to privatization together with nationalism, patriotism, and national sovereignty. According to this objection, *privatization was a threat to and violation of national sovereignty. Anyone who supported privatization was against national sovereignty and independence and was in favor of selling the nation to imperialists.* With respect to the second, and this objection ran through all three speeches, the manner in which Alfonsín was proposing to conduct privatizations, namely the sale of a minority of shares to foreign companies through direct negotiation between the president and the companies, was a violation of government procedure and an effort to ignore "the representatives of the people." *Whatever was done with respect to privatization, it should be done with, through, and by means of the full participation of the Congress.* These two most important objections stand as hallmarks of Eduardo's three antiprivatization speeches. Table 4.4 summarizes Eduardo Menem's argument against the sale of the arms production factories.

TABLE 4.4. Content Analysis of Eduardo Menem's Speech against the Sale of Arms Production Factories, September 8, 1988, Senate Chamber

KEY ARGUMENT: *Privatization is unpatriotic.*

Objection Raised	Number of Mentions
Procedural concerns about ignoring Congress	4
Nationalistic/patriotic/anti-imperialism concerns	6
Legal concerns	1
Arguments against market mechanisms	1
Arguments for greater market mechanisms	4
Alleged secrecy/lack of information	3
Generalized criticism of Alfonsín administration	2
Criticisms of Alfonsín's economic policy	0
Total number of different concerns raised	7
Total number of objections made, including repetitions	21

When Eduardo gave these speeches in mid-1988, no one expected that Carlos Menem would make privatization a hallmark of his presidency less than one year later, nor were Carlos's upcoming efforts to bypass Congress known. In the next chapter, when we compare Eduardo's fourth speech with

the speeches analyzed here, we will find that Eduardo's position was different. But his words here are worth remembering for the next chapter when we
learn how his brother addressed privatization, and they are a good indication
of how Peronism behaves both in power and out of power. At the moment
of these speeches Eduardo presented the positions in these three speeches as
Peronism's *official stance* on privatization, appealing to idealism and to expectations that the state should provide services and employment. To some, the
speeches appeared reasonable, and the position had wide support.

Some of Eduardo's criticisms were correct. Alfonsín had not set out
to privatize the airline or any other state-owned enterprise. Instead, SAS
had taken the initiative and offered to buy shares in Aerolíneas. There had
been no open bidding, and one can imagine that Peronism perceived a
hurried and poorly thought-out policy. In fact, interviews with members
of Alfonsín's administration and party confirm that the SAS offer was an
opportunity that presented itself but was not part of a deliberate policy.
Similarly, petroleum policy had been erratic during Alfonsín's years in
office. Economic policy in general had never been strong under the Alfonsín administration.

Eduardo's procedural objections were also legitimate. Because the
nation had never engaged in large-scale sales of state-owned enterprises,
there was no clear procedure. Given that the companies were owned by the
state, it was possible that the executive did have the authority to sell them.
Alternatively, as part of the nation's budget, perhaps the issue deserved to
be present on the floor of Congress. The issue goes directly to the unusual
power of the president under the Constitution, as reviewed in chapter 2.
This question was also pertinent with respect to the arms production factories that had been placed under the Ministry of Defense. Should such
sales be treated as laws and therefore passed through the Congress as part
of the normal process of lawmaking, or were they military decisions within
the purview of the executive through the Ministry of Defense?[55] As with
many decisions in a newly democratic government, the procedural path
was unclear. Both the executive and Congress were muddling through the
process and trying to figure out how to proceed with a task that at least
some leaders thought was imperative and long overdue.

But there were also contradictions both within and across the speeches.
In the first speech, Eduardo criticized Alfonsín for not relying enough on
market forces and for relying too much on market forces. It is hard to

---

55. Likewise, in his early reforms, Franklin Roosevelt faced some questions about the
authority by which he could make some of the changes he desired. Burns, *Roosevelt: The Lion
and the Fox*.

know from the speeches whether Peronism was for or against relying upon market forces in the privatization process. This contradiction arises within the first speech itself and in connection with the last. Although Eduardo assumed an antiprivatization position in April 1988, by September the hostility of his party to privatization was equivocal. In the second speech there is no mention of market forces and no position for or against them, so the party's position between April and May 1988 was inconsistent on this subject. In the third speech, Eduardo claimed that his party was not even opposed to privatization at all but rather to the changes in decision-making power that privatization would entail. Between April and September, Eduardo changed his position about the most poorly run and unprofitable state companies. In April 1988 he had proposed improving them by changing their administration; by September, he was proposing that they should be the first enterprises sold.

Eduardo also reversed himself across these three speeches. In April 1988, Peronism was absolutely opposed to any privatization. By September, Eduardo's speech was much less accusatory and inflammatory, and the position of his party was more flexible. The third speech is the most confused of all. There he again objected to the sale of "national property" in the form of Aerolíneas and the telephone company but simultaneously called for the sale of the worst functioning companies, of which these two were certainly prime examples.[56]

Across five months, these speeches indicate that Peronism was changing its official position on privatization. Or perhaps, at least before September 1988, the party did not have an official position on privatization. Certainly the inefficiencies and dangers of the state companies were clear, as was the need for improved service. For example, planes owned by the airlines were sometimes unfit to fly. But Peronism was also presenting a series of concerns that reflected widespread popular sentiment in Argentine society about sovereignty, national defense, national patrimony, proper procedure, and the appropriate role of Congress.

Whether Peronism was self-contradictory, confused, or simply trying to make political headway and sustain chaos by opposing everything the Radical administration attempted, in the end the Peronist Party success-

---

56. For example, newspaper coverage during this period reported that shortly after an Aerolíneas plane had taken off from a small city airport, Jorge Newberry, for a domestic flight, the door had fallen off the aircraft. The plane was forced to return to Newberry and was unable to make the planned flight because the door of the passenger compartment could not be closed. Likewise, the telephone company ENTel made customers wait ten years before they could have a new telephone line installed (*La Nación*, Buenos Aires, 1988). This low level of service was common across all state-owned enterprises in the 1980s.

fully stopped the privatizations in 1988. Alfonsín's efforts at privatization failed completely. He did not privatize the industries for which he had offers, and he did not sell any shares to foreign companies. He did not put forward for congressional consideration any bills for privatizing any of the three major industries for which he had offers. Eduardo's speeches gave the impression that no steps toward privatization would ever pass Congress and that Peronism would oppose any efforts to privatize.[57]

Moreover, Alfonsín was running out of time. Already, by the middle of 1988, the 1989 presidential election campaign was under way, and he had become a lame duck. If he had ever had the political power to push through privatization, he certainly did not have it now. By May 1989, Carlos Menem and the Peronist Party had won the election and Alfonsín was simply in a holding pattern, waiting for the next president to take office. Therefore, as his presidency ended, Alfonsín dropped his partial privatization program and left the economy without a clear program to resolve the extensive problems. The grave economic crisis had already caused Alfonsín to lose popular support long before the Peronist attack on privatization from within Congress. Alfonsín decided that leaving office early would be better, so he asked president-elect Carlos Menem to assume the presidency six months early.[58] Menem did so, becoming president of Argentina in July 1989. Many aspects of policy begun here continued with Carlos Menem, occupying his entire ten-year, two-term presidency. Yet there is a sense in which Carlos's privatization agenda originated in these final months of Alfonsín's presidency. The failures that Alfonsín experienced and the sources of opposition he encountered were lessons for Carlos Menem, who was watching from the sidelines.

In the aftermath of the initial Peronist opposition to privatization, Alfonsín found himself greatly restricted in his ability to address the growing economic crisis that had by now engulfed his administration. In August 1988, he nevertheless launched the Plan Primavera, a last-ditch effort to halt the inflationary cycle and bring some relief to the economy. By the agreements reached under this plan some businesses put price controls in place to help restrain inflation and other measures were taken to decrease speculation. For the most part, the Plan was not successful, and decisions

---

57. U.S. presidents are also far less likely to get their proposals through Congress in hard economic times. See Peterson, *Legislating Together*, 145.

58. In her interesting study of Latin American presidents who have resigned before the end of their terms, Hochstetler finds that 40 percent of elected presidents have faced challenges to their presidencies and 23 percent actually stepped down early in response to the efforts to remove them prematurely. See Kathryn Hochstetler, "Rethinking Presidentialism: Challenges and Presidential Falls in South America," *Comparative Politics* 34, no. 4 (2006): 401–18.

by international lending agencies to deny further loans to Argentina only worsened the economic situation. As Alfonsín ended his term in office the value of the peso was falling quickly and inflation was becoming hyper-inflation. The end of his presidency looked ignominious, for although he had moved the nation forward dramatically in terms of democracy, he had failed to manage the economy. The implementation of the Plan indicates that Alfonsín was aware of the economic crisis and tried to take steps to confront it. The Plan also illustrated the extent to which the outgoing president was both ineffectual in managing the economy and somewhat helpless before multiple other factors, such as Peronist opposition and the lack of international support, both of which simultaneously undermined his presidency.

Conclusion

We conclude part II here. This conclusion presents an overview of all of the Alfonsín years and considers the role of institutions within the context of their foundational intent. The praise for institutional democratization that we could make after the human rights policy must be qualified now after examining the role of institutions in the other policies of the Alfonsín administration. Democratization by institutions continued throughout these later years, but the presidential system revealed its complexities more fully. The democratization process itself was subjected to the checks and balances that presidential democracy is supposed to provide, and if the founders of the U.S. presidential system desired checks against power, they did not intend authoritarian checks to be used against democratic power. This is an eventuality the U.S. founders did not anticipate.

In response to Congress's success in checking the presidency and stopping labor reform, the Alfonsín administration stepped outside the presidential system entirely and reverted to corporatism, a vertical approach familiar in Argentina. Casela used corporate control and access to create union support for a more limited labor reform bill. Union acquiescence then allowed Congress to have enough constituency support to pass a weaker labor reform bill. It was a use of nondemocratic means to move toward democratic ends, and it operated quite outside the Madisonian system.

But Peronist control of the Senate left the administration no alternative. Unreasonable control of a legislature is, in fact, one problem Madison anticipated. In his study of factions, he saw the danger that one group could dominate a representative institution in an unfair manner, and he considered this problem when he wrote about factionalism within the legislature. His response to this danger was to rely upon the process of deliberation itself within the representative context. Dialogue, he thought, would bring forward the most reasonable position, as the legislators listened to each other. Representatives, he thought, unlike individual actors in a direct, participatory democracy, would be more dispassionate and less subject to unreason. Moreover, he argued, the size of the American democracy itself would bring forward a variety of different factions from different geographic regions of the country and these would balance each other so that no single faction could rule the day.[59]

Madison was wrong in his confidence that different regional factions would balance each other out so that reason and democracy could prevail. We know now that less than one hundred years after he made his argument one faction of the United States, the South, dominated both the legislature and national politics in a manner that did not allow either reason or democracy to prevail.[60] The institutions did not manage to contain either the aggression or the nondemocratic agenda of the united Southern states. They did not allow deliberation to resolve the conflict. That failure brought on civil war. American institutions are not always equal to the task of containing an extreme faction or of protecting democracy.

Much the same can be said for Argentina where the nondemocratic faction is even larger than was the U.S. South. In the Argentine legislature Peronism dominated beginning in 1987. In the lower chamber Peronism's numerical majority resulted from midterm elections, but in the Senate Peronist power resulted from entrenched Peronist control in the provinces. Peronist supremacy inside many provinces, writes Edward Gibson, is the outcome of authoritarian mechanisms of control inside subnational governments throughout much of the country. Moreover, the Argentine Senate, one of the most malapportioned in the world, favors the far-flung rural provinces, which are the most Peronist-dominated.[61] So again, Madison

---

59. Federalist #10.

60. Burns, *Deadlock of Democracy*, esp. chaps. 1–4.

61. Gibson, *Boundary Control*. Moreover, when electoral reform emerges in Argentina, the incumbent Peronist Party has been shown to win even more seats. This circumstance shows that the problematic circumstance of a single-party state produces multiple ripple effects on Argentina's institutions, making it difficult for the country to extract itself from its authoritarian past. Also see Mark P. Jones and Wonjae Hwang, "Provincial Party Bosses: Keystone of the Argentina Congress," in *Argentine Democracy: The Politics of Institutional Weakness*, ed. Steven Levitsky and María Victoria Murillo (University Park: Pennsylvania State University Press, 2005), 115–38. On electoral reform in Argentina, see Ernesto Calvo and Juan Pablo Micozzi, "The Governor's Backyard: A Seat Vote Model of Electoral Reform for Subnational Multi-Party Races," *Journal of Politics* 67, no. 4 (November 2005): 1050–74.

was wrong and perhaps even naïve to conclude that sectional factions from different parts of the country would balance each other out for the overall benefit of democracy itself. In neither the United States nor in Argentina have the institutions been equal to the task of containing the nondemocratic designs of a large faction.

As a result, the Congress Alfonsín faced contained powerful antidemocratic forces. His challenges were not confined to an aggressive labor force and a dysfunctional economy. They also included an opposition party that was obstructionist at best, and antidemocratic at worst. Peronism did not play fair with Alfonsín, either as a labor proponent or as a political party. Peronism was unfair in allowing militant labor to act unchecked, and it was both unfair and disingenuous in its opposition to privatization.[62] Alfonsín could have responded with presidential decrees, with more executive power rather than less. He was unwilling to respond to Peronism in that way. His determination to use the existing institutions left him competing on an unlevel playing field and limited his democratic reforms. The Peronist challenge went beyond party opposition. It included a willingness to change postures and draw on labor to undermine the democratic government, all with an eye to maximizing the party's 1989 electoral chances.

But while the representative institutions produced severe limits upon Argentina's efforts to democratize, they were, nevertheless, the nation's only real resource. The contribution of civil society to democracy during Alfonsín's presidency was less positive and became more problematic with time. After an early stand for human rights, civil society, as embodied in the labor unions, primarily threatened democracy. This chapter has not described an extensive process of grassroots pressure for reform. In fact, grassroots and popular sectors opposed the reforms studied here. The labor unions strongly resisted the government's efforts at democratization of the unions, and these same groups resisted privatization. In the face of labor militancy, no popular groups mobilized against labor, nor did civilian groups press Congress to pass the Mucci bill. Civil society remained silent as these struggles unfolded. Efforts toward democracy during the Alfonsín

---

62. In the United States, Lyndon Johnson has become known for his reversals of position on civil rights. Early in his career, he opposed all civil rights legislation. Later in his career, in his final years in the Senate and as president, he became the great promoter of civil rights. In Johnson's case, as in the case of Peronism, the vacillation of position was due entirely to a drive for power. Johnson wanted the presidency; Peronism and the Menem brothers wanted power. All were willing to change their position if doing so would gain them power. However, the question remains both about Johnson and about the Menems and Peronism: What is their real position, and do they even have one? On Johnson, see Robert Caro, *The Years of Lyndon Johnson: Master of the Senate* (New York: Alfred A. Knopf, 2002).

years came primarily from above and were unsupported, resisted, or partially resisted from below.

The failure of civil society to take a continuing strong position in mobilized support of the democratic government left democratization proceeding primarily inside the state's institutions, particularly the Congress, which then made errors and opened the door to abuses of power inside the legislature. Yet the U.S. designers of the presidential system Argentina was using would likely have argued that having a problematic Congress was still better than none at all. They did not construct a legislature anticipating that it would always make the best decisions or that it would always include members with good intentions. Congress can be wrong even when it does not include authoritarian actors. The founders of the presidential system constructed a legislature because it provides a democratic process and a forum for dialogue. Its very openness then leaves it vulnerable to authoritarian actors within.

Despite their limits, the institutions of state still provided both the impetus for reform and the forum within which policy could be discussed and formulated. Here we see Argentine leaders muddling through to some degree of reform and some level of progress toward democracy. Some labor reform was achieved, and privatization became a topic of legitimate conversation even if many still rejected it as policy. Even Peronism changed and softened its privatization position on the Senate floor. An institutional arrangement that would permit "muddling through" was exactly what the United States founders hoped to achieve, even if they underestimated the obstacles along the way. Alfonsín contributed greatly to Argentina's democratization and economic modernization simply by opening these two issues for discussion. Quite apart from the level of actual policy success he achieved, he pointed the way toward Argentina's next tasks. In part III we will find that Menem and the Peronist Party were savvy enough to take up those same tasks while proclaiming their opposition to them.

Before turning to the Menem years, it is useful to consider Alfonsín's presidency from the perspective of Madison's comments about leadership. In Federalist #10 he wrote, "The enlightened statesman might not always be available," and therefore institutions were needed to check the president's power. Here we have seen something more akin to Peronist depravity, using the institutions of Congress to destroy the initiative of good leadership. That then becomes another danger in Madison's system of checks and balances. Once the checks and balances are in place, they can be used to good or ill purpose.

Was Alfonsín an enlightened statesman? I suggest that he exhibited more of the characteristics of such a leader than did Menem or any other Argentine president since, up to the time of this writing. His determination to work with and through Congress and his skill at achieving policy by that means was part of his statesmanship. While he was limited and some thought him capable of megalomania, he came closer to having a broader vision about *both* democratic reform *and* democratic process than has any Argentine president since. He was more balanced in his use of power, more self-restrained, and less dominated by the lust for power than most Argentine presidents since. Certainly he was a good leader. Perhaps he was an enlightened statesman.[63] Yet he was not able to overcome the authoritarian agenda of Peronism. He made an enormous contribution, one that has not been matched since. He also faced unparalleled limits upon that contribution from the authoritarian forces that opposed him. In that duel we sense the magnitude of the challenge Argentina faced as it democratized through institutions. In Federalist #51 Madison famously wrote, "If men were angels, no government would be necessary." Clearly Argentina, like most nations, is short on angels. In the face of human deficiencies, good government becomes Argentina's best hope and good leadership is highly desirable.

---

63. This paragraph draws upon an interview with Raúl Alfonsín, conducted in his home, on May 23, 1993. I was exceedingly fortunate to gain this interview. Alfonsín was an impressive man. He was not perfect, but he was visionary, earnest, courageous, and well-intentioned. I respected him. I am indebted to members of the Radical Party for arranging this interview.

PART III

The Menem Years

FIVE

Presidential Innovation and Congressional Cooperation

Privatization Succeeds

Early in the presidency of Carlos Menem the military attempted another coup, led by Seineldín. Menem called his cabinet together and asked for their advice. His minister of defense, Humberto Romero, recommended making a pact with the military. His secretary general recommended "prudence." Others advised negotiation. Menem ignored them all. Instead he called [Martín] Balza, head of the army, and asked him to take his troops to the barracks being held by the rebel troops engaged in the uprising and instruct the rebels to lay down their arms and surrender. He also told Balza that if the rebels did not do as they were told, Balza should fire on them. Balza went to the barracks and called for Seineldín's surrender. Seineldín refused. Balza ordered his men to aim at the rebels and fire. Balza's troops took aim at the rebels and fired. Several rebels died. Then the rebels surrendered. On that day the democratic transition ended.[1]

—Rodolfo Díaz

He could easily have ruled by emergency decree; the country would have cheered. Instead he would at least try to work with Congress, which remained unpopular but in his mind still essential to the credibility of any of his reforms.

—Jonathan Alter on Franklin Roosevelt[2]

---

1. Díaz explains that this occasion was the first time an active military officer obeyed a civilian president and repressed another military man who was in rebellion. Interview, Buenos Aires, March 14, 2008.

2. Jonathan Alter, *The Defining Moment: FDR's Hundred Days and the Triumph of Hope* (New York: Simon and Schuster, 2006), 226.

In part III we study the Menem years, a ten-year period I define as the second phase of Argentina's democratic transition. A dual party system still existed in Argentina during this decade, and that backdrop made oppositional challenge to the presidency possible. This chapter concentrates on economic reform. Chapters 6 and 7 consider economic and social measures taken to alleviate the costs of these reforms. We begin here with the 1989 election and the challenges Argentina faced then. We continue by considering ongoing democratization efforts, and then the bulk of the chapter concentrates on the economic reforms themselves.

Madison's observations about good government inform our view of the Menem years and underscore their limits in the progress toward democracy. In Federalist #51 Madison wrote, "You must first enable the government to control the governed; and in the next place, oblige it to control itself."[3] Labor militancy under Alfonsín had illustrated the need to control the governed, a goal Menem achieved early. But he was much more reluctant to control himself. Our polity-centered approach trains two lenses upon the policy process. It allows us to see the polity moving toward democratization and the struggles inside that process. It also allows us to study the development of subpolicies that contributed to the larger democratization goal.

As Argentina reached its first civilian transfer of power in July 1999, it also faced a "collapse of the state" or the "collapse of assisted capitalism."[4] Hyperinflation had reached 5,000 percent per year. Between August 1988 and July 1989, consumer prices had risen 3,610 percent and wholesale prices by 5,062 percent. Then, in early 1990, consumer prices rose much further: 7,920 percent in January, 6,160 percent in February, and 9,550 percent in March. Between March 1989 and March 1990, the Consumer

---

3. Federalist #51, "The Social Foundations of Political Freedom," in *The Federalist Papers*, by John Jay, Alexander Hamilton, and James Madison (New York: Washington Square Press, 1972), 122.

4. The term "assisted capitalism" implies that capitalism without assistance (in the form of extensive social support) is unsustainable. This attitude had gotten the Argentine state into the position of attempting to provide universal employment with disastrous economic consequences.

Such policies are not unique to Argentina. Kohli writes that India attempted something similar. He suggests that such policies are not appropriate because they require the state to support one sector of society above any other. That position then decreases the state's ability to represent a broad array of interests, the task of a democratic state. Thus, while developmentalist policies appear to support the poor, over the long run they are, in effect, antithetical to democracy itself. See Atul Kohli, *Democracy and Discontent: India's Growing Crisis of Governability* (Cambridge: Cambridge University Press, 1990).

Price Index rose 23,140 percent.[5] Under the dictatorship, Argentina had accumulated an enormous international debt, which added to inflation. Part of that debt was the ongoing state effort to subsidize inefficient service industries. Had Alfonsín been allowed to begin privatization late in his term, Argentina would by now have begun to see results in lowered inflation rates.[6] Instead the economy worsened throughout his final months. The denial in 1988 of an IMF loan and unfavorable lending rates frustrated the nation's attempts to retain its repayment schedule. Treasury reserves had dropped to historic lows.

When a political or economic system collapses people pay a high price in lost jobs, physical displacement, illness, death, or victimization by crime. Charles Tilly argues that states have high or low capacities to serve and protect their populations. Both authoritarian and democratic states can have high capacity, but considerable social upheaval and a loss of state capacity attends the movement from one to the other. Once a new democratic polity gains a high capacity, it will more effectively serve the citizens or control crime, but in a transition considerable social chaos is likely to emerge.[7] In the United States the Civil War caused the collapse of the Southern system, including its polity and its plantation economy. In the immediate aftermath, everyone, including even former slaves, suffered malnutrition, starvation, unemployment, disease, and death until the Northern authorities developed institutional mechanisms to deal with their plight and former slaves integrated themselves into the new free labor economy.[8] These observations frame our understanding of Argentina's challenge. While the state was still learning to become democratic it moved from providing universal employment to a market economy. This change caused unemployment, poverty, illness, and malnutrition.

This collapse defined the 1989 electoral contest. Many positive developments toward the end of Alfonsín's term went unnoticed, including the Union Law, competitive elections inside many unions, and the trial of Gen-

---

5. Smith, "State, Market and Neoliberalism in Post-transition Argentina," 7.

6. Daniel Heymann and Fernando Navajas argue that the deficit contributed directly to the hyperinflation so that, had Alfonsín been allowed to privatize, inflation would have begun to decrease by this time. See "Conflicto distributivo y déficit fiscal: Notas sobre la experience argentina,' in *Inflación Rebelde en America Latina*, ed. José Pablo Arellano (Santiago, Chile: Cieplan-Hachette, 1990), 141.

7. Charles Tilly, *The Politics of Collective Violence* (New York: Cambridge University Press, 2003).

8. Jim Downs, *Sick from Freedom: African-American Illness and Suffering during the Civil War and Reconstruction* (Oxford: Oxford University Press, 2012).

eral Galtieri. Public and press attention went entirely to the economy, and the Peronists appeared poised to win the election. Yet there was also unease about a Peronist presidency. Radicalism was perceived both domestically and abroad as a party deeply committed to democracy and the rule of law, even if it did not manage the economy as skillfully as desired.[9] Peronism, by contrast, was sometimes authoritarian and had un uncomfortable relationship with democracy. There were economic doubts as well. Peronism was the original creator of "assisted capitalism." Perón had first nationalized the state-owned enterprises and started the state toward universal employment.[10] Menem had supported traditional Peronist policies as a senator representing La Rioja Province. There was nothing in his background that would lead observers to expect a dramatic departure from Peronist economic policies once he became president. In the Senate Peronism had already taken a hostile position toward privatization. International lending sectors viewed Menem's impending victory with trepidation.

Yet Menem looked like the only electoral option in Argentina and had substantial support. If he won, it would be difficult to oppose him on the basis of the past nondemocratic performance of his party. Instead, when he won, Alfonsín set aside doubts and asked him to assume the presidency six months early, in July rather than December 1989. Menem agreed upon one condition: that the Radical congressional bloc support his policies for the six-month period. When the bloc agreed it gave the civilian transfer of power greater legitimacy and lessened the likelihood of a military coup.[11] In attending to Congress in this way, Menem seemed willing to work within the presidential system of checks and balances, an attitude that alleviated some of the concerns about his commitment to democracy.[12]

---

9. Rebecca Bill Chavez, *The Rule of Law in Nascent Democracies: Judicial Politics in Argentina* (Stanford: Stanford University Press, 2004).

10. Although Perón's labor creation policies were now causing economic collapse, concerns about employment were not the only factor influencing his economic policies. Far from being entirely prolabor, Perón was also influenced by the powerful economic group, Bunge y Born, associated with Alejandro Bunge. He carried out agro-export policies that advantaged them. See Claudio Belini, "El grupo Bunge y la politica económica del primer peronismo, 1943–1952," *Latin American Research Review* 41, no. 1 (2006): 27–50.

11. Roniger and Sznajder write that some elements of the military had some democratic convictions, which began to emerge after the return to democracy. See *Legacy of Human Rights Violations in the Southern Cone*, 66. The task for Alfonsín and Menem was to empower those subsectors of the military while easing out those who did not believe in democracy.

12. Menem was functioning in a less than fully institutionalized political system. By its very nature, Argentina's lack of institutionalization further contributed to the lack of accountability. See Melo, Pereira, and Figueiredo, "Political and Institutional Checks on Corruption."

The Larger Democratization Project:
Military Subordination and Democratic Decrees

If Menem and Alfonsín emphasized different subpolicies—economics versus human rights—they agreed on the need to push forward the larger democratization project. Like Alfonsín, and as the opening quotation to this chapter indicates, Menem faced military insubordination.[13] One section of the military attempted a coup against him on March 12, 1990, less than a year after Menem had assumed the presidency. This was the fourth military attempt against democracy since 1983. Menem collected his cabinet to hear their advice and then overrode their suggestions to concede or negotiate. He ordered General Balza, the commander of the army, to surround the rebels and demand their surrender.[14] If they did not surrender immediately, Balza was to order his troops to fire on them and shoot to kill. Balza did as he was ordered by his commander in chief, and Balza's troops did as they were ordered by their general. In the face of such firepower, the rebels surrendered.[15] There has not been another attempted coup since then.

If this step established civilian control of the military, Menem's next step sent a very different message. In 1991 he issued presidential pardons to all officers who had been found guilty under the human rights trials and were serving life sentences.[16] The pardons extended to leftist terrorists who

---

13. In part, the reasons for such defiance were the same ones that had imperiled the Alfonsín presidency: budget reductions. Alfonsín had greatly reduced the military budget and Menem sought to continue that pattern. While in power the military had increased arms imports from forty million dollars in 1977 to 360 million by 1987, an 800 percent increase in one decade. Neither civilian government had any intention of continuing that kind of expenditure.

14. Horacio Jaunarena, Alfonsín's minister of defense, gives Menem credit for finalizing the task of obtaining civilian control over the military. Jaunarena is a Radical. Yet his open recognition of Menem's contribution in this regard exemplifies the extent to which this task, perhaps more than any other, was shared and supported across partisan lines. In his interviews Juanarena was honest in recognizing the contribution of each of these two presidents.

15. General Balza is nationally and internationally recognized for having been the first general within the Argentine army to have publicly recognized that the Dirty War was wrong. His public statement to that effect, and his apology to the victims of human rights abuse, represents the kind of act of reconciliation that students of reconciliation studies consider essential to the overall process of social healing in the aftermath of human rights violations. See Eric Yamamoto, Sandra Hye Yun Kim, and Abigail M. Holden, "American Reparations Theory at the Crossroads," *California Western Law Review* 44, no. 1 (Fall 2007): 1–85. Balza's statement caused him to become the focus of civilian attention and he was promoted to the post of commander of the army over more senior officers based in part on the statement and the apology. In retrospect, the promotion of Balza appears to have been a good decision because, at the point of crisis and military challenge to democracy, Balza proved himself reliable and loyal in his support for the civilian regime.

16. More than five years after the end of Menem's administration, in July 2005, the Argen-

were serving life sentences. This step brought substantial popular criticism and still does today. Those who suspected Peronist cooperation with the military saw the pardons as evidence of Peronism's close relationship with the military.[17] Menem ignored this public criticism. With the coup neutralized and pardons issued, he had no further agenda for reducing military involvement in Argentine society.[18] He praised the military publicly, while continuing Alfonsín's policy of decreasing the military budget.[19] Seeking to give the military a task that would keep them busy and of which they could be proud, he involved the military in international peacekeeping efforts.[20]

These initiatives would have been his legacy except for one unforeseen event. Late in his presidency a young conscript, Omar Carrasco, died while in military training in March 1994. His body was found in the city of Zapala, Neuquén province, in a manner reminiscent of the Dirty War. Forensic investigation revealed that he had been beaten to death. In response to Carrasco's death, Argentina erupted in protests, forcing the institutions to respond.[21] The issue of the draft resurfaced. Human rights organizations and family groups mobilized. Civilian leaders argued that the military could not be trusted with the lives of society's youth. Conscription

tine Supreme Court nullified Menem's amnesty laws, declaring them unconstitutional and in violation of international law. See Bonner, *Sustaining Human Rights*, 129. Amnesty for Argentina's military had not been part of the nation's democratization process. In contrast, South Africa was only able to move toward democracy by agreeing to grant amnesty to those who had engaged in human rights violations during apartheid. See Eric K. Yamamoto, *Interracial Justice: Conflict and Reconciliation in Post-Civil Rights America* (New York: New York University Press, 1999), 259.

17. Menem also asked the courts to reverse many legal decisions made under Alfonsín so that the laws in effect during the military dictatorship now had validity on par with laws made under democracy. See Nino, *Radical Evil*, 48.

18. Fitch argues that military policy was a secondary priority for Menem, standing behind his concerns about the economy. See Fitch, *Armed Forces*, 142–43. Pion-Berlin sees little difference between Alfonsín's and Menem's policies toward the military. Both had major successes in budget reduction, but both failed to accomplish significant defense reform. At the time his book was published in 1997 Pion-Berlin still considered that Argentina's military leaders did not accept civilian supremacy. He suggested that Argentina's civilian governments were acting in a manner that allowed them to avoid a coup, but that coup avoidance and civilian supremacy were not the same thing. He argued that civilian governments had been able to avoid another coup because international opinion stood against Argentina's military, domestic support for a coup was absent, and many military officers and soldiers would have preferred to disassociate themselves from their authoritarian past. See *Through Corridors of Power*, 14 and 16–17.

19. Fitch, *Armed Forces*, 142–43.

20. Fitch, *Armed Forces*, 95.

21. Angry popular protest against anything that resembles the human rights violations of the past is a distinct feature of Argentina's democracy today. It serves a positive purpose in restraining the temptation by power holders to use violence, intimidation, and threats of violence for political purpose. Leslie E. Anderson, "Clientelism, Semiclientelism, and Pluralism: Toward a Theory of Grassroots Autonomy," manuscript under review.

should end. Having tabled the issue under the Radicals for fear that pursuing it would produce a coup, Congress now hurriedly ended the draft in response to an angry civil society. The military became a volunteer force, asking for support and even participation from a society that rejected the armed forces now more thoroughly than ever before.

TABLE 5.1. Presidential Decrees Issued by Menem for Democratic Purpose

	Decrees Issued	
Year Issued	N	(%)
1989 (July–Dec. only)	1	.8
1990	4	3.3
1991	6	5.0
1992	15	12.5
1993	18	15.0
1994	17	14.2
1995	14	11.7
1996	6	5.0
1997	10	8.3
1998	10	8.3
1999	19	15.8
Total	120	99.9[a]

[a]These percentages do not add to 100 due to the rounding of percentages.

Menem also attended to Argentina's democratic image abroad and to union democratization at home, addressing these issues through decrees. In international affairs he aligned the nation with the older industrial democracies and with democratization efforts worldwide. He was quick to support any United Nations resolutions in favor of democracy, and many of his decrees served this symbolic purpose. For example, on August 13, 1990, he issued Decree 1560/90, offering Argentina's support for the UN resolution condemning Iraq's invasion and occupation of Kuwait. On the domestic front, Menem pushed forward union democratization with decrees. This was a significant step away from Perón's system that had enhanced government control of unions by allowing only one union per sector. Decree 1753/91 of September 2, 1991, modified a congressional law (23.929) on labor union representation in collective bargaining commissions. In Article 1, the decree said that the collective bargaining commission would allow the presence and participation of more than one labor union for each sector. Decree 1755/91, also issued September 2, 1991, enhanced representation inside the unions as well. It stipulated that all political parties would be allowed to send representatives to the meetings of the undersecretary of government action. The undersecretary of government action is considered a member of the Cabinet and was a representative of the Ministry of Labor. The Ministry could communicate with the labor unions through these meetings. This decree (1755/91) was brief, only two pages long, and had no companion law from Congress. Yet it clearly had the democratic purpose of expanding participation and representation in the everyday routine of the executive branch. It also further democratized the unions by allowing more than one representative from each union.

Table 5.1 lists Menem's decrees issued for democratic purpose. All of these decrees moved away from the monolithic control over each sector established by Perón, and added to the democratization process already under way inside some unions. Thus the overall result of some of Menem's decrees was to make law the portions of Alfonsín's labor reform that Congress had rejected in the Union Law. Menem did not give Congress a chance to reject these reforms a third time: he accomplished them by decree. Congressional consent might not have been forthcoming from the Peronist-dominated legislature in which many representatives, particularly in the Senate, owed their seats to the hierarchical labor control system present throughout Argentina. The move toward multiple unions per sector also weakened state control of the unions because the state could no longer threaten uncooperative unions with removal from their official representative function; alternative unions would already be part of the sector representation. Clearly Menem felt that his own control over labor was sufficiently strong that he no longer needed Perón's old, corporatist measures. In this phase of democratization, Argentina used both its legislative and executive resources. In ending the draft it was Congress that wrote the new law, in response to social protest. In foreign affairs and in sending the military abroad the presidency took the lead. But in furthering union democratization Menem clearly bypassed Congress, unwilling to have another debacle similar to the defeat of the Mucci bill. In each case the nation used the institutional resources at its disposal to move forward with the democratization task.

Early Economic Policy: First Steps

We turn now to the main subpolicy on Menem's agenda: economic reform. The causes of Argentina's economic disaster were deep. By 1989 Argentina had gone fifteen years with no economic growth.[22] The state was trying to manage communication, transportation, and industrial production without

---

22. Díaz, *Prosperidad o Ilusion?*, 43.

the capital necessary to make these industries efficient or the administrative knowledge to run them properly.[23] One part of the mismanagement was bloated payrolls, an outcome of the expectation that the state should provide universal employment. Another part was the cumbersome regulations the state imposed on private enterprises. Yet a third cause of the economic disaster were the subsidies going from the state to inefficient companies that could not stay afloat otherwise. Argentina needed both deregulation and privatization.

Nationalization and poor management had created this collapse. The first move toward nationalization had come in the 1920s when the first Radical president, Hipólito Yrigoyen, sought to nationalize the mines. But most services were nationalized during Perón's two-term presidency of 1946–55. Perón also subscribed to the notion that the state was responsible for the lives of its citizens.[24] By the time of his second presidency, 1973–74, the state had become the principal economic actor.[25] It was the primary producer of goods, played a key role in resource redistribution, and was a principal employer. Argentina called this "assisted capitalism"; its result was inefficient state firms and private companies that could not survive without state subsidies.[26]

Menem's first steps addressed inflation. Despite the death of his first minister of the economy and the resignation of the second, Menem pressed

---

23. Overinvolvement of the state in the national economy to an extent that was economically unviable was a common problem in Latin America and not one confined either to Argentina or to Peronist policy. In Argentina this problem dated back to the original Peronist years of 1946–55. In Chile, hyperinvolvement by the state dated back as far as 1939. Both nations had found this level of state economic involvement impossible to maintain, and both nations moved to decrease the state's role. Both privatized unproductive state industries. Chile moved earlier and more slowly in this direction, extending these reforms from the 1960s to the 1980s. Argentina moved toward these types of reforms only in the 1990s. A key reason for Argentina's later progress in this regard was the power of labor to resist privatization through the unions, which were less strong in Chile. Coming much later and long overdue, Argentina's reforms then created more hardship. On Argentina, see Díaz, *Prosperidad o Ilusión?*, 44. On Chile, see Ffrench, *Economic Reforms in Chile*, 2, 27, and 32.

24. In his study of looting and theft in Argentina in 2001, Javier Auyero claimed that many citizens believe and believed then that they are entitled to state support or to luxury food items or both. See Javier Auyero, *Routine Politics and Violence in Argentina: The Gray Zone* (New York: Cambridge University Press, 2007), esp. chap. 5. For a theoretical perspective on the lootings, see Anderson, "Oppositional Consciousness," *Polity* (2009).

25. Perón was allowed to return to Argentina from exile in Spain in 1973. He was prohibited from running for the presidency in March of that year but his designated candidate, Hector Campora, won. Campora resigned in July 1973 and Perón was then allowed to run for the presidency. He won with 62 percent of the vote but died in office of a heart attack in 1974.

26. Díaz, *Prosperidad*, 66, 70.

ahead.[27] Antonio Erman González became his third minister of the economy, and an early economic policy emerged. The ministry devalued the currency twice, once by 54 percent and again by 170 percent. An exchange rate of 665 australes per $1 matched the black market in an effort to bring dollars into the treasury. Menem's administration negotiated with businesses for a temporary halt in price increases, a measure designed to ease inflation. Eventually the price control agreement included 350 companies that promised to hold prices in check in exchange for lowered interest rates.[28] In an effort to reduce the subsidies that were bankrupting the state, Menem increased the price of petroleum products, transport, and electricity between 200 percent to 640 percent. He cut the public deficit further by suspending tax breaks for industry for 180 days and raised export taxes 5 percent. The value-added tax rose to 13 percent and was extended to cover most goods and services. Payments to contractors for public works were suspended, and many public agencies were slated for elimination or reorganization.

These reforms were also accompanied by employment creation programs and social or economic relief.[29] In response to the need for speed, Menem issued decrees for emergency social relief or to control hyperinflation.[30] Menem issued more than five times as many decrees concerning the economy as did Alfonsín. His decrees covered emergency food, clothing, and housing for the poor and the unemployed. He also took emergency

27. See the *Los Angeles Times*, "News: The World," July 19, 1989, and "Argentine Economic Chief Quits," December 15, 1989.

28. Smith, "State, Market and Neoliberalism in Post-transition Argentina: 1–17, esp. 7.

29. Augustina Giraudy, "The Distributive Politics of Emergency Employment Programs in Argentina (1993–2002)," *Latin American Research Review* 42, no. 2 (2007): 33–55. One problem with these programs was the clientelistic distribution of employment, another indicator of how Peronism uses power. The workfare programs in Argentina in the 1990s were then used again in the 2000s. See Rebecca Weitz-Shapiro, "Partisanship and Protest: The Politics of Workfare Distribution in Argentina," *Latin American Research Review* 41, no. 3 (2006): 122–47. For an additional study of the clientelistic distribution of employment benefits in Argentina, see Karen Remmer, "The Political Economy of Patronage: Expenditure Patterns in the Argentine Provinces, 1983–2003," *Journal of Politics* 69, no. 2 (May 2007): 363–77.

30. Smith argues that Menem was not able to stop hyperinflation immediately. Smith, "State Market." The United States president is also likely to use an executive order when there is a need for speed. Mayer, *With the Stroke of a Pen*, 60. In fact, in supporting extraordinary war powers given to Roosevelt at the point of war, Speaker Sam Rayburn argued explicitly for the need for speed: "There is not time to debate endlessly the relative merits of much disputed . . . bills or amendments. Either we give the President the flexible powers necessary to help Britain, or, by our inaction, we strengthen Hitler's power to conquer Britain and attack us." Sam Rayburn speech, NBC Blue Network, February 9, 1941, quoted in Hardeman and Bacon, *Rayburn*, 259. Yet Rayburn also rejected, at a more general level, the "administrative efficiency of a dictator" (335), indicating that he understood the temporary circumstances of high presidential power in crisis and the need to restrain power in normal times.

measures to help calm the economy itself when possible. The types of decrees issued and the numbers of them are detailed in table 5.2.

But emergency economic relief could only help citizens survive in the short term. Such measures did not address the underlying problem of a deeply dysfunctional economy. Menem understood that Argentina needed fundamental economic reform, beginning with privatization. Privatization on the scale that Argentina needed was a reform so momentous that it compares with the emergency economic measures taken by Franklin Roosevelt in response to the Great Depression. Both Menem and Roosevelt felt that they needed special powers to deal with the crises they faced. Each asked Congress for enhanced delegative powers to deal with the emergency. Delegative powers lie within the second category of presidential powers described in chapter 2.[31]

TABLE 5.2. Economic Decrees Issued by Menem and Alfonsín

Type of Economic Decree	Alfonsín (1983–89)		Menem (1989–99)	
	N	(%)	N	(%)
Immediate crisis relief	19	13.6	98	12.1
Long-term economic reform (taxes, industry)	100	71.4	432	53.5
Reform of the state/privatization	21	15.0	278	34.4
Total	140	100	808	100

Menem claimed that the state of the economy, hyperinflation, and spiraling wage-price increases were a national emergency. He asked Congress for powers to act by decree, including on privatization.[32] Congress gave him

31. Mayer, *With the Stroke of a Pen*, chap. 2 and p. 71. Students of the Roosevelt presidency suggest that FDR's success in assuming powers far beyond those he was constitutionally authorized to have was owing to the emergency of World War II. See Edward S. Corwin, *The President: Office and Powers* (New York: New York University Press, 1948).

On the other hand, an example of sweeping presidential powers without war was John F. Kennedy's use of an executive order to establish the Peace Corps and his use of discretionary presidential funds to support it. No emergency comparable to World War II existed then, although Kennedy probably felt an urgent need to prevent the occurrence in Latin America of another revolution like the one in Cuba, and he saw the Peace Corps as a means toward that prevention. Kennedy's order is listed as Executive Order 10924, 26 Federal Register 1789 (March 2, 1961). On his use of discretionary funds, see Louis Fisher, *Presidential Spending Power* (Princeton: Princeton University Press, 1975), 67–68. On Kennedy's concern about Latin America, see Schlesinger Jr., *Thousand Days*. Also see Burns, *Roosevelt: The Lion and the Fox*, 190, and Hardeman and Bacon, *Rayburn*, 257–58 and 279. In general, in times of crisis, Congress tends to grant the president wide leeway. See Andrew Rudalevige, "The Executive Branch and the Legislative Process," in *Executive Branch*, ed. Aberbach and Peterson, 435.

32. All presidents seek to present themselves as offering bold new policy. Franklin Roosevelt offered the New Deal while John Kennedy offered the New Frontier. In Menem's case,

the authority to issue decrees of necessity and urgency (DNU), responding to the urgency of the crisis and the need for speed. Now the executive could decide whether a situation was a crisis that warranted fast action. If he decided that specific circumstances required speed, he could now do more than taking temporary emergency measures—Menem could make law through a DNU. Additionally, DNUs permitted the executive to modify or repeal existing laws if Menem perceived a crisis and a need for rapid action. This delegation of power law reflected the crisis atmosphere in Argentina at the time. It also demonstrated congressional confidence in the new president and in his capacities for self-restraint and good judgment.

But Menem did not immediately proceed with privatizations by decree. As in the second opening quote to this chapter, he started by working with Congress. Despite holding extraordinary powers, Menem was unwilling to conduct the entire privatization process by decree. He took seriously the need for congressional approval, and in his appeal to the legislature he looked like an American president doing the same. He introduced into Congress two major laws of economic reform. These were Law 23.697, the Law of Economic Emergency,[33] and Law 23.696, the Reform of the State. On July 26 and 27, 1989, Eduardo Menem presented the first of these bills to the Senate.[34] Carlos Menem's work with Congress through his brother,

---

as in Roosevelt's, the realities of crisis demanded a bold new approach, whereas in the Kennedy case, widespread economic collapse was not present. Yet the image of executive initiative is essential in creating a view of presidential power and effectiveness. On Kennedy's New Frontier, see Schlesinger, *Thousand Days*, 210–12.

33. Upon taking office in 1933, Franklin Roosevelt said that if his emergency rescue program was not quickly approved by Congress he would ask Congress for broad executive powers to wage war against the economic emergency "as great as the power that would be given to me if we were in fact invaded by a foreign foe." See Alter, *Defining*, 3.

34. In the U.S. presidential system, presidents have often found that they have a much greater likelihood of getting their policy program or a specific bill past Congress if they can draw upon the support and talents of an extremely skilled legislative leader inside the chambers of Congress. That legislator then serves as a partner to the president, working the chamber floor, presenting the bill or bills, and trying to muster votes for its passage. This legislative partner is essential to the president in getting the executive program passed.

Sam Rayburn, Speaker of the House, played this role for FDR and also for John Kennedy. Lyndon Johnson, as Senate Majority Leader, played this role for Kennedy in civil rights legislation. Nancy Pelosi played this role for Barack Obama on health care reform. Eduardo Menem, as Senate Majority Leader, played this role in Argentina for his brother, Carlos. Although Eduardo's self-reversals of position inspired distrust, his role in promoting his brother's agenda was not an abuse of power and lay well within the normal bounds of executive-legislative partnership in getting an important presidential program past Congress. See Hardeman and Bacon, *Rayburn*. On Johnson, see Caro, *Years of Lyndon Johnson*. On Pelosi, see Ronald M. Peters and Cindy Simon Rosenthal, *Speaker Nancy Pelosi and the New American Politics* (Oxford: Oxford University Press, 2010). And on Menem, see Menem, *Nueve Años en el Senado de la Nación*. The cost of publishing the book was paid for by Eduardo Menem himself.

Eduardo, represents both an attempt to push the edge of his own powers and a careful effort not to overreach and provoke a negative congressional response.[35] The bill proposed granting the president a range of powers to create new laws, eliminate old ones, and transform others, all with an eye toward resolving the national economic emergency swiftly.[36] It also introduced privatization.

With this bill Peronism reversed itself on privatization. Eduardo proposed that the major state companies be sold in their entirety. The bill named the first privatization targets: YPF, the petroleum company; and ENTel, the state telephone company. The reader will recall that Eduardo had challenged the privatization of both of these companies only a few months earlier. The bill likewise targeted Ferrocariles Argentinos, the inefficient railroad company whose nationalization dated back to Perón; Aerolíneas Argentinas, the national airline in which SAS had attempted to purchase 40 percent of shares; State Gas; and Water and Power. This group was followed by the word "etcetera," which left a wide berth to include other companies. Picking up on Peronist deputy José Luis Manzano's idea from earlier years, a portion of shares in each company would be sold to workers and the rest to private companies. In point of fact, workers were losing jobs or facing the declining buying power of their incomes. In such circumstances they were unlikely to have extra disposable income to invest even in profitable companies, much less in failing enterprises. Nonetheless, the provision allowing workers to buy shares was symbolically important because it appeared to offer workers a role in privatization.

Mark Peterson's study of the presidency suggests that often the most controversial proposals are the most needed and that multiple influences determine a president's agenda.[37] Presidents mold their own expectations and agenda by looking at the success or failure of bills proposed in the past. They may also allow their agenda to be shaped by consultations with Congress before actually proposing their own program.[38] These observations also describe Menem's behavior in his first months in office and help us understand his choices. Certainly Menem was responding to crises, and the

---

35. Howell argues that presidents are more likely to take unilateral action during periods when government is unified, as it most certainly was in 1989. See William G. Howell, *Power without Persuasion: The Politics of Direct Presidential Action* (Princeton: Princeton University Press, 2003), xv and chap. 1.

36. Díaz, *Prosperidad o Ilusion?*, 45. Among other measures, the Law of Economic Emergency prohibited further deficit financing of state enterprises and gave a level playing field to domestic and foreign businesses, rather than perpetually favoring the former.

37. Peterson, *Legislating Together*, 275.

38. Peterson, *Legislating Together*, esp. chap. 2.

controversial proposal of privatizations was also a much-needed proposal. But his behavior also reflected the earlier congressional debates over privatization, including Alfonsín's unsuccessful efforts. The idea of privatization had already been suggested before Menem took office and Menem was picking up where Alfonsín left off. Alfonsín's failure to privatize these same companies helped Menem anticipate the opposition he would encounter. The Peronist Party had already declared its opposition to privatization. Indeed, it was the original proponent of nationalized industries and state-sponsored universal employment. The Radicals, on the other hand, had been the first party to recognize the need for privatization. The treatment they had received at the hands of Peronism gave them no incentive to support Menem now.

Having watched Alfonsín try and fail with privatization and having watched his own party destroy Alfonsín's efforts, Menem now returned to that same policy far better prepared than Alfonsín had been. Menem's first task was to gain support for the policy from his own party, which held the congressional majority and opposed privatization. This task would be difficult. Peronism opposed privatization for ideological and pragmatic reasons both. Many Peronists believed that the state should provide universal employment. Privatization would end that responsibility. Additionally, privatization would hit the legislators' core supportive constituency and key source of electoral strength: labor.

The bill Eduardo introduced, which would become the Law of Economic Emergency, granted economic independence to the Central Bank, a step that removed economic policy creation from the political realm and liberated the bank to create policies upon economic grounds. The step brought a significant reduction in tax breaks for inefficient industries.[39] The bill that would become the Reform of the State Law granted the president powers to reduce the state's bloated payrolls. Many of the ministries and agencies targeted by the Reform of the State Law were not part of any service company and would have remained untouched by privatization. Once again, Eduardo presented the bill and the argument for it to Congress.[40]

---

39. These tax breaks and other state subsidies to business were the "Program of Industrial Promotion," strongly supported by Perón and later by Peronism in general. It had allowed inefficient industries with bloated payrolls to stay afloat, providing employment for unneeded workers. Díaz, *Prosperidad o Ilusion?*, 45 and 73.

40. One of the arguments in support of the position that Carlos Menem held too much concentrated power focuses upon his brother, Eduardo, who served as Senate Majority Leader and de facto vice president throughout Carlos Menem's ten-year presidency. It is certainly true that the Menem brothers held considerable power together and, additionally, they were

If we are to understand how the polity as a whole accomplished this major reform then we need to comprehend the role of the Peronist Party. How did the party that had put nationalization in place and supported universal employment for decades now reverse itself on both and bring the Peronist legislators along? The key step toward this goal was the argument in favor of privatization on the floor of Congress. While Peronism was and is a verticalist party, even President Menem could not dictate the vote of the Peronist legislators in Congress. If he was going to include Congress then he needed to persuade. In that effort he turned again to the oratory of his brother, Eduardo.

Eduardo's presentation of these two laws represented a major change

---

persuasive, skilled leaders who could use that power to maximum effect. However, the fact of concentrated power among brothers within one family is hardly confined to Argentina. The behavior of the Menem brothers can be compared with that of the Kennedy brothers. John Kennedy went so far as to appoint his own brother, Robert, to the position of attorney general, on the request of their father! In appointing his brother to a position within the executive branch, John Kennedy concentrated power in his own family even more than did the Menem brothers, who had each been elected to their separate posts. The Kennedy network extended even further than the Menem network. Before Robert was appointed as attorney general he served a brief period in the Senate; both Carlos Menem and John Kennedy had younger brothers who were senators. When Robert left the Senate to join the administration, however, yet another Kennedy brother remained in the Senate. Edward Kennedy, who was elected to the Senate in 1962, continued to serve in the Senate throughout John Kennedy's administration and for several decades thereafter until his death in 2009.

In the Kennedy case, many observers credit Robert with providing a level-headed influence upon John, including in the potentially disastrous situation of the Cuban Missile Crisis; many experts feel that JFK handled the situation better with Robert than he would have done without him. Eduardo also often had a calming effect upon Carlos. Eduardo was the more dispassionate brother. Additionally, Robert Kennedy brought a higher and more intense level of commitment to civil rights than John displayed. And Robert "presided over a thorough liquidation of the McCarthyite heritage." Therefore, Robert's presence in his brother's administration actually increased the dedication of the Kennedy administration to justice and civil rights. On the other hand, Ted Kennedy did not assume a central role in pushing forward his brother's agenda in Congress; indeed, John Kennedy had problematic relations with Congress despite having a brother in the Senate. However, Ted Kennedy was the person who put forward John's civil rights bill in the Senate. It had already been introduced in the House but was introduced in the Senate after John's assassination. Ted continued to be a voice for civil rights in the Senate long after the deaths of John and Robert. In the Kennedy case this kind of power concentration probably had a positive and balancing effect rather than a negative one.

Yet we are correct to scrutinize the concentration of power within families in a nation where the rule of law is tenuous, as it is in Argentina and especially among Peronists, who do not follow the law. Power configurations that are not ideal in an old and established democracy may have a less negative effect than they have in newer democracies where the rule of law is not fully established. On Peronist power and the rule of law in Argentina, see Anderson, "Single-Party Predominance." On the Kennedy case, see Schlesinger, *Thousand Days*, 142, 697–98, and Arthur M. Schlesinger Jr., *Robert Kennedy and His Times*, vol. 2 (Boston: Houghton Mifflin, 1978), and Peter S. Canellos, *Last Lion: The Fall and Rise of Ted Kennedy* (New York: Simon and Schuster, 2009), esp. 98, 112–13, and 122.

both from Peronism's position just a few months earlier and from its historical support for universal employment. Such a step required explanation and necessitated support from a skeptical legislature. Now Eduardo showed a professionalism absent from the speeches he had made in 1988. The 1988 speeches provoked an emotional response from listeners. In particular, the April 1988 speech had been petulant, ideological, and silly. There are many inconsistencies between Eduardo's 1988 speeches and the 1989 speech, but the most important were two key reversals. One was the change in Peronism's fundamental position on the state role in the economy; the other concerned Eduardo's broad understanding of national well-being. In 1988, he had argued that privatization amounted to the selling of the nation's heritage to foreign interests: anyone supporting privatization in 1988 was a sellout to imperialism. Now he argued that the economic chaos of dysfunctional state companies was endangering democracy: anyone who wanted to save democracy would support privatization. Now Eduardo acknowledged that Argentina desperately needed to reduce the state's role in the economy: the survival of democracy depended on it. This 1989 speech reads like the effort of an experienced legislative party making a case to Congress. It demonstrated an awareness of the problems of the nation and was an effort to provide leadership toward effective policy. Argentina was at a crossroads, a moment the military might use as an excuse to intervene. The military had removed Argentina's civilian governments previously on the basis of smaller economic crises than this one. While Peronism had contributed to crisis in 1988, now, as the incumbent party, it was suddenly concerned to avoid a coup.

One argument that Eduardo had made in 1988 against Alfonsín's privatization program was not immediately contradicted in 1989. In 1988 Eduardo had criticized Alfonsín for bypassing "the representatives of the people," and he had called for a greater role for the Congress in privatization decisions. Now, as his brother embarked upon a more extreme version of the same policy, Carlos Menem appeared to be incorporating the Congress. He had asked for Radical support even before assuming the presidency. He had then asked for congressional support for extraordinary powers to confront the crisis. When he had an actual privatization bill written, he had the bill presented to the Congress through the Senate majority leader.[41]

---

41. Whether presidents who put through unpopular policies receive congressional support is the subject of considerable study in Latin America's new democracies. Many scholars have focused upon the obvious factor of a party's numbers in Congress. However, recent work has refined our ability to scrutinize presidential strength by drawing attention to three addi-

In this speech Eduardo hoped to preempt Peronist objections to the bill.[42] He acknowledged that his own party had originally nationalized these industries and services, but, pointing to perestroika, he said that the role of the state in society was changing.[43] There was a need for pragmatism, he said, and all parties understood that there were few options open to them in the crisis.[44] He explained Peronism's reversal from the inflammatory, combative, accusatory position he had taken a few months earlier. He acknowledged that Peronism had historically been a "statist party."[45]

---

tional factors: whether the president is putting forward an extremist or centrist set of policies, whether the president has included opposition party members within his cabinet, and whether the legislature can override a presidential veto. In addition to having a majority in Congress, Carlos Menem had each of these three additional factors in his favor. He had included some members of opposition parties in his cabinet, and he had also included members of the opposing faction of Peronism in his cabinet. His privatization agenda, while not considered a centrist policy, was nonetheless one shared by the main Radical opposition, for they had been the first party to present the policy. And finally, the opposition did not remotely approach the numbers that would have been needed to override a Menem veto. Thus, quite apart from his legislative majority, particularly in the Senate, Carlos Menem enjoyed these several strengths that have been found to sustain presidential policy elsewhere in Latin America. On presidential legislative majorities and their role in policy implementation, see Jones, *Electoral Laws and the Survival of Presidential Democracies*. For a study of other presidential strengths enabling policy implementation, see Gabriel L. Negretto, "Minority Presidents and Democratic Performance in Latin America," *Latin American Politics and Society* 48, no. 3 (September 2006): 63–92.

42. In using his Senate seat to launch and defend major national policy, Eduardo Menem acted more in a manner that shared executive power rather than as a check upon executive power or as a defender of provincial interests. Part of the complexity of the Senate and of individual senatorial roles is that they are expected to play all of these roles at different points in time. See Daniel Wirls and Stephen Wirls, *The Invention of the United States Senate* (Baltimore: Johns Hopkins University Press, 2004), 174–79.

43. Chilean society also went through privatization reform but did so under the Pinochet dictatorship. Today, there is less expectation in Chile that the state should be interventionist, and Chilean society is both more wealthy and more frugal. See Peter Siavelis, *The President and Congress in Post-Authoritarian Chile: Institutional Constraints to Democratic Consolidation* (University Park: Pennsylvania State University Press, 2000), 85–87.

44. Eduardo Menem did not mention Chile, possibly because he did not want listeners to consider that his policy and those of the Chilean dictator, Pinochet, were similar. Yet we know that Pinochet was, in fact, undertaking similar reforms. Ffrench, *Economic Reforms in Chile*.

45. William H. Simon suggests that deliberation, often touted as a pillar of democracy, is itself worthless if it is conducted in bad faith. Bad faith can be exercised in many ways but disingenuousness or the use of intimidation are two examples of deliberation in bad faith. If the chambers of Congress are supposed to be fora for deliberation, then Eduardo Menem and Peronism more generally might well have been acting, and deliberating, in bad faith by making false accusations and by reversing their position so totally. On deliberation in bad faith and on the abuses of the deliberative process, see William H. Simon, "Three Limitations of Deliberative Democracy: Identity Politics, Bad Faith, and Indeterminacy," and Ian Shapiro, "Enough of Deliberation: Politics Is about Interests and Power," both in *Deliberative Politics: Essays on Democracy and Disagreement*, ed. Stephen Macedo (New York: Oxford University Press, 1999). Although she is not negative about deliberation, Jane Mansbridge does acknowl-

He recognized that critics would accuse Peronism of abandoning its "stat-ist" position. In point of fact, however, by 1954 Perón himself had begun to back away from some of his own policies of nationalization and had consid-ered a reduced state role in the economy.[46] Eduardo had found something in the rhetoric of Perón himself that indicated support for a reduced state economic role. Perón's own words would now make it easier for Peronist senators to accept Menem's agenda. Perón was known for his contradic-tions and reversals of position. While many might call this deception, con-fusion, and manipulation, Perón himself called it "pragmatism."[47] Eduardo likewise used the word "pragmatism" to describe the new Peronist privati-zation policy.[48] Perón's policy on the role of the state had been "pragmatic,"

---

edge that participatory democracy and the deliberation that goes with it both require a robust level of equality as a starting point. See Jane Mansbridge, "Carol Patemen: Radical Liberal?," and John Medearis, "Deliberative Democracy, Subordination, and the Welfare State," in *The Illusion of Consent: Engaging with Carol Pateman*, ed. Daniel O'Neill, Mary Lyndon Shanley, and Iris Marion Young (University Park: Pennsylvania State University Press, 2008). For an alternative perspective that sees deliberation as primarily positive and the capacity for deliberation as a measure of the degree to which a society is democratic, see John Dryzek, "Democratization as Deliberative Capacity Building," *Comparative Political Studies* 42, no. 11 (November 2009): 1379–1402.

46. See Perón's 1954 speech in the lower chamber, Diario de Sessiones, Camara de Diputa-dos, 1954, in support of Law 13.653/54. This law was later revised, and the new law was Law 14.380/54. Perón's speech is also referenced in Eduardo Menem, *Nueve Años*, 430. Nicholas Shumway argues that self-contradiction and switching sides are cultural traits in Argentina. See Shumway, *Invention of Argentina*, 30–32. Reversals of position were also a tactic used by Lyndon Johnson and for similar purposes: the drive for power. Johnson is well known for his reversals of position on civil rights where he opposed them early in his career but supported them later in his career, when supporting civil rights was necessary for him to gain the presi-dency. But Johnson performed other reversals as well. He sometimes pretended to be a liberal but also destroyed the career and life of Leland Olds, a liberal, because doing so promoted his own position among the southern Senators and Johnson was driving for power in the Senate. Johnson was even willing to use McCarthyite tactics to destroy Olds. Johnson was so expert at changing colors that he even convinced Hubert Humphrey that he was a liberal while many of his actions were anything but liberal. Was Johnson a liberal or not? Or was he just power driven? These questions remain, just as questions about the real position of Perón and Peronism remain. On Johnson's reversals on civil rights, see Caro, *Years of President Johnson*, 34–39, and chaps. 7 and 8. On the destruction of Leland Olds, see chap. 10. On Humphrey, see 455–58.

47. Steven Levitsky adopts this description of Peronist vacillation. See his *Transforming Labor-Based Parties in Latin America: Argentine Peronism in Comparative Perspective* (Cambridge: Cambridge University Press, 2003), and "Crisis, Party Adaptation and Regime Stability in Argentina: The Case of Peronism, 1989–1994," *Party Politics* 4, no. 4 (2008): 445–70.

48. The Worker's Party (PT) in Brazil also reversed its stand on privatization: as the legis-lative opposition, it was against privatization, but once the party won the presidency, it sup-ported the move. However, the PT's reversal never included the level of denial and deceit that characterized Peronism's behavior. On the PT in Brazil, see Wendy Hunter, *The Transforma-tion of the Worker's Party in Brazil, 1989–2009* (Cambridge: Cambridge University Press, 2010).

not "dogmatic," supporting state intervention into the economy when it was needed and opposing it when it was not. By connecting his own rhetoric to the words of Perón, Eduardo prevented his own party bloc from arguing that he and the president were now backing away from Peronism's original position.[49]

Eduardo also sought to sway Radical senators to his side, a difficult task because he had only recently destroyed their efforts to privatize. He reached out to them, suggesting that both parties were in agreement on the need to preserve democracy. He wished the Radical bloc good luck in offering efficacious and constructive opposition. He felt certain he could rely upon the Radicals to help the Peronists in the process of democratic consolidation that everyone supported. He reminded the Radicals that the nation stood at a historic moment whereby his own party had been asked by their outgoing president to assume control of the government six months early because of the national crisis, reminding the Radical bloc of their agreement to support the Peronist program in the first six months of the new presidency. Eduardo then laid out a brief summary of the many problems that had engulfed the recent Radical presidency: hyperinflation was rampant; Argentines were 3.7 percent poorer now than they had been five years earlier; there had been recent raids on supermarkets. He said the government would need to move quickly. The speech was an admission that the adjustment of Peronism's policy position that the Radicals had called for was now happening.

Regarding the mechanics of the proposed privatizations, Menem referred to Articles 17 and 18 of the Constitution, calling for "transparency in all administrative procedures" and the need to inform the press at every stage of the process.[50] He said that the administration would ask Congress to set up a bipartisan committee of six members from each of the two major parties to be chosen by the party. This committee would be periodically informed of the progress of privatizations to see whether they were being

---

49. In his speech, Eduardo Menem attempted to separate Peronist action from that of Alfonsín in the previous administration. "This is not a case," he said, "in which the executive can act alone" (in Spanish, "cortar solo"); E. Menem, *Nueve Años*, 438. Eduardo also said that, according to the law, the executive can declare an enterprise "subject to privatization" but only with the "corroboration of the national Parliament" (439), again separating the anticipated actions of his own party from the privatization efforts Alfonsín had tried and that Menem had blocked. See E. Menem, July 27–28 speech in *Nueve Años*, 438–39. Also see Juan Perón, *Habla Perón* (Buenos Aires: Editorial Freeland, 1973).

50. Here again, Eduardo attempted to draw a distinction between the secretive actions Alfonsín took in privatizing the defense industries and the transparent efforts Peronism intended to follow: *Nueve Años*, 439.

conducted within the bounds of the law.[51] Eduardo's speech was very long. The first third of the speech was dedicated to persuasion and to the presentation of arguments designed to elicit the votes of the listeners. The last two-thirds of the speech consisted primarily of references to the legal basis for the privatizations.[52]

Because the privatizations would take place under Carlos Menem's emergency powers, Eduardo anticipated objections by acknowledging that the rule of law would not permit an indefinite state of emergency. The state of emergency would be transitory.[53] Bids for the purchase of company shares would be taken publicly and within the principle of transparency. All television and radio stations would be privatized with the exception of one radio and one television channel that would remain under state control. Additionally, there would be a return to the use of tolls on certain bridges.[54] Key points in the speech were the inclusion of worker shares in every privatization, the need to address unemployment and job creation, and the need for speed.[55] Eduardo ended his speech by characterizing various kinds of anticipated opposition in a negative fashion. He grounded the bill in Articles 4–7, specifically Articles 6 and 7 of Law 20.774, the Law of Labor Contract, which empower the executive via the legislature to transform the ownership of enterprises owned by the state. This power is precisely what Eduardo had claimed that Alfonsín had lacked. Table 5.3 summarizes Eduardo's speech favoring privatization.

Eduardo's speech was effective and both bills passed. The Economic Emergency Law was debated and approved in the Senate in ten days, passing the upper chamber on July 22, 1989. The law then moved to the lower chamber, where it was debated between August 23 and 25, 1989. It passed the lower chamber on September 1, 1989. The Reform of the State Law was presented to the Senate on July 26–27 and approved. It then went to

---

51. This bipartisan committee was set up but had very little real impact on the process because it was only able to use the limited information that Carlos Menem provided and because the privatizations proceeded at such a fast pace that there was no time to examine them closely. Moreover, the bipartisan committee had no veto power over the president's actions. See Mariana Llanos, *Privatization and Democracy in Argentina: An Analysis of President-Congress Relations* (Houndmills, Basingstoke, Hampshire, UK: Palgrave, 2002).

52. Here Eduardo referred to Chapter IV of the bill itself wherein the bill states that a certain percentage of shares sold will be sold to workers in each company. E. Menem, *Nueve Años*, 443. He referred as well to Law 21.392, regarding the refinancing of foreign debt, and to Law 20.705, which allowed him to include businesses of which the state owned only a part of the total shares. E. Menem, *Nueve Años*, 449.

53. E. Menem, *Nueve Años*, 443–53.

54. E. Menem, *Nueve Años*, 451.

55. E. Menem, *Nueve Años*, 450–51.

the lower chamber and was approved on August 10, 1989.[56] In the lower chamber approval was achieved through the use of the agreement that the parties had made prior to Carlos Menem's early assumption of office.[57]

TABLE 5.3. Content Analysis of Eduardo Menem's Speech for Privatization Policy, July 26–27, 1989, Senate Chamber

KEY ARGUMENT: *Privatization is necessary to save democracy. Anyone who opposes privatization does not support democracy.*

KEY CHARACTERISTICS: *carefully grounded in law*

Reasons Given	Number of Mentions
State deficit	4
Economic crisis	17
Need for a new role for the state in the economy	19
Movement by other nations to consider reduced state role	3
Threat to democracy from economic chaos	5
Radical Party itself had supported privatization	3
Perón himself had supported reduced state role	3
Popular anticipation and support for privatization	4
Inefficient industries[a]	3
Worker shares	3
Total number of different arguments supporting privatization	10

[a]The reader will recall that the previous year Eduardo had denied that Argentina's industries were inefficient and suggested that selling them to foreign capital would not increase their efficiency.

Carlos Menem had now covered his bases twice. If the public service industries fell under the national patrimony and he already had the power to privatize them, he might proceed now without Congress. But his own party had questioned that authority when Alfonsín had tried to use it for privatization. So now, without resolving that issue, of which different interpretations existed, Menem had protected himself a second time by gaining congressional approval for these two major bills that specifically granted him the power to privatize. Doubly authorized, Menem then privatized a first set of services and industries.

56. Díaz, *Prosperidad o Ilusion?*, 77–78.

57. For a discussion of this agreement inside the lower chamber, see Llanos, *Privatization and Democracy*, 77 and chap. 4, note 16. Llanos suggests that this kind of cooperation and coordination between the Peronist and Radical Parties was quite unusual but was owing to the extreme level of economic crisis and collapse and the generalized sense inside the Congress that unusual action was needed.

Ranis finds that in the early stages of privatization, the Peronist Congress was more out of step with public opinion than was Menem himself. For example, the Peronist-dominated Congress opposed some privatization measures, such as the telephone and airline companies, while the majority of public opinion (73% and 56%, respectively) supported privatization. See Ranis, *Class, Democracy*, 211.

Putting Privatization in Place: Phase I

In her careful study of privatizations, Mariana Llanos subdivides Menem's privatization policy into three phases.[58] The first, which began with the laws of Economic Emergency and State Reform, was the most hurried. The most important step by Congress in phase I was its decision to grant Menem broad delegative powers, which eased the argument over whether the sale of state enterprises was legal and which branch of government was empowered to make the decision.

Next, Menem sought union and business support, again learning from Alfonsín's failures. He used labor's vertical organization to announce policy. He gathered the top leaders of all the largest unions.[59] He listed all the companies that would be partially or totally privatized. A significant portion of workers in each would be laid off. He noted that all workers laid off would receive a severance payment and would be allowed to purchase a portion of the shares in each privatized company. Labor leaders felt shocked and betrayed.[60] Some vowed to oppose the new policy with strikes and other forms of resistance. Others hoped to work with the government in the process of privatization so that the loss of jobs would be minimized. Yet their power to resist was limited. By tying their loyalty to the Peronist Party, they had no alternative political representatives to whom they could turn. Casela had warned them that their interests were not well served by rigid loyalty to any single party, because parties, including Peronism, had their own fate and future to safeguard. Menem sought labor support but left little room for opposition.

By contrast, the rewards of privatization policy for the business sector were more evident. While many businesses lost subsidies and tax breaks, the business community as a whole now had the chance to own the poten-

58. Llanos, *Privatization and Democracy*, 100–103.

59. In Britain, labor organizations are also subsumed under national organizations known as peak associations. The effect is similar in that a few top labor representatives can represent all or most of the working class. The difference between Britain and Argentina lies in the fact that at the time in question the state controlled which union spoke for which sector of labor. Additionally, habitually each union had been vertically organized in its internal structure so that the top man in each sector faced no leadership challenges and could dictate the behavior of his union. Both of these characteristics had been modified by the end of the Menem administration. With respect to Argentina, one has to wonder when, if ever, the unions will finally learn that the vertical, hierarchical organization style that ties them into the state is not in the best interests of the workers themselves. We revisit this question in chapter 6.

60. Interviews with Oscar Lescano (Luz y Fuerza), Buenos Aires, April 9, 2008; Jose Pedraza (Ferroviarios),Buenos Aires, April 16, 2008, June 23, 2009; Venegas (UATE) Buenos Aires, March 22, 2008; and Francisco Nenna (CTERA), Buenos Aires, March 4, 2008, April 24, 2009.

tially profitable state enterprises on a fully private basis. Menem assured business that, while foreign companies would bid for each state enterprise, a domestic buyer would also be involved in nearly every sale.

The first sales included several factories previously owned by the military and now owned by the Ministry of Defense.[61] One was Altos Hornos de Zaplá, a steel plant in the northern province of Jujuy.[62] Again, Menem's political skill is evident here, as is his ability to learn from Alfonsín's mistakes. Alfonsín had begun his privatization efforts with Aerolíneas Argentinas, the national airline. That scenario provoked opposition based on patriotism. By beginning with the sale of former defense industries, Carlos Menem reminded the public of the military dictatorship, including its extensive wealth acquired through state-owned factories. If any of the privatizations could rally favorable public opinion, the sale of former military factories would do so. While the reaction of labor and business was negative, equivocal, or qualified, the public response soon became positive. From positive ratings in the 50s, Menem's positives now soared to 82 percent. The public, it seemed, was more than ready to embrace private provision of many state services. People were tired of the low-quality service from state enterprises.

While Menem had laid the groundwork inside Congress and with business and labor, observers now assess the first stage in the privatization process, between mid-1989 and late 1990, as the stage conducted with the least care and with the greatest number of problems. In particular, Menem was accused of moving too quickly with these early sales, and suspicions of corruption abounded. Additionally, the legal constraints upon the new owners that would characterize later sales were absent in these early sales.

Privatization Encounters Resistance: Phase II

Although Congress had granted Menem the power to proceed, it soon reconsidered its decision. Menem overused his delegative powers and issued DNUs on decisions that were not urgent. Congress used the limited powers of a bicameral committee on privatizations to watch closely the process of privatizations and to ask the executive or cabinet members for information about the sales but it could not stop the sales.[63] After the first

---

61. Pion-Berlin, *Through Corridors*, 125; Smith, "State, Market and Neoliberalism in Post-transition Argentina," 8–9.

62. Llanos, *Privatization and Democracy*, 96.

63. Llanos, *Privatization and Democracy*, 100.

privatizations in phase I, the policy began to encounter resistance from Congress, the judiciary, and some sectors of the public. The press accused Menem of carrying out privatization in a haphazard, unprofessional, uncontrolled, and corrupt manner. The judiciary responded to corruption accusations and claimed that Menem was bypassing judicial authority and constitutional law.[64] They sought greater oversight of the sales. Menem's struggle with the judiciary began here. He reacted to attempted judicial oversight by creating an upper-level criminal tribunal empowered to reverse any criminal court in the country, thus protecting himself from corruption indictments.[65] Another judicial challenge was constitutional. Some judges observed that Menem's use of DNUs and the line-item veto violated the Constitution.[66] Congress had authorized these acts in the context of emergency and they fell under "delegated powers," but Menem used these measures with great latitude. He used the line-item veto sixty-one times between 1989 and 1995.[67] Moreover, while DNUs were supposed to be issued only when Congress was out of session, 38 percent of Menem's DNUs were issued while Congress was in ordinary session, and 62 percent of them were issued while Congress was in extraordinary session (a session that had run over the time limit of a normal session.)

For the most part, Menem was able to ignore efforts at judicial constraint. His ability to resist judicial restraint was heightened by three factors: (a) a crisis context in which he had good reason to reach for greater executive powers; (b) an institutional context where Congress itself had facilitated his powers beyond what some justices considered legal; and (c) a political context in which Peronism faced a continual decline of party opposition. The tension between the executive and the judiciary that emerged here was never resolved and haunts Argentina today.

Opposition also came from state workers. Menem was privatizing the services provided by his own government, and thus the habits of his own employees were being challenged. Workers around him were losing their jobs. To diminish internal resistance Menem instituted a parallel admin-

---

64. Unlike Argentina, Brazil, another country with severe corruption problems, has created a layer of the judiciary specifically directed to deal with corruption issues. Brazil has instituted audit institutions as a formal check against corruption. See Melo, Pereira, and Figueirado, "Political and Institutional Checks on Corruption."

65. Llanos, *Privatization and Democracy*, 75. Also see Juan Linz and Alfred Stepan, *Problems of Democratic Transitions and Consolidation: Southern Europe, South America, and Post-Communist Europe* (Baltimore: Johns Hopkins University Press, 1996), 201.

66. Franklin Roosevelt likewise wanted a line-item veto, but he never got it. See Burns, *Roosevelt: Lion and the Fox*, 373–74.

67. Chavez, *Rule of Law in Nascent Democracies*, 70.

istration. An "intervener" was given the power to enter an agency and override the top administrators there. The interveners answered directly to Menem or to members of his cabinet, with the result that the concentration of power in the executive grew even higher and became even less accountable or transparent.

Although Menem resisted challenges to his authority, he also modified his own approach, beginning with phase II of the privatizations. He named a new minister of the economy, Domingo Cavallo. Cavallo changed the privatization procedure through careful planning and increased transparency. He also pegged the peso to the U.S. dollar, a policy known as "convertibility." It inflated the peso's buying power at the moment of greatest economic hardship. Convertibility divided the public, softening the blow of privatization for those still working and giving them reason to support the administration. Although convertibility was disastrous for long-term economic stability, it was politically useful in the moment and kept the public quiet as the sale of state enterprises moved forward and many Argentines lost their jobs.[68]

Judicial concerns about legality also carried more weight once Cavallo became minister of the economy. Policy implementation became more cautious and deliberate. The decisions made were more open to scrutiny and closer to legal bounds. Bidding opportunities became more open and accusations of closed deals and corruption decreased. The quality of the process of sales improved and the professionalism of the new companies taking over state enterprises increased. For example, the privatization of gas and electricity was designed with advice from the World Bank. These cases included extensive rules regulating the transport and distribution of these two services because of the danger perceived in allowing any single company to have a monopoly on their delivery. In seeking to achieve this regulation, Congress established regulatory agencies for these cases.[69] Similarly, the privatization of some pension programs sought to control the actions of a large number of private pension administrators; again,

---

68. Eventually, great but delayed economic hardship was also created when the peso was allowed to float and return to its actual value. Menem delayed the devaluation of the peso until after he left office. Devaluation produced popular unrest against the new Radical government headed by Fernando de la Rúa. Chile followed a more incremental approach to devaluation. There, small 10 percent devaluations came over time. Such incremental devaluations in Argentina would also have caused Menem to become less popular, a consequence Menem wanted to avoid. On the long-term economic problems of convertibility, see Sebastian Edwards, *Left Behind: Latin America and the False Promise of Populism* (Chicago: University of Chicago Press, 2010), 8–11 and 15.

69. Llanos, *Privatization and Democracy*, 101–2.

Congress solved this problem through the creation of regulatory agencies. The final aspect of this second phase, privatization of the ports, was done through placing control of the ports in private hands (concessions) and by bringing local control to bear on the function of ports (decentralization). The first was also considered to be an aspect of the Reform of the State Law because it took a function that had previously been controlled by the government and placed it in private hands.

In phase II the role of Congress increased. Phase I of the privatizations, including the Economic Emergency Law and the Reform of the State Law, had involved Congress only in initiating privatization policy and delegating more powers to the president. The details of each privatization case were left to the executive.[70] But with respect to privatization of the ports, gas and electricity, and pensions, Congress was involved in writing regulations and specifying oversight to accompany the privatizations.[71] Yet in both the first and second phases of privatization, Congress played a role in writing executive proposals. In neither phase could the executive override congressional approval entirely. But Congress did not vehemently oppose the executive agenda. Many Peronist legislators admired and respected Carlos Menem and were prepared to follow his leadership, while the UCR had been the first party to recognize the need for privatizations.

Phase III: Final Privatizations

While the institutions of state and various other actors inside the polity disagreed with all or part of Menem's economic agenda, he had a strong following in the public. His policies did not cause so much hardship that he lost worker support. Workers, after all, had no real alternative. Instead, he sensed correctly that he could win a second term in office. In 1994 he sought and received a constitutional change that would allow him to run for a second term. In 1995, five and one-half years after assuming the presidency, Carlos Menem ran for reelection and won. Phase III of his privatization agenda corresponds to his second term. The privatizations concluded in Menem's first term had brought a temporary reduction in the national deficit, but the debt increased in 1994, and Menem felt that further priva-

---

70. One detail that particularly irritated critics of the privatization policy was that a number of Argentine companies were being "privatized" by being sold to state monopolies in Spain. One criticism was that these early privatizations favored powerful economic groups with huge unearned profits. Smith, "State Market," 8–9.

71. Llanos, *Privatization and Democracy*, 102.

tizations were necessary. Additionally, in 1995 the Argentine economy felt the shock waves of Mexico's peso devaluation. Moreover, domestic tax collection, primarily based on a sales tax, was particularly vulnerable to recessionary pressures.

However, Menem now found himself in a less favorable political position. Although he had won the election, he faced greater institutional opposition. The crisis had been alleviated but it had not disappeared. Inflation had decreased but still threatened. Criticism came from the Left and from groups who were paying high social costs. As Menem pressed forward with phase III, his popularity began to fall, finally dropping to 20 percent in 1997.[72] Menem was caught between opposing demands. If he continued privatization, the Left would maintain its opposition and criticisms. But if he discontinued privatization the Right would accuse him of failing in midstream to complete the neoliberal reforms. The criticism Menem faced reduced his ability to act alone, find congressional support for extraordinary measures, and rely on emergency laws or decrees. Instead, in his second term he was required to use normal legislative paths more extensively than he had done earlier, and opponents of his policies in Congress had more latitude within which to challenge his agenda or change aspects of specific privatizations.[73] As a result, phase III features a much greater and more oppositional role for Congress.

Five privatization bills were debated in Congress during the first two years of Menem's second presidential term: the post office, the Yacyretá hydroelectric dam, nuclear power plants, airports, and the mortgage bank.[74] Unlike Menem's first presidential term, these proposed privatizations did not attain immediate congressional approval. Two of them, the nuclear power plants and the mortgage bank, were approved by both chambers and became law, but the post office, airports, and hydroelectric dam, after approval in the Senate, faced opposition in the lower chamber. With respect to the post office, lower chamber hesitation came as a result of legislative intervention by Cavallo, who asserted, in a lengthy speech in the lower chamber, that the bill as approved by the Senate contained considerable latitude for Mafioso activities associated with the post office czar, Alfredo Yabrán.[75] Lower chamber disapproval was aroused not in

---

72. Centro de Estudios Unión para la Nueva Mayoría (a public opinion firm), cited in Llanos, *Privatization and Democracy*, 158.

73. FDR likewise faced a more rebellious Congress in 1939 than he had done early in his first term. See Hardeman and Bacon, *Rayburn*, 230–31.

74. The post-office privatization had been submitted to Congress in Menem's second term and had passed committee.

75. Yabrán was subsequently investigated for his various illegal activities and a warrant was

opposition to the president's policy but in opposition to the specifics of the bill as approved in the Senate. The privatization of the airports also faced lower chamber opposition because of the suspicion that the sale involved corruption. The Yacyretá hydroelectric privatization involved a dam on the border between Argentina and Paraguay. Menem wanted to sell the dam to Paraguay because he considered it a drain on national resources. Opposition to its privatization was led by deputies from the provinces located on that border who did not find the fiscal deficit sufficient reason to sell the dam.

Menem responded to congressional opposition by finding a way toward privatization anyway. In the case of the dam, he privatized management of the enterprise because he could not effect sale of the property entirely. When congressional approval of the post office privatization was denied, Menem privatized the post office anyway under the original Reform of the State Law. He also removed Cavallo and replaced him with a more compliant minister of the economy, Roque Fernández, who had a low political profile and could not command the public attention Cavallo enjoyed. Finally, Menem used a DNU to privatize the airports.

Although Menem succeeded in his privatization agenda during phase III, his success was complicated and costly. First, the opposition he faced in Congress revealed the strengthening role of the legislature that had begun to emerge during his presidency. If Menem managed to find means to maneuver around the Congress, he did not do so, or was unable to do so when confronted with a legislature that was no longer willing and compliant. Second, his decision to privatize enterprises without congressional approval or by means of the unusual delegative powers Congress had given him earlier further undermined his public image and helped contribute to public skepticism about his leadership. Third, Menem's failure to win congressional approval for these three bills reveals the beginning of the decline of his personal influence within his own party, another indicator of the gradual movement away from his leadership.[76]

---

issued for his arrest. Yabrán fled from the police and a nationwide hunt for him began. He subsequently committed suicide rather than allowing himself to be taken into custody. Many observers concluded that the suicide was an admission of guilt, although his death meant that Yabrán was never tried. Yabrán was also widely suspected of having ordered the mafioso-style execution of photojournalist José Luis Cabezas (January 1997) who had been investigating Yabrán's post office activities and the suspicions of corruption against him.

76. In *Privatization and Democracy*, Llanos argues, for example, that the later privatization decrees were indicative of Menem's growing weakness rather than his delegative strength because they showed that he had lost his capacity to persuade his party to accept his position, at least in the Chamber of Deputies. Her argument corresponds to the work of Kenneth Mayer, who hypothesized in his research that U.S. presidents are more likely to issue

Our assessment of the phase III privatizations is complex. The post office, airports, and the dam were inefficient and needed improvement. The postal service was as dismal as the railroads and phone service had been. Legislative opposition was not to privatization but to perceived corruption.[77] In the face of that constraint, Menem was defiant. He was unwilling to yield to Congress. Instead, he pushed his policies through using means that had by now become questionable. He achieved his goal at the cost of his own reputation. Menem is unpopular today despite all he did for a nation in crisis. Part of the explanation for his unpopularity lies in the way he handled these last privatizations. Part of the struggle over phase III of the privatizations concerned the regulation of the companies that had purchased the services and regulation of the provision of services themselves.[78]

Despite congressional involvement, the view that Menem governed outside the law remained and colors views of him today. This perception of him as an autocrat or worse is partially due to his treatment of the judiciary and partially due to his personal style and attitude. Menem never voluntarily restrained his own drive for power; in demonstrating that he wanted more power, he drew attention away from the reality of the institutional context within which he functioned. He wanted more and more power. He faced more and more opposition. The very qualities of self-confidence, mastery, and command that had given him the boldness to undertake privatizations in the first place now began to play to his disadvantage. He was increasingly perceived as a power monger who would permit no opposition

executive orders when they are weakened either by a loss of support in Congress or by a loss of public support or both. This particular hypothesis was not fully supported by Mayer's research. U.S. presidents issued more executive orders when they had lost public support but not necessarily when they had lost congressional support. By contrast, Menem's loss of congressional support was accompanied by a larger number of corresponding decrees. Mayer's hypothesis is more fully supported by the findings from Argentina. See Mayer, *With the Stroke of a Pen*, chap. 3, esp. 91 and 96–102.

77. The image of corruption that has lasted of Menem and of his presidency is lamentable and reprehensible. However, corruption need not be permanent and can be eliminated or greatly decreased. A first step in that direction is a negative public reaction and generalized condemnation of the practice. However much Argentina generally and Peronism specifically are dogged by corrupt images, at least the public has responded negatively, a first step toward cleaner government. By contrast, Chinese society does not even appear to object to deliberate governmental corruption. See Melanie Manion, *Corruption by Design: Building Clean Government in Mainland China and Hong Kong* (Cambridge: Harvard University Press, 2004), 5 and 13 and chap. 2.

78. Likewise, the power of regulation is a subject of tension in the United States, although there it is often the executive branch that seeks regulatory power while, in Argentina's privatization process, Congress sought more regulatory power. See Mayer, *With the Stroke of a Pen*, chap. 4. Regulamentation is one of Mayer's case studies of the struggle for greater executive power. The case study is covered in 122–34.

and no restraint. Yet the institutional realities around him were more qualified and nuanced.

An Overview of the Privatizations Policy

This chapter has narrated momentous economic reform in Argentina,
changes that averted a coup, allowed the nation to continue its democratization, and normalized the economy. The decisions, negotiations, and
outcomes were worked out through the nation's democratic institutions of
state, where we saw both a power struggle among institutions and forward
movement on policy. Table 5.4 summarizes the privatizations policy and
captures the magnitude of the economic reform.

In the immediate term, the reforms produced indicators of economic
success. Over the decade of the 1990s, the national economy grew by
about 40 percent. Inflation dropped from 5,000 percent annually in 1989
to nearly zero. Foreign investment in the economy grew in eight out of the
ten years of Menem's presidency. Per capita income rose from $8,000 to
$12,000 per year. Poverty dropped from 47.3 percent of the population to
26.7 percent. The percentage of the national budget dedicated to industrial
subsidies dropped from 4.7 percent to 0.5 percent.[79] Table 5.5 summarizes
the macroeconomic results of the reforms. All of the important industries
and services had been either partially or fully privatized, but some economic problems remained. The airline, Aerolíneas Argentinas, continued
to operate at a loss. The railroads were never fully or successfully privatized
and the northern half of the country lost railroad service, leaving towns
isolated and ruining local economies. Yet, overall, Argentina was better off
in 2000 that it had been in 1989.[80]

Over the longer term, these policies produced high social costs in lost
jobs and poverty. Cavallo addressed those costs partially with his convertibility plan, although that plan was not a long-term solution. We consider
social costs and measures more closely in the next two chapters. There
would also be more social turmoil following the seventeen years of transi-

---

79. Díaz, *Prosperidad o Ilusión?*, 54.

80. Peter Siavelis argues that presidents can have strong institutional powers, strong partisan powers, or both, or neither. Strong partisan powers means that the president enjoys a
large, loyal following in Congress while strong institutional powers mean that the president
has wide authority given to him by the law. Menem began his presidency with both and continued to have wide institutional powers throughout his two terms. However, he gradually
lost partisan support even among his own party. Siavelis applies his argument to Chile. See
Siavelis, *President and Congress in Post-Authoritarian Chile.*

TABLE 5.4. Public Enterprises to Be Privatized under Menem Policy

Company or Public Enterprise	Changes Proposed[a]
Public Enterprises	
Aerolíneas Argentinas	TP, PP
Water and Energy	C
Buenos Aires Catering	TP
Ecological Coordination Metropolitan Area	TP, PP, C
Conarsur	TP
National Highways	C
Federal Electric Energy Company	administrative changes only
Argentine Maritime Lines	TP, PP
National Mail and Telegraph	C
National Telecommunications	TP
Argentine Railroads	C
State Gas	C
Media	
TV Chanel 11	TP
TV Chanel 13	TP
Belgrano Radio	TP
Excelsior Radio	TP
ATC Chanel 7	TP
National Radio Buenos Aires	excepted[c]
Argentine Radio to the Exterior	excepted
National Radio Service	excepted
Ministry of Defense Companies[b]	
Naval Factories Darsena North	TP
Forja Argentina	TP
Argentine Coal Industry	TP
Petrochemicals Rio Tercero	TP
Polisur	TP
Monomeros Vinilicos	TP
Petropol	TP
Induclor	TP
National Sanitary Works	C
Optar	TP
Segba	C
Cultural and Recreation Services and Urban	
Maintenance, City of Buenos Aires	TP, PP, C
Subterranean Rail, Buenos Aires	TP, PP
Coal Exploration Company	TP, PP
Oil Exploration Company (YPF)	C[d]
assisted recovery	SM

Source: Data from Mariana Llanos, *Privatization and Democracy in Argentina: An Analysis of President-Congress Relations* (Houndmills, Basingstoke, Hampshire, UK: Palgrave, 2002), 93–94.

[a]TP = total privatization; PP = partial privatization; C = concession; SM = mixed society.

[b]The number of companies previously owned by the military gives the reader some sense of the overwhelming presence of military power in Argentina prior to the privatizations. Many of these companies had only marginal relevance to actual defense activities but were still controlled by the military. Whatever might be said about Menem's personal autocratic governing style, the mere removal of this number of companies from the hands of the military constituted a clear step toward democracy.

[c]"Excepted" means that the law banned the privatization of these entities or companies. Excepted media were those that had to remain public companies, fulfilling a public mission so that the state would retain ownership of at least some media companies.

[d]The privatization of YPF, the state-owned petroleum industry, was also quite controversial at the time and Congress would not have agreed to privatize it in its entirety. Therefore Menem acted carefully, privatizing only exploration and exploitation activities but not the entire company. This care is reflected in the letter "C" in the table, indicating the concession of partial privatization and not total privatization. YPF also qualified for "assisted recovery," that is, continued support from the state when many other companies were denied access to any continued state assistance. I appreciate clarification from Mariana Llanos on this note and the previous one.

TABLE 5.5. Argentina: GNP and Comparative Price Change, 1983–2000

Year	GNP Growth Rate (%)	Comparative Price Change
1983	3.7	433.7
1984	1.8	688.0
1985	–6.9	385.4
1986	7.1	81.9
1987	2.6	174.8
1988	–1.9	387.7
1989	–6.9	4,924.0
1990	–1.8	1,344.0
1991	10.6	84.0
1992	9.6	17.5
1993	5.7	7.4
1994	8.0	3.9
1995	–4.0	1.6
1996	4.8	.1
1997	8.6	.3
1998	4.2	.7
1999	3.0	–1.8
2000		–.7

Source: Data from International Monetary Fund, Statistical Abstract of Latin America, vol. 38 (2002).

tion, after Menem left power and convertibility ended. However, we should not lose sight of what was accomplished using institutional means. Guided by a self-assured leader, the nation's institutions of state accomplished these reforms, avoiding military intervention and democratic breakdown. The nation emerged from Menem's presidency with a stronger national economy and more competitive and usable public services. Its standing among the international financial institutions and lending agencies rose, and the nation became more attractive for foreign investment and loans.

The economic reforms mattered for another reason as well. Many scholars have found a connection between long-term, sustained economic growth and democracy. Spreading economic wealth widely allows large numbers of individuals to participate politically and strengthens democracy. But others have suggested the reverse: a free polity helps spread wealth more widely.[81] Insofar as Menem normalized democracy, he did

81. An early argument suggesting that the dispersal of economic resources helps democracy develop is found in Barrington Moore's *Social Origins of Dictatorship and Democracy: Lord and Peasant in the Making of the Modern World* (Boston: Beacon Press, 1966). An argument for the reverse causality but one that also supports the connection between a strong economy and democracy is found in Dani Rodrik, *One Economics, Many Recipes: Globalization, Institutions,*

more than keep the military at bay. He also enhanced the economic foundation of democracy. Insofar as he undermined democracy, he also weakened his own reforms. In point of fact, he did both.

Conclusion

At the outset of this chapter we considered Madison's advice that good government needed to control both the governed and itself. Menem embraced the first part of Madison's recommendation but, to a considerable extent, rejected the second. The founders of the American presidential system that Argentina has chosen to emulate intended to provide for such an eventuality through the system of checks and balances. Menem presented a test of that system. His rejection of constraints upon his power left the other institutions of state seeking to control him, a task they accomplished only partially. Yet as we scrutinize the relations among these institutions, we can discern a recognizable system of checks and balances fulfilling part of its function, despite all that Menem did to resist those checks. Throughout the privatization policy, each branch contested for more influence rather than less. Each branch restrained the others . . . somewhat. The outcome was complex and nuanced. Menem was clearly a heavy-handed president.[82] He was also capable, determined, and daring, a combination Argentina desperately needed in 1989. He was not—and was not allowed to become—a dictator.

Menem's drive toward power existed within an institutional design that favored the presidency over all other institutions. He was more than ready to take advantage of that design. He came from a party with a long history of pragmatic policy delivery and limited democratic loyalty. He faced a declining and weakening adversary in the Radical Party. All of these fac-

---

and Economic Growth (Princeton: Princeton University Press, 2007). Rodrik says that strong but flexible liberal economics enhances democratization. A related argument that democracy enhances economic growth better than authoritarianism is found in Carles Boix, *Political Parties, Growth and Equality: Conservative and Social Democratic Economic Strategies in the World Economy* (New York: Cambridge University Press, 1998). Kohli takes the opposite position and suggests that authoritarian regimes do the best job at promoting economic growth. Atul Kohli, *State Directed Development: Political Power and Industrialization in the Global Periphery* (Cambridge: Cambridge University Press, 2004).

82. See Delia Rubio and Mateo Goretti, "When the President Governs Alone: The Decretazo in Argentina, 1989–1993," in *Executive Decree Authority*, ed. John M. Carey and Matthew Soberg Sugart (Cambridge: Cambridge University Press, 1998), 36. Their study reveals that Menem vetoed thirty-seven bills in their entirety and partially vetoed an additional forty-one bills.

tors also worked to enhance his power, quite beyond the crisis itself and his personality. Usually we lack the empirical evidence we have here about relations among institutions during a democratization process. Having that evidence now shows that the process was more institutionally balanced than it appeared from the outside. If the outcome was not fully balanced, it was also not a complete victory for the president.

Executive/judicial relations reveal the worst aspects of Menem's power drive. There are two angles on this tension. In the struggle against Menem, the judiciary was weak in ways that are true for all presidential systems, as discussed in chapter 2. But the Argentine judiciary was weaker still for reasons peculiar to the national political context at the time. Let us consider these two angles further. First, in any presidential system, the judiciary is both stronger and weaker than the legislature in its ability to constrain the president. The judiciary is stronger because it does not have the collective action problems of a legislature. It can more quickly decide to check presidential power. But it is weaker because it has neither powers of enforcement nor an electoral mandate.[83] In a new democracy this weakness matters more because, even when it has reached a decision, the judiciary has no independent enforcement powers. Lacking an electoral mandate, the judiciary relies upon the rule of law for its authority. Yet in a new democracy, it is precisely the rule of law that is contested and under development. Menem understood this and took cagey advantage of the judiciary's weakness within the presidential system. He calculated that he could dominate the judiciary more easily than he could the legislature simply by naming magistrates. Therefore, while he showed some respect for Congress and made efforts to work with it, he showed little respect for the judiciary and tried to undermine judicial autonomy at every turn, either by replacing judges who opposed him or by naming judges who would support him.[84]

83. Howell, *Power without Persuasion*, esp. 138–39 and chap. 6. Howell writes that, at the national level, courts can rely upon the president to enforce their rulings. As an example, Howell points to the famous Supreme Court decision to desegregate the schools of Little Rock, Arkansas, which Eisenhower then enforced using the National Guard (140–41). But the president is unlikely to enforce any Court ruling when the ruling counters his or her own agenda. And the U.S. Supreme Court itself began to back away from its strong civil rights position when Nixon showed himself unwilling to enforce Court decisions (143).

84. One mechanism for ensuring judicial autonomy is police protection of prosecutors who are responsible, under the civil law system, for investigating crimes. During Menem's presidency the level of police protection for prosecutors declined from one police officer per prosecutor to one officer per twelve prosecutors. As a result, prosecutors could be intimidated and threatened. In a visible case against Menem where the public prosecutor, Pablo Lanusse, was pursuing the investigation of a case of gold contraband in which Menem's own involvement was suspected, both Lanusse and his sister were subject to violent attacks and intimidation. Finally, an attacker used a knife to carve the word "ORO" (gold, in English) into the

But in a manner peculiar to Argentina's democratic development, the judiciary was additionally weakened by the efforts of Congress itself. When Congress acted initially to increase presidential powers, it simultaneously weakened the judiciary. Later, when Congress rejuvenated itself, it did not simultaneously rejuvenate the courts. Instead, it did just the opposite. As Congress became more completely dominated by Peronism, Menem became more able to use the legislature to enact measures restricting the judiciary. Violations of judicial autonomy then further increased Menem's latitude to pursue his policy without regard for legal boundaries. Because of its own errors in limiting judicial power and authority, the Congress remained the principal restraint upon many aspects of Menem's privatization agenda; in most instances, the judiciary proved unwilling or unable to challenge him.[85]

Menem's tension with the other branches of state was part of the overall process of institutional creation in the new democratic context. He sought to expand presidential powers; those who advocated more strength for the legislature or judiciary sought to limit those powers. This struggle exists in every presidential democracy and continues far beyond the democratization stage. It was the core dilemma of Menem's presidency. On the one hand, Argentina confronted severe crisis and potential collapse. Speed, authority, and self-confident leadership solved the crisis. On the other hand, the danger of concentrated authority is the tendency to abuse power and reach for more. On the occasion of his second inaugural speech in 1864, Lincoln said, "It has long been a grave question whether any government, not too strong for the liberties of its people, can be strong enough to maintain its own existence in great emergencies."[86] Here we consider the same danger in reverse: whether a government strong enough to solve a great emergency will become too strong to respect the liberties of its people. This is the core dilemma of the Menem years.

Comparing Menem with presidents facing crisis elsewhere in the Western Hemisphere lends perspective on his behavior. When Franklin Roosevelt faced crisis he overreached his own power in a manner he felt was

---

face of Lanusse's sister. Soon afterward Lanusse dropped the case, which was never resolved. Chavez, *Rule of Law*, 76.

On Menem's relationship with the judiciary, also see Gretchen Helmke, "Enduring Uncertainty: Court-Executive Relations in Argentina during the 1990s and Beyond," in *Argentine Democracy: The Politics of Institutional Weakness*, ed. Steven Levitsky and María Victoria Murillo (University Park: Pennsylvania State University Press, 2005), 139–164. Helmke writes that after Menem's presidency the courts reasserted their independence.

85. Chavez, *Rule of Law*, chap. 2.

86. Paludan, *Presidency of Abraham Lincoln*, 291.

legitimate. Among the favorite examples of this behavior was his effort to reform the Supreme Court so that it would not undermine his New Deal policy. FDR sought to add more justices who would support his policies, but Congress blocked him from naming more justices. In many other instances, however, that kind of institutional restraint was not necessary. As in the second opening quote to this chapter, Roosevelt was often more willing to exercise self-restraint than Menem. For example, Menem also sought to reduce judicial restraint upon his own behavior, although, unlike Roosevelt, part of Menem's agenda was corruption as well as furthering his political and economic agenda. Unlike the U.S. Congress, when Menem sought to limit judicial influence, the Argentine Congress did *not* protect the judiciary. Ironically, whereas protection of the judicial system by the U.S. Congress undermined progressive reforms, judicial protection by Argentina's Congress would certainly have enhanced democratic progress. These are the dilemmas of institutional power constraint within a presidential system.

On the other hand, comparisons with other Latin American presidents show that Menem could have been far worse and could have done more damage. Three Latin American examples place him in a favorable light. In Peru, when faced with congressional opposition, President Alberto Fujimori simply closed Congress.[87] That act was far beyond anything that even Menem was prepared to do. Despite its closure, Peru's Congress eventually resurrected itself and then issued a warrant for Fujimori's arrest. So perhaps it was just as well that Menem did not resist Congress any more than he did. More troubling still is the behavior of Hugo Chávez in Venezuela. Chávez used popular elections to give himself ever-increasing terms in office. The reduced accountability he achieved then allowed him to undermine further the institutions of state.[88] While Chávez has died, the problem of institutional decline that he initiated remains present in Venezuela, and there is no evidence that Chávez's successor, Nicolás Maduro, has any more respect for democratic institutions than did Chávez.

Venezuela's democratic future looks a little brighter after the recent electoral victory of the opposition party. Democracy offers different kinds of constraints on power. Where institutional constraint fails but the electoral calendar continues, a new electoral outcome may restrain an overbearing executive. This may be happening in Venezuela now. And finally

---

87. Charles D. Kenny, *Fujimori's Coup and the Breakdown of Democracy in Latin America* (Notre Dame, IN: University of Notre Dame Press, 2004).

88. Javier Corrales and Michael Penfold, *Dragon in the Tropics: Hugo Chávez and the Political Economy of Revolution in Venezuela* (Washington, DC: Brookings Institution Press, 2011).

there is the example of Nicaragua. President Daniel Ortega is actively seeking to undermine the nation's institutions, although with less success so far than either Chávez or Fujimori. Ortega is relying largely on abuses of the electoral system. These include making it difficult for opposition voters to register, delivering necessary voting documents to opposition voters late, intimidation at election time, stealing elections, repression, and violence.[89] He also relies on a closed primary, domination of his own party, and Venezuelan money to keep himself in power.[90] Menem did not use electoral manipulation the way Ortega has done and he lacked external financial backing in his own effort to hold on to power. So, while he looks worse than Roosevelt, he looks better than the other Latin American presidents considered here.

The next chapter looks closely at another power balance: that between the Peronist Party and its labor constituency. That scrutiny returns our attention to the role of civil society in Argentina's democratization. If Congress had been stronger in the power balance studied here it would have represented labor more effectively. Instead, Menem resorted to the predemocratic model of corporate relations that had defined Peronism for decades. While that solution bypassed the democratic institutions of state and reverted to old-style Peronist corporatism, it was not entirely autocratic. It still allowed for dialogue and labor participation in what was ultimately an institutional solution.

---

89. Similarly, in maintaining authoritarianism the United States South created multiple barriers to suffrage, including the white primary, literacy and educational requirements for voter registration, the poll tax, intimidation, and violence. See Mickey, *Paths Out of Dixie*, chap. 3 and also pp. 113 and 159.

90. Anderson and Park (forthcoming, 2016).

SIX

A Return to the
Corporate Method

Labor Reform Anew

An "historic compromise" allowed the Depression to lift. Labor gave up its aspirations for socialization of the economy. In exchange, it got the welfare state, collective bargaining, and acceptance into the political system.

> —Peter Gourevitch, on the Great Depression in the
>   United States[1]

Argentine workers had a redistributive mentality, thinking they had a right to a certain percentage of the GNP but not focused on increasing productivity.

> —Peter Ranis[2]

Once the framework laws for privatization—the Law of Economic Emergency and the Reform of the State Law—had passed Congress, the Menem administration addressed the specifics of labor reform. As a general package, labor reform was intended to impose upon labor the discipline he was outlining for the entire economy, but unexpectedly his labor reforms also dovetailed with some of the labor democratization measures Alfonsín had begun. Specifics within the package included laws on how redun-

---

1. Peter Gourevitch, *Politics in Hard Times: Comparative Responses to International Economic Crisis* (Ithaca: Cornell University Press, 1986), 168.
2. Ranis, *Class Democracy and Labor in Contemporary Argentina*.

dant employees would leave, regulations for the discipline of those who remained, and measures to soften the cost for all, insofar as that was possible in the context of economic crisis. This stage of Argentina's democratization by institutions differs from previous reform efforts. On the one hand, labor reform again exemplifies institutional transition because the initiative came from the state and met with resistance from below. On the other hand, these details were hammered out inside the Cabinet in direct negotiations with labor leaders rather than in Congress. Menem's methods here were corporate and outside the system of checks and balances, just as Casela's labor reform efforts had also been achieved through corporatism. In a fully institutionalized democratic government, Congress would have played a more central role, particularly given its dominance by Peronists in both chambers.

Instead, the Menem administration was able to write the reforms using the corporate relationship between Peronism and workers, an institutional configuration that fits uneasily within a democratic society. That relationship was yet another example of the continuity with a nondemocratic past that accompanies democratization by institutions. Additionally, the reduction of Argentina's legislature to the policy-making level of a parliament weakened Congress's contribution to these reforms. Nevertheless, without the corporate structure of top-down control, the reforms explored here might have been impossible because labor resistance was so high and because many members of Congress also opposed these reforms. Moreover, the reform process allowed for unofficial dialogue between the state and one sector of civil society.

This chapter again examines the question of checks upon power within a presidential system. In his study of early American democracy James MacGregor Burns suggests that James Madison and Thomas Jefferson disagreed over the best mechanism for checking presidential power. Madison relied on an institutionalized system, one which, in Argentina, functioned imperfectly, as we saw in the last chapter. Jefferson, however, was more inclined to trust civil society to check power, particularly through the function of parties.[3] Here was a moment when civil society might have worked as Jefferson imagined to check presidential power. Civil society in Argentina, specifically the working class, might have resisted the reforms studied here had they been able to turn to another party. But that did not happen because Argentina's working class has always tied itself to Peronism, and Peronism was the source of the reforms. Additionally, as this chapter will

---

3. Burns, *Deadlock of Democracy*.

show, checking Menem's power by resisting these reforms was probably
not in the interest of democracy, and might well have ended democracy
entirely. So Jefferson's insights encounter problems: civil society resistance
was neither possible nor desirable. Instead, reforms were pushed forward
without checks from either the institutions or from civil society; ironically,
democracy survived anyway. It is a case in which the failure of checks on
power proved the most salubrious for democracy. Yet it raises haunting
questions about Argentina's ability to check power when failure to do so
could constitute a threat to democracy.

Corporate Labor Control: Perón's System
and Menem's Dismantlement

This chapter continues our polity-centered view of democratization and
labor reform. That view reveals that aspects of the polity continued to be
corporate rather than democratic. It also illustrates Peronism's political
skill in operating inside that corporate structure. The chapter reveals the
many sides of Peronism, both its undemocratic corporate mechanisms and
its visionary abilities to spearhead modernization. Chapter 4 considered
Argentina's corporate system of labor control and Casela's use of that system to impose moderate democratization inside the unions. That chapter
did not consider the essential cornerstone of labor boss power—benefits—
because Alfonsín lacked the resources to reform that power. The limited
nature of his labor democratization owed partly to the fact that he was
unable to alter the benefits system inside the unions and labor bosses continued to control the purse strings for all labor benefits.

In this portion of his reforms Menem now tackled that issue. He
approached the question not because he wanted labor democratization,
Alfonsín's goal, but because he sought to reform the economy and make it
more efficient by eliminating redundant workers. Making such a reform
politically feasible meant reforming the system of labor benefits. Perón
had set up a corporate system of benefits for workers in the 1940s. Workers enjoyed social benefits through their unions; in return they supported
the regime. That vertical, paternalistic governing style caused Perón to
nationalize many industries and services and to employ huge sectors of
the population, often redundantly. Now a new Peronist president understood that universal employment and extensive social services through
the unions were no longer economically viable: they had become a threat
to democracy itself. The party that had set up the corporate welfare sys-

tem needed to dismantle it. Leaders understood why doing so was necessary while workers saw their own personal interests and opposed such reforms. The process explored in this chapter is the process whereby Menem's government convinced Argentina's powerful working class to accept these reforms.[4]

Menem approached the process of privatization more prepared than Alfonsín had been for the difficulties of the task. His plan included four key components: (a) a severance package offered to workers who were losing their jobs; (b) a transfer of social benefits from union provision to state responsibility; (c) a plan for worker shares in privatized companies; and, somewhat later, (d) convertibility, which greatly enhanced the purchasing power of those still employed. This chapter explores how these measures were implemented and reveals why labor opposition was low. A key part of the answer is negotiation. The reforms were accomplished, at least in part, through negotiation inside the executive branch. We explore that dialogue here. The institution of state that played the central role was the executive branch, more specifically, the cabinet, especially the Ministry of Labor. This chapter builds upon interviews with all of Menem's ministers of labor and with the heads of most of the nation's major labor unions, providing perspectives from each side.

Another reason for the restrained labor response was adequate planning. Menem had prepared the groundwork for his policy much more carefully than Alfonsín had. Whereas Alfonsín had stumbled into privatization, Menem had planned the policy and gained international support. Before approaching either the workers or Congress, he asked the international lending agencies for loans based on his promise to privatize. The loans funded the severance packages and were supposed to protect workers for a period of time while they searched for new lines of work. Many workers saw the package as a bonanza that would be more than sufficient to tide them over while they sought new employment. But many labor leaders knew the severance packages were inadequate. Accepting them would lead to long-term hardship.

This chapter is a sequel not only to chapter 5 but also to chapter 4, which addressed Alfonsín's efforts to democratize labor. The success of the negotiations described here drew partially upon the corporate relations

---

4. On the use of old alliances to facilitate neoliberal reform, also see Sebastian Etchemendy, "Old Actors in New Markets: Transforming the Populist/Industrial Coalition in Argentina, 1989–2001," in *Argentine Democracy: The Politics of Institutional Weakness*, ed. Steven Levitsky and María Victoria Murillo (University Park: Pennsylvania State University Press, 2005), 62–87.

that labor has historically maintained with Peronism and partly upon the success of Alfonsín's earlier efforts to democratize the unions. The changes described here entailed major differences in the way leadership was exercised inside the unions, as well as alterations to the working life of union members. Although Menem might not have intended, or perhaps did not intend, these reforms to be steps in the process of national democratization, it was an outcome of his reforms, both in making the nation more attractive and open to business investment and in democratizing the unions. In the end, the labor reforms represent one of the most democratic legacies of Menem's presidency.[5]

This chapter also considers what these reforms failed to accomplish, ways in which Menem missed important opportunities for further democratization and for incorporating greater support from Congress and civil society. Students of democracy and human rights have suggested that societies torn by human rights violations in the recent past can heal themselves by tying retroactive justice into social policy. Specifically, social policy of the sort explored in this chapter can benefit victims' families. Doing so can help broaden popular support for the social policy even as reparations help the nation heal. Menem and his ministers missed this opportunity and were unable to build a coalition in support of social policy. As a result, Menem left office carrying an image of callousness toward the victims of the military dictatorship and toward the poor; the nation itself missed a chance to improve its democratization process by incorporating an element of reconciliation.

Addressing Labor

In corporate style, Menem called together the top labor leaders and announced that the government was preparing to privatize some government-run services.[6] Many reported later that they were totally

---

5. In her study of subnational government in Argentina, Chavez finds that provinces with a more democratic image are more likely to attract business investment, while provinces with a harsh authoritarian image are less likely to receive business investment (*Rule of Law*, 2004). Similarly, in the democratization of the United States South, states with a national profile of intense racism and violence received less business investment. See Mickey, *Paths Out of Dixie*, prologue to part 3, and chap. 6, esp. pp. 185 and 213.

6. Market reforms throughout Latin America were generally easier where the state had a corporate relationship with labor because the state could use its control mechanisms to punish dissident unions. Menem preferred to use his vertical power to persuade union leaders to cooperate, but he knew and they knew that he also had more coercive tools at his discretion. On corporate control elsewhere in Latin America, see Paul G. Buchanan, "Preauthoritarian

unprepared for the president's new message. Labor had supported Menem's election because his rhetoric reminded them of Perón's original message. Moreover, the Peronist Party had recently opposed privatization, as Eduardo Menem's Senate speeches indicate. Now Carlos Menem reversed his party's position completely. Labor leaders were shocked. Oscar Lescano said that he and his union felt "[b]etrayed. Totally. We thought we were going to move forward together. But Eduardo Menem talked to us about globalization and Carlos Menem talked about the need to modernize the economy. We had expected something very different."[7]

Menem explained the reasons for his policy. He talked about the state of the economy, which was evident all around them. Hyperinflation had hit the working class as hard as it had hit anyone. A common saying went that wages were rising at the speed of a person climbing the stairs while prices rose at the speed of an elevator. In laying out his anticipated privatization policy, Menem appealed to the labor leaders, asking for their support and "accompaniment," rather than simply dictating to them the nature of the new policy.[8] Although he was determined to pursue privatization and he saw the nation as lacking any alternative, he was nonetheless willing to listen to objections from labor leaders and to compromise on some particulars. His message was, "Here. Come with me on this path forward and work with me as we go. We will go forward with this policy; that we will do, with or without your input. But as a Peronist and as a sympathizer with the working class, I am asking you to accompany me in this project."[9] These

---

Institutions and Postauthoritarian Outcomes: Labor Politics in Chile and Uruguay," *Latin American Politics and Society* 50, no. 1 (Spring 2008): 59–89, at 84. This approach also describes the Swedish system where a more democratic form of corporatism brings labor peak associations into the policy creation process. See Peter Swenson, *Capitalists against Markets: The Making of Labor Markets and Welfare States in the United States and Sweden* (Oxford: Oxford University Press, 2002), and *Fair Shares: Unions, Pay and Politics in Sweden and West Germany* (Ithaca: Cornell University Press, 1989).

7. Interview with Oscar Lescano, Buenos Aires, Light and Power, March 28, 2008. Here we see the extent of vertical control over workers that Menem enjoyed. He would use this power both to pacify labor and to offer a minimal social safety net. Pierson argues that in most places the coming of the modern welfare state has been associated with parties that stand to the left of center. However, the fascist corporate state also was a source of welfare reforms for reasons of control. Christopher Pierson, *Beyond the Welfare State: The New Political Economy of Welfare*, 3rd ed. (University Park: Pennsylvania State University Press, 2007), 34–35.

8. Miriam Golden writes in *Labor Divided* (69) that austerity measures in Italy that did not benefit labor were likewise presented as a project of unity, "a common job" in which labor was being asked for its support rather than being dictated to by the ruling classes.

9. Peronists often use the term "acompañar" or "acompañarme," translated as "accompany," or "accompany me," or "keep company with me, walk with me, stay with me, move forward with me, and we will walk through this together." Menem was prone to use this kind of language. It was in close keeping with the historical rhetoric of Peronism that bases itself

words reveal Menem's leadership skills. He was determined to put his policy in place, and there was an iron fist behind his words. But the iron fist wore a velvet glove. There was still some small room for compromise and dialogue. Where labor leaders were willing to work with the government, privatization would be made less harsh rather than more so. The choice of how to respond now belonged to labor.[10]

Already, Peronism's hold on labor had prepared the groundwork for privatization of state-owned companies and for growing unemployment. Part of that groundwork included reforming labor union leadership to make leadership more flexible. Ubaldini had been replaced by Oscar Lescano, chosen as CGT leader because he was open to dialogue, willing to work with the government, reluctant to assume an uncompromising position, and always willing to listen to the other side.[11] Lescano did not agree with the privatization policies but saw different options for labor response. Unlike Ubaldini, he could see the larger picture. Labor could either "stand outside on the street and scream," he said, boycotting the negotiation process and having no influence over the specifics, or they could "come inside, sit down at the table, and talk," in the hopes of having some influence on the ultimate shape of the privatization process and its specifics.[12] The reader will note here that Lescano also used corporate language to describe the process. He also chose compromise. He came under serious criticism

---

on the special bond between the national political leader and labor. Labor unionists also use this language among themselves. They even used it with me when I came to their union headquarters to interview them and to hear their side of this story. It is a language of solidarity and togetherness. Now, Menem used it to ask for labor support as, very probably, only a Peronist leader could have done. Interview with Venegas, UATE, Buenos Aires, March 22, 2008.

10. Interview with Oscar Lescano, Buenos Aires, March 28, 2008. Many descriptions of the experience of the Argentine working class in the 1990s emphasize the extent to which labor was deceived by Menem and deprived of its historically favored position in Argentina's society and economy. However, Mark Anner has suggested that labor in Latin America had considerable choice in how it responded to economic restructuring like that which occurred in Argentina. Labor had the choice of whether to emphasize collective bargaining, whether to accept union fragmentation, and whether to seek collective labor law reform. Unions that were most able to protect their members and weather the changes produced by the global economy were those that emphasized collective bargaining rights. Such an emphasis required that union leaders look beyond labor laws alone and attend to the construction of long-term processes that involved labor in continued negotiations. See Anner's article, "Meeting the Challenges of Industrial Restructuring."

11. Enrique Rodríguez, one of the individuals who served as Minister of Labor under Menem and a man who worked within the Labor Ministry for several years beforehand, noted that "Peronism always chooses what (who) is best for it in the moment. When it is out of power it chooses the most combative leader; when it is in power it chooses the person most willing to dialogue." Interview with Rodríguez, Buenos Aires, May 14, 2008.

12. Interview, Buenos Aires, March 28, 2008, Luz y Fuerza headquarters, San Telmo.

for this choice. Other labor leaders felt that he had been too willing to compromise. In the 2000s, after many of the privatization reforms had occurred, Lescano felt that unions that negotiated came out of the privatization process with advantages and concessions that they otherwise would not have had. Unions and leaders who took a rigid position of opposition were hit harder by the privatization process, and their workers suffered more.[13] Yet workers were also consumers. By the time Menem took office, the spiral of inflation had hurt everyone. If labor did not fully understand how inefficient production practices had contributed to economic collapse, they could certainly understand that inflation frustrated any attempt to make ends meet on their salaries.[14] Because of inflation there was some worker understanding of the need for privatization.[15]

Part of the privatization process necessitated firing some workers. While Menem's government did not actually remove redundant labor from state service companies, he and labor union leaders all expected that the new owners of the companies would remove unneeded workers. Therefore both Menem and the labor leaders wanted to put in place mechanisms that would allow labor to absorb these unattractive events without launching the massive strikes that had taken place under the Alfonsín government and that had endangered democracy then. These preventive mechanisms included severance packages. Many individual workers thought these packages generous while some labor leaders saw them as totally inadequate.[16] A key part of the severance packages was continued access to social benefits. Without these packages, including long-term access to benefits, worker

---

13. Unions that disagreed with Lescano's compromising approach include UATRE (Union Argentina de Trabajadores Rurales y Estibadores) and CTERA. UATRE represented agricultural workers while CTERA represented the K-12 teachers union nationwide.

Whereas Menem's reforms consisted of reining in labor and using negotiations, FDR's program consisted of reining in business. Again, negotiations were used, although they were conducted by the legislative branch, and specifically by Speaker Sam Rayburn, rather than by members of the cabinet. See, for example, the description of Rayburn's negotiations with Wall Street financial tycoons as he moved to put in place regulations of the financial industry. Hardeman and Bacon, *Rayburn*, 150–55.

14. Peter Gourevitch also finds that workers have interests as consumers as well as needs as workers. These alternative needs can cause them to move either direction on some policies. Moreover, labor governments have always needed to make choices between their labor supporters and members of the middle class or business who might be part of their winning coalition. See *Politics in Hard Times*, 114–15 and 206.

15. Everyone recognized that something needed to be done, but everyone also sought to protect their own interests and to force the costs of economic liberalization onto other social sectors. As a result, Menem faced opposition from business and state workers and industries, as well as from the working class. Smith, "State, Market, and Neoliberalism in Post-transition Argentina," 5.

16. Interview with José Pedraza, Buenos Aires, Railroad Workers Union, April 16, 2008.

acquiescence would have been impossible. Therefore Menem transferred to the state responsibility for many of the social services the unions had previously provided, a policy that amounted to a key step toward a more universal welfare state. With this transfer, and by offering workers a new source of benefits, combined with the severance packages, Menem was able to induce many workers to leave their jobs voluntarily.

One of the great ironies of the social reforms was their democratizing potential. Alfonsín had tried to democratize the unions by removing control over benefits from labor bosses, but he lacked the resources to democratize social benefits by having the state provide them, a step that would have moved the nation toward a welfare state then. Now came Menem with a highly similar agenda but different motives. Whereas Alfonsín had sought control over benefits in order to democratize labor (the unions were undemocratic) Menem sought to offer (seek state control over) benefits for the good of labor so that those who were laid off would still receive social benefits (the workers were good and deserved benefits). Menem's rhetoric was different and more appealing to the workers. The economic reasoning was sound. But the end result—*a loss of economic power by the traditional labor bosses*—was the same. But Menem's rhetoric did not include advertising his reforms as steps toward a universal welfare state, although they were precisely that.

Not all of Menem's plan was in place at the outset. One important piece that came later was the convertibility plan. It pegged the Argentine peso to the U.S. dollar, greatly inflating the former. As long as convertibility was in place, it offered working class Argentines a greatly increased level of buying power. Workers who still had their jobs saw their income reach much further than before, while those who accepted a severance package likewise saw the value of that package extend far beyond anything they could have hoped for in the past. Although convertibility was an economic policy that benefited all Argentine citizens, not merely the working class, the expansion of buying power was most important among those who had the greatest reason to resist the government's policies and who had the organizational capacity to cause national chaos. Granting workers an inflated buying capacity went a considerable distance toward pacifying them in what might otherwise have been an explosive and difficult time of enormous economic change. Convertibility brought with it a high cost for Argentina at the international level, and even domestically it proved to be unsustainable over the long term. It greatly inflated the cost of Argentine goods on the international market. Exports fell, and Argentina lost ground in international competition. Eventually the peso was returned to its real value, but for the reform period convertibility eased worker acquiescence.

A final part of the privatization policy was the sale of company shares to workers themselves.[17] This policy was primarily for show. Many workers did not want and could not afford shares in failing companies. But this policy was a concession to the ideological forces opposing privatization, forces that Peronism itself had whipped to a frenzy in 1988. Worker shares mollified nationalism and addressed the sale of "the national patrimony" to "foreigners" and "foreign capitalists." Worker shares were first suggested by a Peronist deputy, José Luis Manzano, in the lower chamber during the Alfonsín presidency, but they were never implemented because privatization never happened. Now, under Menem Rodolfo Díaz suggested the inclusion of worker shares. The idea was presented as a bill of law and passed Congress.

Subsequent Steps toward Labor Reform

Once the initial reform was a success, further reform became possible. One example was a policy known as "flexibilization" of labor or "polifunctionality." Labor rigidity and self-protectiveness had resulted from the labor laws passed under Perón. Under those laws, workers were hired for specific positions and the law did not allow a company to move workers to another position in accordance with market demands. These laws had made Argentina one of the most rigid labor markets in the world and one that was not attractive to foreign businesses. Menem and Cavallo, his fourth labor minister, reduced rigidity with flexibility. "Labor flexibilization" allowed companies to move labor to new positions. For example, within the railroad companies, under the old laws a ticket collector could work only as a ticket collector and could not be asked to do any other kind of work.

---

17. Mark Peterson writes that, in seeking to get legislation through Congress, presidents sometimes incorporate a provision that will bring on board enough legislators to garner the votes needed to get a bill passed even when the president does not really want that provision included or does not particularly care one way or the other. Including worker-purchased shares in the privatizations bills constituted just such a provision. It was not really economically meaningful, for not enough shares would be purchased by workers to make any significant difference, and most workers could not afford to purchase shares in failing companies, or would not have wanted to do so even if they could. But the simple inclusion of such a provision deprived leftist opponents to the privatization proposals of a rallying point that could have been used to engender press opposition. On the use of this tactic by U.S. presidents, see Peterson, *Legislating Together*, 63.

Under the new laws, a railroad company with too many ticket collectors could ask a ticket collector to do manual labor, such as track repair, if more labor was needed in that area. Within the labor unions, this flexibility fell under heavy criticism because older workers had often risen to a level of seniority that allowed them to have physically less demanding positions, such as ticket collector. Under the flexibility laws, older workers lost that protection and could be asked to do any work that needed doing. From the perspective of the new private companies, this kind of flexibility was the only way to make the new companies economically viable and to keep labor employed. Employees who still had jobs had to be willing to do whatever needed doing.

As part of the effort to contain labor conflict, Menem introduced a rhetoric of "consumer rights," a notion that had not previously been influential in Argentina. "Consumer rights" was an appealing idea that brought in a large constituency base apart from the unions. Consumers, or average Argentine citizens, said Menem, had a right to live their lives in relative peace and stability. Consumers had a right *not* to have their lives perpetually upended and chaos imposed by repeated labor strikes and unending labor militancy, as had happened during the Alfonsín years. Menem juxtaposed "consumer rights" against the age-old notion of "labor rights" that had predominated from the 1940s onward.[18]

Menem then classified some industries and services, such as transportation, as "essential services" because their smooth functioning allowed citizens to enjoy stable lives, get to work and school, and care for themselves and their families. Menem took a harder line with workers in "essential" industries. He would not tolerate labor disruption in these services and was more draconian in his efforts to force striking workers back to work. As a Peronist whose first loyalty might have been to labor, Menem was able to portray himself as a populist concerned with the welfare of average citizens while also using a heavy hand against labor strikes. This rhetoric provided space within which Menem could defend his antistrike behavior. Additionally, of course, workers are also consumers. The rhetoric thus pitted workers against one another. When Menem tried to prevent workers from striking or forced striking workers back to work, he did so with the support of

18. "Consumers" normally include a significant number of individuals who are middle class while "labor" precisely refers to that sector. By introducing the idea of consumer rights into his agenda, Menem broadened his potential support base to include members of the middle class as well as workers. Many architects of the welfare state in other nations have advised the inclusion of perks and services that go to the middle class, as well as to the poor. Otherwise, public support for a welfare state would be politically inadequate to sustain one. See Medearis, "Deliberative Democracy, Subordination, and the Welfare State."

at least some other members of the working class, namely those who were consumers of the service or industry being threatened by a strike.[19]

Miriam Golden has shown, in the Italian case, that close ties between labor and a specific party are not always beneficial for either labor or the party. The demands of party survival (broadening the electoral base) may be quite different from the needs of labor (issues of employment, wages, and benefits). The divergence between these two sets of goals becomes even clearer in moments of austerity and economic crisis. At such times, labor and political parties should go their separate ways, and labor must be free to change their votes. This freedom is precisely what Casela told labor bosses they needed. But Argentine labor did not heed that warning, and labor in Argentina has never separated itself from Peronism.[20] That choice then allowed Menem to use those close ties to force reform.

Had labor been more independent, Menem would not have been able to wield such a high level of control, including the capacity to break strikes or the ability to change labor leadership at the national level when he faced an intransigent, myopic leader. Had labor unions been more autonomous, they might have fought back against Menem's reforms by throwing their political support to another party. This reality produced both positive and negative consequences. From the perspective of labor, workers lost in the process of privatization and over the course of the Menem years. But from the perspective of democracy and the modernization of Argentina's economy, the dependence of labor upon Peronism had positive long-term consequences. There is a deep irony to the story of Menem's labor reforms. The fascist-inspired model of vertical control instituted by Perón was used by Menem (and earlier by Alfonsín) to democratize labor and modernize the economy. A more modern and autonomous labor force would have been able to resist or even stop these same reforms. And again, as in the story about privatization, a president of questionable democratic loyalty used nondemocratic institutional arrangements to bring a greater degree of democracy and modernity to Argentina.[21]

---

19. Several interviewees from within Menem's cabinet noted that the notion of "consumer rights" drew upon an Italian model in which the same rhetoric had been used in similar circumstances in Italy.

20. Peter Ranis likewise argues that Argentine labor needs to separate itself from the Peronist Party because the party does not necessarily defend labor interests. However, writes Ranis, this separation is impossible at the current time because there is no left of center political party. In fact, Ranis found in his interviews that workers did not even understand class interests and class conflict. Instead, workers associated "leftism" with being antiverticalist and therefore with a kind of disloyalty to Perón. See Ranis, *Class, Democracy*, xxii, 5, and 121.

21. One irony of the Menem reforms was that they were implemented in order to make capitalism work in a situation in which it had become nonfunctional. This reality flies in the

An Institutional Approach to Reform

If the executive branch was central to the reform process, a key aspect of success was the personalities of the ministers inside Menem's cabinet. Of particular importance were the ministers of labor. They comprised the face of the Menem government that interacted most closely with labor and the unions during the process of labor reform. Menem was willing to bring the best men into his cabinet, regardless of factionalism within his party.[22] An early example of this attitude was his choice of Jorge Triaca as minister of labor.[23] Menem had presented himself as a member of the "orthodox" faction of Peronism while Triaca came from the "renovating" faction.[24] The Renovationists have a more social democratic view of Peronism and labor.[25] Triaca's first subsecretary of labor was Rodolfo Díaz, while the second subsecretary of labor was Enrique Rodriguez. As with Alfonsín's administration, the post of labor minister was exhausting because of the perpetual conflicts with labor. Labor ministers did not stay in office for long. Over the course of Menem's first administration, each of these three men served a term as labor minister when the one above him resigned. Yet the three

---

face of arguments that welfare is not compatible with capitalism, an idea that began with Adam Smith. But, like Menem's reforms, early welfare efforts in Europe were likewise seen as market-supporting measures, not market-usurping measures. See Pierson, *Beyond the Welfare State*, chap. 1, esp. 38.

22. Likewise, John Kennedy chose good men for his cabinet and gave them room to work. He did not try to run everything personally. Franklin Roosevelt also chose his cabinet with a bipartisan approach, looking for expertise rather than for purely partisan loyalties. On Kennedy, see Schlesinger, *Thousand Days*, 686. On Roosevelt, see Alter, *Defining Moment*, 167–73.

23. The Latin American left has characterized Triaca as "signaling a strong tilt to the Right in favor of conservative, anti-reform sectors of the Peronist labor movement." I see him differently and would characterize him as a realist rather than a rightist. He clearly saw that the pattern of spending, nonproductivity, and destructive strike activity were combining to bankrupt the economy and jeopardize democracy. While being aware that the reforms would enact a price over the short term, Triaca felt that the long-term results would be more positive and that, in any event, the current state of affairs could not continue. As an example of characterizing Triaca as a rightist, see Smith, "State, Market and Neoliberalism in Post-transition Argentina," 8. My own interpretation of Triaca is based upon several interviews of him in his office in Buenos Aires. He was an admirer of the Kennedy brothers, particularly John and Robert, whose picture dominated one wall of his office. I saw Triaca as moderate, reasonable, and generally able to see both sides of an issue. Also see note # 26.

24. Menem was willing to work with whoever seemed most capable, even if the person came from the opposing faction of Peronism or from outside of Peronism entirely, as we will see in chapter 7 with his choice of Antonio Salonia as Minister of Education. In her study of presidential legislating capacities in Latin America, Gabriel Negretto argues that a willingness to include representatives from multiple parties in the cabinet is part of a recipe for legislative success. See Negretto, "Minority Presidents and Democratic Performance in Latin America."

25. Ranis, *Class, Democracy*, 65.

were close in terms of policy and had great respect for each other. Policy remained steady even as the top post changed hands. Extensive interviews with these three individuals offer a close look at corporate labor relations and at the creation of labor policy during the Menem presidency.[26]

First, these former ministers made clear that this was not a situation in which the government dictated and labor unions obeyed. Such a subservient relationship could not have been achieved in Argentina anyway, and Menem was smart enough to know that dictating to the unions was more likely to cause conflict than cooperation. Accordingly, as privatization advanced, the new laws that changed and reset salaries and benefits were made in negotiation with unions.[27] Menem had warned the unions that privatization was a fact of the future, and he had asked for their cooperation and support. The level of cooperation from each union varied. But at the level of the Labor Ministry and in negotiation with the top people inside that ministry, labor had a chance to influence the course of events. The fact that unions were invited to provide input at this early stage is an important part of the reason Menem was able to avoid many strikes that would certainly have been forthcoming had labor felt entirely excluded.[28]

For example, under the second minister of labor, Rodolfo Díaz, the ministry wrote the Law of Employment, which protected labor from blackmarket workers. The term "black marker workers" was used in Argentina at that time to describe non-union workers who would work below minimum wage. In the United States labor movement they are called "scabs."

---

26. I interviewed Jorge Triaca in Buenos Aires on March 17, 2008, and again on April 10 and April 18, 2008. I interviewed Rodolfo Díaz in Buenos Aires on March 13, 2008, and April 2, 2008. I interviewed Enrique Rodríguez in Buenos Aires on May 4, 2008, and May 25, 2008. In addition to granting extended interviews, Triaca also facilitated my access to key labor leaders, in particular with an initial meeting with Oscar Lescano, Light and Power.

27. A key criticism of state-based reform is that it is top down, to the exclusion of input from popular sectors that are the targets of reform. Certainly, Menem's privatization policies were top down, but they were not constructed to the exclusion of labor; in fact, insofar as labor was willing to participate rather than obstruct policy, labor input was taken into account as much as possible. For criticisms of top-down reform that lacks popular input, see Jonathan Fox, *The Politics of Food in Mexico: State Power and Social Mobilization* (Ithaca: Cornell University Press, 1992). Fox's criticism addresses the Mexican food policy, Sistema Alimentario Mexicano (Mexican Food System) (79–82). For a more general critique of these types of policies, see James C. Scott, *Seeing Like a State* (New Haven: Yale University Press, 1998).

28. Negotiation and compromise are hallmarks of democracy, and Menem's administration deserves credit for its capacity to use these skills to achieve the significant labor reform that it accomplished. Influential leaders in the United States, such as Sam Rayburn and Lyndon Johnson, have also been recognized as great negotiators. Recent work on the United States finds that the newest generation of great negotiators is epitomized by former Speaker Nancy Pelosi, who also has great skills in negotiation and has used those skills to accomplish impressive reforms. See Peters and Rosenthal, *Speaker Nancy Pelosi*.

Díaz also produced the Retirement Law, giving workers a protected guarantee of retirement and pension coverage. Díaz oversaw the creation of the controversial Law of Flexibility or "labor flexibilization plan." It met with a negative response from many labor unions, yet it would have been even more controversial had labor leaders not been involved in its composition. Díaz oversaw the Law on Stimulation and Legalization of Social Development, a series of plans to stimulate employment. Throughout the Menem years the Labor Ministry also worked to revise the tax laws and to enforce tax collection. These changes addressed the state's need for income without asking labor to absorb all of the cost.[29] These examples illustrate the close ties between the Menem government and labor as the policy of privatization moved forward. While journalist reports suggested that Menem's government was treating labor with disdain, the reality of daily policy making was quite different. Labor reform was piecemeal policy making with full labor involvement.

The willingness of the Labor Ministry to work with labor did not always spell success. Unions had different attitudes toward privatization at different points in the process, including extreme intransigence, total cooperation, and everything in between. The railroad industry was one of the most difficult, and railroad workers were intransigent. Early in the first Menem presidency, while Triaca was labor minister, the railroad workers went on strike. Menem refused to negotiate with them, and Triaca followed that directive. Menem suggested that railroads on strike could simply be closed down because the industry was too dilapidated to provide reasonable service to the country. Railroads had become expendable. Despite this official directive, Second Subsecretary of Labor Enrique Rodríguez decided that he would negotiate with the railroad workers. He did so on his own initiative and with the knowledge and acceptance of both Triaca, the labor minister, and Díaz, the first subsecretary of labor. Rodríguez, along with Triaca and Díaz, knew that he was defying Menem's orders. Rodríguez, however, did not want to see the lines closed without at least some effort to talk with the workers. So he told his superiors that he was going to talk with the railroad workers, even at the risk of being fired by Menem.

Rodríguez then went to talk with the railroad workers and found variation within the unions there. He reported that the locomotive drivers were

---

29. Sebastian Edwards and Alejandra Cox Edwards find that decreasing the tax on labor in the formal sector slightly increases the income of labor in the informal sector. There was also a small positive effect on employment. See *Social Security Privatization Reform and Labor Markets: The Case of Chile*, Working Paper 8924 (Cambridge, MA: National Bureau of Economic Research, 2002).

the most intransigent but the signal workers were much more willing to dialogue. Rodríguez was able to work out a compromise with the railroad workers, and the strike ended. Menem was not happy over Rodriguez's defiance of his own orders, but he was pleased that the strike was over. He did not fire Rodriguez; indeed, over time, Rodriguez was promoted all the way up to Minister of Labor. The story illustrates the extent to which members of Menem's executive branch had a level of autonomy that is not widely known and could act within that latitude to move policy forward.[30] Despite this momentary success, the railroads were hit hard by privatization. Among the most dilapidated and outdated of all nationally owned enterprises, they were also the most expensive to upgrade.[31] Rail services reached many of the far-flung regions, tying them into the nation. But the government had invested almost nothing in railroad improvement for decades; doing so now was out of the question.[32]

The details of railroad privatization illustrate the pragmatism and flexibility that brought Menem success. The rails were subdivided into metropolitan and commuter rails versus long-distance lines. The long-distance lines were divided again between northern and southern routes. The most profitable lines, if updated, were the commuter rails near Buenos Aires. Among the long-distance lines, southern routes were potentially more profitable because the civilian population in the south is wealthier and

---

30. An interesting caveat to this story comes from the involvement of Rodríguez's young daughter, who was a child at the time of the strike. As the story goes, Menem phoned Rodríguez's home precisely during the hours that Rodríguez was talking with the railroad workers in direct contravention of the president's orders. Menem's phone call may have been coincidental, but Menem might have gotten wind of Rodríguez's disobedience and called to confirm it.

When the president called, Rodríguez's daughter answered the phone to say that her father was not at home. When the president asked where Rodríguez was, she answered naïvely, "Oh, he's talking with the railroad workers." That evening at dinner, she reported to her father that the president had called. Rodríguez was obviously concerned that he might lose his job for his disobedience. The president had told him not to negotiate with the railroad workers. His daughter replied, "Well, Dad, you weren't negotiating; you were just having a dialogue with them." The distinction stuck, even if it was not strictly true. Rodríguez reported to Menem his daughter's swift turn of phrase, and Menem explained that he would not fire Rodríguez because, after all, he had only been having a dialogue with the railroad workers. He had not been negotiating with them at all.

31. In fact, the decision to nationalize the railroads was questionable from the outset. Back in 1946, when Perón moved to nationalize all industries, one of his own administrators, Miguel Miranda, a successful industrialist, opposed the purchase of the railroads even as he oversaw the nationalization of a large number of public services. Miranda did not want to buy the railroads because he thought they were already obsolete in 1946. Perón insisted on purchasing them anyway. From that moment onward the railroads continued to deteriorate and to place a fiscal drain on the national treasury. See Rein, *In the Shadow of Perón*, 48–53.

32. Interview with José Pedraza, Union Ferroviario, Buenos Aires, April 25, 2008.

can pay higher fares. The least profit potential lay in the northern, long-distance routes where citizen poverty would preclude higher fares.

Initially, Menem proposed to sell all the lines quickly, simply dumping them on the private market. But no buyer of national or international origins emerged, although the government went through several rounds of soliciting bids. Menem then tried to sell portions of the lines, subdividing them as described above. When still no one came forward, his agenda was to close the rails entirely, making Argentina a nation without railroads. Vehement labor protest caused him to reconsider. He tried a third time and eventually found buyers for the metropolitan lines. He also found a Brazilian company that would purchase and renovate the southern and western long-distance lines. Menem was never able to find a buyer for the northern lines. Faced with the certainty that the northern rails would close, the rail workers themselves came forward with a cooperative proposal to purchase the lines. Menem responded by closing parts of the northern lines and selling the remainder to the workers. Railroad union leaders say that this solution never worked and that public use of the northern lines has all but disappeared. But the outcome exemplifies compromise between Menem's government and one of the nation's oldest unions. It also carried with it the added benefit that if the new arrangement did not work, as indeed it has not, then labor had been given a chance to save their own jobs while the state was released from expensive subsidies to an industry it could not afford.[33]

Congress in the Labor Reforms

In a fully functional presidential democracy where Congress plays the role of a Congress, the process of making legislation would have fallen to Congress. But Argentina was not a fully functional democracy, and even when it does function Congress plays a role more like that of a parliament than of a Congress, with the prerogative of initiating legislation falling to the executive. Additionally, as we saw in chapter 4, when Congress was asked to reform labor it refused to support many aspects of labor reform. The much-needed Mucci bill was defeated and replaced by a weaker labor reform

---

33. Mark Peterson notes that presidents sometimes find their agenda significantly "diluted" as a result of congressional consultation and of presidential estimates of the likely congressional reaction. *Legislating Together*, 66. In this case, Menem's agenda of closing the lines was diluted by popular responses, union actions, and by the behavior of his own cabinet member, Enrique Rodríguez.

law. Thus the realities of policy making in Argentina's polity reduced the importance of Congress with respect to labor reform policy but did not preclude Congress entirely.

Instead, each piece of labor legislation hammered out inside the Ministry of Labor was then introduced to Congress and passed into law. Legislators in each chamber worked with the ministry to introduce bills and shepherd them through. In the Senate, Peronists Oraldo Britos and Rodriguez Saa introduced many labor bills. In the lower chamber, Peronist deputy Osvaldo Borda often introduced bills because he was the head of the Committee on Labor. Radical deputies Casela (former labor minister under Alfonsín) introduced some bills as did Fernando De la Rúa (later elected president). Bills were debated within each chamber and approved there. However, the real negotiation had already taken place inside the executive branch. Once bills were presented to Congress, there was enough acquiescence by labor to allow Peronist legislators to approve them without fear of labor backlash. It was corporate policy making rather than congressional law creation. Yet Argentina's Constitution places legislative initiative with the executive, as in a parliamentary system, so the pattern was within the constitutional design of Argentina's presidential system.

Had Peronist deputies in Congress represented labor in deliberative processes, the workers might have been better represented than they were through corporate inclusion of labor leaders. Members of Congress can become quite specialized in matters that concern the committees on which they sit. Instead, by representing themselves inside the cabinet, the unions made some serious mistakes that would subsequently hurt labor. One example is the minimum wage. The Ministry of Labor took a long-term perspective and wanted to peg the minimum wage to industry profits, a profit-sharing scheme. The ministry anticipated that the sweeping economic reforms would soon produce very high profit levels for the newly privatized companies. By the late 2000s, these anticipated profits had become reality. But in the 1990s the labor unions rejected any profit-sharing arrangement. They preferred to peg the minimum wage to the cost of living. Labor's position was a much more cautious and minimalist approach that was very self-protective. It guaranteed workers a living, but it denied them any participation in the upcoming profit bonanza.[34] It also

---

34. In his interviews with me and in his dialogue with the labor unions, Rodriquez made the argument that Argentina's labor leaders are outmoded in their perspective on labor goals. In the instance described here, quite apart from the inability to see the advantages of profit sharing, labor leaders also focused only on bread and butter issues such as wages. But in other societies where labor is more forward looking in its negotiations with industry, labor is also

kept them in a situation where they had no incentives to increase productivity.[35] Congressional representatives would have had more time to study the economics of profit sharing. They might have seen the long term and the bigger picture and done better at representing labor interests. At least Madison thought that they would.

Reflecting on these negotiations, Rodríguez remarked that union leaders had been closed-minded. They lacked vision and could not imagine a path toward creating wealth among workers, as through Scandinavian-style profit-sharing.[36] Union leaders could never understand that worker and company interests can be made compatible.[37] Companies cannot and will not raise wages if they are barely surviving financially. But companies that are realizing high profits can afford to raise wages significantly. Rodriquez suggested that Argentina's labor unions are old-fashioned, rigid, and uninformed about the modern world. "They have plenty of lawyers to defend them," he said, "But they lack social advisors and sociologists who can teach them how the modern economy and society interact." This example reveals divisions between union leadership and the administration. Menem and his cabinet were trying to move Argentina's economy forward into the modern world. Argentina's labor unions were still stuck in the self-protective, minimalist mentality of the 1940s.[38] Tying the minimum wage to living costs

---

able to consider normative issues such as pay differentials among workers and the appropriate size of those differences. These considerations were likewise absent from the demands made by labor in Argentina. On normative considerations among labor leaders, see Swenson, *Fair Shares*.

35. A problem for Argentine labor has always been its lack of interest in productivity, a position that isolates it from political coalitions with other social sectors. All other sectors, including business, consumers, and the middle class, prefer to see higher productivity. Gourevitch, *Politics in Hard Times*, 206.

36. Swenson, *Capitalists against Markets*.

37. Peter Ranis argues that workers had a "redistributive mentality," thinking that they had a "*right*" to a certain percentage of the national GNP; they were not at all focused upon actually increasing national productivity or the total size of the GNP. Workers did not see productivity as their responsibility. I have called this position having a sense of entitlement but no sense of responsibility. Ranis writes that this basic mentality is the one that Alfonsín sought to change. On worker attitudes, see Ranis, *Class, Democracy*, 62–63. The unions' position reflects the "us" and "them" mentality that describes the Peronist working class. Anderson, *Social Capital in Developing Democracies*, chap. 3. Ethelbert Haskins sees a similar attitude among African Americans in the United States today. See his *Victim Psychosis in the Center City Ghettos* (Denver: Outskirts Press, 2010).

38. One criticism that has been made of Menem's reforms and their aftermath has been that the income gap has grown in Argentina. Workers have fallen further behind the middle and upper classes than they were prior to the reforms. We see here that workers and labor unions themselves played a role in creating that outcome. They preferred to negotiate for cost-of-living wage increases in their new contracts rather than for wage increases pegged to company profits. Rodríguez's argument here is that labor unions failed, through rigidity,

also kept labor interests linked to low productivity, whereas profit-sharing would have linked labor interests with raising productivity.

If Rodríguez thought the unions old-fashioned, one can only imagine what they would have been like had Alfonsín not tried to democratize their internal leadership and had Menem's administration been forced to deal with all of the original caudillos who were still in control of labor when the nation returned to democracy. In their interviews with me, Menem's administrators gave significant credit to the Radical administration, which had taken the first steps to modernize the unions. Given the antipathy between Radicalism and Peronism, the sense of mutual cooperation and respect that emerged in the interviews is notable. Menem's administrators knew what Alfonsín had accomplished, even if Menem would never admit publicly that Alfonsín had ever made any contribution at all. Similarly, Peronist administrators credited Casela for having eliminated the top echelons of labor leadership in many unions, a step that caused the unions to be less intransigent and more willing to entertain the possibility of labor's changed role in a modern economy.[39] Rodríguez also credited Ideler Tonelli, the labor minister toward the end of Alfonsín's administration, for his effort to make peace with Ubaldini. This effort might have been hopeless because of Ubaldini's combative style. But Tonelli had tried, and Rodríguez knew he had tried because, as Ubaldini's lawyer, he had accompanied the labor leader to the government meeting with Minister Tonelli. This attempt is yet another example of the extent to which reforms begun under Alfonsín were finished under Menem while other reforms made by Menem might have been impossible if not for the initial progress made by Alfonsín.

Conclusion

This chapter, combined with chapter 4, reveals the magnitude of the labor reforms accomplished during Argentina's democratic transition years, reforms that were essential to the democratization process.[40] The compari-

---

narrow-mindedness, and an old-fashioned approach, to negotiate the best possible contract for their members.

39. Interviews with Rodolfo Díaz (March 13, 2008) and Enrique Rodríguez (May 4, 2008), both in Buenos Aires.

40. Economic modernization reforms comparable to the ones described here were also undertaken in Chile, with the enormous difference that Chile's reforms took place under an authoritarian regime headed by the military. On Chile's modernization reforms, see René Cortazar, ed., *Inflación rebelde en América Latina* (Santiago de Chile: CIEPLAN, Hachette, 1990); René Cortazar and Jose Able Arellano, eds., *Políticas Macro-económicas: Una Perspectivea*

son with the United States suggested in one of the opening quotes for this chapter is particularly relevant here because of the similarity between the economic crisis Menem faced and the economic crisis of the Great Depression. The Peter Gourevitch quote opening this chapter says that labor in the United States surrendered its ideal of a socialized economy in exchange for political acceptance. Similarly, Argentine labor surrendered its ideal of universal employment and began to accept a degree of democratic governance. In return it gained some social acceptance and took initial steps toward democracy and economic modernity. This historic compromise in Argentina was comparable to FDR's achievements under the New Deal. But Menem did not take full advantage of the opportunity history presented to construct an Argentine New Deal, creating the paradox of great reform that fell short of transformative reform. His reforms fell short of profit-sharing and did not raise the living standard of the working class.

Within that overarching paradox lay several smaller ones. One was the use of nondemocratic institutional means to achieve a democratic end. The Ministry of Labor incorporated labor input into the reform process using relationship patterns developed in the nondemocratic past that gave the democratic government corporate control over labor. Corporate relations are not always and not necessarily nondemocratic. In Sweden, they have been used in a more democratic fashion to involve labor in macro-system reforms.[41] But in Argentina corporate relations have historically been more vertical and less democratic. The Ministry of Labor used that structure to accomplish reform, to engage in dialogue and insist upon reform when labor would have refused. Thus economic modernization and democratic process were achieved through nondemocratic institutional mechanisms. This book shows that institutions bring with them patterns from an authoritarian past while also providing mechanisms for a democratic future. Labor reform exemplifies how that can happen.

Menem's reforms left his own party in an awkward position. Peronism subscribes to vertical, caudillistic channels of control. But the economic changes that the nation needed demanded transparency and accountability. While Peronist leaders wanted their vertical, nonaccountable, and hierarchical control, they found themselves faced with demands for economic and political openness that proved essential to economic modernization. They were essential in selling the dinosaur companies, in reforming labor policy, and in other aspects of economic law. They were essential in mak-

---

Latinoamericana (Santiago de Chile: Corporación de Investigaciones Económicas para Latinoamerica, 1988); Cortazar, Foxley, and Tokman, *Llegados del Monetarismo*.

41. Swenson, *Capitalists against Markets*.

ing the newly privatized companies function efficiently. In short, economic modernization went hand in hand with democracy. Peronism was ready to oversee the former; it was much less eager to oversee the latter. This clash between Peronism's verticalism and its pragmatic ability to see and implement needed solutions dominated the Menem years and has not been resolved even today. In fact, the contradiction came to characterize Menem's administration. The fundamental tension between the desire for hierarchical control and the dawning awareness among Peronists of the need for openness and transparency to aid economic development became a defining tension of the Menem years and of the legacy he left behind.

Another paradox of the reforms undertaken here was that an authoritarian party with limited democratic loyalty had become the driving force in moving social services away from corporate control and toward state provision. Precisely because Peronism had set up the corporate system of social services through the unions, only Peronism could dismantle it. Moreover, workers were not going to tolerate the loss of those services entirely. At least some services to at least some citizens would have to be replaced through the state. The provision of pensions, unemployment protection, and social services is a task normally associated with the welfare state, particularly the wealthy states of advanced industrial democracies. The welfare state has often emerged from an advanced level of democracy and is considered by some to be the highest form of democracy.[42] But in Argentina we find state services emerging out of a nondemocratic history.[43] Steps toward one of the most advanced forms of democracy were led by a party that does not even fully subscribe to the most basic elements of democracy, such as the rule of law.

These various paradoxes emerge because a Latin American tradition of centralized control—embodied in the corporate model inherited from Peronism—was combined with the presidential system of power balance copied from the United States. The nondemocratic thrust of the first tradition was perpetually at odds with the democratic purpose of the other. The result was a contradictory, paradoxical process that still created a desir-

---

42. Pierson, *Beyond the Welfare State*; on the welfare state in Latin America, see Evelyn Huber, Thomas Mustillo, and John D. Stephens, "Politics and Social Spending in Latin America," *Journal of Politics* 70, no. 2 (April 2008): 420–36, and Evelyn Huber, "Successful Social Policy Regimes? Political Economy, Politics, and the Structure of Social Policy in Argentina, Chile, Uruguay and Costa Rica," paper presented at the conference "Democratic Governance in Latin America," University of Notre Dame, October 7, 2005.

43. Welfare services in Germany came first through Bismarck and later through the Nazis before eventually evolving into being democratic, welfare-state services. We discuss this evolution further in the Conclusion.

able end. In that process a leader with only limited loyalty to democracy nonetheless took key steps toward democracy. Argentina had fallen into a vicious cycle of economic disaster, labor combativeness, political chaos, and military coups. Menem broke this pattern by placing the economy on a stable economic footing and weakening labor's power to close it down. The resulting stability greatly reduced the chances of chaos or another military coup. Menem took separate steps against the military directly to discourage further coup attempts.

A similar set of reforms might have been possible using Congress as Alfonsín did on human rights and labor reform. Menem never gave that option a chance because the corporate route was available, familiar, and he did not value the democratic process in its own right. Also, Congress had not acquitted itself well as a policy-making forum with its defeat of the Mucci bill. The Senate remained as undemocratic in the years considered here as it had been under Alfonsín, and Menem was not willing to waste time giving the Senate another chance to defeat reform. Additionally, a decision on Menem's part to use the democratic process rather than the corporate route would have required a coalition-building approach in which he built support for his reform inside Congress and across society at large. This is what Alfonsín did with respect to human rights policy. Menem had the tools to build such a coalition and the rhetoric to sell it at his fingertips, left for him by Alfonsín's unfinished human rights policy. Menem could have tied labor reform into an overall agenda of democratized social services and special benefits for the families and children of the disappeared. His reform package could easily have incorporated small additional benefits for children of the disappeared at relatively little cost. It would have been an Argentine New Deal that also remembered the disappeared.[44] Such a coalition might well have given Menem the congressional support to enact labor reform through Congress instead of through the executive using corporatism. Success in such a goal also would have given Menem the legacy of greatness he desired. But oddly, the man who could build a coalition inside his own party could not or would not do the same for the nation as a whole. The result left civil society opposing the labor reforms when it might have been led to support them.

We cannot know if Menem would have succeeded had he tried this approach. In other parts of Latin America labor has also opposed the kinds of reform Menem put in place.[45] But other Latin American nations have not

---

44. For example, human rights policy in Chile has included reparations for the families of the disappeared. See Collins, *Post-transitional Justice*.

45. Levitsky and Mainwaring, "Organized Labor and Democracy in Latin America."

moved extensive social services to the state and have not built labor reform upon a commendable early human rights policy. These two facts gave Menem a coalition-building advantage that he failed to use. We will never know whether a leader of superior vision and greater coalition-building capacities could have accomplished Argentina's reforms differently.

We move now to a final paradox in the next chapter. If Menem and his party were caught in the contradiction between the habits of hierarchical control and the modern need for transparency and openness, nowhere is the tension between domination and control on the one hand and free-wheeling criticism and diverse ideas on the other hand more evident than in the world of education. Authoritarians cannot dominate a world where education is free, open, and sophisticated. And yet high-quality, accessible education is precisely what Menem tried to achieve. As an autocratic president he oversaw unparalleled reforms to education. In doing so, he may have laid the groundwork for the termination of his party's control over Argentine society, although that outcome is still not visible on the horizon. The next chapter considers educational reforms.

SEVEN

Executive Vision and Congressional Resistance

Educational Reform

The basis of our government is the opinion of the people. . . . And so . . . the whole people must take upon themselves the education of the whole people, and must be willing to bear the expense of it.

—Thomas Jefferson and John Adams[1]

[A] democratic state of education tries to teach virtue . . . *democratic virtue*, the ability to deliberate and hence to participate in social reproduction.

—Amy Gutmann[2]

In this final chapter on the Menem years we study his reforms to Argentina's K-12 educational system and university access.[3] Unlike privatization

---

1. Lester J. Cappon, ed., *The Adams-Jefferson Letters: The Complete Correspondence between Thomas Jefferson and Abigail and John Adams* (New York: Simon and Shuster, 1971), 480, cited in Andrew DelBanco, *College, What It Was, Is, and Should Be* (Princeton: Princeton University Press, 2012), 28.

2. Amy Gutmann, *Democratic Education* (Princeton: Princeton University Press, 1987), 46.

3. This chapter is based on multiple interviews with teachers, leaders, and former leaders of the teachers' union, CTERA, and with former members of Menem's Ministry of Education. Menem's presidency had four ministers of education: Antonio Francisco Salonia (July 1989–December 1992); Jorge Alberto Rodríguez (December 1992–April 1996); Susana Beatriz Decibe (April 1996–May 1999) and Manuel Guillermo Garcia Solá (May 10, 1999–December 10, 1999). I also interviewed university professors at the University of Buenos Aires and at several private colleges. In 2008, my position as a Fulbright Scholar and

and labor reform, Menem's educational reforms have received relatively little attention.[4] That neglect is unfortunate because they reveal a progressive side to the Menem administration that has gone unrecognized.[5] The educational reforms are also important because of the information they provide about democratization by institutions. The vision and initiative for them came from the executive branch, specifically from the Ministry of Education, which oversaw the changes to higher education. But Congress played a central role in writing law for the K-12 reforms. As with the other reforms studied in this book, we use the polity-centered approach to understand what happened here. Again we find reformist vision coming from the executive branch while Congress was more problematic in its role. We see as well the innovative capacity of Menem's ministers.

The education reforms matter for democratization because of the connection between education and democracy. Amy Gutmann, Dennis Thompson, and their contributors argue that education and democracy are inseparable because education enhances deliberation[6] and gives citizens more capacity to resist oppression.[7] Additionally, education connects to democracy by being part of the welfare state. Most students of the modern welfare state suggest that broad state support for public education is the first plank in a welfare system.[8] Argentina had already taken steps in

---

teacher in a doctoral seminar at the UBA placed me in a position of having extensive access to the internal dialogue inside the UBA over the creation of doctoral programs in Argentina. I also spent extensive time in the library of the Ministry of Culture and Education where there are sources on the development of education in Argentina.

4. Alfonsín had made some educational changes, but the ones studied here were more comprehensive.

5. Here, again, the Menem reforms depart from traditional neoliberal reforms, which never focus on increasing human capital or on improving education. See Michel Duquette, *Building New Democracies: Economic and Social Reform in Brazil, Chile and Mexico* (Toronto: University of Toronto Press, 1999), esp. 196–202.

6. Gutmann, *Democratic Education*. See also Amy Gutmann, ed., *Democracy and the Welfare State* (Princeton: Princeton University Press, 1988), and Amy Gutmann and Dennis Thompson, *Democracy and Disagreement* (Cambridge: Harvard University Press, 1996). Gutmann and Thompson posit an essential connection between education and deliberation.

Education is widely perceived as reducing popular vulnerability to clientelism. It also enhances democratic, bridging social capital. On education and clientelism, see Jonathan Fox, "The Difficult Transition from Clientelism to Citizenship: Lessons from Mexico," *World Politics* 46, no. 2 (1994): 151–84, and Anderson, "Clientelism, Semiclientelism, and Pluralism." On education and social capital, see Anderson, *Social Capital*. Andrew Delbanco argues that education, particularly higher education, is basic to democracy itself. See his *College: What It Was, Is, and Should Be.*

7. Anderson and Dodd, *Learning Democracy*, esp. chaps. 2 and 9. Also see Vanessa Siddle Walker, *Their Highest Potential: An African American School Community in the Segregated South* (Chapel Hill: University of North Carolina Press, 1996), 203.

8. Pierson, *Beyond the Welfare State*.

this direction. The movement of social services from the unions to the state, which we saw in the previous chapter, was one step toward a welfare state in Argentina; educational reform was another. These reforms tie in to the labor reforms considered in the previous chapter for another reason as well: education provided an alternative future for those who had lost jobs as a result of privatization. These reforms opened a world of opportunity for the working class.

The education reforms were similar to privatization and the democratization of labor in some ways but unlike them in others. On the one hand, privatization and reduction of state responsibility were key to Menem's overall approach. The reforms modernized education, gave young people the skills needed in the new economy, and reduced the hierarchical and authoritarian forms of control that had characterized education previously.[9] They provided opportunities for skill development among working-class adults and offered a long-term option to those who had lost their jobs. On the other hand, the reforms to education were forward-looking and less characterized by immediate necessity in the face of crisis than were the privatizations. They were voluntary and optional and, for that reason, required the skill of a president able to work with Congress without holding disproportionate power.

As with privatization and labor reform, the educational reforms were not what the nation would have expected from Peronism. Perón saw primary and secondary education as a means to inculcate the population into becoming his passive, obedient followers.[10] He had created technical schools where workers could learn a trade. The foundation of Perón's understanding of education had always been an effort to use education as a system of control.[11] Predictably, he had been at odds with the nation's universities,

9. Alberto C. Taquini, *La Transformación de la Educación Superior Argentina: De las Nuevas Universidades a los Colegios Universitarios* (Buenos Aires: Academia Nacional de Educación, 2000), 37–43.

10. Anderson, *Social Capital in Developing Democracies*.

11. The effort to control the popular masses by restricting access to education or by manipulating education dates back long before Perón, back to efforts to resist the influence of the French Revolution. In writing against the French Revolution, Edmund Burke sought to preserve a society of hierarchy and subordination, which he saw as essential to social order. Famous for his comment about "the swinish multitude," Burke wrote to convince a popular audience to resist the ideals of the French Revolution. His predicament was that ignorance, once dispelled, is impossible to reestablish. He understood that education was foundational to democracy. Likewise, Menem's educational reforms were fundamentally democratic. In response to Burke, the radicals of the day, who defended democracy, argued that democracy was not about bloodshed and leveling, as Burke suggested, but about human dignity. On Burke, see Don Herzog, *Poisoning the Minds of the Lower Orders* (Princeton: Princeton University Press, 1998), 36, 85, and 514, and chap. 12. On arguments for and against the French

always the level of education least susceptible to control.[12] University students and professors had opposed Perón for his authoritarian and fascist characteristics while he had responded to such challenges by intervening and micromanaging the universities. He fired tenured professors and cut funding for dissident students.[13] That Peronism would solicit reforms that opened educational access and decentralized control was counterintuitive.

With education reform, Menem had a chance to work with Congress in a nonemergency situation, building a coalition in support of a much-needed reform. Menem failed to do that, despite the Peronist majority in both houses, and his failure contrasts with Alfonsín's successes even when faced with an opposition-dominated Congress. Instead, Congress went off in a different direction, with disastrous results. As with human rights law during the early Alfonsín years, Congress made reform more complicated and time-consuming than it otherwise would have been. But the congressional method was one of dialogue and deliberation, and, unlike Alfonsín, Menem proved unable to work with Congress toward policy. Congressional policy then elicited a vehemently negative response from one sector of society: the teacher's union, CTERA (Central de Trabajadores de la Educación de la República Argentina). Here the special delegative powers Menem had enjoyed with privatization did not apply, and the corporate powers he had used to control labor were absent. Lacking such superior power, even with majoritarian control of Congress, Menem could not put effective reform in place.

Like privatization, the timing of Menem's educational reforms fits with broad regional dynamics. Merilee Grindle has called the 1990s economic reforms "first generation" reforms while the educational reforms, coming somewhat later, were "second generation" reforms.[14] Her term has more

---

Revolution, see Daniel O'Neill, *The Burke-Wollstonecraft Debate: Savagery, Civilization, and Democracy* (University Park: Pennsylvania State University Press, 2007). From this perspective, Burke would have opposed Menem's educational reforms.

12. Argentina's national universities have suffered a long history of political interference, of which Peronism was only one phase. See Tulio Halperin Donghi, *Historia de la Universidad de Buenos Aires* (Buenos Aires: Eudeba, 1962).

13. In the aftermath of such an experience, Argentina's universities have been particularly concerned to have their autonomy protected from the national government, and some feel that the universities still do not have adequate protection from government intervention. See Jose Luis Cantini, *La Autonomia y Autarquia de las Universidades Nacionales* (Buenos Aires: Academia Nacional de Educación, 1997), 15 and 97–102. On the other hand, in being shielded from oversight, much like a private university, Argentina's research universities, like the University of Buenos Aires, sometimes engage in authoritarian and questionable practices, as, for example, with regard to tenure.

14. Merilee S. Grindle, *Despite the Odds: The Contentious Politics of Education Reform* (Princeton: Princeton University Press, 2004), 7.

to do with sequencing than timing because many nations reformed their economies first and their educational systems later. In the 1990s several other important Latin American nations also reformed their educational systems. Grindle has found that both the source of energy for education reform and the location of resistance in five countries (Mexico, Bolivia, Brazil [Minas Gerais], Nicaragua, and Ecuador) were similar to what we find in Argentina: initiative came from the Ministry of Education; resistance came from civil society.[15] Unlike the five countries Grindle studies, Argentina also reformed its university system. This was Menem's most important educational accomplishment. The conclusion to this chapter returns to some of the similarities between Argentina and Grindle's findings about educational reform elsewhere in Latin America.

The reforms discussed here are visionary and would have been even more constructive had they not become bogged down in unnecessary complexity inside Congress. Yet they were not presented as part of a progressive package connected with the process of social healing begun under Alfonsín. Had they been presented in that light they might have elicited less opposition. In failing to sell the reform either to Congress or to society at large, Menem revealed the limits of his leadership capacities in a democratic society.

Preparing the Groundwork

The reader will remember that Menem assumed office six months early and had only three months to name his cabinet. Nevertheless, educational reform was on his agenda. He invited Antonio Salonia to be his Minister of Education. Salonia had been subsecretary of education in the 1950s under President Frondizi (1958–62), but had not been part of Perón's government. Salonia was loosely connected with the Radical Party but called himself a "developmentalist."[16] Menem's choice of Salonia, like his selection of

---

15. Grindle does not attempt to study all of Brazil but, instead, focuses upon the state of Minas Gerais as her Brazilian example. *Despite the Odds*, 23.

16. During Frondizi's presidency the Radical Party had divided because Frondizi wanted to reach out to Peronism and reincorporate the banned and proscribed movement back into the mainstream politics of the nation. Salonia had supported Frondizi in this goal. Frondizi's faction of the Radical Party was the Union Civica Radical Intransigente (UCRI, or the Intransigent Radical Civic Union). The hard-core anti-Peronist Radical faction was the Union Civica Radical del Pueblo (UCRP, or the People's Radical Civic Unión). My understanding of Salonia's and Menem's conversations about educational reform draws upon interviews with Antonio Salonia. I interviewed him several times at the school where he was the principal in Buenos Aires (on April 27, May 16, and May 21, 2008).

Jorge Triaca as Minister of Labor, exemplified his willingness to staff his cabinet with men of vision, regardless of their specific political loyalties.[17] Frondizi's presidency had overseen the creation of a few private liberal arts colleges, known as "private universities," that awarded only bachelor's degrees.[18] They were a parallel, complementary system for awarding the bachelor's degree outside of the state-run system. The number of private colleges created under Frondizi did not meet the need for classroom seats, and few colleges had been founded since. Argentina's higher education system fell far short of providing the number of seats the nation needed. Menem's educational agenda picked up where Frondizi's program had left off, starting with higher education. Working through the Ministry of Education, Argentina would accredit a series of private colleges. Each proposal for a college would be reviewed by the ministry. The national government was the only entity that could legally accredit new colleges, or "universities," as they were called in Argentina. The process of review for accreditation would allow the government to control quality. Again we see how Menem's presidential agenda was influenced by a previous democratic government, a characteristic that Mark Peterson ascribes to presidents in the United States. Here Menem picked up where a much earlier president had left off; part of Menem's agenda was shaped by Frondizi's efforts, including those that failed.[19]

In conversations before Menem took office, Salonia argued that the proposed system of private colleges would not undermine the prestigious public university system that Argentina already had and was not an effort

---

17. John Kennedy was also known for bringing into his administration men who had previously been opponents and for convincing them to work with him. See Schlesinger, *Thousand Days*, 687. A key example of this pattern was his decision to make Johnson his vice president, despite the distance and tension that had existed between them. See Caro, *Master of the Senate*.

18. Frondizi argued that private education could bring greater choice to Argentine education. The idea met with vehement resistance. Antonio F. Salonia, "Decentralización Educativa, Participación y Democracia: Escuela Autonóma y Ciudanía Responsable," in *Educación y Política en la Argentina* (Buenos Aires: Academia Nacional de Educación, Santillana, 2002), 167–212.

19. Mark Peterson writes that understanding a president's personal agenda is difficult because he or she creates that agenda in the context of knowing what has been tried before, what policies have succeeded or failed, and what options exist in the immediate context. Menem knew that privatization reforms to education had been attempted in the past and had succeeded only to a limited extent. He also knew what values and goals Salonia would hold if he were brought into the administration. Likewise, Menem was aware that Argentina's higher educational system was woefully inadequate to its task, and he hoped to modernize it, just as he sought to modernize the economy. Thus, to say that Menem was persuaded by Salonia's ideas ignores the possibility that Menem was already leaning in the direction that Salonia would want to go. He was persuaded, rather, that Salonia would and could launch the kind of educational reforms that were in keeping with the rest of Menem's overall agenda.

to drain resources away from the national university. The private colleges would be self-supporting to a considerable extent and would have access to many sources of funding unavailable to the public universities. For example, tuition was free at the public universities, but the private colleges would charge tuition. This revenue would provide an important source of financial support for the private colleges. Salonia argued as well that the quality of education in the private colleges could be quite high because of state oversight. Therefore, the private colleges would augment and not undermine the quality of higher education in Argentina. At the base of his argument, however, Salonia exhibited a belief in the value of private education at the university and college level. His opinion was that private education was a benefit in its own right and that alternative, private sources for obtaining a university education should be available in Argentina, quite apart from the state-run public education system.

Salonia argued for openness in higher education, and he suggested that developing a series of high-quality liberal arts colleges was the way to achieve greater openness. Increased access would allow students to choose where they went to school and allow faculty members to seek work in a variety of institutions. Neither the educational paths of the students nor the career paths of the faculty would be constrained to a single model within a state system of public higher education. Different colleges would be able to specialize in different academic areas. Specialization would then allow students to pick and choose where they went to school, selecting a college that was particularly strong in the subject(s) they wanted to study. Specialization would also allow faculty to migrate to schools that emphasized their own areas of expertise, and groups of specialized faculty could congregate in the same institution and provide each other a higher level of mutual support than would otherwise be possible.

Having a series of private liberal arts colleges accredited to award the BA would expand the number of seats available inside the system of higher education and not place the entire burden of providing higher education on the state. This argument was particularly pertinent in the atmosphere of economic collapse that predominated as Menem won the election, assembled his cabinet, and prepared to take office. In that context, the state clearly did not have the resources to expand the availability of a university education at the level that was necessary in the modernized economy Menem envisioned. Passing a portion of the responsibility for higher education off to the private sector, while continuing to support the public universities with as many resources as possible, was a way of expanding access to higher education across the entire population. The argument was for a "both/and" approach—for private colleges and the University of Buenos Aires as well as other public universities nationwide.[20] A desire for privatization of part of Argentina's system of higher education fit with Menem's overall agenda of privatization and a reduction of the state burden.

Private colleges would allow Argentina to develop some schools oriented around core values shared by sectors of the population. Some college students might like to attend a Jewish college and have a college education that incorporates Jewish values or aspects of religious education. Under the state public university system this option was impossible because the public universities were constitutionally mandated to be secular. But Salonia believed that the freedom to choose religious education should be available to Argentina's young people. The existence of private colleges, some of which could be managed by churches or religious institutions, would allow this freedom of choice in higher education. It would also provide

---

20. Gutmann also favors a "both/and" approach to higher education, arguing that both public and private universities make essential contributions to democracy. She argues that private universities are more protected from the winds of politics and the destructiveness of momentary fads that overtake public opinion. For example, the antitax phobia that spread through the United States and various individual states in the 1990s resulted in antitax laws and anti–property tax laws that had a devastating effect on state universities. Moreover, the use of ballot referenda to make these changes allowed the antitax voices to bypass the normal political process of dialogue and debate that normally takes place inside the institutions of state government. These winds of public opinion can and do devastate public universities and public university systems. In 1992, an antitax amendment passed in Colorado by referendum greatly limited the resources available to the University of Colorado. Over the next several years, the university suffered a decline from which it has never recovered. In some departments, including political science, there was a massive exodus of excellent faculty who easily found jobs in more hospitable state environments. This scenario has recurred in many other states. Meanwhile, argue Gutmann and Thompson, private universities are free of the threat that comes from public opinion fads because they depend less upon public resources.

On the other hand, private universities can develop closed and protected systems of decision making that exclude certain individuals, minorities, or women and, being free of public scrutiny, can perpetuate such discrimination for long periods of time. Public universities, in contrast, being perpetually subject to public scrutiny, theoretically have a much harder time engaging in that type of prejudice and exclusion for a long time. There are, of course, exceptions to these general rules. There are situations in which a private university has achieved a higher degree of openness and tolerance while a public university has both lower resources and a higher degree of internal exclusion and prejudice. These differences are then attributable to regional and contextual pressures. A private university in a progressive region might achieve greater openness than a public university in a backward, conservative region.

At the same time, a severe economic downturn can devastate private universities, as it did in the United States in the late 2000s. At times, public universities might weather an economic downturn better because of their lower private endowments and greater diversity in their funding sources. These various considerations are several of the advantages and disadvantages that Gutmann points out as generalized rules about higher education and reasons that society is best served by having both a private and a public system of higher education. See Gutmann, *Democratic Education*.

yet another source of resources for higher education and another channel through which nonstate resources could be funneled into higher education. Through this channel, churches, synagogues, and other religious organizations could fund or help fund colleges of their choice. At the same time, however, the quality of these colleges would be overseen at the point of establishment and periodically reviewed by the Ministry of Education. The accreditation and periodic reaccreditation process would ensure that these colleges met a certain basic minimum standard for the provision of high quality education and did not sacrifice educational quality while seeking some degree of religious education.

Freedom of choice was a fundamental element of the educational reforms, choice for students and their families and choice for faculty members as well. Salonia would later call the law he proposed the "Freedom to Teach" law, although that literal translation is confusing and misleading.[21] A more appropriate translation would be the "Law on Academic Freedom," which more accurately captures the intent of the law. The closed, rigid, hierarchical university system that had grown up inside an authoritarian nation with only one system of higher education had allowed power abuse to go undetected and unchecked within Argentina's universities. All universities and university systems are subject to a certain amount of "old boy networking," by which certain individuals attain favors (or promotion, or tenure) because of their personal networks; others in positions of power are able to close out or punish individuals who disagree with them or who have challenged their power or their particular academic perspective. These abuses were rampant inside the state university system. Academic freedom and even academic quality were often sacrificed to "old boy" power-holders. Tellingly, the term "academic freedom" does not even translate into Spanish, but this was one goal of the proposed reforms.

The various arguments that Salonia made in favor of private education resonated with Menem's economic goals. Menem sought to free the state from being the sole provider of services across a variety of sectors. While freedom of choice and academic freedom were Salonia's goals, lessening the state's burden was Menem's. Menem was pleased with many of Salonia's arguments. He gave the new minister of education considerable latitude on educational reform. Salonia served as Minister of Education from 1989 to

---

21. La Ley de Libertad de Enseñanza. A similar law was approved in 1958, Law 14.557. However, like many laws on the books in Argentina, it had little real impact because too few universities existed to give students and professors educational and professional options. The effort during the Menem years was to make the law have substantive impact by offering real university options.

1992, outlasting many of the other first ministers that Menem chose for the other offices.

Academic Freedom and Beyond: Reforms to Higher Education and Vocational Training

Menem's reforms began with increased support for the universities. Despite the prevailing economic crisis, between 1991 and 1996 investment in public universities grew from $783,991 to $1,771,484 annually (see table 7.1). Moreover, nine colleges were created between the beginning of Menem's first term in office in 1989 and the first year of his second term in 1996 (see table 7.2)

The Creation of Private Liberal Arts Colleges

We begin by looking at the process of higher education reform, another example of institutionally driven democratization. The Ministry of Education put out a call for college proposals and received a strong response. In the first year it reviewed many proposals. Most were rejected; several dozen were accepted and those applicants received permission to establish a college. Private colleges soon blossomed, particularly in Buenos Aires. All were smaller than the University of Buenos Aires (UBA) and many specialized in the social sciences, business education, or prelaw. Some were quite expensive and exclusive while others were larger and less expensive. As in the United States, the private colleges offered a more limited selection of courses than the public universities but featured smaller class sizes and closer faculty attention. Among them were colleges with a religious affiliation.

TABLE 7.1. Budget for National Universities, by Year, 1991–1996

Year	Budget in Millions of Dollars
1991	783,991
1992	990,446
1993	1,395,235
1994	1,617,977
1995	1,716,291
1996	1,771,484

Source: Annuario de Estadisticas Universitarios (Buenos Aires: Ministerio de Cultura y Educación, 1996), 147.

TABLE 7.2. Name and Founding Date
of National (State-Funded) Universities,
Argentina

Name of University	Date Created
Cordoba	1613
Buenos Aires	1821
La Plata	1890
Tucumán	1912
Litoral	1919
Cuyo	1939
Technológica	1948
Sur	1956
Nordeste	1956
Rosario	1968
Río Cuarto	1971
Comahue	1971
Salta	1972
Catamarca	1972
Lomas de Zamora	1972
Luján	1972
La Pampa	1973
Misiones	1973
San Juan	1973
San Luis	1973
Santiago del Estero	1973
Entre Ríos	1973
Jujuy	1973
Centro	1974
Mar del Plata	1975
Patagonia	1980
Formosa	1988
La Matanza	1989
Quilmes	1989
General San Martin	1992
La Rioja	1994
Patagonia Austral	1994
Villa María	1995
General Sarmiento	1995
Lanús	1995
Tres de Febrero	1995

Source: Nuevas Universidades Para un Nuevo Pais (Buenos Aires: Editorial Estrada, 1971); and *Universidad y Sistema Educativo: Libertad y Compromiso* (Buenos Aires: Editorial Cinae, 1983).

Fears that private colleges would vacate the public universities were unfounded. There was more demand for seats in university and college classrooms than the public universities could provide. Enrollment in higher education grew. The private colleges were intended as places of under-graduate training. However, some developed master's programs. None undertook doctoral training. The UBA lacked enough faculty to provide supervision for dissertations in the various fields of social science and the humanities but began awarding a cross-disciplinary PhD. Prior to that step the doctorate had not been available in Argentina, and students seeking it studied abroad.[22] In many instances, they never returned. The educational reforms also placed pressure on the UBA and other public universities to improve undergraduate education and faculty treatment.

Another important result is that Argentina now has more academic employment options for faculty. Some schools emphasized the percentage of their faculty who hold the doctorate as a point of attraction for students. Moreover, the process of oversight and reaccreditation that these schools must undergo regularly is now taking into account the percentage of faculty who hold doctorates. These multiple employment options mean that Argentina suffers less brain drain than it has in the past.[23] Argentina still

---

22. The doctorate awarded by the UBA as of this study is not at all comparable to the specialized doctorate awarded in the United States in the various fields of social science and the humanities. Students do not receive in-depth training in any field of the social sciences and do not take comprehensive exams to demonstrate their mastery of the field. However, students do conduct extensive research for a dissertation, and the dissertation, both at the research stage and during writing, is closely supervised by a doctoral chair and committee. In this sense, the UBA program allows students to move forward with research and with an original contribution in their area of expertise. The advent of serious research in Argentina constitutes a significant step forward. Although the Argentine doctorate is not at all competitive by international standards, it is a significant step forward by domestic standards. It allows the country to move toward training their own research scholars rather than depending on foreign universities to train their scholars, researchers, and university teachers.

In the spring semester of 2008, I had the privilege of serving as a Fulbright Scholar at the University of Buenos Aires in Argentina. Apart from conducting the research for this book, my responsibilities included teaching a doctoral-level seminar in political science (comparative politics) for students who had already been admitted to the doctoral program at the UBA. The UBA doctoral seminar was a completely delightful experience. The students were of high quality and could have held their own in most doctoral programs in the United States. Additionally, I spent many hours talking with Pablo Alabarceres, rector of the doctoral program in the social sciences at the UBA. We discussed both the strengths and limitations of the program he oversaw and compared its various details to the details of doctoral training in the United States. I am indebted to him for much of the knowledge and insight I have gained about the current state of higher education and doctoral training in Argentina. Other conversations with Andrés Fontana, Dean of Graduate Studies at the University of Belgrano, helped me understand both the contributions and the limitations of the private colleges.

23. Brain drain is still a serious problem for Argentina, and the Academy of Education

has room for improvement in making its academic positions attractive to faculty. In particular, it needs to improve salaries and award tenure, two key advantages of academic employment abroad that continue to keep faculty who have the doctorate from returning to Argentina. Another is research support. But the simple fact of offering alternative choices for academic employment represents a significant step forward from the 1980s, when the public universities were the only source of academic employment in Argentina.

Not all of Salonia's university reforms were successful. He proposed, for example, that undergraduate students at the University of Buenos Aires should pay tuition, or even a small fraction of the cost of their education, for attending class at the public university. His proposal was also directed toward the other public universities. In this proposal, he encountered intransigent opposition. Although the UBA and other universities pay their faculty a tiny salary, ideological commitments to free university education predominated. Undergraduate students, most of whom are middle class, do not pay tuition at the public universities; graduate students are required to pay tuition. In this disagreement, the public universities fell back on the argument that they were and should be autonomous, even though paying tuition would greatly improve the quality of the education.

Community Colleges and Vocational Training

The decision to establish a series of private liberal arts colleges represented an important educational reform for Argentina, one that brought many advantages. However, the reform itself could also be criticized on the basis of class: it primarily benefits the middle class. In response to this challenge, Law 24.521 created community colleges in different locations throughout the nation. These new institutions allowed access to higher education for students who would have been disinclined or unable to enroll full time in a university or liberal arts college.[24] This reform touched workers who could now enter college long after they had left high school and even while they were working full time. This change expanded the opportunity structure for workers. One of the original criticisms that Peronism had made of the nation's university system in the 1940s was that it primarily served

---

keeps careful account of the number of doctorate holders who leave Argentina for employment abroad. The Academy of Education figures include numbers of Argentines awarded PhD degrees and, among them, the number who have returned to Argentina permanently versus the number who have remained abroad.

24. On the creation of community colleges, see Taquini, *La Transformación*, esp. 187–224.

the middle class while closing out workers. Community colleges addressed this criticism. Menem's administration improved the quality of university education and also increased university access.

A third reform focused on the Workers University, established by Perón in the 1940s. The Ministry of Education revamped it to deliver vocational education skills selected in communication with the Ministry of the Economy and the ongoing effort there to privatize, modernize, and improve efficiency in industry. The Ministry of Education also established vocational training centers in other parts of Argentina. Community colleges and vocational schools expanded opportunities for labor, although Menem did poorly in advertising these opportunities when he gathered labor leaders together to announce privatization. It was not his only failure of rhetoric or of public presentation of his policies.

The reforms to higher education were remarkable as a goal but limited in the process by which they were put in place. They established much-needed reform at the level of higher education, reforms that broadened access and gave workers and young people opportunities they had never had before. But, ironically, the very newness of the reforms, the creation of something new rather than the reform of a system already in place, meant that they could be conducted in a top-down fashion from within the Menem administration and without the involvement of Congress. The reform itself was democratic while the method of putting it in place remained highly centralized. This had also been true of Menem's labor reforms. This top-down approach would change as the Ministry of Education moved toward reforming K-12 education, where the need to involve Congress was much greater.

K-12 Reforms

The initiative for K-12 reform came from the Ministry of Education in response to a recommendation from the United Nations. UNESCO sent a team of visitors who proposed that Argentina emulate an education decentralization reform already in place in Spain.[25] The reform would allow provinces to make changes to the local curriculum in accordance with local needs and priorities.[26] Following the Spanish example and the UN suggestion, the Ministry of Education proposed a bill that permit-

---

25. Increased local participation has been shown to be important in increasing the quality of K-12 education. See Siddle Walker, *Their Highest Potential*.

26. A key problem with Argentina's educational system was the lack of participation among

ted decentralization of the educational system already in place. The hope
was to make primary and secondary education more relevant to particular
localities and to decrease centralized control from the federal government.
It was to have been a democratic reform to K-12 education just as the
previous reform had democratized higher education. But reform to K-12
education was more complicated and involved interests from all over the
country. It could not be put in place by the Ministry of Education alone.
Instead it required coalition building across both Congress and society
itself. Moreover, Menem was asking Congress to give up some portion of
its power: its centralized control over education. Menem asked the Ministry of Education to draft a law and send it to Congress, but he failed to lay
the groundwork for congressional support.

An extended process developed inside the legislature in response to the
proposed law. The reader will recall the nearly four years of debate over
labor reform after Congress rejected the Mucci bill. Now Congress established committees to rewrite the education bill. The committee process
alone took two years. Subsequently, the bill saw extensive debate and further reform on the floor of the legislature. Instead of small decentralization
changes, Congress's bill changed the K-12 educational system. In place of
primary and secondary education, not unlike grade school, middle school,
and high school in the United States, Congress established a "polimodal"
system of one year of kindergarten, seven years of "basic" education, and
two years of secondary training. The changes increased the number of primary years of education by one and decreased the number of secondary
years by one. The changes also required teachers to instruct in a variety of
new technical areas for which they were not trained.[27] The Law on Federalization of Education made K-12 education much more complex and
greatly increased the demands on teachers.[28]

The only part of the original ministry bill that survived legislative changes was the section on federalization. Under the new law, fiscal
responsibility for K-12 education would pass from the federal government
to the provinces. Therefore, schools all over Argentina moved into a situation of fewer fiscal resources and greater demands and complexity inside

---

the provinces in designing local education. The reform was intended to address this issue.
Salonia, "Decentralización," 194.

27. For the reasoning behind the polimodal system, see Mabel M. de Rosetti, *La Teoría de
los Polisistemas en el Área Educativa* (Buenos Aires: Academia Nacionál de Educación, 1996).

28. For the text of the law and comments on it, see Alfredo M. van Gelderen, *La Ley Federal
de Educación de la República Argentina* (Buenos Aires: Academia Nacionál de Educación, 1996).

the classroom. It was far more than either Menem or Salonia intended. Salonia came to oppose this bill but had no veto power; Menem refused to veto the law. It went into effect and received widespread opposition all over Argentina.

Vehement opposition to the new law came from CTERA, the largest national teacher's union.[29] CTERA has sympathetic ties to the Peronist labor unions but is more leftist and less bound to the Peronist Party. CTERA's greater independence lies in its history. It was a self-starting union organized at the grassroots level after Perón left power and without help or guidance from the state. CTERA was founded in 1957, and teachers organized themselves first along provincial lines. They unified themselves into the national union in 1973. Their organizational background is horizontal rather than vertical, and the history of their organization is characterized by grassroots initiative and base-level leadership. They have never been tied to the state or the Peronist Party in the same manner as the blue-collar labor unions.[30]

Menem lacked the corporate control over CTERA that he held over the labor unions. CTERA's independence made it impossible for him to exercise the same level of control, even if he had had a rationale for it. He had no law that allowed him to remove the head of CTERA for disagreeing with the government. Multiple teachers' unions and grassroots elections would have immediately provided alternative leadership. Moreover, educational reform was less urgent than economic reform, and there was no reason for Menem to exercise corporate control over the teachers even if he had wanted to. Instead, Menem needed a different kind of skill, one that depended primarily upon the capacity to build a voluntary coalition. He needed to build a coalition of supportive voices inside society, especially among teachers and parents. He needed to build support for his reform

---

29. Salonia suggests that educational reform in Argentina requires a continuous process of dialogue and participation. Federal laws should never be treated as absolutes. See Antonio Salonia, "El Sistema de Técnicos y Burocratas al Sistema Abierto y Participativo," in Academia Nacionál, *Educación y Política en Argentina* (Buenos Aires: Academia Nacionál de Educación, 2002), 285–87, and esp. 291.

30. Vazquez and Balduzzi, *De apóstoles a trabajadores: Luchas por la unidad sindical docente 1953–1973. Historia de CTERA I* (Buenos Aires: Instituto de Investigaciones Pedagógicas Marina Vilte, Confederacion de Trabajadores de la Education en la Republica Argentina, 2000). In an extended interview with Francisco Nenna, adjunct secretary (the number 2 leader) of CTERA, Nenna commented, comparing CTERA with the blue-collar unions, "We are different from the Peronist unions. We are trying to move away from personalism. We emphasize cooperation more fully. We see ourselves as a team, and we try to work together as such." Also see note 31.

policy, just as any democratic administration in any presidential democracy needs to build a coalition around any major reform. Menem needed and did not have rhetoric that would sell his reform broadly.

CTERA's opposition focused on the expense of the reforms, the demands made on teachers, and low salaries. They were outraged that the law did not substantially increase salaries; they now demanded higher salaries, particularly in view of the new teaching requirements. CTERA was also predisposed to oppose any reform in which Salonia had been involved. Although CTERA is not part of the system of higher education, many CTERA leaders opposed the creation of private universities on ideological grounds, believing that all education should be free. They had also opposed all of Menem's privatization reforms for similar ideological reasons. Opposition to the Law on Federalization of Education was their chance to strike out at both Menem and Salonia.

There were also legitimate grounds for the teachers' opposition, just as there had been legitimate grounds for worker opposition to privatization. The teachers recognized that the reforms would greatly increase the expense of delivering basic education. They recognized, as well, that the reform was targeting the local level without providing adequate fiscal provisions for resources at that level. Congress had written law without working closely with the Ministries of Education and the Economy to make sure that the resources needed to implement the reforms would be available at the provincial level. They had also failed to solicit the opinion and expertise of teachers in their constituencies. Ironically, the executive branch, in creating labor reform, had solicited more input from labor than Congress had solicited from teachers in writing education reform. Congress had created an impossible situation. It had passed a law that reflected little awareness of local realities and that was disconnected from the resource base available for education at that time. Additional opposition came from the provinces. The polimodal aspect of reform, more than decentralization, generated provincial opposition. Local authorities would have embraced an opportunity to have more control over local education, but they were not willing to make extensive additional demands on their teachers. The polimodal reforms required more classrooms and other kinds of physical plant changes for which the provinces did not have the resources and for which the Congress did not provide the resources.

K-12 education reform, like human rights policy, was a moment during the transition years where Congress was given the latitude to write policy, something it would have in a classic presidential system but which it does not have in the parliamentary guise that system assumes in Argentina. In each case, Congress committed major blunders. Were Argentina's Congress granted more opportunities actually to write policy, as the U.S. Congress does, it would undoubtedly become more skilled at doing so and less likely to create cumbersome policies that subsequently need to be undone.

There were also some progressive elements to K-12 educational policy as written by Congress. The teachers also opposed these. The reader will remember that there had been conflict between Menem and the labor unions on the Law on Flexibilization of Labor, a movement toward making labor requirements less rigid inside the workplace. Once "flexibility" had been introduced, companies could move workers around to achieve maximum efficiency and productivity. In the conflict with the teachers' union, the Menem government experienced a similar battle. Under the old system, seniority predominated, allowing more senior teachers to take the best posts and to control their more junior colleagues. Under the old system, only seniority and work experience mattered in teaching appointments and promotions. Now Congress established a teacher-oriented version of labor flexibilization. Stellar teaching accomplishments, innovation, and creativity could justify placing a new teacher in a desirable teaching position even if that new teacher were younger and less experienced than other candidates. CTERA adamantly opposed this reform. They argued that this new method of selecting teachers for posts broke the internal unity of the teachers' union. Quite possibly, what it actually broke was the absolutist control of the old hierarchy inside the school system.[31]

Another objection to the Law of Federalization of Education concerned the uneven nature of resources available nationwide. According to the law as it emerged from Congress, there would be extensive differences in the resources available for primary and secondary education across the provinces. This difference would emerge from the federalization aspect of the bill. Under the reform, wealthy provinces would retain their own resources and put them into education while less wealthy provinces would have fewer resources to support education. The original system had avoided this disparity. While education had been controlled by the federal government, all resources for preuniversity education were funneled through the central government. In that process, resources were spread evenly across the provinces and an equalization process resulted. Wealthier provinces received fewer resources from the central government than they had put in, and

---

31. In subsequent years, this aspect of the reform has been more difficult to reverse. While the polimodular aspect of educational reform is being abandoned, rewarding teachers based solely on seniority has decreased. Interview with Francisco Nenna, Buenos Aires, CTERA headquarters, April 25, 2008.

poorer provinces received more resources than they had contributed. The result was that educational quality across the nation was more even than it would otherwise have been. With the Law of Federalization of Education, this leveling process ended.

Although Salonia opposed the polimodal reforms to education and had proposed a much simpler set of changes, he did not foresee the extreme reaction from teachers nationwide. A large part of that response concerned salaries. During the Menem years, teachers' salaries were notoriously low; teachers could not live on the wages they received.[32] When they opposed the educational reforms, a significant dimension of their discourse addressed salary issues. They wanted higher salaries, and any reform that did not include a raise was not acceptable to them. However, the Ministry of Education lacked the authority to raise teachers' salaries, and the Ministry of the Economy refused to do so. CTERA might have concentrated too much energy on salaries when the overall picture of educational reform was more complex. However, the Ministry of Education might have been more successful with the reforms had they brought the teachers into dialogue, just as the Ministry of Labor had done with the union leaders. Instead, unlike the privatization reforms, dialogue was left to Congress, where teachers were not adequately included.

As with the reform packages offered labor, with the educational reforms Menem missed an opportunity for inclusive rhetoric and coalition building that might have dispelled opposition. The educational reforms might have received more support had they been presented as part of an overall social reform package that linked state responsibility for worker benefits, increased public access to and involvement with education, and included steps toward reparational justice. That approach might have been particularly effective against a truly leftist opponent, which the labor unions were not. CTERA might have felt uncomfortable opposing a reform package that included special educational benefits for children of the disappeared and educational opportunities for newly unemployed workers. Instead, presented as a top-down reform and lacking a better rhetorical appeal, the reform became yet another example where reforms initiated by the state met opposition in civil society.

---

32. This is a controversial point. Is K-12 teaching a part-time (three-quarters) job that offers a supplementary income in conjunction with the income of another breadwinner in the family? If so, then teachers do not need to live on their salaries. Or is teaching a full-time job intended to be able to support a family? Grindle addresses this issue when she suggests that Latin America's teachers were *not* underpaid, given the hours they worked. Argentina's teachers clearly felt that teaching was a full-time job, and one for which the salary should be high enough to support a family.

In the face of this uproar, Salonia offered to resign. He suggested that a Peronist Minister of Education might be able to accomplish more. Menem accepted Salonia's resignation and appointed a new minister, Jorge Rodriguez. Salonia's resignation did not end the conflict between CTERA and Menem's government. The worst aspect of that confrontation came later. In 1997, several years after Salonia's resignation, CTERA launched a "permanent" two-year strike against the Menem government over teachers' salaries. This strike lasted from 1997 to 1999, during which time the teachers camped permanently on the plaza in front of the Congress, living in a series of large white tents. To their credit, they had finally begun to see the Congress, rather than the executive, as the source of the reform to which they objected so vehemently. According to CTERA, this strike was managed so that classes were never disrupted, but the strike was a permanent statement of opposition to Menem's educational policies. The teachers rotated so that some were always living on the plaza "on strike" while, back in their home districts, others worked overtime to cover their classes. According to CTERA, this long-term, sustained strike against Menem made a significant contribution to ending the Menem presidency, rendering impossible the third term he so desperately desired. The permanent CTERA strike became one more reflection of public opinion, indicating that public patience with Menem and his reforms had finally ended. CTERA was very proud of its role in helping to remove Menem from office.

Viewed in conjunction with the labor reforms studied in the previous chapter, the educational reforms reveal some surprising and counterintuitive findings. In the previous chapter the Menem administration largely bypassed Congress in making labor reform. Although each labor law was passed through Congress and approved there, the real debate and dialogue needed to gain labor support took place inside the Labor Ministry rather than in Congress, where Madison thought useful deliberation would occur. Yet when Congress was given the chance to be included once again in making law, Congress was less effective at dialogue than was the executive branch and the Ministry of Labor. Congress, of course, had multiple constituency concerns of its own. Legislators may have had reasons for making the polimodal changes they made. After all, Menem was asking Congress to give up power in one of the few policy areas where it still retained influence. But the Law on the Federalization of Education was approved without adequate dialogue or public explanation. Madison had hoped for something better from a legislature.

The Educational Reforms in Comparative Context

Before concluding this chapter, we are able to consider Argentina's educational reforms in a comparative context owing to the work of Merilee Grindle. Just as privatization was on the agenda across other Latin American nations, so was educational reform in the 1990s.[33] Grindle also found that teachers and teachers' unions constituted the most vociferous opposition to educational reform in other countries. Teachers resisted any reforms that diminished their control over changes and improvements in the classroom. They resisted the involvement of other actors, including parents and local communities, even when consumers had an obvious interest in educational improvement. Teachers' unions resisted reform that did not focus primarily on salaries, and they resisted reform for ideological reasons.[34] All of these characteristics describe the response of Argentina's teachers, particularly CTERA, to Menem's reforms, although Argentina was not one of Grindle's cases. If CTERA was particularly prone to extreme and dogmatic opposition to reform, it was certainly not alone in its resistance.[35]

Full consideration of CTERA's opposition to educational reform depends on recognition that Argentina already had one of the best primary educational systems in Latin America before Menem's arrival. UNESCO statistics placed Argentina at the top of most educational achievement charts in Latin America. Argentina had low rates of illiteracy, already only 14 percent in 1950 and down to 4 percent in 1990, before the Menem reforms. Additionally, while many Latin American nations had inefficient primary school systems, with students in seventh grade demonstrating only fourth-grade learning levels, Argentina had one of the most efficient primary educational systems in the region. Moreover, Argentina stood at the top of student achievement levels in language learning and mathematics.[36] These statistics place CTERA's position in regional perspective and offer a strong argument for raising salaries.

Additionally, Grindle writes that all teachers' unions on the continent claimed that teachers were underpaid. The truth of that claim bears investigation. Salaries were low if one considers annual pay rates, but they were not low if one factors in the number of hours worked across a calendar year, including months when schools are closed.[37] Grindle's argument here refers

---

33. Grindle, *Despite the Odds*.
34. Grindle, *Despite the Odds*, 58–59, 127–30, 134–39, and 165.
35. Grindle, *Despite the Odds*, 135.
36. UNESCO, *The Right to Education: Toward Education for All throughout Life* (Paris: UNESCO, 2000), 30, 141; Laboratorio Latinoamericano de Evaluación de la Calidad de Educación, 1998, 50–51, cited in Grindle, *Despite the Odds*, 30–33.
37. Grindle, *Despite the Odds*, 127–30. See also at note 32.

to the weeks of the year when schools are closed. K-12 teachers do not teach during the summer and also have no research or publishing responsibilities. She is essentially considering teaching a part-time job. However, the extent to which salaries were low also varied by country, and independent assessments by the International Labour Organization confirmed CTERA's position that teachers' salaries in Argentina were extremely low.[38] These points also place CTERA's opposition in perspective.

What is more difficult to understand or explain is CTERA's hostile reaction to the reforms to university education that did not affect their workday world at all. Grindle has written that some teacher opposition to educational reforms was purely ideological, linked to a leftist rejection of neoliberal reforms more generally, including privatization. The teachers' opposition to Salonia's creation of private universities can be explained in this manner. It seems more unreasonable than CTERA's response to the proposed K-12 reforms. CTERA believed in public education for its own sake; from that ideological perspective, any move toward private education was unacceptable.[39] Neither Salonia nor Menem shared that position.

Grindle suggests that all reforms speak to groups of winners and losers. In the case of educational reforms more generally, the winners were parents, children, and the public at large while the teachers clearly saw themselves as losers, whether or not they actually were.[40] In the struggle over reform, each side brings to bear its own perspective on winning or losing. Educational reform in Latin America was difficult, as it was in Argentina, because those who perceived themselves as losers, the teachers, were highly organized and had a long-term direct channel of influence into the ministries of education. The potential winners, however, were not organized and were often not even aware that they stood to gain from successful reform.

The same is broadly true about reform to higher education in Argentina, although whether anyone there was a direct loser is not at all clear. Faculty and staff at the UBA could have seen themselves as potential losers, but they did not launch the extensive opposition to the reforms that CTERA did. The teachers themselves were also not direct losers; indeed, their reasons for opposition to the higher education reforms were ideological rather than derived from personal concerns. Winners in the case of university reform were clearly not organized prior to the reforms because the new universities and their faculty and student bodies did not even exist at that point. But the fact that they were winners quickly became apparent once the new universities began functioning. The results of the university

---

38. Grindle, *Despite the Odds*, 130.
39. Grindle, *Despite the Odds*, 135.
40. Grindle, *Despite the Odds*, 11.

reform were different from K-12 reform: large sets of winners were readily visible while clear losers were not. This could be another reason why Salonia's reforms to higher education were more successful than his reforms to K-12 education.

This overview of educational reform elsewhere in Latin America helps us see why Argentina's educational reform was so difficult, why it was the object of opposition, where that opposition was legitimate and where it was not, and how reform differed below and at the level of higher education. Menem gave Salonia a chance to try his reforms. Salonia's success was much greater at the university level than elsewhere. Nevertheless, the reforms brought considerable positive change. Again, vision and ideas had originated within the nation's institutions, specifically from within the executive branch. Society itself resisted those reforms and was partially successful in limiting their effect. But opposition was not completely successful, and, in particular, the reforms to higher education have left a positive legacy for the nation.

Conclusion

We now conclude both this chapter and our study of the Menem years. We have a more complete view of the possibilities of democratization by institutions and we can place the educational reforms in the context of the other major reforms accomplished in the 1990s. Campaign promises and senatorial grandstanding aside, Menem entered office with a wide agenda of reform and modernization.[41] That agenda included major changes to the economy, the role of the state in society, the government's relationship with labor and the military, social services and education. To accomplish such an agenda via the institutions of state required the broadest possible coalition of support.

But Menem was less capable than Alfonsín at building broad coalitions in support of reform policy. It was a weakness that became more consequential as his administration aged and the economic crisis diminished. It became most apparent with the K-12 educational reforms. Early in his presidency Menem combined high delegative powers with crisis and built an adequate coalition in Congress from the vantage point of superior power. Given disproportionate institutional power, he was able to get his privatization reforms past Congress, although congressional support

41. Menem's inaugural speech, for example, said nothing about the broad program of economic modernization he planned to pursue. See Congreso de la Nacion, Argentina, Camara de Senadores, *Diario de Sesiones* (Buenos Aires, 1989).

diminished with time. When it came to labor reform, he largely bypassed Congress and used corporate power instead. Then Congress served mostly as a rubber stamp. He did not build a coalition, but, again, from a position of superior power, Menem could succeed. And even with higher education reform, there was legitimate reason to bypass Congress because the administration was establishing new colleges, which only the Ministry of Education could accredit, and because the affected constituency was small. But with K-12 reforms, Menem's inability to build broad support finally produced significant problems. Here he lacked either delegative powers or corporate powers and therefore entered the policy-making process from a position of greater equality. From that position he was unable to build the support he needed either within society or in Congress.

When Menem faced opposition from the teachers, he needed a coalition of support from parents. Grindle has argued that educational reform elsewhere in Latin America struggled because the teachers saw themselves as losers in the reform effort, whether or not they actually were, while the potential winners—parents, children, local citizens more generally—were not organized in support of the reforms and did not even know they were happening. Menem needed to reach out to that group, ask them to contact Congress, and build a civil society coalition in support of his reform agenda. He did not do so, and may not even have known how. As a result, the reforms went awry.

The debacle in Congress over K-12 reform should not cause us to lose sight of the value of the educational reforms as a whole. They were a step toward modernization, and the system that emerged more closely resembles an advanced industrial democracy. This is particularly true given the reforms to higher education. Menem catapulted Argentina's university system into the twenty-first century in a remarkably short period of time. At a time when higher education is under attack in many places in the United States, Argentina's effort to improve its university system raises questions about which nation is moving forward and which is not. In his impassioned plea for the preservation of higher education in the United States, Andrew Delbanco notes, "We owe it to posterity to preserve and protect this institution. Democracy depends upon it."[42]

In the educational reforms, we again see the bold exercise of executive leadership. Reform originated at the top, between the president and his minister, and then moved downward into society. As with the other reforms, grassroots sectors of society, in this case K-12 teachers, resisted reform. The struggle between Salonia and the teachers underscores both

---

42. DelBanco, *College*, 177.

the advantages and limits of institutionally driven, top-down democratization. The institutionally driven style of reform gave Salonia the authority and power to implement his vision for higher education. But when the executive branch relinquished the initiative and turned the task of writing legislation over to Congress, failure began. To make this reform succeed the executive needed to know how to work within the system of democratic institutions instead of always defying it. Menem needed to solicit and build support.

The fate of the education reforms helps explain the negative perception of Menem. His reform was democratic but his methods were not. His ability to achieve his goals through democratic means was limited. Menem did not understand the democratic process even if many of his goals enhanced democracy. Although he could successfully build a coalition inside his own party, he could not do the same in society at large or within the democratic institutions of state. Yet the rhetoric for success was only a short step away and had already been handed to him by Alfonsín.

Following on the heels of state social services, the educational reforms were a second step toward a modest welfare state and could have been presented as such both to society and to Congress. Menem had already placed unemployment coverage, health insurance, and old age pensions under state responsibility. In established democracies all of these services are part of a modern welfare state. Now the state also had greatly expanded access to higher education and was seeking to decentralize and thereby improve the quality of K-12 education.[43] As with the reforms to social services, the educational reforms could have offered small additional benefits to the children of the disappeared. That offer would have helped build congressional and social support for them.

This chapter again exemplifies the democratic potential and the autocratic failure of the Menem presidency. He found a minister of unusual vision for educational reforms that enhanced democracy, which, if they had passed, would have enhanced it further. But Menem's method was so autocratic, so steeped in habits of central control, and so unable to build coalitions around him that he failed to work successfully with Congress even when his own party controlled both chambers. Billing the educational reforms as part of the reform package would also have contributed to social healing. Menem failed to frame the educational reforms in the most positive light and preempt civil society opposition. He needed a civil society coalition of support from those who could have benefited from

---

43. Amy Gutmann has argued that K-12 public education is the first pillar of the modern welfare state. See "Distributing Public Education in a Democracy," in Amy Gutmann, *Democracy and the Welfare State* (Princeton: Princeton University Press, 1988), 107–30.

decentralized reforms. While Salonia certainly presented his reforms in a way that emphasized greater choice and access, his appeal was to Menem alone. Both leaders could have gone one step further and appealed to society itself. That appeal would have been public and general, via the media, rather than closed inside a corporate meeting room. It would have exemplified transparency and openness, characteristics quite foreign to Peronism but increasingly essential in a democratic society. Menem had already revealed himself as a skilled rhetorician. He could have presented the educational reforms, particularly the new universities and community colleges, as another form of increased access to social distribution, tied in to other progressive reforms like support for children of the disappeared and social healing. Doing so would have softened or at least weakened the opposition of the harshest critics, particularly the K-12 teachers' union. If CTERA had confronted a governmental ministry that used a rhetoric of access, social redistribution, and social healing the union would have had more difficulty demonizing either Salonia or Menem. But Peronism was weighed down by its own historical baggage. It is unskilled even at finding, much less claiming, the moral high ground. Had Menem done that, the teachers would then have been left needing to explain why they opposed reforms that increased educational access and social redistribution, enhanced local interests and helped social healing.[44] Casting the educational reforms in a language of progressive politics would have made Menem's legacy more positive.

We now end our study of the Menem years. His presidency was filled with paradox. His reforms were democratic in expanding access to higher education, in the effort to decentralize K-12 education, and in removing social services to the state. They were democratic in breaking labor's destructive hold over society. They were democratic in enhancing economic modernity, of which privatization was an essential first step. Menem was much less successful in the use of democratic process, both with respect to building congressional support or in appealing to civil society.

The Menem years have also furthered our understanding of democra-

---

44. David Crocker recommends that societies democratizing in the aftermath of gross human rights violations should offer compensation or restitution to individuals whose rights have been violated, or to their families. Such compensation should come in the form of an income bonus or medical services or enhanced educational opportunities, as, for example, in the form of a scholarship. David A. Crocker, "Truth Commissions, Transitional Justice, and Civil Society," in *Truth v. Justice: The Morality of Truth Commissions*, ed. Robert I. Rotberg and Dennis Thompson (Princeton: Princeton University Press, 2000), 99–121, esp. 106. In fact, in the aftermath of human rights violations in Chile, the Rettig Commission recommended special educational subsidies for young people who are from the families of the disappeared. See Collins, *Post-transitional Justice*.

tization by institutions and of Argentina's unique polity, partly presidential, partly parliamentary, and partly still corporate. Throughout Menem's presidency the impetus for reform came from the state. His presidency, like Alfonsín's, accomplished steps toward democratization through the use of institutions. But Menem was less able than Alfonsín to build broad support for his policies across Congress and society at large. History carried baggage for Menem, just as it did for Alfonsín. The shortcoming of the Radicals as a party and of Alfonsín as a president was their inability to develop and implement pragmatic policy, especially as concerns the economy. It cost them the presidency and has destroyed their party. The shortcoming of the Peronists as a party and of Menem as president was their inability to find a normatively appealing reason for their policies and to use rhetoric to that effect to create broad support. That failure of vision, combined with his corruption and insatiable lust for power, cost Menem the legacy of greatness he craved.

I have argued throughout this book that civil society failed to support democratization consistently during the transition years. But civil society was changing and by the end of Menem's presidency more opportunity to engage civil society might have been present. The absence of positive civil society input was partly the result of the institutional democratization process itself. A process that had not incorporated civil society when civil society was nonconstructive now failed to incorporate civil society when civil society might have been more open and constructive. The crisis was now past and democracy had begun to normalize. As a popular president leading the nation's largest political party, Menem could have done more to bring civil society on board with his reforms. He could have done that by using welfare state and human rights rhetoric to present an Argentine version of the New Deal. Menem never really gave civil society a chance to support his policies. Coming to the crisis from a hierarchical tradition where leaders are preprogrammed to prevail, he never even tried. Had he been willing to frame his reforms progressively, set aside his Peronist pride, and tie his reforms into Alfonsín's first steps toward retroactive justice, had he been willing to sell his reforms to civil society across the entire package and not just with privatization, he might well have achieved more civil society support for the reforms and more fortification for the democratic process.

PART IV

Overview and Conclusions

EIGHT

An Empirical Analysis of Executive Power

"[O]ut of the crooked timber of humanity no straight thing was ever made."

—Immanuel Kant[1]

This book has shown that Argentina's presidential system greatly favors the president within the balance of power. Within the institutional design of Argentina's presidential system, Alfonsín and Menem acted largely within their purview. Even when Congress flexed its muscles and challenged presidential power or policy, the end result was not always or not necessarily good for policy or for democracy. This was because players in Congress were sometimes nondemocratic, incompetent, or simply inexperienced. The primary responsibility for the reforms studied here and for the democratization process itself fell to the presidents. Given the fact that these two presidents had great power and sometimes should have exercised even more power, it is important to examine empirically how presidential power was used during these years. Previous chapters have looked at presidential decrees on specific policies. Here we take a broader view of presidential decrees across both presidencies, all policies, and seventeen years.

Argentina's presidents are empowered to drive the legislative agenda, but they are also allowed to make law by decree. Part of their power to

1. *Idea for a Universal History with a Cosmopolitan Purpose*, Proposition 6.

issue decrees is constitutional while part is delegated, as it was specifically in Menem's case, in response to economic crisis. Similar patterns exist in the United States. U.S. presidents have the power to issue executive orders, and in times of crisis Congress has given them additional such powers. As an indicator of the level of unilateral executive power, the executive order is the subject of scrutiny by scholars of the U.S. presidency. We can likewise scrutinize presidential decrees as an indicator of unilateral executive power in Argentina. This chapter looks at the use of decrees by Argentina's presidents and compares it with the use of executive orders by U.S. presidents.

Considerable controversy existed in Argentina over the use of presidential decrees, particularly by Carlos Menem.[2] In the United States, unilateral presidential action through executive orders has likewise excited suspicion. U.S. presidents have used executive orders to protect the nation in an emergency or for expediency when congressional obstruction thwarted them. Sometimes presidents in the United States have been delegated authority by Congress to use executive orders. In other cases, presidents have issued executive orders precisely because Congress refused to act or to move forward on a specific issue.

The Executive Order in the United States

The history of the executive order is found in the tradition of centralized, monarchical power, exactly the power the founders of the United States sought to constrain. Indeed, executive orders began in the royal tradition of the prerogative of the monarch or the "authority of the crown."[3] For that very reason they are both grounds for caution and an efficient mode of unilateral action. In the nineteenth century, when the U.S. presidency was still relatively weak owing to the cautiousness of the founding years, the use of executive orders was still new. This would change with President Lincoln. Early in his first term, at the start of the Civil War, Lincoln issued a series of orders that launched the war effort, including mustering troops, paying out treasury funds to expedite the recruitment process, and denying postal service to persons considered disloyal to the Union.[4] Dur-

---

2. The new government elected in Argentina in 2015 does not have a congressional majority, just as Alfonsín did not toward the end of his term. The new government has implemented several of its main measures through decrees. These were revised by a constitutional commission inside Congress but were, nonetheless, controversial.

3. Cooper, *By Order*, 5–6.

4. Paludan, *Presidency*, chaps. 3 and 4.

ing this time he also suspended the writ of habeas corpus. This step was potentially a threat to democracy because the writ had been inherited from the British tradition of popular government and had originally been set up to protect the population from monarchical power.[5] Lincoln suspended the writ when preparations for war were happening all around him and active sabotage of those efforts had occurred. The suspension was used to arrest persons suspected of treason, in working either against the Union war effort or for the Confederate states that had seceded.[6] Lincoln saw his task as a crisis-oriented one of saving the Union. He also acted in the first three months of the war when Congress was not in session. Questions about his actions revolved around whether anyone could suspend the writ and specifically whether the president had the authority to do so. When Congress reconvened in early 1861, it ratified many of the actions Lincoln had taken to initiate and promote the war effort, but it remained silent on the suspension of the writ of habeas corpus, neither ratifying nor rejecting Lincoln's action. Subsequently, in 1863 and after the war had been running for nearly three years, Congress passed the Habeas Corpus Act, which granted the president the authority to suspend the writ, thus ratifying his order many months after the fact.

In 1933, Congress gave FDR broad legislative powers. In that year he used those powers to confront the economic crisis.[7] Starting in 1940, he then used his war powers first to help the allies against Germany and then to promote the national war effort itself. In both cases FDR had the consent of Congress broadly speaking, although he would soon confront congressional opposition on various particulars.[8] But both Truman and Ken-

---

5. Lincoln's act was challenged on legal grounds by Chief Justice Roger Taney, who argued publicly that the president lacked the authority to suspend the writ. Lincoln, who was himself a lawyer, responded that the Constitution was too important to be left up to interpretation by a justice who defended slavery while denying the president's authority to save the Union. Paludan says that Lincoln was correct in his interpretation of the Constitution and that Taney was wrong. Lincoln's interpretation of the Constitution was supported by several well-known legal authorities, including "the professor of Constitutional law at Harvard, the leading Constitutional law lawyer in Congress and leaders of the American bar." Nevertheless, Lincoln's action remained startling and controversial. Paludan, *Presidency*, 71–79.

6. Paludan further argues that although the suspension of the writ was itself an extreme act, it was generally enforced lightly *Presidency*, 73–75.

7. When FDR was sworn in as president in March 1933, there were 14 million unemployed in the United States, 5,000 banks had closed, 100,000 businesses were bankrupt, and the "[l]ifelong savings of millions of individuals" had been wiped out. "In the air was a feeling of panic and doubt whether this nation, or any nation, could survive as a democracy." Hardeman and Bacon, *Rayburn*, 147.

8. FDR also used unilateral presidential action to intern 170,000 Japanese Americans. Today the United States is still wrestling over the ethics of this action. On internment, see

nedy issued executive orders to establish civil rights legislation precisely because Congress, and more specifically the Senate, dominated by Southern senators, refused to pass any civil rights bills.[9] In these cases executive orders were used for progressive purposes but without the consent of both chambers of Congress.[10] On the other hand, Reagan issued an executive order in February 1981 that caused sweeping reform of the federal regulatory process and greatly scaled back the ability of the government to regulate agencies and processes for any reason.[11] In essence Reagan used broad executive power to undermine and restrict the power of the executive branch more generally.

In one of the more extreme examples of the use of presidential power, Kennedy issued an executive order to establish the Peace Corps and then used discretionary presidential funds to finance it.[12] His decision to do so seems more questionable than FDR's executive orders or Truman's and Kennedy's orders on civil rights; with respect to the Peace Corps, Congress had not delegated Kennedy the authority to act in this fashion and he had not confronted congressional obstruction on this particular issue. However, he had met sustained opposition more generally to progressive measures from the Dixiecrat senators that FDR and Truman had faced previously. In Kennedy's case the southern senators used procedural measures to block his entire program from being considered on the floor of the House. Dixiecrats dominated the House Rules Committee and used that power to prevent Kennedy's program from coming up for debate. Sam Rayburn, Speaker of the House and a Texas Democrat who did support Kennedy, finally solved that problem by enlarging the size of the Rules Committee but only after a long, hard fight.[13] The rules of House procedure are not meant to be used to block the entire agenda of an elected president, but Dixiecrats were using them in precisely this manner. Kennedy might have felt that a Peace Corps bill would have met with the same obstruction as all of the other progressive measures he had proposed, and he might also have felt a need for speed after the Cuban Revolution. Whatever his reasons,

Cooper, *By Order*, 39–40. On reparations, see Yamamoto, Kim, and Holden, "American Reparations Theory."

9. Mayer, *With the Stroke of a Pen*, 5, 8, 190. The practice of creating civil rights law by executive order began with FDR but was taken much further by Truman and Kennedy. Mayer, *With the Stroke of a Pen*, 88. See also Caro, *Master of the Senate*, chap. 6.

10. The House of Representatives did, in fact, pass civil rights legislation multiple times during the 1940s and 1950s but the bills always died on the Senate floor due to the opposition of southern senators.

11. Mayer, *With the Stroke of a Pen*, 35, 126–30.

12. Mayer, *With the Stroke of a Pen*, 88.

13. Hardeman and Bacon, *Rayburn*, 448–65.

he acted unilaterally, and Congress subsequently approved his act. These examples illustrate that executive orders in the United States, and the reasons for them, fit no single category or description. Some have been progressive and others conservative. Some have potentially threatened democracy while also saving the nation. Some have had congressional consent while others have been explicitly against the wishes of one congressional chamber. Executive orders are complex and multifaceted. The extent to which they can be justified lies very much in the perception and values of the observer. But because of their complexity, they cannot be either condemned or embraced in blanket fashion. Instead, they must be considered in context.[14]

Much the same can be said about the presidential decrees issued during the years under consideration here, including many of those issued by Menem. Both Alfonsín and Menem faced crisis and the need for speed that often accompanies crisis. They also enjoyed support from Congress and also encountered obstructive opposition in Congress. This book has shown that both were true at different times during the seventeen-year transition period. Additionally, unlike in the United States, these two presidents had to deal with an inexperienced Congress that made many mistakes. Chapter 7 showed that those mistakes destroyed Menem's and Salonia's efforts to put in place progressive educational reforms recommended by the United Nations. All of these factors shaped the context in which they issued their presidential decrees.

Upon assuming power in December 1983, Alfonsín stepped knowingly and willingly into a crisis from which he knew he might not emerge alive. Only ten years earlier, in Argentina's immediate neighboring country of Chile, the military had bombed the presidential palace, home to the democratically elected president, Salvador Allende. Allende died in the bombing. There was no guarantee that something similar would not occur in Argentina during Alfonsín's presidency. Indeed, we know in retrospect that the Argentine military was far more murderous than the Chilean military, so concerns for Alfonsín's life were well founded.[15] By the time that

---

14. The first two presidents of the new "democratic" Russia, Mikhail Gorbachev and Boris Yeltsin, issued decrees that bypassed the legislature to advance the cause of reform (under Gorbachev, Russia was still called the Soviet Union). Their use of decrees in the face of an intransigent Communist Party and an obstructionist legislature raises the question of whether Russian presidents should be allowed to use illiberal means to achieve liberal ends. See Huskey, *Presidential Power*, 7, 20–21.

15. Many sources estimate that 30,000 Argentines were disappeared by the military dictatorship and 3,000 Chileans were disappeared by the Pinochet regime. Argentina's population at the time was about thirty million; Chile's was about ten million.

Menem assumed office in mid-1989, the threat of a military coup was at least as strong as, if not stronger than, it had been in 1983. By 1989, civilian punishment had angered the military to the point of rage among some officers. The inefficient services of the state-run economy combined with repeated labor strikes had caused economic and social chaos, circumstances that Argentina's military had repeatedly used in the past to justify taking power. Although the military had retreated humiliated in 1983, by 1989 their historic brazenness had returned. They had already attempted several coups against Alfonsín. Menem confronted as high a probability of death as Alfonsín and, unlike Alfonsín, he also faced an economy in crisis on par with the Great Depression that prevailed when FDR took office. For both Argentine presidents, crisis was severe and unprecedented, as was the effort to deal with it using democratic procedures.[16]

Within this context, it appears both unsurprising and understandable that the president could and should have extensive decision-making power. The crisis context also helps us understand the need for swift action to alleviate chaos and suffering. The atmosphere into which these two Argentine presidents stepped was similar. In fact, Menem took an action that FDR did not: before moving on major economic policy matters, Menem asked the Congress to grant him "extraordinary powers" to deal with the economic crisis. And in a legalized fashion the Argentine Congress did so. It wrote, debated, and passed into law a bill granting Menem temporary but extraordinary power, even beyond what he already had within the institutional configuration described above. The congressional law gave Menem explicit permission to issue "decrees of urgency" associated with the crisis. Only after that bill did Menem proceed with his policies and with his extensive use of decrees.

Our evaluation of the use of executive authority by Menem and Alfonsín, including the issuance of decrees, should be viewed within this context.[17] One way to view decrees is to consider them part of the construction of an institution—and we are certainly observing the process of constructing Argentina's new democracy. Specifically, we are looking at the construction of the presidency, including efforts to push the limits of presidential power and corresponding efforts to limit that power.[18] Table 8.1 looks

16. FDR considered himself to be drawing upon the legacy of Lincoln, who had himself exceeded normal constitutional limits upon his powers in the crisis of the Civil War. James, "Evolution of the Presidency," 15.

17. Chile also has a history of responding to problems of governability by increasing executive authority. See Siavelis, *President and Congress in Post-Authoritarian Chile*.

18. On the use of executive orders by U.S. presidents to help create the institution of the presidency, see Mayer, *With the Stroke of a Pen*, chap. 4.

at the numbers of decrees issued by these two presidents during each year of their respective terms.

TABLE 8.1. Presidential Decrees Issued, 1983–1999

	Year	N	(%)
Alfonsín	1983 (Dec. only)	7	0.9
	1984	156	18.9
	1985	163	19.8
	1986	156	18.9
	1987	150	18.2
	1988	125	15.2
	1989 (Jan.–June)	67	8.1
	Total	824	100
Menem	1989 (July–Dec.)	48	1.8
	1990	198	7.3
	1991	303	11.2
	1992	323	11.9
	1993	337	12.4
	1994	331	12.2
	1995	299	11.0
	1996	262	9.7
	1997	236	8.7
	1998	191	7.0
	1999	185	6.8
	Total	2,713	100

Source: Data from the SAIJ website (Argentine Website for Legal Information), www.saij.gob.ar

Alfonsín served as president for five and a half years, from December 1983 until July 1989. After he resigned six months early, Menem took office and served for ten years, winning reelection in 1995. Table 8.1 illustrates that Menem was much more inclined to use presidential decrees than Alfonsín. If Menem, serving a term double the length of Alfonsín's presidency, had simply doubled the number of Alfonsín's decrees, he would have issued between 1,650 and 1,700 decrees. In fact, Menem issued 2,713 decrees.[19] Even taking into account Menem's longer term in office, the data

---

19. In his study of executive power, William Howell used a database of executive orders and found that between 1920 and 1998 U.S. presidents issued 10,203 executive orders or approximately 130 executive orders per year. "Executive order" is the U.S. term for a presidential decree. Using Howell's database for comparison, Menem, and even Alfonsín, appear to have used this power more extensively than U.S. presidents during the time period Howell studied. U.S. presidents, of course, were working within an established democracy while both Alfonsín and Menem were trying to get democracy running. Howell, *Power without Persuasion*.

But the sheer number of decrees or executive orders is somewhat misleading for another

show that he issued more decrees per year and far more decrees overall than Alfonsín.

This comparison has caused observers to conclude that Menem was an autocrat and Alfonsín was not. But the situation was more complex. In part III we saw some of the reasons why Menem resorted to presidential decrees so often. Part II also showed that democracy might have been better served had Alfonsín used decrees more. Yet that conclusion does not tell us specifically what kinds of decrees these presidents issued. To answer that question we begin by looking at the kinds of decrees that Alfonsín and Menem issued. Although Menem probably overused his decree-making powers, the overuse was not as extreme as the numbers indicate, and there were institutional and practical reasons for many of them. There was also a difference in style and energy level that defined Menem and also contributed to his decrees. Observers have tended to conclude that Menem overstepped his authority and did so even within the context of the latitude he enjoyed through Argentina's institutional design. The extent to which he did overstep his powers is scrutinized here.

Table 8.2 lists the types of decrees each president issued and the executive/legislative relationship reflected in those decrees. Let us look at each category in table 8.2. In the first category, "administration of executive branch and foreign policy," stand a series of decrees that allowed each president to determine how his ministries were behaving. These decrees reflected executive branch functions and were beyond the purview of Congress. Decrees in this category mandated what procedures ministries would follow and how they would work together on particular policies. Many

---

reason as well. In both the United States and Argentina many executive orders or decrees are internal bureaucratic decisions about the daily functioning of government. In the United States Kenneth Mayer also scrutinized executive orders as one indicator of executive power. He tried to distinguish between major and minor orders. Mayer found that between 1936 and 1999 U.S. presidents issued 1,028 executive orders of substantive interest for his study (81). By that comparison as well Menem appears to have overused his decree-issuing authority. However, for his data analysis, Mayer constructed a database that included only "substantive orders," a determination he made using a series of congressional publications to separate important and "substantive" orders from trivial ones, of which there were many more. For example, early in the FDR presidency, Roosevelt's newly established executive agencies, such as the National Recovery Administration, issued nearly 3,000 executive orders in their early efforts to save the economy. Truman also issued many executive orders after 1945. These executive orders were essential because they allowed the government to govern but were not major policy initiatives. Accordingly, Mayer excluded them from his database. In contrast, I am counting all presidential decrees issued by Menem or Alfonsín. This difference in the method of counting makes the number of decrees Menem issued look quite different. In fact, U.S. presidents issued many hundreds of decrees that Mayer excluded from his substantive data set. See Mayer, *With the Stroke of a Pen*, 66–81.

decrees in this category were bureaucratic instruments that allowed the executive branch to function, comparable to the executive orders issued for the administration of the National Recovery Act in the early years of the FDR presidency.[20] These decrees were designed to make the executive bureaucracy function more smoothly or allow it to perform a duty it had not previously undertaken.

TABLE 8.2. Level of Congressional Involvement in Presidential Decrees, Alfonsín and Menem Presidencies

Alfonsín Presidency: 1983–1989		
Decrees having . . .	*N*	(%)
1. no congressional involvement:		
administration of executive branch/foreign policy[a]	249	30.2
2. carte blanche involvement	4	.5
3. Regulamentary decree (signs into law a bill Congress has already passed)	73	8.9
4. administration of existing policy:		
congressional awareness, no regulamentary law[b]	473	57.4
5. been overturned by later decree	21	2.5
6. been overturned by Congress	1	.1
7. missing	3	.4
Total	824	100
Menem Presidency: 1989–1999		
Decrees having . . .	*N*	(%)
1. no congressional involvement:		
administration of executive branch/foreign policy	882	32.5
2. carte blanche involvement	3	.1
3. Regulamentary decree (signs into law a bill Congress has already passed)	172	6.3
4. administration of existing policy:		
congressional awareness, no regulamentary law	1,508	55.6
5. been overturned by later decree	129	4.8
6. been overturned by Congress	15	.6
7. opens or prolongs congressional session	1	.0
8. missing	3	.1
Total	2,713	100

[a]There is no indication in the record that Congress had any awareness of these decrees or was attending to the content of them.

[b]In cases listed in this category Congress indicated that it was aware that the president was issuing the decree but did not find a need to debate and pass a partner bill into law. This might have happened due to the minor nature of the decree or urgency or because the decree was an addition to a larger decree that had already been debated and passed into law by Congress. In cases of a regulated decree, the president had to conform to certain expectations from the Congress in dictating the decree. If those expectations were not met, the Congress was free to step in subsequently and overturn or change the decree. In these instances, presidents preferred not to lose the time involved in congressional debate after the fact and, therefore, conformed to congressional expectations in issuing these decrees.

20. Mayer, *With the Stroke of a Pen*, 81.

Decrees in category 1 were never addressed by Congress and became law without congressional oversight, but they were not a misuse of presidential powers. For example, Decree 2808, issued by Alfonsín on September 6, 1984, revised the guidelines by which state employees working abroad could submit applications for foreign travel related to official business. The guidelines covered costs of foreign airfare and transportation while abroad, medical insurance, reimbursement allowances, and exchange rates. Another example of this type of decree is Decree 287, also issued by Alfonsín on March 3, 1986. It established an agricultural technological plan for the National Agricultural Technology Institute, which itself was under the Ministry of Agriculture. Decree 287 stated that INTA would decide agricultural technological policy. It also established which kinds of INTA contracts could go to private companies and which were confined to public companies.

In each of these two decrees issued by Alfonsín an argument could be made that greater oversight by Congress was advisable. Yet, in the context of that moment, such oversight could have been more problematic than helpful. These decrees were issued, along with the administrative rules accompanying them, at a time when most constructive governmental and administrative behavior had been suspended for more than seven years. Speed was often of the essence in getting the government running at all. Alfonsín might well have argued, in defense of these decrees, in the following way: "Well, we are trying to get things done around here. We are trying to get a country started." In this context, the details of full democratic governance were sometimes suspended in the interests of setting some guidelines swiftly, allowing agencies of the federal government to function. Specific oversight of these guidelines could wait until Congress had time to establish a committee authorized to conduct it. At that later date, if such a committee were ever set up, changes could be made and administrative rules or guidelines altered. But at least for the time being, these kinds of decrees avoided paralysis and allowed the process of constructive governance to move forward. It was an understandably imperfect solution given the challenges of the early democratization process.

Yet there is no doubt that this free-wheeling approach to governance left room for abuses. Indeed, times of crisis underscore the importance of leaders and their own *inner* commitment to democracy. A leader might use his or her power to undermine or subvert the procedures of democracy or might voluntarily stay within democratic bounds as much as possible.[21] In

---

21. Examples on each side of that question help us understand the importance of leadership personality. In the United States FDR had multiple opportunities early in his presi-

the Alfonsín years, the nature of Argentina's crisis concerned the establishment of functional democratic government. By the time of Menem's presidency the nature of the crisis had changed, forcing Menem to prioritize the economy. Like Alfonsín, Menem acted swiftly when he perceived an emergency, issuing numerous decrees designed to manage the economic emergency quickly.[22] In the face of the bureaucratic red tape for which the Argentine state is famous, Menem issued a decree that released loans that had already been approved. As a result, companies that were functional and profitable could begin to work sooner. A similar example was Decree 91, issued by Menem on January 7, 1991. It canceled the debts of the atomic energy commission. This kind of decision fell directly under the purview of the president for two reasons. First, it involved an agency in a ministry of the executive branch; second, the step was taken in direct response to the financial emergency. Either reason would have been sufficient for Menem to act. Yet from the more relaxed perspective of a developed democracy and a less crisis-driven context, cancellation of debts in this manner might have been better handled by a congressional committee.

This situation demonstrates two separate influences toward the concentration of authority and decision making in the hands of the executive. One was institutional; the other historical and contextual. The fact that many agencies of the government report to ministries controlled by the executive branch in Argentina offered an institutional setting whereby the president could make many decisions that would be subject to oversight if power were less institutionally concentrated in the executive under Argentina's institutional design. Second, the atmosphere of crisis also gave

---

dency to use the economic crisis to expand his powers and subvert democratic procedures and institutions. Instead, he chose to keep his own behavior within democratic boundaries. By contrast, Indira Gandhi (head of India's largest party, the Congress Party, and repeatedly elected to president), chose to the use elections themselves to undermine democracy in India. She did so by using her charisma and personal popularity to build the party into a hierarchical machine dependent on her control while undermining and then eliminating the party's own democratic procedures, such as internal elections. Hugo Chávez did something similar in Venezuela, although he operated primarily as a charismatic, populist leader, appealing directly to the population and side-stepping the party system. On FDR, see Alter, *Defining Moment*. On India, see Ashutosh Varshney, *Civic Life and Ethnic Conflict in India* (New Haven: Yale University Press, 2003). On Venezuela, see Corrales and Penfold, *Dragon in the Tropics*.

22. Alfonsín also issued economic decrees designed to address the financial crisis. For example, Decree 581, issued by Alfonsín on May 9, 1989, authorized the Central Bank to receive contributions or donations from productive sectors of the economy. Decree 581/89 made note of the economic emergency and stated the grave need to act in the face of that emergency. Productive sectors of the economy needed to have at their disposal minimal funds that had already been approved for them. This decree authorized the release of these funds and instructed the bank to release the monies involved.

the executive and his ministers and advisers every reason to make urgent decisions swiftly. In Menem's case the crisis had a name: "the economic emergency." Menem had specifically been given "necessary and urgent" powers in the face of that emergency, and in many decrees such as 49/91 he referred to the necessary and urgent context in which the decree had been issued.[23] In Alfonsín's case, the crisis did not have a specific name but was no less real. Alfonsín was trying to erect a democratic government in the aftermath of dictatorship. From both presidents, based on the decrees listed in this category one gathers the sense of crisis and urgency. These presidents were trying to run a country, to do what they could and do so immediately. The luxuries of balanced power faded in the context of this predominant sense of crisis and urgency.

The placement of many foreign policy decisions within this category follows from the expectation as well that Argentine foreign policy is run by the president. In the United States, the president also has extensive latitude in conducting foreign policy. Under this expectation, various administrative tasks of foreign policy were covered by these decrees. For example, Decree 970, issued by Menem in May 1993, mandated a monthly increase in the housing allowance allotment for public servants working abroad, such as in embassies. Similarly, Decree 428, issued by Menem in March 1992, gave diplomatic recognition to Croatia. This category also included symbolic decrees whereby the president makes a statement of solidarity with a nation in trouble. For example, in January 2010, the Argentine president might have issued a decree stating solidarity with Haiti after the island was hit by an earthquake, or in September 2001, the president might have issued a solidarity statement in support of the United States after the twin towers in New York were hit by terrorists.[24] These decrees emanate from the presidency because of its peculiar power to make decisions about foreign policy and about Argentina's position in the community of nations.

---

23. There are many examples of the U.S. president acting in a manner that appears unilateral but actually results from legislative action giving him the needed latitude. A recent example, which involved financial crisis, came in 1993 and 1994 when Bill Clinton decided to bail out the Mexican economy. He acted quickly, in the context of a crisis, and to prevent the widespread economic chaos that would have followed had Mexico been allowed to go bankrupt. He acted, moreover, in accordance with legislation passed by Congress during the New Deal, which gave him the appropriate latitude. In fact, Clinton's act came in response to pressure from Republican legislators who felt certain that they could not muster the number of votes needed on the floor of Congress to pass a law to bail out the Mexican economy. Swift action by Clinton appeared to be the only option. I am grateful to Steven Boyle for providing this example.

24. I thank Aníbal Corrado for helping me with these two examples of what solidarity decrees look like.

But by virtue of being solidarity statements, they are not an abuse of power and do not need to pass through Congress. They are not laws.

If we subtract from the number of decrees all of those issued in this first category, the use of decrees by these presidents looks different. Over 30 percent of them were administrative measures pertaining to the executive branch, often in crisis, or foreign policy. Excluding these decrees, Alfonsín issued 575 other types of decrees and Menem issued 1,831.

We look next at category 2 in table 8.2, what I have called "carte blanche decrees." These decrees reflected presidential use of delegative powers. Alfonsín issued only four decrees of this kind and Menem issued only three. These decrees are coded "carte blanche" because they responded to a directive from the Congress. However, that congressional statement or directive was minimal and usually consisted of a title and a single sentence on one page. These directives were not the result of a law that had been debated at length in Congress. Instead, they simply directed the president to issue a decree on a specific subject. The presidential decree then referenced the original congressional law, such as it was, as the reason for this decree.[25] I have used the term "carte blanche decrees" because Congress, once having called for the decree, appeared to exercise no oversight on the resulting presidential decree.

Let us look at several examples of the decrees in this category. Decree 328 of March 8, 1988, was an addendum to Law 20.744,[26] the 1973 Law of Labor Contract.[27] It laid out the guidelines that unions were expected to follow before going on strike or otherwise reducing their hours on the job. The decree also specified the conditions under which employees could be fired. Chapters 4 and 6 revealed that labor strikes were a key problem for the Alfonsín administration, but they were also a threat for Menem. Strikes became a serious threat to democracy during the last two years of Alfonsín's presidency.[28] We know, therefore, that Decree 328/88 addressed an extremely urgent matter. Yet here we find Congress directing the executive to take swift action and issue a decree that would be an addendum to a law already on the books. Its specificities would have far-reaching impact, yet Congress subtracted itself from the picture. One can surmise that

---

25. These original congressional laws were not always still on the books and do not appear on the SAIJ (Sitio Argentino de Información Jurídica) website for Argentine legal information.

26. No longer on the SAIJ website.

27. Ley de Contrato de Trabajo.

28. Labor strikes in Latin America more generally have frequently endangered democracy because of the chaos they create and the opportunity they create for military intervention. Levitsky and Mainwaring, "Organized Labor and Democracy in Latin America."

Congress itself was taking advantage of the swift action made possible by decrees and, in this case, ordering the executive to take action in response to labor strikes rather than taking the time to put an addendum through debate on both floors of Congress.

Also in this second category is Decree 1537, issued in 1991 by Menem. It likewise responded to a law, number 23.697. Menem's decree suspended subsidies and subventions from the national treasury to religious publications. This suspension included reduced postal rates and applied to Catholic publications as well as other religious publications not issued or sold for profit. This decree is notable for its deliberate inclusion of Catholicism. Although officially a secular state, Argentina's government has, on many occasions, offered subsidies to the Catholic Church (e.g., Catholic schools) that it would not offer to other religions. This decree specifically singled out the Catholic Church as one organization that would be included in Decree 1537/91, ending this particular subsidy. This cost-saving measure relied for its legitimacy upon the state's official secularism. Two further decrees issued by Menem on December 28, 1994, Decrees 2376/94 and 2377/94, responded to both a previous law and a previous decree. Decree 2766/94 created a national registry of public hospitals; Decree 2377/94 gave provisional authorization for the establishment of a University of the Congress.

Given the small number of carte blanche decrees that responded to congressional directives, drawing conclusions about the character of these decrees is difficult. What does appear certain, however, is the need for speed and the desire to avoid a lengthy congressional debate. In the case of Decree 328/88, issued by Alfonsín, that desire for speed might well have come in response to the chaotic situation created by frequent labor strikes. In the case of Decrees 1537/91 and 2377/94, speed appears to have been desirable because the administrative step was relatively small—the suspension of postal subsidies or the creation of a new university. These examples clearly show that Congress and the executive were working together. They are not examples of an executive acting alone, overruling or bypassing congressional authority. Following the single-page directive from Congress came a more extensive executive-issued decree on the specific policy called for in the carte blanch decree. In category 3 stand decrees that elicited a bill and then a law in Congress that accompanied the relevant executive order. We discuss category 3 below.

Category 4 is the largest category for both presidents: 57 percent of Alfonsín's decrees and 55.6 percent of Menem's. These decrees were administrative, like those in the first category, but they were different from category 1 in that they pertained to policy or law that was already in existence. They went beyond the administration of the executive branch itself, but they did not create entirely new laws. They facilitated the administration of policies and laws already in existence. For example, Decree 348, issued by Alfonsín in 1985, stated that cooperation on sanitation improvement measures for the southern province of Chubut would take place between the Ministry of Health and the provincial government, represented in Buenos Aires by the House for the Province of Chubut.[29] Similarly, Decree 353, issued by Menem in February 1992, authorized financing to build housing on military bases. After the reorganization of the military under the Alfonsín presidency, independent military autonomy and control over its own factories, vacation resorts, and many other aspects of decision making were sharply curtailed. Beginning with the Alfonsín years, decision-making power and control over the military fell under the Ministry of Defense and, therefore, the executive branch. Accordingly, administrative decisions such as building military housing now fell to the executive. This kind of decree epitomized civilian control over the military; it removed from military hands decisions, powers, and economic latitude that would never rest with the military in a democracy. Far from being an example of authoritarian presidential power, this kind of decree, common in the Alfonsín years, actually reduced authoritarianism by increasing civilian control over the military.

Categories 5 and 6 include decrees that had been overturned at the time of the creation of this database. Decrees in category 5 were overturned by a subsequent executive decree, often one promoting the same policy but making it more extensive or specific in its application. The fact that a decree was overturned in this manner is not an indication that the policy was rejected. Often, the policy was embraced and elaborated by a subsequent presidential decree. Decrees in category 6 are ones that were subsequently overturned by a congressional law. In the bottom half of table

---

29. Each Argentine province has a "House of the Province of ____ [Neuquén, Chubut, Jujuy, and so forth]" located in a favorable place in the center of Buenos Aires. These "houses of the provinces" look like travel agencies advertising the area and helping domestic or foreign tourists plan visits there. The houses of the provinces also act as real estate agencies, facilitating the purchase of property. Additionally, however, the houses serve as conduits between the provincial governments and the representatives of the province in the national government. Each one has extensive ties with the legislators from its province, particularly with the senators, and serves as a go-between for executive policy, such as health care policy, as it pertains to the province. In this case, Alfonsín's Decree 348 of 1985 brought the House of the Province of Chubut into a minimal level of involvement in health, sanitation, and development work being administered by the central government through the Ministry of Health for the Province of Chubut.

8.2, category 7 exists only for the Menem presidency and contains only one decree by which the president opened or extended a congressional session. Far from being an example of unbridled presidential action, through this last category Menem extended congressional involvement in governance.

This overview shows that presidential decrees were not necessarily examples of unchecked presidential power or authoritarianism. Instead, they were tools used by both the president and the legislature that were often a part of everyday governance. The ease with which they were issued also allowed them to increase government efficiency. The Argentine system made many of these decrees more appropriate than they would have been in other presidential democracies. The fact that Argentina is a federal system and has high levels of power concentrated in the ministries increased the necessity for decrees. The context of crisis then further increased this necessity. Some decrees definitely reflected a misuse of president power, but many did not.

As we can see from table 8.2, the level of congressional involvement was roughly similar across both presidencies, and the percentages in each category are comparable. That fact challenges the assumption that Menem worked alone, following a dramatically different posture toward the Congress, and that Alfonsín worked with the Congress. The major difference between the two presidents lies in the numbers of decrees issued, not in their distribution across categories.

Categories 1 and 4 merit further comment. Combined, both categories comprise more than 80 percent of decrees issued by each president, although the sheer numbers of decrees issued by Menem during his 10.5 years in office is far greater than the number of decrees issued by Alfonsín during his 5.5 years in office. Both of these categories contain administrative decrees and concern administrative decisions either within or beyond the executive branch. Neither category contains major legal initiatives representing new laws or policies.

Now we can address category 3, which includes decrees regulating and signing into law bills passed by Congress. In Argentina, bills cannot become law without being regulated and signed by the president. Presidential regulation of a bill passed by Congress might include an instance when Congress adopts a new bill regulating alcohol consumption. The president, who is both the executive and the chief of public bureaucracy, has to sign a decree accompanying the bill in order to make the bill work as law. The president's decree details who enforces the new law, when the law takes effect, how much money will be used for enforcement, where the money will come from, and other practical details of administration. If a bill is approved by Congress it has a particular level of legitimacy and power. Yet the bill is not law until the president signs a regulamentary decree that allows the law to be enforced.[30]

This example of a regulamentary decree involves the enforcement of a single law. Yet other regulamentary decrees were important in the initiation of democratic governance, and they were often attached to a decree or law from the military dictatorship. For example, Decree 943/84 of March 29, 1984, issued by Alfonsín, referred in its text to the Proceso years, the military's own term for its dictatorship of 1976–83. This decree followed a congressional bill and, together with that bill, created the Federal Council of Culture and Education (Consejo Federal de Cultura y Education). On its surface the decree looks like the simple creation of a cultural institute. But in its text the decree also says that laws passed during the Proceso have only provisional authority. As a result, those dictatorship laws remained in effect for practical purposes, but they also might be replaced or overturned in due course if the new democratic government encountered situations where they violated civil rights. This kind of wording preserved space for the democratic government to attend to these military laws in the future, as time allowed, without requiring the government to take time out of everyday urgencies to review all of the military laws at once. Decree 1152/84 of April 13, 1984, addresses the use of fertilizers. Like the hypothetical example given above of an alcohol consumption law, this decree did not take a major step toward democratic governance but still exemplifies the coordination of executive and legislative action. Similarly, Decree 95/85 of January 15, 1985, was issued by Alfonsín in response to a congressional bill. Regulating the activities of rural farm workers picking and cultivating cotton, this decree was covered by the press because of its relevance for the working class.

Under Menem, Decree 515/90 of March 19, 1990, regulated Law 23.763, the 1989 budget. This decree was important, not for its demonstration of unbridled presidential power but as an example of executive/legislative cooperation. First, the decree indicates that Congress was the government branch that passed the annual budget. This extremely important task grants extensive power to Congress. As with other bills under Argentina's presidential system, however, even the budget bill could not become law without an accompanying presidential decree. This particular decree related to only a small piece of the overall budget bill. Law 23.763 provided

---

30. In this hypothetical example, we see the executive filling the role of law enforcement. This task normally falls to the executive in any presidential democracy. I appreciate this example from Aníbal Corrado.

funding from the national budget to support political parties. Here we see the executive regulating into law a bill that Congress had already approved. Similarly, Decree 541 of March 23, 1990, regulated Law 23.697, which was the Economic Emergency Law that extended special powers to Menem. Drawing upon that law, this decree extended taxes and credit to the mining industry. Decree 583/90 of March 29, 1990, regulated Law 23.767 and provided immediate crisis relief in the form of food, toilets, and housing to the poorest sectors of the national population. It shows speed and urgency in crisis, not autocratic presidential power.

Decrees in category 3 sometimes responded to laws left over from the military dictatorship and sometimes initiated key social steps to address the national economic crisis. At other times, these same decrees simply placed into law an administrative bill that had worked its way through Congress and now needed presidential regulation to become law. In this manner, decrees in category 3 were sometimes administrative, even mundane, but they sometimes enacted major new policies. This category, which is the third row in both halves of table 8.2, shows empirical evidence of congressional involvement in policy making. During the Menem years, for example, each of the policies privatizing major industries, such as the telephone company, passed through this dual process. First the president issued a decree that indicated the specifics of the policy as he wished to see it implemented. Then Congress debated the decree as if it were a bill presented to the legislature. Through the course of debate in both chambers, the specifics of the decree were changed, always with close oversight by the executive branch. In the end, a counterpart law was passed by Congress supporting the presidential decree and converting the law from being one by decree to being one through legislative action. Often, this procedure was followed because of urgency, which frequently characterized the Menem presidency. Additionally, the decree gave the president advantages in the precise wording of the law he wanted to see passed. This category gives some credence to the impression that Alfonsín was more willing to work with the Congress while Menem was less willing to do so. Nearly 9 percent of Alfonsín's decrees went through this process; only 6.3 percent of Menem's decrees did. Yet the difference is not large, and the overall percentage of decrees managed in this fashion was small. The fact that this category contained the most important decrees of either presidency helps us understand, better than the overall numbers do, why Alfonsín was perceived as more democratic than Menem.

During Menem's presidency and thereafter, the Argentine press carried out an unending campaign accusing Menem of governing by decree. That accusation has taken root in scholarly and popular understandings of his presidency and has become the basis of the well-known idea of a "delegative president."[31] Yet the data in table 8.2 indicate that the situation was more complex than this simple accusation would suggest. First, we see that both presidents worked with Congress on major policy initiatives. Second, many of the decrees issued concerned administrative matters that did not warrant the time entailed in congressional debate and approval. Third, the mechanics of law creation in Argentina require a presidential decree in order for Congress to do its job; indeed, in the case of regulamentary decrees, Congress asked the president to issue a decree.

Yet it is appropriate to scrutinize the decrees and the large number of them. This scrutiny is appropriate not because Menem sometimes made law by decree when Congress would have preferred to be involved, but because all Argentine presidents hold extensive executive powers on par with an executive in a parliamentary system but without the constraints of a parliament.[32] Moreover, in a presidential democracy like the United States, where the power of Congress is greater, or in any democracy where extreme crisis was not present, many of the decisions made by decree, even the administrative decisions, could have been cause for debate and disagreement.[33] Some of that debate would appropriately have fallen within

---

31. Guillermo O'Donnell, "Delegative Democracy," *Journal of Democracy* 5, no. 1 (1994): 55–69.

32. Richard Rose argues that a prime minister is actually much more powerful than a president because, by virtue of having her own party in power in the legislature, she can push legislation through and enact policy much more thoroughly than can a president. Rose also suggests that the parliamentary system originated in Europe, which, like Latin America, has a more hierarchical and collective leadership tradition while the U.S. leadership tradition is more individualist, producing a presidency that is supposed to be checked by the legislature. The parliamentary institutional system exaggerates executive power. For example, both Margaret Thatcher and Tony Blair won landslide majorities in Parliament but received less than 44 percent of the popular vote. See "Giving Direction to Government in Comparative Perspective," in *Executive Branch*, ed. Joel D. Aberbach and Mark A. Peterson (Oxford: Oxford University Press, 2005), 73–76. In contrast to Juan Linz's recommendation of parliamentarism for Latin America, by Rose's argument parliamentarism in Latin America would only serve to concentrate power more thoroughly in the executive.

Concentration of power in the executive even within a presidential system is not unique to Argentina. The president in Chile also has extensive powers, including the power to control the legislative agenda. The Chilean executive even has a clearinghouse or filter office that coordinates all legislation originating in the executive branch. These powers have been granted to the Chilean president as a result of the institutional changes made during the Pinochet dictatorship. See Siavelis, *President and Congress*, 56–59.

33. Ana Maria Mustapic argues that the Argentine constitution was designed to create a powerful presidency because in 1853, when the Constitution was written, the nation had just finished thirty years of chaos under the dictatorship of Juan Manuel de Rosas. A powerful presidency was perceived as a path toward stability. See "Oficialista y diputados: Las rela-

the authority of the Congress, but other matters, such as relations with the provincial governments, might have been cause for debate about federal/state relations.

Looking at the decree categories across both presidencies gives us additional perspective on how executive power was used. Table 8.2 showed that many decrees were constructive and contributed to the process of democratic governance. Table 8.3 (opposite page) shows that the content of the decrees corresponded with major urgencies in newly democratic Argentina. For example, Menem's decrees concentrated on the economy more than Alfonsín's did, although both presidents attended to the economy in their decrees. Additionally, Alfonsín issued a larger percentage of administrative decrees, as befits the first democratic administration following a dictatorship. Overall, however, the decrees of both presidents are widely distributed and reflect the breadth of concerns that fall under presidential purview.

Toward the bottom of table 8.3 is the category "administration of executive branch." This category corresponds to the routine matters that fall to the presidency, are important for the everyday business of government, but are not momentous or indicative of unbridled presidential powers. FDR, who was one of the first U.S. presidents to use executive orders extensively, addressed many routine matters through such administrative orders. These relatively minor orders took up so much of his time that they were later delegated to other officials. This category inflates the number of decrees issued by Argentine presidents but does not represent an inappropriate use of power.[34] Most executive orders in the United States and presidential decrees in Argentina are more important than the ones in this administrative category.

---

ciones Ejecutive-Legislative en la Argentina," *Desarollo Economico: Revista de Ciencias Sociales* 39, no. 156 (January–March 2000): 571–95. See also Carlos Nino, "El hiperpresidencialismo argentino y las concepciones de la democracia," in *El Presidencialismo puesto a prueba*, ed. Carlos Nino (Madrid: Centro de Estudios Constitucionales, 1992). By contrast, the U.S. presidency was set up to be a weaker office. See Joel D. Aberbach and Mark A. Peterson, "Presidents and Bureaucrats: The Executive Branch and American Democracy," in *The Executive Branch*, ed. Joel D. Aberbach and Mark A. Peterson (Oxford: Oxford University Press, 2005).

34. During the FDR presidency administrative orders, such as the establishment of customs ports of entry, were ultimately delegated away from the president. In Argentina, Menem was required to issue a number of decrees administrating the operation of ports of entry. On FDR, see Mayer, *With the Stroke of a Pen*, 76.

TABLE 8.3. Categories of Decrees by President (Number of Decrees and Percentage of Total)

Category	Alfonsín (1983–89)		Menem (1989–99)	
	N	(%)	N	(%)
Economics				
immediate crisis relief	19	2.3	98	3.6
long-term economic reform (taxes, industry)	100	12.1	432	15.9
reform of the state/privatization	21	2.5	278	10.2
Labor Reform				
employment creation	20	2.4	82	3.0
union discipline	6	.7	11	.4
other	4	.5	15	.6
Social support—long-term programs	42	5.1	161	5.9
Industry	43	5.2	226	8.3
Agriculture	43	5.2	43	1.6
Transportation (highways, rail, air, shipping)	26	3.2	157	5.8
Reform of Federal Relations				
decentralization (power, money, responsibility transferred to provinces)	22	2.7	114	4.2
intervention in provinces	4	.5	11	.4
Military	47	5.7	89	3.3
Environment (pollution, parks, cleanup)	11	1.3	54	2.0
Justice				
legal system	38	4.6	82	3.0
penal laws, jails	33	4.0	76	2.8
Education (universities, high schools)	72	8.7	115	4.2
Culture and the arts	12	1.5	51	1.9
Administration of executive branch	142	17.2	263	9.7
Communication	21	2.5	79	2.9
Health care/medicine	35	4.2	88	3.2
Sports	8	1.0	28	1.0
International Relations	54	6.6	154	5.7
Missing	1	.1	6	.2
Total	824	100	2,713	100

Note: We can place the total number of decrees listed here in comparative perspective by considering that Franklin Roosevelt's National Recovery Administration issued nearly 3,000 administrative orders in its first year. See Erwin Griswold, "Government in Ignorance of the Law," 199; Department of Commerce, Division of Press Intelligence, *Subject Index of Executive Orders*, March 8, 1933–October 1, 1935, and October 1, 1935–September 1, 1936. Papers of Samuel Rosenman, Folder: Subject Index of Executive Orders, FDR Library. Cited in Kenneth R. Mayer, *With the Stroke of a Pen: Executive Orders and Presidential Power* (Princeton: Princeton University Press, 2001), 68.

Conclusion

These data on executive decrees during the transition years show that presidential power was used in a multifaceted, complex fashion that fell primarily within the prerogative of the presidency and sometimes enhanced democracy, allowing it to function more smoothly. The analysis does not reveal extensive, authoritarian misuse of decree power. Press coverage of Argentina's transition years trumpeted an authoritarian overuse of executive decrees, especially by Menem, but that view is not supported by the data analyzed here. Instead, the extent to which executive power was overused in Argentina can more easily be understood by reference to the entire polity, including both the institutional design and how that design is used in Argentina. The presidential system itself is revised in Argentina to reduce legislative powers to those of a parliament in most situations, while those same revisions exaggerate executive powers beyond the intention of the Westminster model. Additionally, those revisions, problematic in their own right, are then grafted onto a polity still exhibiting important corporate characteristics. The extent to which either or both presidents of the transition years misused power is not uncovered by the empirical analysis examined here but, rather, by a contextual understanding of the entire polity, the institutional design, and the background and history of the political parties that played key roles in the democratic transition.

CHAPTER 9

Presidential Checks
and Balances in the
Democratization Process

The greatest test of a human being is to give him power and watch
him use it.
   —Sam Rayburn, Speaker, U.S. House of Representatives

The best way to know a man is to watch him with power.
   —Jorge Solana, Argentine senator, Province of Neuquén

As we conclude our examination of Argentina's democratization by institutions, we can say that these seventeen years were simultaneously impressive
and problematic, inspiring and troubling. They show us what possibilities
exist and what the limitations are with democratization by institutions. The
Argentine transition oversaw momentous political, economic, and social
change that brought key steps toward democracy and left behind many
aspects of the nation's authoritarian past. The process itself deserves our
careful study because it was primarily conducted through the formal institutions of state without external intervention or international oversight
and often in the face of citizen resistance. We did not find in Argentina's
democratization process the presence of cohesive citizen groups demanding democratic reforms. Nor did we discover a vast array of progressive
social groups pushing for democratic change. After the earliest years of

democracy's return, when civil society was involved in the transition, popular groups primarily showed resistance to or disgruntled acceptance of the various reforms. Insofar as our theories have led us to expect civil society to play a positive role in democratization, Argentina's experience challenges that assumption and causes us to look at institutions instead of civil society as a source of democratic innovation.

Argentina shows that democratization by institutions is possible. In fact, the process considered here was advantageous and successful on several levels. Institutional democratization was gradual, avoiding extreme disruption and violence. It provided a set of guidelines for actors to follow and a set of solutions for problems. Most important, working within these institutions provided society with a *process* for addressing problems as they emerged. And, as imperfect as it was, the institutional process was better than anything Argentina had tried in the past. Indeed, where civil society does not provide the impetus for democratization, institutions become the only option, short of international intervention as, for example, after defeat in war.

Gerhard Loewenberg tells us that both the presidential and parliamentary systems were outgrowths of their own historical settings. In Europe the legislature evolved in the heart of monarchy where the task at hand was to reduce that central power gradually while incrementally introducing a governing mechanism reflecting the will of the people. The result was a parliament where legislative and executive powers are intertwined, and it is difficult to say where one ends and the other begins. By contrast, the presidential system grew up in the American colonies where local government began through local assemblies because the monarch was often far removed. But over time those local assemblies learned to problem-solve and to govern, taking popular opinion into account from the outset. They also became a source of resistance to monarchical power. They became the model upon which the founders of the United States constructed presidentialism. The result was a democratic system that prioritized the legislature and originally produced only a weak president. That system has evolved into having a stronger presidency while always retaining a powerful legislature.[1] From such a background, presidential and legislative powers are easily distinguishable, and it is the legislature that drives the governing agenda.

Latin America's presidential system evolves out of a third tradition entirely. Latin American nations inherited a superhierarchical and cen-

---

1. Gerhard Loewenberg, *On Legislatures* (Boulder: Paradigm, 2011), esp. chap. 1.

tralized system from the colonial experience and did not reject it as the American colonies did. Instead, hierarchy and centralized control were embraced by the new Latin American nations, often producing dictatorship. The presidential system was then imported from the United States and mapped on top of the hierarchical traditions of Latin America. The result is a system in which two historical traditions battle each other. The Latin American institutional design is an outwardly presidential system, with strongly hierarchical trappings and a legislature that has the formal authority to be independent but that is greatly constrained by the political context and traditions.

In Argentina the mapping of presidentialism onto a tradition of centralized hierarchy has produced something that is not quite a parliamentary system but does not function exactly as a presidential system either. In many moments Argentina's president is stronger than either a classical, presidential-system president or a prime minister while the Congress can be weaker than a parliament. But not always: Argentina's transition years show that there are moments when the Congress can rise to towering strengths, pushing aside executive guidance or restraint. In those moments it acts like a Congress, not like a parliament. But because it only formulates policy periodically it lacks the skill, experience, and committee structure of the U.S. Congress. Lacking the expertise of the US Congress, Argentina's Congress makes many mistakes. And afterward it recedes again, shrinking back into the position of a parliament, following the executive and forgoing the power to make policy.[2]

Argentina's Congress had moments of towering strength both at the beginning and at the end of this book. First, with respect to human rights policy and then with respect to K-12 reform, it wrestled the initiative away from the executive branch and made policy on its own, as a Congress is expected to do in a typical presidential system. At such moments, faced with a more powerful legislature than Argentina's presidents normally expect, the president needs to know how to build a coalition of congressional support if he or she is to retain any influence at all, something Alfonsín understood but Menem did not. Since the president has so much independent power and is required to build coalitions only rarely, Argentine presidents

---

2. Some observers of Argentina's Congress feel that only executive power—as in the presidency or in a governorship—really matters and legislative power is a weak power that belongs only to "losers." This attitude causes legislators to try to leave the Congress as soon as possible and to try instead for a higher level of executive power. The departure of legislators then leaves Congress with a low rate of seniority and a high rate of inexperience. These characteristics then leave Congress more likely to make mistakes.

do not develop this skill as thoroughly as do their American counterparts. The Argentine system, which does not exactly fit either the parliamentary model or the presidential model but has elements of both, does not offer regular opportunities for presidents to learn to build coalitions. As a distinct configuration of institutional power, emerging from a distinct history and moving forward in ways that do not exactly follow either presidentialism or parliamentarism, the Argentine system will have to find or build its own process whereby presidents learn to build coalitions. Presidents will be forced to learn this skill if Congress acts congressional more often and recedes into subordination less often, so, in this sense, the Argentine system will need to make its own history.

Argentina's institutional design was adequate for democratization but could have been better. If it had followed its own blueprint more closely it might have worked better. More restraints upon the presidency and more power in Congress and the courts could have prevented some of Menem's excesses, as well as the extent to which those excesses have expanded since his departure. In considering the possibilities for government to restrain power, James Madison advised against relying upon an enlightened statesman to lead a nation out of trouble. An enlightened statesman *might* be available, but, then again, perhaps not. Therefore, he wrote, it is the fact of representative government that provides the key protection against the dangers of power abuse, the institution itself and not the individual within it.[3] Insofar as the Argentine system has weakened Congress and empowered the presidency within an institutional arrangement that already favors a strong executive, then that system has gone directly against what Madison advised when he developed the U.S. institutional design. This book has shown how high a price Argentina has paid for its disregard of that warning.

The United States, itself, has also disregarded Madison's warning periodically and turned to powerful presidents in times of crisis. In at least some of those moments, strong presidential power has been an asset. Strong presidential power was an asset for Argentina at times during both of these presidencies. We also see from the Argentine example that there were times during these transition years when the crisis called for more rather than less presidential power. Madison may have underestimated the demands created by crisis. Hamilton, however, seemed more aware of the value of strong presidential leadership. Both Alfonsín and Menem provided that leadership. Each then imposed his personality upon the insti-

---

3. James Madison, Federalist #10, "Factions: Their Cause and Control," in *The Federalist Papers*.

tutional design. Menem was all too eager to seize the power that the insti-tutional configuration gave him, but Alfonsín was probably too reticent. In transitions and crises, strong presidential powers are required, as other democracies have shown. Moments when a presidential decree was not used but might well have been appropriate included the democratization of labor, early privatization, and the K-12 educational reforms. For instance, Menem could have used a decree to raise teachers' salaries. But a decree at some of these moments, for example, the democratization of labor, might have encountered strong resistance from sectors of civil society, risking a military coup. That fear may have restrained these presidents from using such decrees.

This dilemma characterizes every presidential democracy: in a crisis, strong executive power is convenient and may be the only force that can save the state and restore some degree of normalcy. But once a crisis ends, strong executive power can become the problem rather than the solution, the newest threat to the democratic state. In confronting this dilemma, Argentina joins the ranks of democracies everywhere that have met a cri-sis and resolved it. But unlike many democracies, Argentina lacks exten-sive democratic resources in the citizenry, particularly the bridging social capital and horizontal ties that would cause protest to advance democracy.[4] Such democratic capacities in society itself can be very important during the long periods in between elections. Argentina must resolve the presi-dential dilemma while also contending with social antagonism, the heritage of a ferocious authoritarian past and the continuities that flow therefrom.

One of the strongest examples of extensive executive power was Men-em's privatization policy and his labor and educational reforms, which accompanied that policy. While exemplifying strong executive power, these steps were also among the greatest accomplishments of these transition years. Not only did they make the economy functional, a step that ulti-mately supports democracy itself, but they also included increasing state support for higher education and the transfer of social service distribution to the state, both steps toward democracy.

In advanced industrial democracies, support for education is considered the first plank in the welfare state and, as such, intricately connected to democracy. Amy Gutmann writes that public support for education was already a reality in the United States long before the country became a welfare state, and that made its incorporation into the welfare state easier. Access to education and governmental support for it is a basic facet of

---

4. Anderson, "Democratization and Oppositional Consciousness."

both democracy and the welfare state. Improved access to public education for most Argentines is precisely what Menem achieved with the education reforms, especially the reforms to higher education.[5]

Menem's reforms of social services also moved Argentina in a democratic direction, although that outcome was an accidental side effect of his policies rather than the central goal. Social services are not confined to democracies, and their existence does not mean that democracy is the goal. In point of fact, the opposite can be true. Nazism offered social support services while reaching for power, but it cut back those services once it had consolidated power and the Second World War had begun.[6] Similarly, Perón offered social support services partly as a means of tying both the unions and the workers to himself, keeping them under state control. Menem's movement away from that model inched Argentina in a democratic direction, as defined by Gosta Epsing-Anderson. Epsing-Anderson argues that welfare states can be more or less democratic, depending on the distribution system used. Table 9.1 presents the levels of his argument and places Argentina within those levels in relation to democracy. Within that argument, during the years examined in this study Argentina moved from Level I to Level II but still falls short of the most democratic level which is Level III.

TABLE 9.1. Welfare Systems and Their Relation to Democracy

System Characteristics	Level 1	Level II	Level III
Style of inclusion:	corporate, member-oriented welfare	needs-based welfare	universal welfare based on citizenship
Level of inclusion:	members only, exclusion of nonmembers	more inclusion	highest level of inclusion
Examples:	Bismarckian and Nazi Germany, Peronist Argentina	United States, contemporary Argentina	France, Sweden
Relationship to democracy:	least democratic	more democratic	most democratic

Source: Gosta Epsing-Anderson, *The Three World of Welfare Capitalism* (Princeton: Princeton University Press, 1990).

5. Amy Gutmann, "Distributing Public Education in a Democracy," in *Democracy and the Welfare State*, ed. Amy Gutmann (Princeton: Princeton University Press, 1988), 107. Gutmann further argues that higher education in particular has a special relationship with democracy: neither can exist without the other. Notably, an essential part of the Menem reforms to education came at the university level. On higher education and democracy, see Gutmann, *Democratic Education*, chap. 6.

6. Ralph H. Bowen, *German Theories of the Corporative State with Special Reference to the Period 1870–1919* (New York: McGraw Hill, 1947); C. W. Guillebaud, *The Social Policy of Nazi Germany* (Cambridge: Cambridge University Press, 1941).

This movement toward a more democratic manner of distributing social services was a reform led by a nondemocratic party and an overbearing president for pragmatic economic reasons rather than the normative reasons that have driven welfare reform in many advanced democracies. President Menem and Peronism were quite unable to offer a normative rationale for their policies. Menem would have gained more support for his policy had he given it a normative rationale as well as an economic one. Yet despite his failing in this regard, the outcome was still a first step toward state provision of social services. This ironic outcome illustrates the complicated nature of the powerful president in times of crisis. Had Congress stopped privatization under Menem the way it did under Alfonsín, it would also have robbed Argentina of this desirable step in the provision of social services.

The Working of Democracy

Stepping back from the Argentine case to consider theoretical perspectives on democratic function helps us understand the advantages of democratization by institutions. Although Argentina's presidential system has revised the system copied from the United States, a recognizable presidential democracy of institutional checks and balances still exists in Argentina. It is at least as imperfect in Argentina as it is in the United States, and it does not always yield good solutions. But it does allow a kind of muddling through toward policy solutions, although at times that muddling includes a good deal of mudslinging. The system functions adequately for gradual democratization, and it was all Argentina had at the time of transition. It was good enough.

It also brought some advantages that the founders of the United States did not anticipate. Jack Knight and James Johnson have argued that democracy is the best form of government based on the pragmatic notion that it is superior to all other forms of government in problem-solving. Conflict and disagreement, they suggest, are everywhere; in fact, they are normal rather than exceptional. Therefore, the ability to resolve conflict and coordinate action to facilitate moving forward on specific tasks is one of the most important services that a government can provide.[7] Their pragmatic argument for democracy fits Argentina's transition period well, particularly the Menem years. Problem-solving and the coordination of policy were strong

7. Jack Knight and James Johnson, *The Priority of Democracy: Political Consequences of Pragmatism* (Princeton: Princeton University Press, 2011).

points of the Menem presidency. Pragmatic problem-solving was not an asset emphasized by the founders of the presidential system, but institutional democratization also brought that asset to Argentina.

As Charles Tilly reminds us, democratization is never a neat, consistent forward process.[8] It may well involve two steps forward and one step back. It might also entail forward movement on some dimensions and backward movement on others. It may bring contradictions, particularly when guided by a contradictory party. Democratization led by a party ambivalent toward democracy itself is bound to feature contradictions, backsliding, and authoritarian behaviors. In democratization by institutions, the institutions themselves are both part of the problem and part of the solution. No real world democracy can ever claim to be a fully just society.[9] Each has problems, drawbacks, and injustices sewn into the democratic fabric. Nevertheless, and despite such imperfections, a democratic society is superior and preferable, a better place to live, one that offers more opportunities, fewer threats, and a safer existence than any other form of government. These characteristics certainly describe Argentina after the transition years studied here more than before or during that transition.

Democracies are often superior at resolving conflict. As a nation with a long history of poor conflict resolution, Argentina is certainly better today at resolving conflict among different sectors of society than it was before 1983. Democracy has both pragmatic as well as normative value. If the leadership of Peronism has been deficient on normative grounds, it has been quite useful on pragmatic grounds. Speaking pragmatically, the nation is today more able to foster cooperation, find and implement policy solutions, and coordinate itself toward common goals. This is no small achievement, particularly when we consider where the nation was in 1983. Much of this improved capacity came as a result of using the state's institutions to accomplish reform.

Beyond Transition

Democratization in Argentina struggles forward with the contradictory legacies the transition left behind. In its effort to fix itself, it caused new problems that it now must resolve. The nation benefits from momentous reform derived through a less than fully democratic process. The post-

---

8. Charles Tilly, *Democracy* (Cambridge: Cambridge University Press, 2007).

9. Josiah Ober, *Democracy and Knowledge: Innovation and Learning in Classical Athens* (Princeton: Princeton University Press, 2007).

transition years face challenges left by those years. During the extended crisis of transition, a strong president was precisely what Argentina needed. But after the crisis ended and consolidation began, then a more balanced use of power was in order. The presidential qualities that the nation needed in 1990 had become a threat to democracy by the end of that decade.

The United States has also gone through crisis periods of strong presidential leadership followed by periods of reining in presidential power. The periods after Lincoln and FDR were characterized by more subdued presidencies and an effort to roll back presidential power. After FDR, for example, a two-term limit was imposed upon the presidency. In the 2000s Argentina also struggled with finding the right balance, and the struggle continues today. In 2000 the nation began by ridding itself of Menem. It continued with an overly weak president, Fernando De la Rúa, who could not even face crisis but resigned instead. The nation has not yet found the best balance of executive power because the presidency has now moved to accept nepotism as a manner of succession. This new problem presents a new challenge to the ongoing effort to control the executive in Argentina.

Another problem left over from the transition period is the loss of a two-party system. Today, national elections involve competition between factions of Peronism. Even the 2015 victory of "the opposition" was only a victory of the opposition over Christina Kirchner, not the victory of a separate, strong, institutionalized party. It was the victory of another personalistic coalition including both Peronists and Radicals and it will not be surprising if Macri soon begins to show the same autocratic, personalistic tendencies exhibited by Menem and Christina Kirchner.[10] As V. O. Key illustrated for the U.S. South, this factionalized arrangement is no asset for democracy and releases deeply undemocratic behaviors inside an ostensibly democratic national system.[11] The one-party system has limited Argentina's ability to confront the social costs of the privatization policies and has caused many other problems of power abuse. As long as no other party appears to challenge Peronism, Peronist power abuse will continue. At elections a civil society lacking in democratic resources of its own then faces the nondemocratic option of one personalist party coalition or another. The nation does not have a class-based party system because Peronism alone attempts to represent all classes. But no single party can focus primarily upon the poor and also attend to business interests without

---

10. Some observers are more optimistic than I about the possible return of the Radicals and argue that the 2015 victory may indicate growing strength in the Radical Party. See Coimbra Mesquita and Corrado, "Corrupcion, sistemas mediaticos y gobiernos," 105.

11. V. O. Key, *Southern Politics in State and Nation* (New York: Alfred A. Knopf, 1949).

shortchanging one or the other. In the struggle over Peronist policy, the poor are more likely to lose, as Menem's presidency illustrated.

At the current moment, the best that factionalized Peronism can offer is a rightist candidate (e.g., Menem) who prioritizes neoliberal economics and a leftist candidate (e.g., the Kirchners) who prioritize social concerns, in the hopes that the leftist and rightist sectors of the electorate will be satisfied with alternating levels of attention. The PRI in Mexico, also a catch-all party, tried a similar approach during its eighty years in power. That strategy worked as long as elections were a charade, as they were for most of the twentieth century. Once elections became competitive, however, the PRI's catch-all approach faced problems. The party found itself challenged from both Left and Right and deprived of a majority electoral following. As democracy has continued and elections have become real, the PRI has struggled to redefine itself. It still has trouble relinquishing old habits like vote buying, which may have been determinant in the June 2012 election. Despite continuing old habits, the PRI promised voters that it had reformed itself, and 38 percent believed the promise. But a majority of the electorate did not, and the PRI governs now from the shaky position of a pluralist electoral victory that will require many compromises with adversaries.

The experience of the PRI provides perspective on the position of Peronism and helps us speculate about Argentina's future. At the moment, the PRI faces real electoral competition, forcing it to define and clarify its position. It also faces growing popular willingness to expose its nondemocratic behaviors, such as vote buying, even among voters who sold their votes. The PRI has moved from losing an election to winning a slender plurality. But while it has tried to represent everyone, it has essentially represented no one and has left itself open to attack from both the Left and the Right. Peronism shares many traits with the PRI, including the willingness to buy votes. But Peronism does not face any real electoral competition at the moment, and as long as that remains true it can probably continue to present itself as a catch-all party that represents everyone. It may also face less exposure of its nondemocratic habits in a noncompetitive electoral environment. But if elections became competitive again, Peronism could face challenges from the Left and the Right, as the PRI has done. Then, like the PRI, it might find itself struggling to hold on to an elusive middle ground while challengers clearly committed to the Left or to the Right hold the majority of the electorate. It would certainly be ironic if Peronism's effort to destroy alternative party competition ultimately led to its own demise.

Far more likely, however, is a scenario similar to that of the Republican Party in the United States at the turn of the twentieth century. The GOP battled over its traditional conservatism and a new brand of progressivism led by Teddy Roosevelt.[12] In that standoff, the progressives lost to conservatism, which has prevailed since. Progressive voices turned first to the Bull Moose Party and the independent candidacy of Teddy Roosevelt and later to the Democratic Party itself. The Republican Party then clearly re- defined itself as conservative and has remained that way for one hundred years.

This kind of self-definition and redefinition by parties is all part of the normal process of building, developing, and consolidating democracy. We see the process happening in Argentina and in other new democracies, and we sometimes forget that the older and more established democracies likewise went through similar phases. Parties can struggle internally over "who" they really are, just as the Republican Party did in the United States at the turn of the twentieth century. In that scuffle, parties can also disappear. Over sixty years before the internal Republican struggle in the United States, the Whig Party disappeared altogether, to be replaced by the Republicans. The Whigs no longer had a current agenda with which to appeal for votes while the Republicans did: free soil (land) and the limitation (and eventual abolition) of slavery. In response to such a challenge the Peronists could redefine themselves as either a leftist or rightist party or they be replaced by one of each. Over the long term Peronism will find it difficult to remain a catch-all party because the inner contradictions will consume much of the party's energy. Similarly, Argentina will have difficulty remaining both a single-party state and a democracy.

Coalition formation and factionalism can eventually lead to firmer divisions along stronger and more institutionalized party lines. For example, in the 1960s in the United States, the Democrats in the Deep South divided and factionalized against each other. Some favored reconciliation with the national party, which demanded greater racial equality; others preferred to break with the national party. Eventually some southerners stayed with the national Democratic Party while others toyed temporarily with a new party—the States Rights Party—and eventually joined the Republican Party. If the Peronist/Radical coalition that won in 2015 were to move away from personalistic leadership and institutionalize itself as a separate, left-of-center party it could become the challenge to Peronism that Argentina currently needs.

The problem with the Peronists is that they consider democratic insti-

---

12. On Teddy Roosevelt's effort to turn the Republican Party in a progressive direction, see Edmund Morris, *Colonel Roosevelt* (New York: Random House, 2010), chap. 1.

tutions and the rule of law to be nuisances, impediments to their policies and graft. This attitude can be found in the corruption and autocratic behavior of Menem and Christina Kirchner but also in similar behavior by provincial governors and union leaders. Unless and until someone else, another powerful party perhaps, teaches them the lesson that those institutions protect them as much as they constrain them, then they will continue to have this attitude. But if another power were to arrive in Argentina capable of destroying Peronism entirely, I believe we would suddenly find Peronists to be the greatest of all advocates of the inviolability of institutions and the rule of law because no one is more able to turn on a dime and reverse itself completely than is Peronism.

Another casualty of the transition years is the decline of a normative basis for politics. Peronism is a power-driven party primarily oriented toward pragmatic problem-solving. As a catch-all party, an ideological base for its policies becomes an electoral inconvenience. It does not make an argument for its policies based on what is the normatively right position. It only argues in favor of pragmatism. Pragmatism does matter, of course, and democracies need to solve problems. But politics periodically needs vision and normative inspiration as well. The failure of normative vision on the part of Peronist leaders has left some policies deficient. More normative language in the transition years would have allowed Menem to accomplish more and to leave a more positive legacy. One price for the lack of normative discourse is the human rights situation. Led by Peronism, Argentina has never been able to move forward on a large-scale policy of reparations and social healing. The last time a party took a normative position with respect to formulating major changes to human rights policy was during the Alfonsín administration, which is also the last time the Radicals governed for most of a complete presidential term.[13] The lack of a normative basis for politics affects not only the democracy itself but also the success of specific policies. The normative foundation of democracy is inseparable from its pragmatic value. Leaders

---

13. The Kirchners have overturned some of the laws that halted the human rights trials, allowing trials to continue. They have also established a day of mourning commemorating the disappeared. Symbolism is important. But with respect to concrete steps to address the issue, the Kirchner's approach has primarily been a return to Alfonsín's policies without offering a major new impetus of their own, such as reparations. Human rights issues received renewed attention in Argentina as a result of the naming of the new pope from Argentina, Pope Francis, who, himself, has a questionable past with regard to the issue. See Daniel H. Levine, "A Burden of History," *New York Times*, March 14, 2013; Diego Martinez, "Es la Impunidad Total," *Página 12*, March 15, 2013; and Alejandra Dandan, "Más Que Nunca," *Página 12*, March 25, 2013.

can do more pragmatically if they can use a normative argument to build a broad coalition of support for their policies.

And finally there is the question of civil society. Civil society was instrumental in bringing down the dictatorship and pressing for human rights.[14] Beyond that, however, as the mechanics of policy making began, civil society was often part of the problem rather than being part of a democratic solution. Yet by the end of the Menem years civil society had become more constructive and could have been included in policy making more. The story of the educational reforms illustrates that leaders need to learn how to build democratic coalitions that include sectors of civil society. That approach could elicit more positive involvement from civil society. Civil society is showing signs of awakening and there are examples of constructive popular action.[15] Some workers have taken control of factories closed during privatization, raised the funds to restart them, and taken over production themselves. Gabriela Ippolito-O'Donnell's work in Villa Lugano found neighbors able to unite to pave the streets, and there have been other neighborhood movements that attempt to build unity and services.[16] Each of these citizen efforts faces clientelistic power holders who seek to undermine independent citizen action, so any movement toward autonomous civil action is difficult.[17] But its development is crucial for democratic health, and whether a vibrant civil society can emerge could be the key question in Argentina for the next several decades. Each time the rule of law prevails, citizen trust in the system expands. Each time a citizen group succeeds other citizens are encouraged to try mobilization themselves. As the period of normalcy lengthens in Argentina and citizen groups test the waters with cooperative, mobilized goals, the nation may begin to develop some degree of positive social capital. As citizens learn to trust one another and work together toward political ends, civil society can then become a source of pressure upon the institutions to improve their own function even further, constrain executive power more, and fortify both the rule of law and institutional checking mechanisms.

---

14. Gabriela Ippolito-O'Donnell, "Calidad institucional y sociedad civil en la Argentina," in *Cuanto Importantan las Instituciones? Gobierno, Estado y Actores en la Politica Argentina*, ed. Carlos H. Acuña (Buenos Aires: Siglo Veintiuno Editores, 2013).

15. Enrique Peruzzotti, "The Nature of the New Argentine Democracy: The Delegative Democracy Argument Revisited," *Journal of Latin American Studies* 33, no. 1 (2001): 133–55, and "Broadening the Notion of Democratic Accountability: Participatory Innovation in Latin America," *Polity* (October 2012): 625–42; also see Ippolito-O'Donnell, "Calidad institucional y sociedad civil en la Argentina."

16. Ippolito-O'Donnell, *Right to the City*.

17. Anderson, "Democratization and Oppositional Consciousness."

Most studies of democratization that emphasize the positive role of civil society do not go on to consider how such a grassroots process of democratization can eventually include institutions. We need to consider more carefully how democratic energy from civil society and from state institutions can work together and enhance each other. Democratization need not be either grassroots driven or institutionally driven. It can be both. This study causes us to ask how such a combination can emerge. A nation that has democratized using its institutions now faces the task of incorporating civil society more. Capable leaders who build coalitions of public and legislative support will help move Argentina in that direction. If Argentina's leaders can learn to incorporate civil society more, then institutions will cease to be the nation's primary democratic resource.

Further Latin American Comparisons

Considering the role of institutions in other Latin American democracies helps us assess the value of institutional democratization more thoroughly. Across a region where hierarchical traditions prevail and civil society is sometimes not democratic, the democratization process elsewhere has also been one of institutional innovation. Like Argentina, other Latin American nations have a presidential system mapped on top of a tradition of centralized control. Without the empirical knowledge of the inner workings of those institutions that we have for Argentina, we cannot engage in the detailed scrutiny of institutional democratization done here. Yet that detailed scrutiny is precisely what we need. Mark Jones argues that single-country studies are necessary "because it takes years of study to gain sufficient understanding of a set of institutions to write a competent analysis."[18] We have that depth of analysis for the United States because U.S. scholars only study one country and produce volumes of careful analysis of U.S. institutions. Only similar in-depth analysis of other countries will allow meaningful comparison with the United States. It is difficult to know exactly how other Latin American nations are managing the difficult balance between the two countervailing forces of a presidential system and a centralized, hierarchical political tradition. But we can still see the broad outlines of an institutionally driven democratization process in other nations of the hemisphere. Many of these processes look more problematic than Argentina's.

18. Cited in Crisp and Botero, "Multicountry Studies of Latin American Legislatures," 331.

In Venezuela, actually an older democracy than Argentina, the nation's institutions proved unequal to the task of halting the gradual de-democratization process. Hugo Chávez used the electoral system and the vote of the low-income electorate to increase incrementally the level of power he held and his longevity in office. His behavior offered a frightening example of the abuse that can result when an authoritarian leader emphasizes poverty alleviation at the expense of the democratic political system itself. Chávez purchased the loyalty of the poor with social programs. His approach has been used by many populist authoritarians before him, including Perón and Hitler. The price Venezuela paid for poverty alleviation is the decline of democracy. Chávez effectively dismantled democracy's checks and balances, converting the institutions themselves into his victims. When viewed comparatively, Chávez's behavior is considerably more extreme than Menem's and places Menem's power abuse in perspective.

In comparison to the Venezuelan democracy, Argentina's institutions and its electoral process have done more to curb presidential power. Chavez sought to de-democratize Venezuela and moved a considerable distance in that direction. With his death, and the loss of the charisma that he used for his antidemocratic project, the nation's democratic institutions might have had an opportunity to rejuvenate themselves. However, Nicolas Maduro only continued to weaken the democratic institutions, now using Cuba as a model, and has brought the armed forces into the process of governance.[19] The Venezuelan case is particularly disturbing because the leaders dismantling democracy have extensive popular support. The long-term success of Chavez's and Maduro's efforts to degrade the nation's institutions is unknown because of the opposition's legislative victory in 2015. That outcome may enable Venezuela to revitalize its institutional checking mechanisms.

The Venezuelan case is particularly pertinent for Argentina. Both countries have seen democracy undermined by popular support for a charismatic leader. Venezuelan democracy was several decades old when Chávez appeared. It was older then than Argentina's democracy is now. One might have thought that Venezuela's democracy was safe from the return of authoritarianism, but it was not. In fact, significant sectors of civil society in Venezuela embraced Chávez and supported his efforts to expand his powers. In the face of an electorate that chose a nondemocrat, the institutions

---

19. On Venezuela's future, see Daniel H. Levine and José Molina, "Calidad de la Democracia en Venezuela," *America Latina Hoy* 45 (2013).

of state were powerless to stop him.[20] Argentina's electorate has repeatedly supported nondemocrats, and while Menem was less extreme than Chávez, Perón was probably worse. Therefore, the power of the state's formal institutions to support and protect democracy in the face of an electorate that fails to do so is an important question in Latin America more generally. If Argentina's electorate votes for authoritarianism, as Venezuela's voters have done, the best hope for democracy's survival will again fall to the nation's institutions. Given the history of Argentina's civil society, this scenario is possible.

Peru faced a similar dilemma. The nation likewise sought to democratize itself through the use of its institutions. Like Argentina and Venezuela, a president, this time Alberto Fujimori, sought ever-increasing amounts of power and wanted to dismantle the new democracy in the process. Like Menem, the guise that Fujimori used was crisis: the need to end terrorism and stop Sendero Luminoso's reign of fear. The goal was meritorious, but, unlike Alfonsín, Fujimori was willing to use nondemocratic means. The danger of that choice is the loss of democracy itself. In the face of legislative resistance, Fujimori simply closed down the Congress, disguising his action by misnaming it an "auto-coup." It was nothing of the kind. It was only another ambitious president seeking excessive power and attempting to circumvent the checking mechanisms of a presidential democracy. Fujimori's effort was ultimately unsuccessful. With the support and encouragement of regional international actors, the Congress struck back, removing Fujimori from office entirely and declaring him an outlaw.[21] The judiciary then took up the battle. When they launched an effort to arrest him Fujimori left Peru entirely, compelling the forces of law and order to chase him around the globe before they finally brought him to justice. In comparison to Menem, Fujimori was allowed to go much further toward dismantling

---

20. An article by Jennifer L. Merola and Elizabeth J. Zechmeister unpacks the Chavez situation further. They argue that while Chavez was seen as charismatic and that perception heightened popular support for him, poor performance by Chavez also eroded perceptions of his charisma. Voters who remained influenced by charisma inflated their positive view of Chavez's performance. The authors predicted a gradual decline in popular support for Chavez. The article was written before Chavez's death and gives us some idea of what we could expect for his successor, Maduro, who was considerably less charismatic. See "The Nature, Determinants and Consequences of Chavez' Charisma: Evidence from a Study of Venezuelan Public Opinion," *Comparative Political Studies* 44, no. 11 (January 2011): 28–54. A parliamentary election in 2015 was not determined by charisma, and delivered an opposition victory widely seen as a defeat for Maduro. See http://www.cnn.com/2015/12/07/americas/venezuela-oelections/ (accessed March 2, 2016).

21. Javier Aguayo, "The Legislature Strikes Back in Peru: The Role of Congress in the Demise of Fujimori in 2000," PhD diss., University of Florida, 2004.

democracy before the nation's institutions of state finally stopped him. But like Argentina, it was Peru's institutions, sustained by the international community, that gradually returned the nation to a more democratic path.

Possibly the Latin American nation whose institutions hold out the greatest democratic promise is Chile. There the formal institutions of state have a longer history than elsewhere on the continent. Institutions have gradually introduced and then improved upon democracy. In the aftermath of dictatorship, Chile's institutions themselves were tipped toward the right. As a result, part of Chile's democratization process has been an effort to remove the automatic institutional advantages that Pinochet left for the rightist parties. Chile has needed to level out its institutional playing field. The institutional democratization process in Chile has therefore been slower than Argentina's. But progress is discernible. Gradually the constraints left by Pinochet have been removed, weakened, or counterbalanced, and that process is still ongoing.

Evidence of growing democratic institutional strength is evident in Chile's improved human rights policy. It is true that external events in the democracies of Europe prodded Chile's institutions to get busy. A judge in Spain sought to extradite former dictator, Pinochet, from London where Pinochet had gone to seek medical attention. Britain refused to extradite Pinochet, angering the Spanish authorities and violating their extradition agreement with Spain. The entire affair became an international incident. However, Britain did send Pinochet home, ending his medical visit to London and advising Pinochet not to return. The incident prodded the Chilean judicial authorities into action. Since then, they have responded to international pressure and opinion with vigor. Whereas Chile started out looking deficient in its efforts to resolve questions of retroactive justice, today it appears to be advancing even ahead of Argentina on both retroactive justice and reparations. That advancement is owing to institutional changes, especially inside the judiciary. Nearly thirty years on, Chile's democracy looks to be resolving its institutional constraints and even its human rights problems, also through the use of institutions.[22]

If Chile offers one particularly successful example of the use of institutions for democratization, El Salvador probably provides the least successful example of the same. El Salvador proved unable to democratize itself at all without extensive external intervention. Close supervision by international actors was necessary for democracy to emerge. El Salvador's institutions have been quite unwilling to move on the issue of human

---

22. Collins, *Post-transitional Justice.*

rights, retroactive justice, or retribution.[23] Indeed, the movement toward democracy might not have been possible if retroactive justice had been part of the equation. El Salvador looks to have faced a cruel choice: democracy or retroactive justice, one or the other but not both. The nation has not resolved this quandary, and the institutions of state have contributed less to democracy than have grassroots processes at the local level.[24]

While these examples include only some of the democratization processes currently under way in Latin America, the overview illustrates that Argentina's democratization process shares much in common with democratization processes elsewhere on the continent. It is, in fact, toward the front in the pursuit of positive institutional contribution to the democratization process. If there is a difference, that difference shows that Argentina's institutions have provided more restraint upon power and done so sooner than many of Argentina's hemispheric neighbors. Although Argentina's institutions could certainly function better, they have still exceeded the function of their counterparts elsewhere in the region.

Revisiting the Comparison with the United States

Most studies of democratization do not explicitly compare the democratic reform process to politics in the United States. Yet the comparison with the United States made throughout this book has been useful on several levels. First, as part of its own democratic development, the United States established institutions that enable democratic participation and also restrain power. It was an early example of democratization so it is appropriate to ask whether it provides relevant information for later democratization processes. Second, clearly the Latin American nations thought that the U.S. example was useful because they designed their own institutions as presidential systems. Third, as the discussion makes clear, the United States has moved along the same path toward democratic development that Argentina is currently following and has, during its history, wrestled with crises that threaten democracy or the nation, just as Argentina wrestled during these transition years. Last, as part of its own institutionalization, like Argentina, the United States has turned to the president for leadership in times of severe crisis. That decision has led the United States to wrestle with the dilemma that haunts all presidential democracies: how to use the powers

---

23. Collins, *Post-transitional Justice*.

24. Manning, *Making of Democrats*; and Paul D. Almeida, *Waves of Protest: Popular Struggle in El Salvador, 1925–2005* (Minneapolis: University of Minnesota Press, 2008).

of the president to save the nation while constraining those powers to save democracy. The U.S. struggle is of relevance for all other democracies facing the same dilemmas.[25]

These broad commonalities have led to common specifics. In both nations, the president has shown a tendency to overreach his or her prescribed powers. The president's choice to reach toward more power in both countries has had a rationale in crisis and has been met with opposition from the other branches of state. While the degree of overreach is greater in Argentina, the fact of it is not. U.S. presidents have also used power in questionable ways at particular times. Yet the use of presidential power, as in Argentina, has often resulted in democratic advances. In particular, U.S. presidents have been inclined to use high levels of power or to overreach their power not only when they face crisis but also when they face extensive opposition or obstruction from the other institutions of state. Both of these scenarios occurred during Argentina's democratic transition. That comparison provides perspective on the two Argentine presidents studied here and causes us not to overreact in assessing presidential power in Argentina. Many of their efforts to use power have parallels in the United States. This is true even of Menem's efforts, particularly considering the crisis he faced.

Whereas both Argentina and the United States have looked toward a powerful, self-confident president to resolve crises and save the nation, the United States nonetheless has far more experience than Argentina in shrinking the powers of the presidency to something more appropriate to normal times. In the immediate aftermath of Lincoln's presidency, and especially after FDR, the United States turned toward more self-restrained presidents. Having a two-party system and an alternative party choice makes presidential constraint much easier. But even so, the U.S. today faces ongoing struggles of excessive presidential power such as with concerns about the imperial presidency and about excessive surveillance put in place by George W. Bush.[26]

This comparison with the United States has followed a generally comfortable tenor in which the United States looks good in comparison with Argentina. The United States has mostly managed to avoid the greatest dangers that confront Argentina, and Argentina can learn from studying

---

25. In fact, Robert Mickey explicitly calls for a study of United States politics in comparison with Argentina, Brazil, and Mexico—countries with which it shares much in common because of its protracted battle against authoritarianism in the Deep South. See *Paths Out of Dixie*, 352–53.

26. For a discussion of an excess of power in the United States presidency, see Arthur Schlesinger Jr., *The Imperial Presidency* (Boston: Houghton Mifflin, 1973).

U.S. politics. The United States is "ahead" of Argentina. But recent events in Washington introduce a less comfortable undercurrent to the U.S.-Argentina comparison. Those events have made the United States look more like Argentina than we would prefer to admit. Students of U.S. politics could learn by considering Argentina's democratic struggles.[27]

There were times in the Argentine democratic transition when one actor or several actors did not value democracy above and beyond their own immediate goals, policies, and preferences. Early in the transition years studied here that actor was the military, which had little or no democratic loyalty coming into the transition process, so their behavior is not surprising. But later in the transition years, particularly toward the end of the Alfonsín presidency, the Peronist Party itself displayed limited loyalty to the democratic system. To hold the democratic system itself hostage to political disagreements, or for one party to use the democratic government as a weapon in disagreement over policy, is to endanger democracy itself. Similarly, to refuse to follow the Constitution for partisan reasons weakens the Constitution itself, with potential long-term ramifications. To choose these tactics is to send a message that at least one party values its own position more than it values democracy. Such escalation risks the possibility that other actors will respond by fortifying other institutions of the democratic system beyond a healthy level simply in order to move forward the process of governance and policy implementation. In Washington today, the message of the Republican Party, and particularly of the Tea Party subsection of it, is that it values its own position more than it does the function of democratic government. By shutting down the government and threatening to do so again, Republicans illustrate that they value victory for themselves more than they value democracy itself or the democratic institutions. This is an extreme and dangerous message to send. It invites an extreme response.

In Argentina, Menem used congressional resistance to his policies as an excuse to extend presidential power still further. Obama may respond to the Republicans with a similar reaction. The configuration of Argentina's institutions, weighted as they are toward the presidency in any event, facilitated Menem's choice. But, as we have seen here, the long-term ramifications for Argentina's democracy were not good. Unable to get his policies implemented, his nominees considered, or even to keep the government open, current U.S. president Barack Obama faces a similar dilemma and

27. Lawrence Dodd writes that his understanding of political development in the United States has been informed by watching regime politics in Nicaragua. See "Congress in a Downsian World," *Journal of Politics* (March 2015).

could be tempted to respond in a similar manner: by heightening presidential powers. Voters may like that institutional response now, when it serves a popular president. But it alters the institutional balance of power, and, if taken, it will remain after the popular president leaves. Voters may then feel differently about a more powerful American president when he or she is not so popular.

Similarly, Peronist hardball politics during these transition years and shortly thereafter contributed to the demise of the Radical Party and, with it, the two-party system itself. While Peronists may greet their predominance with glee now, *any* party that faces no competition will gradually lose touch with its voter base. That is happening to Peronism today and may be happening to the Republican Party in the United States. While the Democrats may be playing less of a role in the demise of the Republicans than Peronism played in the demise of Radicalism, the overall outcome could be similar: the decline of two-party competition, also unhealthy for democracy. While the Democrats might celebrate the potential decline of the Republicans, over the long-term single party predominance does not facilitate democracy.

Finally, the tactics of House Republicans in closing down the government entirely has decreased trust in government. In the United States, many voters do not distinguish between the responsibility of the Republicans and that of the Democrats in closing the government. That failure causes an overall distrust in government itself. Surveys in the aftermath of the government shutdown reveal that more Americans distrust those in Washington, all of those in Washington. Argentina provides ample evidence that low levels of trust are not good for democracy. So again, the long-term effect of contemporary Republican tactics may weaken democracy itself. In short, both the Democrats and the Republicans in the United States today could learn from studying what Argentina has done to itself during the transition process studied here. Short-term tactics that weaken the institutional balance of power or events that permanently eliminate opposition have long-term negative ramifications for everyone in a democracy. The hope is that the United States can regain its equilibrium and avoid excessive presidentialism. The Republicans may learn to moderate before they lose more citizen support; in some places, they appear to be doing so, but the jury is still out on these tendencies.

Usually established democracies such as the United States can more easily move between strong presidents and presidential restraint, using powerful presidents in times of crisis but then pulling back from them when a crisis has passed. New democracies usually have less experience with such give and take. They have both the pressures of crises pushing for strong presidential powers and a tradition of centralized control that causes excessive presidentialism to be the default mode even in normal times. But usually is not the same thing as always. Experience does not leave the United States immune from the dangers present in Argentina. The U.S. democracy can monitor itself better by seeing how struggle in Argentina has left democracy weaker than it needed to be. Latin America's democratic consolidation process is likely to be one of learning to pull back from excessive presidentialism despite the dual influences in that direction. The task for the United States today may entail protecting against excessive presidentialism when congressional tactics make it appealing. In the process of curbing Latin American presidentialism, the other institutions of state will be crucial. In the United States, the need to avoid more presidentialism demands moderation on the part of Congress, particularly among the party that opposes the president. In Latin America, when civil society can contribute to executive constraint on an ongoing basis, the task of curbing the executive will be easier; when civil society does not represent a fully democratic influence, the institutions of state will face the task alone. In the United States civil society should also play a crucial role in curbing power, so it is important for the opposition not to alienate citizen trust unnecessarily.

Democratization by Institutions

The role of the state's formal institutions in the democratization process is rapidly becoming one of the most important questions in the study of Latin American politics. In the face of deliberate efforts by elected authoritarians to undermine nascent democracies in the region, the role that democratic institutions can play in promoting and protecting democracy is emerging as a central concern in the hemisphere. When elections themselves yield elected authoritarians, then civil society has abdicated its responsibility to promote democracy. Elections, then, are not enough to preserve democracy. This scenario is particularly probable in the face of the extreme poverty that still prevails among significant portions of the electorate in each nation. In recent elections throughout the region, the poor have frequently shown that they value social services more than they value democracy. Their preference is understandable given the desperation of their personal circumstances.

But over the long run, the choice of authoritarianism and social services will not serve the interests of the poor any more successfully than it serves the interests of the middle class, which is likely to see the Faustian trade-off sooner. It will then fall to the formal institutions of state to constrain those elected executives who do not believe in democracy. It will fall to the legislature and the judiciary to uphold the rule of law and continue the evolution of democracy until the electoral system once again yields a democrat. In emulating the basic institutional design of the United States, most Latin American democracies enjoy a system of checks and balances that can be used to muddle through toward democratization. Understanding that system and how it can be made to work for democracy is a key step in our study of Latin America. In a region where the intricate functioning inside and between institutions is understudied, we find ourselves in urgent need of understanding institutions better and of comprehending how they can play this essential democratic role. This book is a step in that direction.

If we assess Argentina's overall progress toward democratization we can say the following. The military appears to have been retired from public life, which is no small achievement. The hope is that no leader will invite them back into the governance process. As long as the military remains in the barracks, then the struggle between the military· and civilians is over. Now the nation faces a struggle among the civilians themselves. Within that contest, Argentina still has a long way to go. The nation needs an opposition party. It also needs an independent judiciary, one willing to face off against the executive and be guaranteed of survival, both personal and institutional. Argentina falls far short of any balanced equilibrium of power between the judiciary and the executive. Argentina's concentration of power in the executive has to be reduced and power dispersed more broadly. Civil society needs to become more activist, robust, and mobilized.

Democratization by institutions looks to be a slow process, one of generations rather than of years or even decades. But the British example proves that so slow a process does, nevertheless, work. The haughty arrogance of President Christina Kirchner shows that these qualities are not confined to one gender, although they are certainly pronounced within one party. Examples like the resignation of Vice President Eduardo Duhalde and his de facto appointment as Buenos Aires governor—a freewheeling approach to institutional constraints—will have to stop if democracy is to take its next steps forward.[28] At the moment, and partly as a result of these

---

28. This type of behavior within the Peronist Party exemplifies the party's limited loyalty to democratic rules and procedures. It was one reason why opponents of Peronism were concerned about Menem's presidency. In doling out public office as if it were the personal property of the president to distribute as he pleased, Peronism acted as if Argentina's state

transition years, the Argentine executive is not prepared to accept judicial restraint. Yet absolute power corrupts and it corrupts absolutely. Now that the military and labor are under control, the next authoritarian stronghold in need of control is the executive itself. This book has shown that such control is both problematic and gradually possible. It is toward that task that Argentina must turn now.

---

belonged to the president. In the absence of a governor for the Province of Buenos Aires, an open election should have been held in which the vice president was not a candidate. Instead, Duhalde felt no responsibility to complete his term in office as the vice president and instead ran unopposed for the provincial governorship. When he won he stepped down as vice president and became governor of the Province of Buenos Aires. In the crisis context of 1989 no one had the inclination to fuss over such loose handling of democratic rules. It is important to note here that Duhalde's resignation from the vice presidency should also be seen in the context of long-standing conflict between him and Menem. Duhalde did not support Menem's policies and would eventually oppose him as contender for the Peronist presidential candidacy. Given the differences between the president and vice president over policy, both leaders may have felt that it was wiser for Duhalde to leave the administration.

Argentina's nondemocratic pattern over these first thirty years of democracy, and particularly more recently, is for vice presidents to step down into the governorship of the most important province, or of an important province, and from there attempt to make a run for candidacy for the presidency. I am indebted to Aníbal Corrado for this observation.

References

Aberbach, Joel D., and Mark A. Peterson. 2005a. "Presidents and Bureaucrats: The Executive Branch and American Democracy." In *The Executive Branch*, edited by Joel D. Aberbach and Mark A. Peterson. Oxford: Oxford University Press.

Aberbach, Joel D., and Mark A. Peterson. 2005b. "Control and Accountability: Dilemmas of the Executive Branch." In *The Executive Branch*, edited by Joel D. Aberbach and Mark A. Peterson. Oxford: Oxford University Press.

Adelman, Jeremy. 2007. "Between Order and Liberty: Juan Batista Alberdi and the Intellectual Origins of Argentine Constitutionalism." *Latin American Research Review* 42, no. 2: 86–110.

Alter, Jonathan. 2006. *The Defining Moment: FDR's Hundred Days and the Triumph of Hope*. New York: Simon and Schuster.

Ames, Barry. 1987. *Political Survival: Politicians and Public Policy in Latin America*. Berkeley: University of California Press.

Anderson, Leslie E. 1994. *The Political Ecology of the Modern Peasant: Calculation and Community*. Baltimore: Johns Hopkins University Press.

Anderson, Leslie E. 2002. "Of Wild and Cultivated Politics: Conflict and Democracy in Argentina." *International Journal of Politics, Culture and Society* 16, no. 1 (Fall): 99–132.

Anderson, Leslie E. 2006. "The Authoritarian Executive: Horizontal and Vertical Accountability in Nicaragua." *Latin American Politics and Society* 48, no. 2: 141–69.

Anderson, Leslie E. 2009. "The Problem of Single-Party Predominance in an Unconsolidated Democracy: The Example of Argentina." *Perspectives on Politics* 7, no. 4 (December): 767–84.

Anderson, Leslie E. 2010a. *Social Capital in Developing Democracies: Nicaragua and Argentina Compared*. Cambridge: Cambridge University Press.

Anderson, Leslie E. 2010b. "Poverty and Political Empowerment: Local Citizen Political Participation as a Path toward Social Justice in Nicaragua." *Forum on*

Public Policy 2010, no. 4 (December). Available at http://forumonpublicpolicy. com/Vol2010.no4/archive.vol2010.no4/anderson.leslie.pdf

Anderson, Leslie E. 2014. "Democratization and Oppositional Consciousness in Argentina." *Polity* 46, no. 2 (April): 164–81.

Anderson, Leslie E. 2015a. "Clientelism, Semiclientelism, and Pluralism: Towards a Theory of Grassroots Autonomy." Manuscript under review.

Anderson, Leslie E. 2016. *Federal Powers in Democratization: Human and Civil Rights in Argentina and the United States.* Manuscript in progress.

Anderson, Leslie E., and Lawrence C. Dodd. 2005. *Learning Democracy: Citizen Engagement and Electoral Choice in Nicaragua, 1990–2001.* Chicago: University of Chicago Press.

Anderson, Leslie E., and Lawrence C. Dodd. 2009. "Nicaragua: Progress amid Regress?" *Journal of Democracy* 20, no. 3 (July): 153–67.

Anderson, Leslie E., and Won-ho Park. 2016. "International Contributions to Nicaraguan Democracy: The Role of Foreign Municipal Donations for Social Development." *Foreign Policy Analysis.* doi:10.1093/fpa/orw047.

Anderson, Thornton H. 1993. *Creating the Constitution: The Convention of 1787 and the First Congress.* University Park: Pennsylvania State University Press.

Anner, Mark. 2008. "Meeting the Challenges of Industrial Restructuring: Labor Reform and Enforcement in Latin America." *Latin American Politics and Society* 50, no. 2 (Summer): 33–65.

Arnson, Cynthia J., ed. 1999. *Comparative Peace Processes in Latin America.* Washington, DC: Woodrow Wilson Center; Stanford: Stanford University Press.

Auyero, Javier. 2007. *Routine Politics and Violence in Argentina: The Gray Zone.* New York: Cambridge University Press.

Auyero, Javier, Pablo Lapegna, and Fernanda Page Poma. 2009. "Patronage Politics and Contentious Collective Action: A Recursive Relationship." *Latin American Politics and Society* 51, no. 3 (Fall): 1–31.

Auyero, Javier, and Débora Alejandra Swiston. 2009. *Flammable: Environmental Suffering in an Argentine Shantytown.* Oxford: Oxford University Press.

Banco Central de la Republica Argentina, Secretaria de Hacienda. 1976. *Gobierno general: cuenta de ingresos y gasto corrientes.* Vol. 4. Buenos Aires: Banco Central de la Republica Argentina, Secretaria de Hacienda.

Barahona de Brito, Alexandra. 1997. *Human Rights and Democratization in Latin America: Uruguay and Chile.* Oxford: Oxford University Press.

Barkan, Elazar. 1996. "Payback Time: Restitution and the Moral Economy of Nations." *Tikkun* (September 19): 52.

Bates, Robert. 1981. *Markets and States in Tropical Africa.* Berkeley: University of California Press.

Bayard de Volo, Lorraine. 2006. "The Nonmaterial Long-Term Benefits of Collective Action: Empowerment and Social Capital in a Nicaraguan Women's Organization." *Comparative Politics* 38, no. 2 (January): 149–67.

Beer, Caroline C. 2006. "Judicial Performance and the Rule of Law in the Mexican States." *Latin American Politics and Society* 48, no. 3 (September): 33–61.

Belini, Claudio. 2006. "El grupo Bunge y la política económica del primer peronismo, 1943–1952." *Latin American Research Review* 41, no. 1: 27–50.

Bermeo, Nancy. 1994. "Sacrifice, Sequence, and Strength in Successful Dual Transitions: Lessons from Spain." *Journal of Politics* 56, no. 3 (August): 601–27.

Bermeo, Nancy. 2003. *Ordinary People in Extraordinary Times: The Citizenry and the Breakdown of Democracy*. Princeton: Princeton University Press.

Boix, Carles. 1998. *Political Parties, Growth and Equality: Conservative and Social Democratic Economic Strategies in the World Economy*. New York: Cambridge University Press.

Bonner, Michelle. 2007. *Sustaining Human Rights: Women and Argentine Human Rights Organizations*. University Park: Pennsylvania State University Press.

Bowen, Ralph H. 1947. *German Theories of the Corporative State with Special Reference to the Period 1870–1919*. New York: McGraw Hill.

Bowman, Kirk S. 2002. *Militarization, Democracy, and Development: The Perils of Praetorianism in Latin America*. University Park: Pennsylvania State University Press.

Bowman, Kirk S. 2011. "Book Review of Leslie E. Anderson, *Social Capital in Developing Democracies: Nicaragua and Argentina Compared*." *Latin American Politics and Society* 53, no. 3 (Fall): 188–92.

Brinks, Daniel. 2008. *Judicial Responses to Police Killings in Latin America: Inequality and the Rule of Law*. Cambridge: Cambridge University Press.

Brock, Michael. 1973. *The Great Reform Act*. London: Hutchinson and Co.

Bruce, M. 1968. *The Coming of the Welfare State*. 4th ed. London: Batsford.

Brysk, Alison. 1994. *The Politics of Human Rights in Argentina: Protest, Change, and Democratization*. Stanford: Stanford University Press.

Buchanan, Paul G. 2008. "Preauthoritarian Institutions and Postauthoritarian Outcomes: Labor Politics in Chile and Uruguay." *Latin American Politics and Society* 50, no. 1 (Spring): 59–89.

Bunce, Valerie. 1998. *Subversive Institutions: The Design and the Destruction of Socialism and the State*. New York: Cambridge University Press.

Burns, James MacGregor. 1956. *Roosevelt: The Lion and the Fox*. New York: Harcourt Brace Jovanovich.

Burns, James MacGregor Burns. 1963. *The Deadlock of Democracy: Four-Party Politics in America*. Englewood Cliffs, NJ: Prentice-Hall.

Burrin, Phillippe. 1984. "La France dans le Champ Magnetique des Fascismes." *Le Debat* 32: 52–72.

Calvo, Ernesto, and Juan Pablo Micozzi. 2005. "The Governor's Backyard: A Seat Vote Model of Electoral Reform for Subnational Multi-Party Races." *Journal of Politics* 67, no. 4 (November): 1050–74.

Canellos, Peter S. 2009. *Last Lion: The Fall and Rise of Ted Kennedy*. New York: Simon and Schuster.

Cantini, Jose Luis. 1997. *La Autonomia y Autarquia de las Universidades Nacionales*. Buenos Aires: Academia Nacional de Educación.

Cappon, Lester J., ed. 1971. *The Adams-Jefferson Letters: The Complete Correspondence between Thomas Jefferson and Abigail and John Adams*. New York: Simon and Shuster.

Caro, Robert A. 2002. *The Years of Lyndon Johnson: Master of the Senate*. New York: Alfred A. Knopf.

Caro, Robert A. 2012. *The Years of Lyndon Johnson: The Passage of Power.* New York: Knopf.

Carranza, Mario Esteban. 1983. "The Role of Military Expenditure in the Development Process: The Argentine Case 1946–80." *Nordic Journal of Latin American Studies* 12 (1–2): 115–66.

Catterberg, Edgardo. 1991. *Argentina Confronts Politics: Political Culture and Public Opinion in the Argentine Transition to Democracy.* Boulder: Lynn Rienner.

Chambers, Simone. 1996. *Reasonable Democracy.* Ithaca: Cornell University Press.

Chavez, Rebecca Bill. 2004. *The Rule of Law in Nascent Democracies: Judicial Politics in Argentina.* Stanford: Stanford University Press.

Cleary, Matthew, and Susan Stokes. 2006. *Democracy and the Culture of Skepticism: Political Trust in Argentina and Mexico.* New York: Russell Sage.

Cohen, Richard E. 2010. "Pelosi: The Campaign Boss." *National Journal* (May 8).

Coimbra Mesquita, Nuno, and Aníbal Corrado. 2015. "Corrupción, sistemas mediáticos y gobiernos: Contextos de acusación y respuestas del poder public en Argentina y Brasil." *Politai: Revista de Ciencia Politica* 6, part 2 (11): 89–110.

Collins, Cath. 2010. *Post-transitional Justice: Human Rights in Chile and El Salvador.* University Park: Pennsylvania State University Press.

Comissão Nacional da Verdade. 2014. http://www.cnv.gov.br/index.php/outros-destaques/576-verdade-e-reconciliacao-dentro-e-fora

Congreso de la Nacion, Argentina, Camara de Senadores. 1983–99. *Diario de Sesiones.*

Cooper, Phillip J. 2002. *By Order of the President: The Use and Abuse of Executive Direct Action.* Lawrence: University Press of Kansas.

Corrales, Javier, and Michael Penfold. 2011. *Dragon in the Tropics: Hugo Chávez and the Political Economy of Revolution in Venezuela.* Washington, DC: Brookings Institution Press.

Cortazar, René, ed. 1990. *Inflacion rebelde en America Latina.* Santiago, Chile: CIEPLAN (Corporación de Estudios Para Latinoamerica), Hachette.

Cortazar, René, and Jose Able Arellano, eds. 1988. *Politicas Macro-economicas: Una Perspectivea Latinoamericana.* Santiago de Chile: Corporacion de Investigaciones Econoicas para Latinoamerica.

Cortazar, René, Alejandro Foxley, and Victor E. Tokman. 1984. *Llegados del Monetarismo, Argentina y Chile.* Buenos Aires: PREALCOIT Ediciones Soilar.

Corwin, Edward S. 1948. *The President: Office and Powers.* New York: New York University Press.

Crisp, Brian F., and Felipe Botero. 2004. "Multicountry Studies of Latin American Legislatures: A Review Article." *Legislative Studies Quarterly* 29:329–56.

Crocker, David A. 2000. "Truth Commissions, Transitional Justice, and Civil Society." In *Truth v. Justice: The Morality of Truth Commissions,* edited by Robert I. Rotberg and Dennis Thompson, 99–121. Princeton: Princeton University Press.

Dandan, Alejandra. 2013. "Más Que Nunca." *Página 12,* March 25.

Davis, Richard W. 2008. *A Political History of the House of Lords 1811–1846: From the Regency to the Corn Law Repeal.* Stanford: Stanford University Press.

Dawson, John. (1977) 1995. *Healing America's Wounds.* Ventura, CA: Regal Books.

Delbanco, Andrew. 2012. *College: What It Was, Is, and Should Be.* Princeton: Princeton University Press.

de Rosetti, Mabel M. 1996. *La Teoría de los Polisistemas en el Área Educativa.* Buenos Aires: Academia Nacional de Educación.

Díaz, Rodolfo. 2002. *Prosperidad o Ilusion? Las reformas de los 90 en Argentina.* Buenos Aires: Editorial Abaco de Rodolfo Depsalma.

Dodd, Lawrence C. 2015. "Congress in a Downsian World." *Journal of Politics* 77, no. 2 (March): 311–23.

Dominguez, Jorge, and James McCann. 1998. *Democratizing Mexico: Public Opinion and Electoral Choices.* Baltimore: Johns Hopkins University Press.

Dorfman, Ariel. 1991. *Death and the Maiden.* New York: Penguin Books.

Dosh, Paul. 2009. "Tactical Innovation, Democratic Governance and Mixed Motives: Popular Movement Resilience in Peru and Ecuador." *Latin American Politics and Society* 51, no. 1 (Spring): 87–118.

Downs, Anthony. 1957. *An Economic Theory of Democracy.* New York: Harper and Row.

Downs, Jim. 2012. *Sick from Freedom: African-American Illness and Suffering during the Civil War and Reconstruction.* Oxford: Oxford University Press.

Drake, Richard. 1995. *The Aldo Moro Murder Case.* Cambridge: Harvard University Press.

Dryzek, John. 2009. "Democratization as Deliberative Capacity Building." *Comparative Political Studies* 42, no. 11 (November): 1379–1402.

Duquette, Michel. 1999. *Building New Democracies: Economic and Social Reform in Brazil, Chile and Mexico.* Toronto: University of Toronto Press.

Eckstein, Harry. 1992. *Regarding Politics: Essays on Political Theory, Stability, and Change.* Berkeley: University of California Press.

Eckstein, Susan. 1977. *The Poverty of Revolution: The State and the Urban Poor in Mexico.* Princeton: Princeton University Press.

Editorial Cinae. 1983. *Universidad y Sistema Educativo: Libertad y Compromiso.* Buenos Aires.

Editorial Estrada. 1971. *Nuevas Universidades para un Nuevo Pais.* Buenos Aires.

Edwards, Sebastian. 2010. *Left Behind: Latin America and the False Promise of Populism.* Chicago: University of Chicago Press.

Edwards, Sebastian, and Alejandra Cox Edwards. 2002. *Social Security Privatization Reform and Labor Markets: The Case of Chile.* Working Paper 8924. Cambridge: National Bureau of Economic Research.

Elazar, Daniel J. 1970. *Cities of the Prairie: The Metropolitan Frontier and American Politics.* New York: Basic Books.

Elkins, Zachary, Tom Ginsburg, and James Melton. 2009. *The Endurance of National Constitutions.* Cambridge: Cambridge University Press.

Elster, Jon. 1988. "Is There a Right to Work?" In *Democracy and the Welfare State,* edited by Amy Gutmann. Princeton: Princeton University Press.

Encarnación, Omar. 2014. *Democracy without Justice in Spain: The Politics of Forgetting.* University Park: Pennsylvania State University Press.

Epsing-Anderson, Gosta. 1990. *The Three Worlds of Welfare Capitalism,* Princeton: Princeton University Press.

Epstein, Edward. 2010. "Pelosi Gets Good Marks in Two New Books." *Congressional Quarterly Weekly*, May 10.

Etchemendy, Sebastian. 2005. "Old Actors in New Markets: Transforming the Populist/Industrial Coalition in Argentina, 1989–2001." In *Argentine Democracy: The Politics of Institutional Weakness*, edited by Steven Levitsky and María Victoria Murillo, 62–87. University Park: Pennsylvania State University Press.

Evans, Rowland, and Robert Novak. 1966. *Lyndon B. Johnson: The Exercise of Power. A Political Biography*. New York: New American Library.

Falleti, Tulia. 2010. *Decentralization and Subnational Politics in Latin America*. Cambridge: Cambridge University Press.

Ferla, Salvador. 1974. *La Tercera Posicion Ideologica y Apreciaciones Sobre el Retorno de Peron*. Buenos Aires: Ediciones Meridiano.

Ffrench, Ricardo. 2002. *Economic Reforms in Chile: From Dictatorship to Democracy*. Ann Arbor: University of Michigan Press.

Field, Bonnie N. 2006. "Transitions to Democracy in Internal Party Rules: Spain in Comparative Perspective." *Comparative Politics* 39, no. 1 (October): 83–102.

Fisher, Louis. 1975. *Presidential Spending Power*. Princeton: Princeton University Press.

Fitch, John S. 1998. *The Armed Forces and Democracy in Latin America*. Baltimore: Johns Hopkins University Press.

Fitch, John S., and Andrés Fontana. 1990. "Military Policy and Democratic Consolidation in Latin America." Working paper. Buenos Aires: CEDES (Centro de Estudios de Estado y Sociedad).

Forment, Carlos. 2004. *Democracy in Latin America*. Chicago: University of Chicago Press.

Fox, Jonathan. 1992. *The Politics of Food in Mexico: State Power and Social Mobilization*. Ithaca: Cornell University Press.

Fox, Jonathan. 1994. "The Difficult Transition from Clientelism to Citizenship." *World Politics* 46, no. 2 (January 1994): 151–84.

Fox, Jonathan. 2008. *Accountability Politics: Power and Voice in Rural Mexico*. Oxford: Oxford University Press.

Fraser, D. 1973. *The Evolution of the Welfare State*. London: Macmillan.

Fritzsche, Peter. 1998. *Germans into Nazis*. Cambridge: Harvard University Press.

Fullinwider, Robert K. 1998. "Citizenship and Welfare." In *Democracy and the Welfare State*, edited by Amy Gutmann, 261–78. Princeton: Princeton University Press.

Gais, Thomas, and James Fossett. 2005. "Federalism and the Executive Branch." In *The Executive Branch*, edited by Joel D. Aberbach and Mark A. Peterson. Oxford: Oxford University Press.

Galvan, Dennis C. 2004. *The State Must Be Our Master of Fire: How Peasants Craft Culturally Sustainable Development in Senegal*. Berkeley: University of California Press.

Garreton, Manuel Antonio. 2003. *Incomplete Democracy: Political Democratization in Chile and Latin America*. Chapel Hill: University of North Carolina Press.

Germani, Gino. 1978. *Authoritarianism, Fascism, and National Populism*. New Brunswick, NJ: Transaction Books.

Gibson, Edward L. 2012. *Boundary Control: Subnational Authoritarianism in Federal Democracies*. New York: Cambridge University Press.

Ginsburg, Tom. 2003. *Judicial Review in New Democracies: Constitutional Courts in Asian Cases*. New York: Cambridge University Press.

Giraudy, Augustina. 2007. "The Distributive Politics of Emergency Employment Programs in Argentina (1993–2002)." *Latin American Research Review* 42, no. 2: 33–55.

Golden, Miriam. 1988. *Labor Divided: Austerity and Working Class Politics in Contemporary Italy*. Ithaca: Cornell University Press.

Goodhart, Michael. 2008. "A Democratic Defense of Universal Basic Income." In *The Illusion of Consent: Engaging with Carol Pateman*, edited by Daniel O'Neill, Mary Lyndon Shanley, and Iris Marion Young. University Park: Pennsylvania State University Press.

Gough, Ian, and Geoffrey Wood. 2004. "Introduction." In *Insecurity and Welfare Regimes in Asia, Africa and Latin America: Social Policy in Development Contexts*, edited by Ian Gough and Geoffrey Wood, 1–11. Cambridge: Cambridge University Press.

Gourevitch, Peter. 1986. *Politics in Hard Times: Comparative Responses to International Economic Crisis*. Ithaca: Cornell University Press.

Greene, Kenneth F. 2007. *Why Dominant Parties Lose: Mexico's Democratization in Comparative Perspective*. New York: Cambridge University Press.

Griffin, Roger. 1995. *Fascism*. Oxford: Oxford University Press.

Grindle, Merilee S. 2004. *Despite the Odds: The Contentious Politics of Education Reform*. Princeton: Princeton University Press.

Guest, Iain. 1990. *Behind the Disappearances: Argentina's Dirty War against Human Rights and the United Nations*. Philadelphia: University of Pennsylvania Press.

Guillebaud, C. W. 1941. *The Social Policy of Nazi Germany*. Cambridge: Cambridge University Press.

Gutmann, Amy. 1988. "Distributing Public Education in a Democracy." In *Democracy and the Welfare State*, edited by Amy Gutmann. Princeton: Princeton University Press.

Gutmann, Amy, ed. 1988. *Democracy and the Welfare State*. Princeton: Princeton University Press.

Gutmann, Amy. (1987) 1999. *Democratic Education*. 2nd ed. Princeton: Princeton University Press.

Gutmann, Amy, and Dennis Thompson. 1996. *Democracy and Disagreement*. Cambridge: Harvard University Press.

Gutmann, Amy, and Dennis Thompson. 2000. "The Moral Foundations of Truth Commissions." In *Truth v. Justice: The Morality of Truth Commissions*, edited by Robert I. Rotberg and Dennis Thompson, 22–44. Princeton: Princeton University Press.

Gutmann, Amy, and Dennis Thompson. 2004. *Why Deliberative Democracy*. Princeton: Princeton University Press.

Habermas, Jürgen. 1979. *Communication and the Evolution of Society*. Translated by Thomas McCarthy. Boston: Beacon Press.

Habermas, Jürgen. 1996. *Between Facts and Norms: Contributions to a Discourse Theory of Law and Democracy*. Translated by William Rehg. Cambridge: MIT Press.

Hagopian, Frances. 1996. *Traditional Politics and Regime Change in Brazil*. New York: Cambridge University Press.

Halperin Donghi, Tulio. 1962. *Historia de la Universidad de Buenos Aires*. Buenos Aires: Eudeba.

Hardeman, D. B., and Donald C. Bacon. 1987. *Rayburn: A Biography*. Austin: Texas Monthly Press.

Haskins, Ethelbert W. 2010. *Victim Psychosis in the Center City Ghettos*. Denver: Outskirts Press.

Hayner, Patricia. 2001. *Unspeakable Truths: Confronting State Terror and Atrocity*. New York: Routledge.

Helmke, Gretchen. 2005. "Enduring Uncertainty: Court-Executive Relations in Argentina during the 1990s and Beyond." In *Argentine Democracy: The Politics of Institutional Weakness*, edited by Steven Levitsky and María Victoria Murillo, 139–64. University Park: Pennsylvania State University Press.

Hernandez, Antonio Maria. 1995. *Reforma Constitucional de 1994: Labor del Convencional Constituyente*. Buenos Aires: Camara de Diputados de la Nación.

Herrera, María Rosa. 2008. "La Contienda Política en Argentina 1997–2002: Un Ciclo de Protesta." *América Latina Hoy* 48:165–89.

Herzog, Don. 1998. *Poisoning the Minds of the Lower Orders*. Princeton: Princeton University Press.

Herzog, Don. 2006. *Cunning*. Princeton: Princeton University Press.

Heymann, Daniel, and Fernando Navajas. 1990. "Conflicto distributivo y déficit fiscal: Notas sobre la experienca argentina." In *Inflacion rebelde en America Latina*, edited by José Pablo Arellano. Santiago, Chile: CIEPLAN (Corporación de Estudios Para Latinoamerica), Hachette.

Hilgers, Tina. 2008. "Causes and Consequences of Political Clientelism: Mexico's PRD in Comparative Perspective." *Latin American Politics and Society* 51, no. 4 (Winter): 123–53.

Hochstetler, Kathryn. 2006. "Rethinking Presidentialism: Challenges and Presidential Falls in South America." *Comparative Politics* 34, no. 4: 401–18.

Holden, Robert H. 2004. *Armies without Nations: Public Violence and State Formation in Central America, 1821–1960*. Oxford: Oxford University Press.

Holt, Michael, 1978. *The Political Crisis of the 1850s*. New York: W. W. Norton.

Horowitz, Michael J. 1989. "Commentary and Exchanges on Politics and Public Debate." In *The Fettered Presidency: Legal Constraints on the Executive Branch*, edited by L. Gordon Crovitz and Jeremy A. Rabkin. Washington, DC: American Enterprise Institute for Public Policy Research.

Houle, Christian. 2009. "Inequality and Democracy: Why Inequality Harms Consolidation but Does Not Affect Democratization." *World Politics* 61, no. 4 (October): 589–622.

Howell, William G. 2003. *Power without Persuasion: The Politics of Direct Presidential Action*. Princeton: Princeton University Press.

Huber, Evelyn, Thomas Mustillo, and John D. Stephens. 2008. "Politics and Social Spending in Latin America." *Journal of Politics* 70, no. 2 (April): 420–36.

Huber, Evelyn. 2005. "Democratic Governance in Latin America: Successful Social Policy Regimes? Political Economy and the Structure of Social Policy in Argentina, Chile, Uruguay and Costa Rica." Paper presented at the conference "Democratic Governability in Latin America," October 7, University of Notre Dame.

Hunter, Wendy. 2007. "The Nationalization of an Anomaly: The Worker's Party in Brazil." *World Politics* 59 (April): 440–75.

Hunter, Wendy. 2010. *The Transformation of the Worker's Party in Brazil, 1989–2009.* Cambridge: Cambridge University Press.

Huntington, Samuel. 1968. *Political Order in Changing Societies.* New Haven: Yale University Press.

Huskey, Eugene. 1999. *Presidential Power in Russia.* Armonk, NY: M. E. Sharpe.

Ippolito-O'Donnell, Gabriela. 2012. *The Right to the City: Popular Contention in Contemporary Buenos Aires.* Notre Dame, IN: University of Notre Dame Press.

Ippolito-O'Donnell, Gabriela. 2013. "Calidad institucional y sociedad civil en la Argentina." In *Cuanto Importantan las Instituciones? Gobierno, Estado y Actores en la Politica Argentina,* edited by Carlos H. Acuña. Buenos Aires: Siglo Veintiuno Editores.

Itzigsohn, John. 2000. *Developing Poverty: The State, Labor, Market Deregulation, and the Informal Economy in Costa Rica and the Dominican Republic.* University Park: Pennsylvania State University Press.

Jamal, Amaney. 2007. *Barriers to Democracy: The Other Side of Social Capital in Palestine and the Arab World.* Princeton: Princeton University Press.

James, Scott C. 2005. "The Evolution of the Presidency: Between the Promise and the Fear." In *The Executive Branch,* edited by Joel D. Aberbach and Mark A. Peterson. Oxford: Oxford University Press.

Jones, Mark. 1995. *Electoral Laws and the Survival of Presidential Democracies.* Notre Dame, IN: University of Notre Dame Press.

Jones, Mark P., and Wonjae Hwang. 2005. "Provincial Party Bosses: Keystone of the Argentina Congress." In *Argentine Democracy: The Politics of Institutional Weakness,* edited by Steven Levitsky and María Victoria Murillo, 115–38. University Park: Pennsylvania State University Press.

Kahneman, D., and A. Tversky. 1979. "Prospect Theory: An Analysis of Decision under Risk." *Econometrica* 47:263–91.

Karl, Terry Lynn. 1987. "Petroleum and Pacts: The Transition to Democracy in Venezuela." *Latin American Research Review* 22:63–94.

Keck, Margaret, and Kathryn Sikkink. 1998. *Activists beyond Borders: Advocacy Networks in International Politics.* Ithaca: Cornell University Press.

Kenny, Charles D. 2004. *Fujimori's Coup and the Breakdown of Democracy in Latin America.* Notre Dame, IN: University of Notre Dame Press.

Key, V. O., Jr. 1949. With the assistance of Alexander Heard. *Southern Politics in State and Nation.* New York: Knopf.

Klesner, Joseph. 2007. "Social Capital and Political Participation in Latin America: Evidence from Argentina, Chile, Mexico and Peru." *Latin American Research Review* 42, no. 2: 1–32.

Knight, Jack. 1992. *Institutions and Social Conflict.* New York: Cambridge University Press.

Knight, Jack, and James Johnson. 2011. *The Priority of Democracy: Political Consequences of Pragmatism.* Princeton: Princeton University Press.

Kohli, Atul. 1990. *Democracy and Discontent: India's Growing Crisis of Governability*. Cambridge: Cambridge University Press.

Kohli, Atul. 2004. *State Directed Development: Political Power and Industrialization in the Global Periphery*. Cambridge: Cambridge University Press.

Krouse, Richard, and Michael McPherson. 1988. "Capitalism, 'Property-Owning Democracy,' and the Welfare State." In *Democracy and the Welfare State*, edited by Amy Gutman. Princeton: Princeton University Press.

Kumlin, Staffan, and Bo Rothstein. 2005. "Making and Breaking Social Capital: The Impact of Welfare State Institutions." *Comparative Political Studies* 38, no. 4 (May): 339–65.

La Nacion. 1983–89. Buenos Aires.

La Prensa. 1983–89. Buenos Aires.

Ledewitz, Bruce. 1979. "The Uncertain Power of the President to Execute the Laws." *Tennessee Law Review* 46, no. 4 (Summer): 757–806.

Lee, Francis E., and Bruce I. Oppenheimer. 1999. *Sizing Up the Senate: The Unequal Consequences of Equal Representation*. Chicago: University of Chicago Press.

Levine, Daniel H. 1992. *Popular Voices in Latin American Catholicism*. Princeton: Princeton University Press.

Levine, Daniel H. 2013. "A Burden of History." *New York Times*, March 14. http://www.nytimes.com/roomfordebate/2013/03/14/does-pope-franciss-election-signal-a-catholic-comeback-for-latin-america/argentine-catholicism-has-a-burden-to-overcome (accessed March 3, 2016).

Levine, Daniel, and José Molina. 2013. "Calidad de la Democracia en Venezuela." *América Latina Hoy* 45: 157–75.

Levine, Daniel, and Catalina Romero. 2004. "Movimientos Urbanos y Desempoderamiento en Peru y Venezuela." *América Latina Hoy* 36:47–77.

Levinson, Sanford. 2000. "Trials, Commissions, and Investigating Committees." In *Truth v. Justice: The Morality of Truth Commissions*, edited by Robert I. Rotberg and Dennis Thompson, 211–34. Princeton: Princeton University Press.

Levitsky, Steven. 2003. *Transforming Labor-Based Parties in Latin America: Argentine Peronism in Comparative Perspective*. Cambridge: Cambridge University Press.

Levitsky, Steven. 2008. "Crisis, Party Adaptation and Regime Stability in Argentina: The Case of Peronism, 1989–1994." *Party Politics* 4, no. 4: 445–70.

Levitsky, Steven, and Scott Mainwaring. 2006. "Organized Labor and Democracy in Latin America." *Comparative Politics* 39, no. 1 (October): 21–42.

Levitsky, Steven, and María Victoria Murillo. 2005. "Introduction." In *Argentine Democracy: The Politics of Institutional Weakness*, edited by Steven Levitsky and María Victoria Murillo, 1–20. University Park: Pennsylvania State University Press.

Levy, Jack S. 1992. "An Introduction to Prospect Theory." *Political Psychology* 13:171–86.

Lijphart, Arend. 1999. *Patterns of Democracy: Government Forms and Performance in Thirty-Six Countries*. New Haven: Yale University Press.

Linz, Juan J. 1994. "Presidential or Parliamentary Democracy: Does It Make a Difference?" In *The Failure of Presidential Democracy*, edited by Juan J. Linz and Arturo Valenzuela. Baltimore: Johns Hopkins University Press.

Linz, Juan, and Alfred Stepan, eds. 1978. *The Breakdown of Democratic Regimes*. Baltimore: Johns Hopkins University Press.

Linz, Juan, and Alfred Stepan. 1996. *Problems of Democratic Transitions and Consolidation: Southern Europe, South America and Post-Communist Europe*. Baltimore: Johns Hopkins University Press.

Llanos, Mariana. 2002. *Privatization and Democracy in Argentina: An Analysis of President-Congress Relations*. Houndmills, Basingstoke, Hampshire, UK: Palgrave.

Llanos, Mariana, and Francisco Sánchez. 2006. "Council of Elders? The Senate and Its Members in the Southern Cone." *Latin American Research Review* 41, no. 1: 133–52.

Loewenberg, Gerhard. 2011. *On Legislatures: The Puzzle of Representation*. Boulder: Paradigm.

Magaloni, Beatrice. 2006. *Voting for Autocracy: Hegemonic Party Survival and Its Demise in Mexico*. New York: Cambridge University Press.

Mangany, Chabani. 2004. "Transitions." In *On Becoming a Democracy: Transition and Transformation in South African Society*, edited by Chabani Mangany. Leiden, The Netherlands: University of South Africa Press.

Manion, Melanie. 2004. *Corruption by Design: Building Clean Government in Mainland China and Hong Kong*. Cambridge: Harvard University Press.

Manion, Melanie. 2006. "Democracy, Community, Trust: The Impact of Elections in Rural China." *Comparative Political Studies* 39, no. 3 (April): 301–24.

Manning, Carrie. 2008. *The Making of Democrats: Elections and Party Development in Post-War Bosnia, El Salvador and Mozambique*. New York: Palgrave Macmillan.

Mansbridge, Jane. 2008. "Carol Pateman: Radical Liberal?" In *The Illusion of Consent: Engaging with Carol Pateman*, edited by Daniel O'Neill, Mary Lyndon Shanley, and Iris Marion Young. University Park: Pennsylvania State University Press.

Martinez, Diego. 2013. "Es la Impunidad Total." *Página 12*, March 15.

Martínez Franzoni, Juliana. 2008. "Welfare Regimes in Latin America: Capturing Constellations of Markets, Families and Policies." *Latin American Politics and Society* 50, no. 2: 67–100.

Mayer, Kenneth R. 2001. *With the Stroke of a Pen: Executive Orders and Presidential Power*. Princeton: Princeton University Press.

McClennan, Sophia A. 2010. "Beyond *Death and the Maiden*: Ariel Dorfman's Media Criticism and Journalism." *Latin American Research Review* 45, no. 1 (January): 173–88.

Medearis, John. 2008. "Deliberative Democracy, Subordination, and the Welfare State." In *The Illusion of Consent: Engaging with Carol Pateman*, edited by Daniel O'Neill, Mary Lyndon Shanley, and Iris Marion Young. University Park: Pennsylvania State University Press.

Melnick, R. Shep. 2005. "The Courts, Jurisprudence and the Executive Branch." In *The Executive Branch*, edited by Joel D. Aberbach and Mark A. Peterson, 452–85. Oxford: Oxford University Press.

Melo, Marcus André, Carlos Pereira, and Carlos Mauricio Figueiredo. 2009. "Political and Institutional Checks on Corruption: Explaining the Performance of Brazilian Audit Institutions." *Comparative Political Studies* 42, no. 9 (September): 1217–44.

Menem, Eduardo. 1992. *Nueve Años en el Senado de la Nación (1983–1992)*. Buenos Aires: printed by author.

Merola, Jennifer L., and Elizabeth J. Zechmeister. 2011. "The Nature, Determinants and Consequences of Chavez' Charisma: Evidence from a Study of Venezuelan Public Opinion." *Comparative Political Studies* 44, no. 11 (January): 28–54.

Mickey, Robert, 2015. *Paths Out of Dixie: The Democratization of Authoritarian Enclaves in America's Deep South, 1944–1972*. Princeton: Princeton University Press.

Milkis, Sidney M. 2005. "Executive Power and Political Parties: The Dilemmas of Scale in American Democracy." In *The Executive Branch*, edited by Joel Aberbach and Mark Peterson. Oxford: Oxford University Press.

Ministerio de Cultura y Educacion. 1996. *Annuario de Estadisticas Universitarios*. Buenos Aires: Ministerio de Cultura y Educacion.

Molina, José F. 2004. "The Unraveling of Venezuela's Party System: From Party Rule to Personalistic Politics and Deinstitutionalization." In *The Unraveling of Representative Democracy in Venezuela*, edited by Jennifer L. McCoy and David J. Myers. Baltimore: Johns Hopkins University Press.

Moon, J. Donald. 1988. "The Moral Basis of the Democratic Welfare State." In *Democracy and the Welfare State*, edited by Amy Gutmann. Princeton: Princeton University Press, 1988.

Moore, Barrington, Jr. 1966. *Social Origins of Dictatorship and Democracy: Lord and Peasant in the Making of the Modern World*. Boston: Beacon Press.

Moore, Barrington, Jr. 1978. *Injustice: The Social Basis of Obedience and Revolt*. White Plains, NY: M. E. Sharpe.

Morlino, Leonardo. 2005. "Anchors and Democratic Change." *Comparative Political Studies* 38, no. 7 (September): 743–70.

Moss, Chris. 2008. *Patagonia: A Cultural History*. Oxford: Signal Books.

Mustapic, Ana Maria. 2000. "Oficialista y diputados: Las relaciones Executive-Legislativa en la Argentina." *Desarollo Economico: Revista de Ciencias Sociales* 39, no. 156 (January–March): 571–95.

National Commission on Disappeared Persons (CONADEP). 1986. *Nunca Mas: A Report by Argentina's National Commission on Disappeared People*. London: Faber and Faber.

National Education Association. 2010. *Advocate*. Spring. Washington, DC: National Education Association.

Negretto, Gabriel L. 2006. "Minority Presidents and Democratic Performance in Latin America." *Latin American Politics and Society* 48, no. 3 (September): 63–92.

Neustadt, Richard E. 1960. *Presidential Power: The Politics of Leadership*. New York: John Wiley and Sons.

Nino, Carlos. 1992. "El hiperpresidencialismo argentino y las concepciones de la democracia." In *El presidencialismo puesto a prueba*, edited by Carlos Nino. Madrid: Centro de Estudios Constitucionales.

Nino, Carlos. 1996. *Radical Evil on Trial*. New Haven: Yale University Press.

Nohlen, Dieter, and Mario Fernández, eds. 1991. *Presidencialism versus Parlamentarismo*. Caracas, Venezuela: Nueva Sociedad.

Nordlinger, Eric. 1977. *Soldiers in Politics: Military Coups and Government.* Englewood Cliffs, NJ: Prentice Hall.

Norris, Pippa. 2008. *Driving Democracy: Do Power-Sharing Institutions Work?* New York: Cambridge University Press.

Nunn, Kenneth B. 1999. "Rosewood." In *When Sorry Isn't Enough: The Controversy over Apologies and Reparations for Human Injustice,* edited by Roy L. Brooks. New York: New York University Press.

Ober, Josiah. 2007. *Democracy and Knowledge: Innovation and Learning in Classical Athens.* Princeton: Princeton University Press.

O'Donnell, Guillermo. 1994. "Delegative Democracy." *Journal of Democracy* 5, no. 1: 55–69.

O'Donnell, Guillermo. 1999. "Horizontal Accountability in New Democracies." In *The Self-Restraining State: Power and Accountability in New Democracies,* edited by Andreas Schedler, Larry Diamond, and Marc F. Plattner. Boulder: Lynne Rienner.

O'Donnell, Guillermo. 2004. "Why the Rule of Law Matters." *Journal of Democracy* 15, no. 4 (October): 32–46.

O'Donnell, Guillermo, and Philippe Schmitter. 1986. *Transitions from Authoritarian Rule: Tentative Conclusions about Uncertain Democracies.* Baltimore: Johns Hopkins University Press.

Ollier, María Matilde. 2008. "La Institucionalización Democratica en el Callejón: Estabilidad Presidencial en Argentina, 1999–2003." *América Latina Hoy* 49:73–103.

O'Neill, Daniel. 2007. *The Burke-Wollstonecraft Debate: Savagery, Civilization, and Democracy.* University Park: Pennsylvania State University Press.

O'Neill, Daniel, Mary Lyndon Shanley, and Iris Marion Young, eds. 2008. *The Illusion of Consent: Engaging with Carol Pateman.* University Park: Pennsylvania State University Press.

Organization of American States. 2014. "IACHR Welcomes Brazil's Truth Commission Report and Calls on the State to Implement its Recommendations." http://www.oas.org/en/iachr/media_center/PReleases/2014/151.asp

Paludan, Phillip Shaw. 1994. *The Presidency of Abraham Lincoln.* Lawrence: University Press of Kansas.

Paxton, Robert O. 1997. *French Peasant Fascism: Henri Dorgeres's Greenshirts and the Crisis of French Agriculture, 1929–1939.* Oxford: Oxford University Press.

Pelikan, Jaroslav. 2005. "General Introduction: The Executive Branch as an Institution of American Constitutional Democracy." In *The Executive Branch,* edited by Joel D. Aberbach and Mark A. Peterson. Oxford: Oxford University Press.

Penfold-Becerra, Michael. 2007. "Clientelism and Social Funds: Evidence from Chávez's Misiones." *Latin American Politics and Society* 49, no. 4 (December): 63–84.

Pérez-Díaz, Víctor M. 1993. *The Return of Civil Society: The Emergence of Democratic Spain.* Cambridge: Harvard University Press.

Perlman, Janice. 2010. *Favela: Four Decades of Living on the Edge in Rio de Janeiro.* Oxford: Oxford University Press.

Perón, Juan. 1973. *Habla Perón.* Buenos Aires: Editorial Freeland.

Peters, Ronald M., and Cindy Simon Rosenthal. 2010. *Speaker Nancy Pelosi and the New American Politics.* Oxford: Oxford University Press.

Peterson, Mark A. 1990. *Legislating Together: The White House and Capitol Hill from Eisenhower to Reagan*. Cambridge: Harvard University Press.

Pharr, Susan, and Robert Putnam. 2000. *Disaffected Democracies: What's Troubling the Trilateral Countries?* Princeton: Princeton University Press.

Pierson, Christopher. 2007. *Beyond the Welfare State: The New Political Economy of Welfare*, 3rd ed. University Park: Pennsylvania State University Press.

Pion-Berlin, David. 1985. "The Fall of Military Rule in Argentina, 1976–1983." *Journal of Interamerican Studies and World Affairs* 27, no. 3 (Summer): 55–76.

Pion-Berlin, David. 1991. "Between Confrontation and Accommodation: Military and Government Policy in Democratic Argentina." *Journal of Latin American Studies* 23, no. 3 (October): 543–71.

Pion-Berlin, David. 1997. *Through Corridors of Power: Institutions and Civil-Military Relations in Argentina*. University Park: Pennsylvania State University Press.

Pion-Berlin, David. 1998. "The Limits to Military Power: Institutions and Defense Budgeting in Democratic Argentina." *Studies in Comparative International Development* 33, no. 1: 94–115.

Piven, Frances Fox, and Richard Cloward, 1977. *Poor People's Movements: How They Succeed and Why They Fail*. New York: Pantheon Press.

Poletta, Francesca. 2006. *It Was Like a Fever: Storytelling in Protest and Politics*. Chicago: University of Chicago Press.

Polsby, Nelson. 1975. "Legislatures." In *Handbook of Political Science*, vol. 5, edited by F. I. Greenstein and Nelson W. Polsby. Reading, MA: Addison-Wesley.

Polsby, Nelson. 2004. *How Congress Evolves: Social Bases of Institutional Change*. Oxford: Oxford University Press.

Przeworski, Adam, and John Sprague. 1986. *Paper Stones: A History of Electoral Socialism*. Chicago: University of Chicago Press.

Ranis, Peter, 1995. *Class, Democracy, and Labor in Contemporary Argentina*. New Brunswick, NJ: Transaction Press.

Rein, Raanan. 2008. *In the Shadow of Perón: Juan Atilio Bramuglia and the Second Line of Argentina's Populist Movement*. Translated by Martha Grenzeback. Stanford: Stanford University Press. Originally published as *Juan Atilio Bramuglia: Bajo la sombra del líder. La segunda linea de liderazgo peronista*. Buenos Aires: Ediciones Lumiere, 2006.

Remmer, Karen. 2007. "The Political Economy of Patronage: Expenditure Patterns in the Argentine Provinces, 1983–2003." *Journal of Politics* 69, no. 2 (May): 363–77.

Retamozo, Martin. 2006. "Los 'Piqueteros': Trabajo, Subjectividad y Acción Colectiva en el Movimiento de Desocupados en Argentina." *América Latina Hoy* 42:109–28.

Roberts, Kenneth M. 2006. "Populism, Political Conflict and Grass-Roots Organization in Latin America." *Comparative Politics* 38, no. 2 (January): 127–48.

Robins, Steven J., ed. 2005. *Limits to Liberation after Apartheid: Citizenship, Governance and Culture*. Oxford: James Curry.

Robinson, Donald L. 1996. "Presidential Prerogative and the Spirit of American Constitutionalism." In *The Constitution and the Conduct of American Foreign Policy*, edited by David Gray Adler and Larry N. George. Lawrence: University Press of Kansas.

Rodrik, Dani, 2007. *One Economics, Many Recipes: Globalization, Institutions, and Economic Growth.* Princeton: Princeton University Press.

Romero, Simon. 2015. "Draft of Arrest Request for Argentine President Found at Dead Prosecutor's Home." *New York Times.* February 3. http://www.nytimes.com/2015/02/04/world/americas/argentina-albert-nisman-arrest-warrant-cristina-de-kirchner.html?_r=0

Roniger, Luis, and Mario Sznajder. 1999. *The Legacy of Human Rights Violations in the Southern Cone: Argentina, Chile and Uruguay.* Oxford: Oxford University Press.

Rose, Richard, 2005. "Giving Direction to Government in Comparative Perspective." In *The Executive Branch*, edited by Joel D. Aberbach and Mark A. Peterson. Oxford: Oxford University Press.

Rotberg, Robert I., and Dennis Thompson, eds. 2000. *Truth v. Justice: The Morality of Truth Commissions.* Princeton: Princeton University Press.

Rothstein, Bo. 1998. *Just Institutions Matter: The Moral and Political Logic of the Universal Welfare State.* Cambridge: Cambridge University Press.

Rouquie, Alain. 1967. "Le Mouvement Frondizi et le Radicalisme argentin." Paris: Fondation Nationale des Sciences Politiques, Centre d'etude des Relations Internationales.

Rouquie, Alain. 1978. *Pouvoir militaire: Societe politique Republique Argentina.* Paris: Presses de la Fondation Nationale des Sciences Politiques.

Rubio, Delia, and Mateo Goretti. 1998. "When the President Governs Alone: The Decretazo in Argentina, 1989–1993." In *Executive Decree Authority*, edited by John M. Carey and Matthew Soberg Shugart. Cambridge: Cambridge University Press.

Rudalevige, Andrew. 2005. "The Executive Branch and the Legislative Process." In *The Executive Branch*, edited by Joel D. Aberbach and Mark A. Peterson. Oxford: Oxford University Press.

Rudra, Nita. 2007. "Welfare States in Developing Countries: Unique or Universal?" *Journal of Politics* 69, no. 2 (May): 378–96.

Ryan, Alan. 2008. "Participation Revisited: Carol Pateman versus Joseph Schumpeter." In *The Illusion of Consent: Engaging with Carol Pateman*, edited by Daniel O'Neill, Mary Lyndon Shanley, and Iris Marion Young. University Park: Pennsylvania State University Press.

Salonia, Antonio F. 2002a. "Decentralización Educativa, Participación y Democracia: Escuela Autonoma y Ciudania Responsible." In *Educación y Política en la Argentina.* Buenos Aires: Academia Nacional de Educación.

Salonia, Antonio F. 2002b. "El Sistema de Técnicos y Burocratas al Sistema Abierto y Participativo." In *Educación y Política en la Argentina.* Buenos Aires: Academia Nacional de Educación.

Sanchez, Pedro. 1983. *La Presidencia de Illia.* Buenos Aires: Centro Editor de America Latina.

Sarmiento, Domingo Faustino. 1929. "Comentarios de la Constitucion de la Confederación Argentina." Buenos Aires: Talleres graficos argentina de L.J. Rosso. Originally published 1853.

Sartori, Giovani. 1976. *Parties and Party Systems: A Framework for Analysis.* Vol. 1. Cambridge: Cambridge University Press.

Schlesinger, Arthur M., Jr. 1973. *The Imperial Presidency.* Boston: Houghton Mifflin.

Schlesinger, Arthur M., Jr. 1978. *Robert Kennedy and His Times.* Vol. 2. Boston: Houghton Mifflin.

Schlesinger Jr, Arthur M., Jr. 2002. *A Thousand Days: John F. Kennedy in the White House.* Boston: Houghton Mifflin.

Scott, James C. 1998. *Seeing Like a State.* New Haven: Yale University Press.

Senen Gonzalez, Santiago, and Yanina Welp. 1999. "Illia y la Toma de Fabricas." *Todo es Historia* no. 383 (June): 8–23.

Shannon, J. B. 1938a. "Presidential Politics in the South 1938: I." *Journal of Politics* 1 (May): 146–70.

Shannon, J. B. 1938b. "Presidential Politics in the South 1938: II." *Journal of Politics* 1 (August): 278–300.

Shapiro, Ian. 1999a. *Democratic Justice.* New Haven: Yale University Press.

Shapiro, Ian. 1999b. "Enough of Deliberation: Politics Is about Interests and Power." In *Deliberative Politics: Essays on Democracy and Disagreement*, edited by Stephen Macedo. New York: Oxford University Press.

Shapiro, Ian. 2003a. *The Moral Foundations of Politics.* New Haven: Yale University Press.

Shapiro, Ian. 2003b. *The State of Democratic Theory.* Princeton: Princeton University Press.

Shugart, Matthew Soberg, and Scott Mainwaring. 1997. "Presidentialism and Democracy in Latin America: Rethinking the Terms of the Debate." In *Presidentialism and Democracy in Latin America*, ed. Scott Mainwaring and Matthew Soberg Shugart. Cambridge: Cambridge University Press.

Shumway, Nicolas. 1991. *The Invention of Argentina.* Berkeley: University of California Press.

Siavelis, Peter. 2000. *The President and Congress in Post-Authoritarian Chile: Institutional Constraints to Democratic Consolidation.* University Park: Pennsylvania State University Press.

Siddle Walker, Vanessa. 1996. *Their Highest Potential: An African American School Community in the Segregated South.* Chapel Hill: University of North Carolina Press.

Simon, William H. 1999. "Three Limitations of Deliberative Democracy: Identity Politics, Bad Faith, and Indeterminacy." In *Deliberative Politics: Essays on Democracy and Disagreement*, edited by Stephen Macedo. New York: Oxford University Press.

Skocpol, Theda. 1992. *Protecting Soldiers and Mothers: The Political Origins of Social Policy in the United States.* Cambridge: Belknap Press of Harvard University Press.

Skocpol, Theda. 1994. "The Origins of Social Policy in the United States: A Polity-Centered Analysis." In *The Dynamics of American Politics: Approaches and Interpretations*, edited by Lawrence C. Dodd and Calvin Jillson, 182–206. Boulder: Westview Press.

Skowronek, Steven. 1993. *The Politics Presidents Make: Leadership from John Adams to George Bush.* Cambridge: Harvard University Press.

Smith, Frank E. 1964. *Congressman from Mississippi.* New York: Capricorn Books.

Smith, William C. 1991. "State, Market and Neoliberalism in Post-transition Argentina: The Menem Experiment." *Journal of Interamerican Studies and World Affairs* 33, no. 4 (Winter): 1–17.

Stokes, Susan. 2001. *Mandates and Democracy: Neoliberalism by Surprise in Latin America.* New York: Cambridge University Press.

Story, Joseph. 1891. *Commentaries on the Constitution of the United States.* Reprint, 1987, Durham, NC: Carolina Academic Press.

Swenson, Peter. 1989. *Fair Shares: Unions, Pay, and Politics in Sweden and West Germany.* Ithaca: Cornell University Press.

Swenson, Peter. 2002. *Capitalists against Markets: The Making of Labor Markets and Welfare States in the United States and Sweden.* Oxford: Oxford University Press.

Szusterman, Celia. 1993. *Frondizi and the Politics of Developmentalism in Argentina, 1955–62.* Pittsburgh: University of Pittsburgh Press.

Taquini, Alberto C. 2000. *La Transformación de la Educación Superior Argentina: De las Nuevas Universidades a los Colegios Universitarios.* Buenos Aires: Academia Nacional de Educación.

Tcach, Cesar. 2000. "Radicalismo y Fuerzas Armadas (1962–1963): Observaciones desde Cordoba." *Desarollo Economico* 40, no. 157 (April–June): 73–95.

Thompson, E. P. 1971. "The Moral Economy of the English Crowd in the Eighteenth Century." *Past and Present,* no. 50 (February): 76–136.

Tilly, Charles. 2003. *The Politics of Collective Violence.* New York: Cambridge University Press.

Tilly, Charles. 2007. *Democracy.* Cambridge: Cambridge University Press.

Timerman, Jacobo. 1981. *Prisoner without a Name; Cell without a Number.* Translated by Toby Talbot. New York: Alfred Knopf.

UNESCO (United Nations Education, Scientific and Cultural Organization). 2000. *The Right to Education: Toward Education for All throughout Life.* World Education Report, 2000. Paris: UNESCO.

UNESCO and OECD (Organization for Economic Cooperation and Development). 2000. *Investing in Education: Analysis of the 1990 World Education Indicators.* Paris: UNESCO.

van Gelderen, Alfredo M. 1996. *La Ley Federal de Educación de la República Argentina.* Buenos Aires: Academia Nacionál de Educación.

Varshney, Ashutosh. 2003. *Civic Life and Ethnic Conflict in India.* New Haven: Yale University Press.

Vazquez, Silvia Andrea, and Juan Balduzzi. 2000. *De apóstoles a trabajadores: Luchas por la unidad sindical docente 1953–1973. Historia de CTERA I.* Buenos Aires: Instituto de Investigaciones Pedagógicas Marina Vilte, Confederacion de Trabajadores de la Education en la Republica Argentina.

Wang, Chin-Shou, and Charles Kurzman. 2007. "Dilemmas of Electoral Clientelism: Taiwan, 1993." *International Political Science Review* 28, no. 3: 225–45.

Wayne, Steven J. 2005. "Presidential Elections and American Democracy." In *The Executive Branch,* edited by Joel D. Aberbach and Mark A. Peterson. Oxford: Oxford University Press.

Weitz-Shapiro, Rebecca. 2006. "Partisanship and Protest: The Politics of Workfare Distribution in Argentina." *Latin American Research Review* 41, no. 3: 122–48.

Weyland, Kurt. 1996. "Risk Taking in Latin American Economic Restructuring: Lessons from Prospect Theory." *International Studies Quarterly* 40, no. 2 (June): 185–208.

Wilson, Richard A. 2001. *The Politics of Truth and Reconciliation in South Africa: Legitimizing the Post-Apartheid State.* New York: Cambridge University Press.

Wirls, Daniel, and Stephen Wirls. 2004. *The Invention of the United States Senate.* Baltimore: Johns Hopkins University Press.

Wood, Gordon S. 1969. *The Creation of the American Republic, 1776–1787.* Chapel Hill: University of North Carolina Press.

Yamamoto, Eric K. 1999. *Interracial Justice: Conflict and Reconciliation in Post-Civil Rights America.* New York: New York University Press.

Yamamoto, Eric K., Sandra Hye Yun Kim, and Abigail M. Holden. 2007. "American Reparations Theory at the Crossroads." *California Western Law Review* 44, no. 1 (Fall): 1–85.

Yamamoto, Eric K., and Susan K. Serrano. 1999. "Healing Racial Wounds? The Final Report of South Africa's Truth and Reconciliation Commission." In *When Sorry Isn't Enough: The Controversy over Apologies and Reparations for Human Injustice,* edited by Roy L. Brooks. New York: New York University Press.

Zechmeister, Elizabeth J. 2012. "Book Review of Leslie E. Anderson, *Social Capital in Developing Democracies: Nicaragua and Argentina Compared.*" *Perspectives on Politics* 10, no. 2 (June): 507–8.

Index

Note: Page numbers followed by *t* refer to tables.

273